LEARNING FROM INTERNATIONAL PUBLIC MANAGEMENT REFORM

RESEARCH IN PUBLIC POLICY ANALYSIS AND MANAGEMENT

Series Editor: Lawrence R. Jones

Volumes 1–10   Research in Public Policy Analysis
and Management

RESEARCH IN PUBLIC POLICY ANALYSIS AND
MANAGEMENT   VOLUME 11B

LEARNING FROM INTERNATIONAL PUBLIC MANAGEMENT REFORM

EDITED BY

LAWRENCE R. JONES
Naval Postgraduate School, Monterey, California, USA

JAMES GUTHRIE
Macquarie University, Sydney, Australia

PETER STEANE
Macquarie University, Sydney, Australia

2001

JAI
An Imprint of Elsevier Science

Amsterdam – London – New York – Oxford – Paris – Shannon – Tokyo

ELSEVIER SCIENCE Ltd
The Boulevard, Langford Lane
Kidlington, Oxford OX5 1GB, UK

First edition 2001

Library of Congress Cataloging in Publication Data
A catalog record from the Library of Congress has been applied for.

British Library Cataloguing in Publication Data
A catalogue record from the British Library has been applied for.

ISBN: 0-7623-0760-9
    (Vol. 11A & 11B Set: 0-7623-0761-7)

♾ The paper used in this publication meets the requirements of ANSI/NISO Z39.48-1992 (Permanence of Paper).
Printed in The Netherlands.

CONTENTS

PART B

III. LEARNING FROM REFORM IN ASIA

LIST OF TABLES AND FIGURES

LIST OF CONTRIBUTORS – PART B

Kevin Yuk-fai Au is an Assistant Professor in the School of Business, University of Hong Kong.

Allan Barton is Professor in the Department of Commerce, The Australian National University, Canberra, Australia.

Peter DeLeon is a Professor in the Graduate School of Public Affairs, University of Colorado at Denver.

Yvon Dufour is Lecturer at Macquarie Graduate School of Management, Macquarie University, Sydney, Australia.

Bryon Gordon is Senior Evaluator in the Budget Issues Group, Accounting and Information Management Division, U.S. Central Accounting Office (GAO), Washington, D.C.

Mark T. Green is Assistant Professor in the Graduate School of Public Affairs, University of Colorado at Denver.

Lotte Jensen is an Associate Professor of Public Administration in the Institute of Political Science, University of Copenhagen, Denmark.

L. R. Jones is Wagner Professor of Public Management in the Department of Systems Management, Naval Postgraduate School, Monterey, California and Coordinator of the International Public Management Network.

Joanne Kelly is a Visiting Research Fellow at the Expenditure and Management Strategies Sector of the Treasury Board Secretariat of Canada in Ottawa.

Kurt Klaudi Klausen is Professor and Director of the Program in Public Management in the Department of Political Science and Public Management, University of Southern Denmark, Odense.

Lise Lamothe is an Assistant Professor at the Université Laval, Quebec, Canada.

Riccardo Mussari is Professor of Public Management and Accounting at the University of Siena, Italy.

Paul Posner is Director of the Budget Issues Group, Accounting and Information Management Division, U.S. General Accounting Office (GAO), Washington, D.C.

Nancy Roberts is Professor of Strategic Management and Professor of National Security Affairs, Naval Postgraduate School, Monterey, California.

Kuno Schedler is Professor of Public Management in the Institute for Public Services and Tourism, University of St. Gallen, Switzerland and Coordinator of the International Public Management Network.

David Shand is a senior official for the World Bank presently working in the Southeast Asia region.

Randal G. Stewart is Professor of Government and Industrial Relations, University of Sydney, Australia.

Ilan Vertinsky is Professor and Director of the Centre for International Business Studies, University of British Columbia, Vancouver, Canada.

Denis Yu-long Wang is Associate Professor and Director of the Master's of Science Degree Program in International Business, School of Business, Chinese University of Hong Kong.

John Wanna is Professor in the Centre for Australian Public Sector Management, Griffith University, Brisbane, Australia.

Clay Goodloe Wescott, Ph.D. is Senior Public Administration Specialist at the Asian Development Bank, Manila, Philippines.

Yu-Ying Kuo is Assistant Professor in the Department of Public Policy and Management, Shih Hsin University, Taipei, Taiwan.

FOREWORD TO PART B

LEARNING FROM INTERNATIONAL PUBLIC MANAGEMENT REFORM EXPERIENCE

The contents of this book are provided in two volume parts. The first volume part of the book includes chapters 1 through 16: Learning From Reform in Australia, and Learning From Reform in New Zealand. In this, the second volume part, are chapters 17 through 31 organized into three sections: Learning From Reform in Asia, Learning From Comparative and International Reform, and Learning From Public Management Reform: Critical Perspectives on New Public Management. The editors appreciate the quality and number of contributions of the forty-two authors that made the composition of this two-part volume set possible. We believe it adds considerably to new knowledge in the emerging field of international public management.

Lawrence R. Jones
Monterey, California

James Guthrie
Sydney, Australia

Peter Steane
Sydney, Australia

SECTION III

LEARNING FROM REFORM IN ASIA

17. MEASURING GOVERNANCE IN DEVELOPING ASIA[1]

Clay Goodloe Wescott

INTRODUCTION

Is it possible to measure the quality of overall governance in a developing Asian country? Are present measures robust enough to allow the ranking of countries along a continuum from well-governed to poorly-governed? Should these rankings be used by donor agencies and private investors in making investment decisions? Despite the complexity and diversity of approaches of governance systems, there are various qualitative and quantitative tools being used in the region. In this chapter, the advantages and disadvantages of some of these tools will be analyzed, and some lessons will be derived showing how the prudent use of governance indicators can help development agencies and private investors.

Beginning a few years ago, the Asian Development Bank (ADB) started to pay serious attention to governance issues. The Board of the ADB was the first of an international financial institution to adopt and implement a governance policy.

One challenge in approving the new policy came from Article 36 of the ADB's Charter, which states that the Bank, ". . . shall not interfere in the political affairs of any member nor shall they be influenced in their decisions by the political character of the member concerned. Only economic considerations shall be relevant to their decisions . . ."

The term "economic considerations", however, has been widely interpreted by the Bank. Data from recent studies are showing that governance matters for economic development. For example, a survey of governance in around 165

Learning from International Public Management Reform, Volume 11B, pages 295–309.
Copyright © 2001 by Elsevier Science Ltd.
All rights of reproduction in any form reserved.
ISBN: 0-7623-0760-9

countries found that a one standard deviation increase in any one of 6 governance indicators causes a $2\frac{1}{2}$ fold increase in PC income, a 4-fold decrease in infant mortality, and a 15 to 25% increase in literacy.[2] A one-standard deviation increase would be moving from rule of law in Russia to the Czech Republic, or moving in reducing corruption from levels in Indonesia to levels in Korea. This research indicates a causal link between improved governance and improved development performance. Easterly and Levine (1997) compare development performance in Asia and Africa, and find the latter suffered because ethnic conflict encouraged policies fostering rent-seeking rather than economic performance. Van Rijckeghem and Weder (1997) use regression analysis to show that countries with poorly paid public officials tend towards higher corruption.

The link is strongest for the extremes: the worst performers have the worst governance, and the best, the best. The link is harder to prove when comparing countries closer in rank order. For example, China's economic performance has recently been stronger than India's; yet India has a highly developed (though out of date) legal system and many lawyers, while China's legal system is, by comparison, rudimentary. As Dethier (1999) points out, the reason may be that there are informal substitutes for the legal protection and enforcement of property rights which existed long before states and formal legal institutions (e.g. arbitration, reputation, merger, strong-arm tactics, and altruism), highlighting one of the problems of specifying governance indicators.

In addition, there are a host of problems with data, model specification, and statistical estimation that make any analysis of causal links between governance and development performance exceptionally difficult. Take, for example, the case of a posited link between poor civil service pay and corruption, cited above. Broader comparative research indicates that there is a high correlation between the various governance indicators in most data sets. Thus, a significant regression finding between two variables may be "caused" by one or more other factors not being measured. This chapter will not go further into such questions, but rather focus on the task of measuring the quality of governance for its own sake.

Based on the presumption that effective governance is needed for strong development performance, the Bank adopted a policy, *Governance: Sound Development Management*, in August 1995, and an anti-corruption policy in 1998. In addition, by launching a governance website in 1999,[3] and hiring a core group of specialist staff, the Bank has moved proactively to address a broad range of governance issues.

The Bank defines governance as, ". . . the manner in which power is exercised in the management of a country's social and economic resources for development". ADB's emphasis in its governance programming is on dialogue and local ownership. Every effort is made to ensure that governance programs and conditions are:

(a) based on knowledge of the realities in practice rather than on blueprints and preconceptions;
(b) based on genuine dialog rather than just pressure;
(c) implemented forcefully but with a realistic sequence and timetable
(d) designed taking into account the constraints of country capacity to carry them through;
(e) flexible enough so that executing agencies can develop individual sub-projects within programs as and when progress permits;
(f) funded by a higher proportion of grant-funded technical assistance to lending than would be the case for other types of programs.

A central governance challenge is that while the Bank's overarching objective is to reduce poverty in developing member countries (DMCs), many DMC governments are essentially non-democratic. Olson (2000) argues that under autocratic systems, ruling elites block reforms that would disrupt the status quo that allows them to plunder their citizens. Yet Olson acknowledges that the same elites have an "encompassing interest" in the domain they are exploiting: if it prospers, they can extract more for themselves in taxes and other way. And Dollar and Kraay (2000) show the surest way to reduce poverty is economic growth. So there is some reason for hope.

Another way of looking at the challenge is that one might expect even autocratic governments to redistribute some minimum amount in order to ensure that some of the most visible manifestations of poverty are reduced. This would reduce adverse publicity (e.g. bad for business and tourism), and reduce the threat of socio-political instability. However, it is not easy to persuade these governments to transfer large amounts of public resources to poor and weak segments of society that have little political leverage, or to work for pro-poor, sustainable economic growth.

REASONS FOR MEASURING GOVERNANCE

Over the last decade, there has been an increasing interest in measuring governance across nations by investors, donor agencies, and academics. Deleon and Resnick-Terry (1999) explain how earlier efforts by academics such as Binder et. al. (1971) went out of favor in the 1980s as analysts focused on differences in context, and the difficulties these cause in making comparisons. However, over the last decade, measuring governance has come back into favor through a combination of advances in information and communications technology (thus facilitating cross-national data-gathering and research) and advances in public choice theory and institutional economics. The increasing impetus for performance appraisal and efficiency has led to the international search for good practices or "policy pinching", and the inevitable comparative measurement to see if what worked in country "X" works as well in country "Y".

Donor agencies and other investors want comparative governance measurements to help in making sound investment decisions. In the past, agencies allocated official development assistance based mainly on per capita income and population. Poor countries tended to get more aid per capita than better off ones, and small countries more than larger ones – both to compensate them for increased risks, and because the cost of running an aid program in a country dictates a minimum expenditure level, leading to the highest aid allocations per capita in some of the smallest countries. Countries that benefited from aid under these allocation formulae were often not well governed. As official development assistance declines, and is replaced by investment from private investors, pension funds, and the like, development financing is likely to be more and more attracted to countries with favorable governance indicators,[4] thus shifting resources in many cases to a different set of countries.

International agencies also want to find out if governments are abiding by international conventions and treaties they have signed. UNDP (1991) used the Humana Index, for example, taking account of 40 different dimensions of human rights and then scored each country for compliance or non-compliance. The International Parliamentary Union (2000) ranks countries based on the percentage of women in national legislatures. There are also mechanisms for monitoring countries' periodic reports on the Universal Declaration on Human Rights and related conventions[5] outlining legislative, judicial, administrative and other requirements. NGOs such as Freedom House (1999) and Institute for Democracy and Electoral Assistance (1997) monitor comparative progress and setbacks in governance. The Political and Economic Risk Consultancy (1998) rates eleven Asian countries based on perceptions on the quality of media. Governments themselves also measure the governance of their neighbors to assess security risks.[6]

METHODOLOGICAL PROBLEMS WITH MEASURING GOVERNANCE

Governance can be measured in terms of effort or in terms of results.[7] The former is important for morale, and also fairness when international concessional fund allocations are made. A small step forward in a country with weak governance may be more difficult to achieve than a larger step forward in a better governed country; The former deserves some credit for its achievements, however meager in comparative terms.

Yet measures of effort need to be combined with measures of tangible progress towards objectives. There are four types of results: in terms of inputs, outputs, outcomes (including impacts), and process. When results measurement is cost effective and appropriate, one should use whatever combination of indicators that is suitable for the activity, sector, country, and time being measured. Choosing the right combination raises many methodological issues and tradeoffs. For example, there is the common problem that "what you see is not always what you get." Laws and regulations enacted may not be enforced. Anti-corruption units may focus on eliminating political opponents. Policy-makers may ventriloquize commitment to donor-supported policy changes, giving the impression of local ownership of reforms; yet their actual views may be directly opposite. Expatriate advisors may be used not to train counterparts, but to carry out policy formulation and coordination roles, thus sidelining counterparts, who are seen by insecure rulers as potential threats if they know too much. Staff given specialized training may be transferred to assignments where the training is irrelevant for the same reason, thus perpetuating problems of low government effectiveness. Thus, one needs to be careful what one measures, and what inferences are drawn.

Another issue is who does the measuring, and on what authority. A central goal of measuring governance in developing Asia is to encourage countries to improve through a combination of external and internal incentives. External incentives include increased aid allocations and investment, and improved standings in international organizations. Yet many of the measurements used are designed and implemented by external evaluators, and are thus subject to the criticism that they are not sensitive to local contexts, and not locally owned. The Development Assistance Committee of OECD (1998, 1999) is developing methodologies for measuring governance jointly with partner countries in an effort to support country-based processes and improve local ownership.

EXAMPLES OF MEASURING GOVERNANCE IN PRACTICE

Qualitative Reporting

Qualitative reporting can give richness and depth of analysis. It is particularly suitable for measuring outcome and process variables, and may be based on international standards. Such reporting typically analyzes each case separately, may include comparative, quantitative indicators as part of the analysis, and may also rank cases based on the quality of the governance aspects examined. Here are some examples:

Governance Issues Studies

International donor agencies carry out these studies to better understand how governance affects their assistance, and to get pointers on how the assistance can better help improve governance in each developing member country (DMC). Since the ADB governance policy was approved, governance issues have been analyzed in separate sections of Country Assistance Plans and Country Operational Strategy Studies. In addition, the Bank is selectively carrying out separate governance issues studies in developing member countries, which then become the basis for detailed governance strategies for the countries. Studies for Thailand and Cambodia are completed.[8] Other studies are underway in China, Lao PDR, Nepal, Pakistan (a governance issues study team was working in Pakistan during the October 1999 coup), Bangladesh and Vietnam. In addition, the ADB (1999) has completed a major, comparative review of public sector reform in 6 Pacific island countries. The World Bank is carrying out comparable "National Institutional Reviews" in selected countries.

These studies pay particular attention to the extent of transparency in budget preparation, level and trend of non-productive government expenditures and spending on social sector programs, degree of participation in development processes (at national, sector, and project levels), success in fighting corruption, prevalence of legal and bureaucratic factors promoting official secrecy and inhibiting public access to information, and the need to ensure that complex, large, and unusual patterns of financial transactions are monitored and reported. Based on this analysis, the Bank works with developing member countries to formulate strategies and programs to address the key governance issues identified, together with relevant performance indicators.

By tailoring work to each country's specific conditions, they avoid some of the methodological problems discussed earlier. For example, some of them, such as the Cambodia study, have been highly participatory, thus building local ownership for future reforms. They avoid mistaking form for content by going beyond quantitative ratings, and allowing for analysis of distinctive features of country context. They provide a reality check for interpreting standard indicators of overall governance across countries. The disadvantage of these studies is that they can be selective, may be biased by the self-interests of informants, and do not have built in systems for resolving conflicting informant views.

Reporting on Fiscal Transparency

The "Code of Good Practices on Fiscal Transparency" was adopted by the Board of the IMF (1998). The Code includes, "Requirements for a minimum standard of fiscal transparency." This minimum standard is far below the standard found in developed countries, but judged to be the minimum necessary for effective functioning of a government. There are four broad requirements covered: clarity of roles and responsibilities, public availability of information, open budget preparation, execution and reporting, and independent assurances of integrity. This minimum standard has provided a useful basis for both self-diagnosis by countries themselves, and reporting by international donors. For example, it was used as the basis for country reports by 10 Pacific Island Countries facilitated by the IMF and UNDP in 1998, and as the basis for part of the ADB Governance Issues Study for Lao PDR in 1999.

As with some of the Governance Issues Studies, country self-diagnoses can build ownership for ensuing reforms. Based on a standardized questionnaire, they also provide data in a format whereby countries can be compared to each other. Although this reporting looks only at limited aspects of governance, it focuses attention on a reform agenda that can have many positive linkages to other aspects of governance.

Innovation Awards Program

This provides an explicitly competitive opportunity for reporting on governance. The theme of the CAPAM (the Commonwealth Association of Public Administration and Management) International Innovations Awards Program in 1998, was "Service To The Public". CAPAM received 121 submissions to the Program from 24 countries worldwide. The Awards Program was co-sponsored by CAPAM, KPMG, and Binariang, a telecommunications company in Malaysia.

Winners and summary descriptions from CAPAM (1998) included:

(1) Education Guarantee Scheme, Rajiv Gandhi Shiksha Mission, State of Madhya Pradesh (India) – In one year over 16,089 schools were built, or 40 new schools per day. Nearly 500,000 children were served.
(2) Ontario Delivers – Improving the Delivery of Quality Public Service in Ontario (Canada) – Electronic service delivery was adopted, including a

"One-Window" approach, leading to faster service and greater ease of transactions.

(3) New Pension Delivery Systems (South Africa) – The Department of Social Welfare, Free State has cut down time to process applications from three months to as little as two weeks, and serves citizens 7 days a week. Results also include less fraud, less need for long travel to pay points, and better security at pay points.

A subsequent competition is being carried out over the period 1999–2000. This type of reporting is highly participatory, helps to raise the stature of governance reformers, and is a good means of sharing ideas that may be picked up in other countries. The disadvantage is that successful innovations say nothing about the overall governance environment, and are often dependent on exceptional individuals and contextual factors that can't be easily replicated.

Quantitative Reporting
In addition to qualitative reporting, quantitative indicators can give numerical precision (although often not as precise as they seem on the surface). In some cases, these tools can allow cross-country comparisons. Kauffman et. al. (1999) combines many performance indicators into six broad clusters, allowing statistical analysis of the relation between governance and economic performance across a range of countries.

Dethier (1999) points out that most governance variables are proxies, whether qualitative (e.g. perception of corruption) or quantitative, e.g. percentage of total procurement subject to open, competitive bidding. In the case of the former, subjective values are typically ranked on an ordinal scale. The use of proxies runs a high risk of measurement errors and biased estimates. There is also a common problem that some explanatory variables used in studies are poor proxies for describing actual legal and political processes. A good proxy indicator should be relevant, and permit regular observation and "reasonably objective" interpretation to determine the change in its value or status.

Each aspect of governance can be measured in different ways, for different purposes. In the case of corruption, for instance, one can measure the public or experts' perception of corruption, or experiences of corruption, e.g. frequency of bribery in procurement contracts, amount of bribes as a percentage of contract value, frequency of bribery in permit applications, percentage of public sector jobs bought, percentage of public servants income as bribes. Alternatively, one may use costs of public services, costs of construction, assets of leaders, etc. as more indirect (but "harder") proxies of corruption, poor governance and wastage. A good measurement of corruption can present hard data and generate public debate on the issue of corruption. But corruption is only a symptom of underlying weaknesses in governance. Thus complementary diagnostic (either qualitative or quantitative surveys on governance can potentially identify the underlying causes of corruption. For example, whether a public institution bases its hiring and promotion decisions on meritocracy or favoritism and whether there are auditing and oversight mechanisms in budget allocation may explain the extent of corruption in the institution. Dethier (1999) points out that diagnostic surveys can also depoliticize the discussion of corruption by shifting public attention from people to institutions.

Here are some examples of uses of quantitative indicators:

Democracy and Governance Program Indicators

Developed by the Center for Democracy and Governance (1998), U.S. Agency for International Development to measure country and program performance, they are organized under four governance objectives: strengthened rule of law and respect for human rights, more genuine and competitive political processes, increased development of a politically active civil society, and more transparent and accountable governance institutions. Indicators are organized under program "objective" and "intermediate results" being measured. Among the hundreds of indicators listed, one example is: "Judicial salary and benefits as a percentage of what a comparable professional makes in private practice." This comes under the first objective, and the intermediate result: "Effective and fair legal institutions". A suggested guideline is that compensation should ideally be 80–90% of that in private practice. Compensation significantly less than that is a warning flag for rule of law. As with all the indicators, there is an estimate of the cost of obtaining the needed data: in this case, "low" (less then $500).

This approach stresses the need for cost-effective indicators and tradeoffs. For example, to determine the intermediate result: "improved application of the law in commercial cases", one could conduct an expert review of sample cases to see if the law had been appropriately applied. A lower-cost proxy indicator would measure "percentage change in the number of commercial cases filed." The use of this proxy would assume that citizens are more willing to file cases if they think the law will be predictably and fairly applied.

This approach also stresses that indicators be operational: "number of public defenders per 100,000 population," or "percent change in number of cases handled by public defenders," rather than "availability of legal services." Indicators should show the size of the problem when possible: "percent of human rights violations reported investigated/prosecuted" rather than "number of human rights violations reported investigated/prosecuted." Indicators should measure incremental changes where possible, not just the attainment of thresholds: "percent of civil society organizations showing improvement on an index," rather than "percent of civil society organizations that have a written strategic plan." Indicators should also measure the intended result as directly as possible: "percent of citizens understanding basic human rights" rather than "numbers reached by civic education."

USAID developed these indicators to monitor progress in achieving planned results. They were initially tested in four countries with different governance systems, data availability, and data collection expertise. There was no explicit intention to use the indicators to compare governance progress in these or other countries, but rather an effort to come up with a set of indicators robust enough to be suitable for a range of country contexts.

Performance Allocation Rating

The World Bank International Development Association system is based on a country policy and institutional assessment (CPIA) (80%) and a portfolio performance review (20%). The former is based on ratings on a scale of 1–6 of 20 criteria under 4 clusters: economic management, structural policies, policies for reducing inequalities, and public sector management/institutions. Countries whose performance is rated "unsatisfactory" on the governance criteria – criteria from the CPIA and the procurement criterion of the portfolio performance component, are put on a governance watch list. Countries receiving "highly unsatisfactory" ratings on governance criteria have their overall rating cut by a third, called the "governance discount". A country's allocation of concessional financing is then calculated through a formula taking into account per capita GNP and the performance rating. The governance criteria of the CPIA are: property rights and rule-based governance, quality of budgetary and financial management, efficiency of resource mobilization, efficiency of public expenditure, and transparency and accountability, and corruption in the public sector.[9]

Despite the methodological problems indicated earlier in making cross-country comparisons based on governance indicators, the ADB is currently designing a system to measure overall governance in developing member countries. The ADB objective is to stimulate discussion with countries on how governance indicators are moving and why. The approach will be to work in partnership with countries to solve mutually-acknowledged problems.

As with the World Bank, the ADB will adjust the results to take into account special needs of, for example, small (island and landlocked) countries, post-conflict countries, countries facing catastrophes, and countries undertaking far-reaching reforms. Both banks are looking for effective means of balancing country-specific and common standardized criteria, use of published and unpublished information, use of qualitative and quantitative data, and setting the proper balance between measures of effort and measures of results. No single governance indicator gives the whole picture, but one needs to define a manageable set that can be collected and updated within resource limitations.

Moody's (2000) Country Risk Guidelines

These are used as the basis for "sovereign ratings" of a country's creditworthiness, taking into account answers to, inter alia, the following questions:

(1) Is there a substantial risk of political regime change which could lead to a general repudiation of debts – or a risk of civil war/anarchy or foreign invasion?
(2) Does the country have a well-established system of contract law, which allows for successful suits for collection of unpaid debts, seizure of collateral, technical breakdowns?
(3) Does the country have a deep financial system which is effective in making payments and avoiding technical breakdowns?
(4) Is the regulatory/legal environment malleable, corrupt, unpredictable, etc.?
(5) Is there a tendency towards hyperinflation? (Moody's, 2000)

The resulting analysis leads to investment ratings for short- and long-term debt. Some examples of current sovereign rankings in the region for long-term debt include both Investment-Grade (Singapore–Aaa, People's Republic of China–A3, Hong Kong–A3, Rep. of Korea–Baa2, Malaysia–Baa3,), and Speculative-Grade (Fiji–Ba1, Philippines–Ba1, Thailand–Ba1, India–Ba2, Papua New Guinea–B1, Indonesia–B3, Pakistan–Caa1).

Similar to other ratings systems such as PRS Group (2000), S&P (2000), and Simon (1992), this one measures aspects of governance of particular interest to certain types of investors. There is no attempt to build country ownership in the system: indeed the independence of the system from country manipulation is a prime attraction to clients. Instead, countries are encouraged to improve on the indicators being measured, so that they can reduce interest charges and attract more investors.

Transparency International (TI) Corruption and Bribe Payers
Perception Indices

This international NGO released its fifth annual Corruption Perceptions Index (CPI) in 1999, ranking 99 countries based on a compilation of 17 surveys from 10 independent organisations. TI (1999) also released for the first time a Bribe Payers Perceptions Index (BPI). This ranks 19 leading exporting countries in terms of the degree to which their corporations are perceived to be paying bribes abroad. The BPI shows that companies from many leading exporting nations are widely seen as using bribes to win business. The BPI reveals that on a scale of 0–10, where 10 represents a corrupt-free exporting country, the best score among the countries rated was 8.3, while the worst score, representing a great propensity to use bribes, was 3.1. China (including Hong Kong) was seen as having the greatest willingness to pay bribes abroad, followed by South Korea, Taiwan, Italy and Malaysia. Sweden, Australia and Canada achieved the most favorable results.

These indices are valuable for generating publicity, leading to pressure from citizens on businesses and governments to reduce corruption. However, as in most quantitative governance indices, the degree of numerical precision should not be overstated. The comparative data surveys on which the indices are built draw from the experience and perceptions of those most directly confronted with the realities of corruption, e.g. business people, country experts, chambers of commerce etc. As such, they may reflect biases stemming from different country contexts. For example, Nigeria may be ranked more corrupt than China because the former has a much more open press than the latter, with extensive reporting on alleged corruption reinforcing the impression of its scale. While the actual level of corruption in China could be similar, the perception might be that it was lower because it is not as openly reported on or discussed.

One could try to measure corruption in other ways: say by comparing the number of prosecutions or court cases. Yet such cross-country data might again not reflect actual levels of corruption, but rather the quality of prosecutors, courts or the media in exposing corruption.

LESSONS FROM WORK IN PROGRESS ON MEASURING GOVERNANCE

There is increasing interest in measuring governance in developing Asia among development agencies, private investors, citizens, and governments. Despite the complexity and diversity of approaches of governance systems, there are various qualitative and quantitative tools being used in the region, developed thanks to advances in theory and in information and communications technologies making comparative work of this type more feasible and intellectually coherent. The examples discussed here have been selected to highlight some lessons for work in progress. References to other work are included, but given the fast-moving nature of the field, this list is bound to be incomplete.

The first lesson from this work in progress is that the measurement of governance performance over time in a single country is conceptually more straightforward than measuring performance across countries. The U.S.AID indicators discussed have been designed for the former purpose, and would seem to provide a useful toolkit for a wide range of different country contexts. The ADB and World Bank Governance Issues Studies are another example, adding qualitative richness to the task of measuring governance in Asian countries. By focusing on individual countries, they avoid problems of how to make meaningful comparisons between countries in widely different situations.

A second lesson is that cross-country comparisons that group countries into broad clusters are more meaningful than comparisons which rank-order countries. Moody's "investment grade" rating is an example of a broad cluster grouping. The IMF minimum standard on fiscal transparency can also be useful in separating countries that meet the standard from those that do not.

The most useful indicators are clear, relevant, economic, adequate, and monitorable. Such indicators can be helpful for development agencies and private investors if used cautiously.

NOTES

1. The author is Senior Public Administration Specialist, Asian Development Bank. The views expressed in this paper are the author's own, and do not represent those of the ADB.

2. The indicators measure the process by which governments are selected, monitored and replaced, the capacity of the government to effectively formulate and carry out effective policies, and the respect of citizens and the state for laws, regulations and other institutions that govern the economic and social interactions among them. Cf. Kaufmann et al. (1999).

3. See < http://www.adb.org/Governance/ >. The "links" page lists many other websites covering governance issues.

4. This issue has been explored extensively by the Money Matters Institute, at < www.worldpaper.org >

5. They are: Convention Against Torture; Convention on the Elimination of All Forms of Discrimination; Convention on the Rights of the Child; International Convention on the Elimination of All Forms of Racial Discrimination; International Convention on the Protection of the Rights of All Migrants; International Covenant on

Civil and Political Rights; International Covenant on Economic, Social and Cultural Rights.

6. A major research effort within the U.S. government (National Research Council, White House, et al) in the mid–90s tried to establish indicators that would predict the risk of state failure. However, the results were never released because of fears of diplomatic problems (and possibly self-fulfilling prophecies) with the high-risk countries.

7. The section draws from, inter alia, Schiavo-Campo and Sundaram, forthcoming.

8. http://www.adb.org/Documents/Papers/Governance_Thailand/default.asp?p = gov pub >; Kato et al (2000).

9. Other tools in use by the World Bank include, inter alia, Program Expenditure Reform Credits (looking to minimize risks in program lending), Country Financial Accountability Assessment (comparing local accounting and audit standards to international practice), and Country Procurement Assessment Report (sub-set of CFAA). See < http://wbln0018.worldbank.org/prem/ps/iaamarketplace.nsf >

REFERENCES

Asian Development Bank (1999). *Reforms in the Pacific*. Manila: Asian Development Bank.
Binder, L. et al. (1971). *Crises and Sequences in Political Development*. Princeton, NJ: Princeton University Press.
Center for Democracy and Governance (1998). *Handbook on Democracy and Governance Program Indicators*. Washington, D.C.: U.S. Agency for International Development.
Commonwealth Association of Public Administration and Management (CAPAM) (1998). CAPAM International Innovations Awards Programme 1998: Service To The Public – Summaries of the Submissions by The Award Winners, Finalists And Honourable Mentions. http://www.comnet.mt/capam/Intawrd/summarie.htm#Finalists
Deleon, P., & Resnick-Terry, P. (1999). Comparative Policy Analysis: Déjà Vu All Over Again? *Journal of Comparative Policy Analysis: Research and Practice*, *1*, 9–22.
Dethier, J. (1999). Governance and Economic Performance: A Survey, Discussion Papers on Development Policy, No. 5. Bonn, Germany: ZEF.
Development Assistance Committee of OECD (1998). Proposal For Assessing Progress In Participatory Development And Good Governance. Paris: OECD.
Development Assistance Committee of OECD (1999). DAC Informal Experts' Group Meeting on Assessing and Monitoring Performance in Good Governance. Paris: OECD.
Dollar, D., & Kraay, A. (2000). Growth Is Good for the Poor (draft). Washington, D.C.: World Bank. < http://www.worldbank.org/research/growth/pdfiles/growthgoodforpoor.pdf >
Easterly, W., & Levine, R. (1997). Africa's Growth Tragedy: Policies and Ethnic Divisions. *Quarterly Journal of Economics*, *112*, 1203–1250.
Freedom House (1999). *Freedom in the World: The Annual Survey of Political Rights and Civil Liberties, 1998–99*. < http://www.freedomhouse.org/survey99/ >
Institute for Democracy and Electoral Assistance (1997). *Voter Turnout from 1945–1997: A Global Report on Political Participation*. Stockholm: Institute for Democracy and Electoral Assistance.
International Monetary Fund (IMF) (1998). Code of Good Practices on Fiscal Transparency. Washington, D.C.: International Monetary Fund. < http://www.imf.org/fiscal/ >
International Parliamentary Union (2000). *Women in National Parliaments*.

< http://www.ipu.org/wmn-e/classif.htm >

Kato, T., Kaplan, J. A., Sophal, C., & Sopheap, R. (2000). *Cambodia: Enhancing Governance for Sustainable Development.* Working Paper No. 14. Phnom Penh: Cambodia Development Research Institute.

Kaufmann, D., Kraay, A., & Zoido-Lobaton, P. (1999). *Governance Matters.* Washington, D.C.: World Bank. < http://www.worldbank.org/wbi/gac/gac_pdfs/govmatrs.pdf >

Moody's (2000). Sovereign Ratings: A Ratings Guide, New York: Moody's. < http://www.moodys.com/repldata/ratings/ratsov.htm > (May).

Olson, M. (2000). *Power and Prosperity : Outgrowing Communist and Capitalist Dictatorships.* New York: Basic Books.

Political and Economic Risk Consultancy (1998). Shortcomings of the Media in Asia. < http://www.asiarisk.com/library9.html >

PRS Group (2000). *International Country Risk Guide.* East Syracuse, New York: PRS Group.

Schiavo-Campo, S., & Sundaram, P. (2000) (forthcoming). *To Serve and To Preserve: Improving Public Administration in the Competitve World.* Manila: ADB.

Simon, J. (1992). Political-risk analysis for International Banks and Multinational Enterprises. In: R. L. Solberg (Ed.), *Country-Risk Analysis: A Handbook* (pp. 118–132). London: Routledge.

Standard & Poor's Institutional Market Services (2000). COMPUSTAT Global Database. New York: Standard & Poor's.

Transparency International (TI) (2000). Corruption Indexes and Surveys. < http://www.transparency.org/documents/index.html#cpi >

United Nations Development Programme, 1991. *Human Development Report,* New York: Oxford.

Van Rijckeghem, C., & Weder, B. (1997). Corruption and Rate of Temptation: Do Low Wages in the Civil Service Cause Corruption? IMF Working Paper 97/73. Washington, D.C.: International Monetary Fund.

18. NEW PUBLIC MANAGEMENT IN HONG KONG: THE LONG MARCH TOWARD REFORM

K. Au, I. Vertinsky and D. Wang

INTRODUCTION

The story of paradigm shift to what is generally described as the New Public Management (NPM) in Hong Kong has several sub-themes and episodes. It is a story with roots in the late 1960s and early 1970s with periods of lull and renewal characterized by shifting powers and expectations among stakeholders. It is a narrative of reform in which a colonial administration seeks social legitimacy. It is also a story of administrative adjustment to the process of transferring sovereignty, adjustment to a restructuring economy and society, and a time of diffusion of new ideas into the domain of public management. This chapter investigates the antecedent conditions that shaped the reform process in each of its key episodes, the triggers that accelerated it, and the forces that emerged to dampen it.

THE COLONIAL PERIOD: INTERNAL DEVELOPMENTS AND EXTERNAL INFLUENCES

Scott (1998) argues that the origins of managerial efficiency in Hong Kong can be traced to the British government's concern that expenditures in each colony should not exceed its revenue. Once the territory had reached self-sufficiency, the colonial civil service was left largely in control, with little attention from

Learning from International Public Management Reform, Volume 11B, pages 311–335.
ISBN: 0-7623-0760-9

London. The bureaucracy was not held accountable to any local representative institutions, and was not challenged by local politics in any meaningful sense (Cheung, 1997: 720). Indeed for most of its history, party politics was not tolerated in Hong Kong, and until 1985, members of the Legislative Council (except the officials) were appointed by the Governor. "Colonial absolutism had not excluded local participation, but such participation was confined to established elites – mainly business and professional elites" (Cheung, 1997: 721).

The doctrine guiding the government was one of laissez-faire until the 1950s when it was replaced by a doctrine described by the term "positive non-interventionism" coined by Hadden-Cove, the Financial Secretary (1972–1981). The doctrine rested on the premises that: (1) it is futile and damaging to economic growth to intervene in market processes; and (2) it is essential for government to provide only pure public goods and when necessary to undertake actions to protect markets. Huang et. al. (1993: 1419) observed that, based on the ideas of minimum interference and active concern for economic development, the meta-policy in the 1960s and 1970s was to "define its (the government's) role as being to provide the infrastructure within which decisions on entrepreneurial activity remained the prerogatives of the entrepreneur." The emphasis in the domain of social policy was minimum interference and the provision of those services necessary to preserve political stability and economic growth.

This state of affairs came to an end after riots in 1966 and the spillover from the Cultural Revolution highlighted serious flaws in the Hong Kong civil service. The resultant modernization of the colonial civil service in the 1970s significantly expanded the scope of government activities in the areas of education, health, housing and social welfare. Despite pressures from the Finance Branch to check the growth in the public sector, the size of the civil service increased from 1967–1980 by 44%. Its growth, and its expanded responsibilities, led to a significant increase in the proportion of professionals among the civil servants, although power remained concentrated in the small group of civil servants in the general/administrative grade (Scott, 1998). To improve the effectiveness of the government in delivering expanded social programs, the civil service was reorganized through separating policy functions from implementation functions. This followed the recommendations of external consultants (McKinsey and Company) who were hired to facilitate change in 1974. Other recommendations involving financial decentralization met strong resistance from the Finance Branch.

During the late 1970s and early 1980s, two key developments affected the evolution of public management in Hong Kong. Internally, the civil service was pressed to respond to a rapidly emerging service economy (notably financial services) in need of a more sophisticated regulatory apparatus.

Externally the negotiations between the U.K. and PRC about the future of Hong Kong increased uncertainty and pressures on the government to provide stability and defend its legitimacy. The signing in 1984 of the Sino-British agreement did not resolve the uncertainty and created new pressures on the colonial government to maintain economic stability and increase its responsiveness to the population of Hong Kong. The government departed, in practice, from its doctrine of non-interventionism and got involved more aggressively in attempts to foster economic growth. Thus, for example, half of the appropriation of the Industry Department in 1986–87 was earmarked for industrial investment promotion (Huang et al., 1993: 1428). The government also increased its intervention in a variety of areas such as environmental protection, in response to citizens' complaints.

To defend its legitimacy in the transition period the government also introduced some measures to increase representation. In 1984 after a review of representation processes in regional levels, it was decided to extend the electoral process to the central level as was done in the 1970s at the regional and district levels. In 1985 the Legislative Council was reorganized with the introduction of 24 members elected by functional constituencies and an electoral college. On the 27th of May 1987 the government published a Green Paper entitled "The 1987 Review of Developments in Representative Government" followed by the publication of a White Paper which outlined the plan to introduce a number of directly elected members into the Legislature in 1991 (Government of Hong Kong, 1988). While only limited measures to increase the political accountability of the government were introduced the moment was ripe to re-examine the backbone of the government structure – the Civil Service.

THE NEW PUBLIC MANAGEMENT IN HONG KONG: ROUND ONE

The emergence of what is referred to as the "New Public Management" began to dominate the public administration agenda in several countries in the 1980s. In particular, the public management reforms carried out by the Conservative government in the U.K., starting in 1979, served as a model for the Hong Kong government (Pollit, 1996). While "value for money" initiatives and the importance of small government were ingrained in the colonial public administration traditions of Hong Kong, the decentralization that the New Public Management Paradigm requires was alien to British colonial governance traditions, the PRC-preferred model of governance and to Chinese culture. All emphasized a well-controlled hierarchy. The shift to the "New Public Management" also required a significant transformation in the culture of the civil service, from one focused on input-oriented administration to a managerial culture focused on effective outcomes.

A report on Public Sector Reform published in 1989 by the Finance Branch signaled the first comprehensive move of the Hong Kong government to the "New Public Management" (Finance Branch, Government of Hong Kong, 1989).

The Public Sector Reform document articulated the following seven principles:

(1) Regular, systematic review of the whole of public expenditure (zero-base budgeting);
(2) Systematic evaluation of benefits and costs of all government activities and policies and the provision of such information to decision makers to affect policy reviews;
(3) Definition and delegation of responsibility for policy, implementation and resources;
(4) Accountability of managers for all expenditures incurred in support of their policy objectives;
(5) Provision of services through an organization and management framework that is appropriate to the nature of each service;
(6) Improvement of the relationship between related policy and executive functions (policy-agency relationship);
(7) Improvement of the managerial skills of civil servants.

Several pilot projects were launched. The first reviewed the division of responsibility between policy branches and their relevant departments, giving each significantly greater financial authority to manage their budgets and re-deploy savings that accrued. A second project examined the delegation of authority, while a third project involved the creation of trading fund departments, i.e. departments staffed by civil servants but run on a quasi-commercial basis with revenues accruing to separate trading funds. The fourth project focused on statutory corporations established to provide public services, with the goals of clarifying their objectives and increasing their accountability. A review of government operations was also initiated, including the exploration of opportunities for efficiency gains through "contracting out" and review of the benefits and costs of further "corporatization" and privatization initiatives. The review also examined accounting procedures, the introduction of objective-led planning systems, and the introduction of "business managers" to complement the functions of traditional public service administrators.

Implementation of the pilot projects was completed in 1991. In mid–1992, a special unit – the Efficiency Unit – was set up to serve as a focal point for the direction, coordination, and implementation of public sector reform. The arrival of a new governor (Chris Patten) in 1992 brought new vigor to the reform. He added an emphasis on viewing the public as clients, rather than supplicants of the public sector. The Efficiency Unit, along with the Civil Services Branch, was charged with nurturing in the public service "a culture that perceives the public as paying customers and treats them accordingly". The method of achieving this objective was through the introduction of "performance pledges" to all government departments.

To support this change in managerial culture, and help modernize business practices and technologies, a business center was set up to provide internal consulting to the various agencies and departments.

Privatization of government owned assets was also introduced to the reform agenda by Governor Chris Patten. In August 1992, Governor Patten raised the prospect of privatizing the Kowloon-Canton Railway Corporation (KCRC) initiating a debate in Hong Kong about other privatization "candidates" such as the Mass Transit Corp.(MTRC), the Post Office and the Airport Authority. In October 1992, the government confirmed that KCRC is the only utility being considered for privatization with a straight sale or public float among the options considered (South China Morning Post, October 6, 1992). Not surprisingly privatization proposals received a strong endorsement from the General Chamber of Commerce. The Chamber had published a lengthy paper arguing "that privatization should not be regarded as a political football to be kicked around, but as a way to take unnecessary burden off the Government, and therefore the tax-payer" (South China Morning Post, September 20, 1992). The proposals, as expected, mobilized concerns about the appropriateness of selling public assets before the transfer of sovereignty in 1997. Privatization proposals were allowed to die (just to surface several years later). The government has refocused its attention on the establishment of Trading Funds as means for introducing market discipline to government operations.

The form and consequences of establishing Trading Funds for departments providing services on a quasi-commercial basis provide an indicator about the depth of the reform commitment and its effectiveness in improving the productivity of these departments (Huque et al., 1999: 5). Funds could be viewed as one of the critical steps toward introducing major changes through flexibility in management and exposure to open competition. The establishment of Trading Funds required spelling out broad financial objectives, agreed quality standards, a frame of reporting relationship, methods of financing, constraints on the use and disposal of funds and identification of the authority, responsibilities and accountability of managers. The Trading Funds Ordinance of 1993 provided the management framework for the Trading Funds. The Trading Funds established included the Land Registry, the Companies Registry, Sewage Services, the Office of the Telecommunication Authority, the Post Office, and the Electric and Mechanical Services Department.

Apart from the objective of efficiency, the Hong Kong Government demanded the adoption of customer-led orientation. Exposure to competition was regarded as a stimulus, both to the objective of efficiency and the objective of responsiveness to customers. The Trading Funds were required to adopt a much more transparent reporting and planning systems with open Business Plans and Annual Reports. The framework agreements for each Trading Fund allowed the relevant Policy Secretary to monitor the performance and operations of the Fund. The General Manager of the Fund can be fired if he fails to meet the agreement, or penalties can be imposed on the Fund. Typically Funds were instructed to ensure that services offer "value for money", that they meet needs of customers and meet their financial targets. Initially customers did not have a direct involvement in fund decision but their complaints could be reflected through indirect pressure (e.g. through the Policy Secretaries or the Legislative Council). Over time, most Trading Funds have developed means to consult user representatives. The Companies Registry, for example, now holds four meetings a year with its customer Liaison Group which includes members from the Hong Kong Society of Accountants, the Hong Kong Association of Banks, The Law Society and other big Institutions with vested interest in the operation of the Registry (Huque et al., 1999: 28).

Other Funds use focus groups and customer satisfaction surveys to increase their responsiveness. Only the Electrical and Mechanical Services Fund, out of the six funds, was supposed to eventually face market competition. The Post Office, however, gradually saw its natural monopoly eroding as alternative means of communication provided substitutes to mail service. The other four are natural monopolies and thus will not face competition. Pricing decisions by funds, largely, reflected the needs of the funds to meet their financial targets and political pressures from customers. Huque et al. (1999: 38) observed that as departments are gradually transformed into self-accounting units, with increases in customer orientation, the differences between Trading Funds and Departments are disappearing. They suggest that full corporatization of the Funds into public companies with employees without civil servant status will expose them more fully to the discipline of a market regime.

Lam (1997) reports the following achievements of the reform process by 1996:

(1) The customer-driven approach was adopted by the Land Registry. This consisted of an appointment of a customer service manager, regular liaison meetings, customer surveys and newsletters to customers;
(2) The Department of Health appointed a patient relations officer to handle special problems, some amenities for patients were provided in clinics and all departments directly serving the public had adopted performance pledges;
(3) A business-oriented approach to using trading funds was adopted by the Company Registry, and the Land Registry to employ temporary and contract staff to reinvest cash surpluses and work with private sector partners;
(4) Staff participation and commitment was emphasized by the creation of work improvement teams within the Hong Kong Police and Land Registry, by holding tea receptions in the Department of Health and establishing a service quality committee for the police;
(5) Efficiency was increased in the Land Registry by designating each operational division as a cost center;
(6) A quality assurance system was established at the governmental Land Transport Agency in the form of quality control circles;
(7) Work simplification schemes in attempt to raise effectiveness were adopted by the Labor Department;
(8) New human resource management practices were introduced to the Buildings Department with the establishment of a staff development panel, a grade consultation group, and a departmental working committee on training;
(9) A total of 4500 management staff members received training on leadership skills and management change and some 34,000 civil servants received training in customer services.

Some evidence of improved effectiveness is also noted by Lam (1997), especially in the domain of service provision. For example, a savings of 8% was achieved in 1996 through improved programming and the establishment of cost centers. Service targets in this domain were exceeded. Similar achievements are noted in the health and social welfare areas. In all these areas, however, budgets increased, hardly the vision of the "small government" envisaged by the more ideologically motivated versions of the New Public Management.

Increasing decentralization had some counterproductive effects. Lack of coordination between different programs led to policies and programs inconsistent with each other. For example, inconsistent transportation system and housing development plans have led to severe problems of traffic congestion and air pollution in Tuen Mun and Tsuen Wan districts (Lam, 1997). The introduction of reforms through pilot programs have led to marginal changes far short of the total reform articulated in the principles included in the 1989 Public Sector Reform Document that envisioned a global shift from public sector administration to management.

As expected, the more radical proposals to reform the public sector encountered resistance reflecting a variety of factors, such as civil servant responses to lessened employment security, bureaucratic inertia, culture clashes, lack of capacity and inadequate training. Some failures could be attributed to such resistance, while others reflected failures endemic to the New Public Management (Hood, 1996). A dominant factor, however, was the growing presence and influence of China and the uncertainties that the approaching change of régime brought about.

RÉGIME CHANGE

The 1984 Sino-British agreement specified that public servants previously serving in Hong Kong in all government departments, including the Police Department, and members of the judiciary may all remain in employment and continue their service with pay, allowances, benefits and conditions of services no less favorable than before. Thus, the bureaucracy as an institution was intended to continue, as before, relatively unaffected by the transfer of power. (Scott, 1998: 158) Indeed, ". . . the Chinese government has emphasized its wish to inherit a bureaucracy which will retain centralized and hierarchical characteristics" (Scott, 1998: 159). The Civil Service was viewed by it as a means of continued control and a symbol of continuity that was important for the protection of the economic benefits flowing to China, and the additional benefits that might flow in the future.

In contrast the colonial government sought to buttress its legitimacy by bringing reform involving increased decentralization, corporatization and working toward increased responsiveness of the civil service to citizen demands. The clash of expectations by both régimes generated much of the uncertainties surrounding the reforms that started in the early nineties. Indeed, as the 1997 turnover approached the presence and influence of the People's Republic of China (PRC) grew and the motivation of civil servants to pursue implementation of reforms declined.

While increased efficiency as a norm for the civil service was generally accepted many were skeptical about the motives of the colonial government in introducing the reforms. Cheung (1995: 43) argued, for example, that claims for increased efficiency were only rhetorical and that the reform was intended to release public managers from political pressures of transitional politics, not to make them more accountable or responsive. It was also claimed that corporatization, was intended to shield the colonial régime from the increased voice of the emerging political parties.

The value of stability and predictability to Hong Kong elites and to the Chinese government peaked just before and immediately after the transition. The Civil Service became the symbol of continuity under the new, appointed Chief Executive. Only after reassuring the world that indeed "one country, two systems" is a reality, could the new régime re-examine the role and structure of government and contemplate change.

Introduction of some measures of representative government, though very limited, meant an increase in political accountability and continued demands for a responsive government. The institutions developed in the 1990s to bring about reform and the know-how accumulated implementing some reform measures, provided an infrastructure for a new reform movement once the political conditions were appropriate. A short period of stability and relative non-intervention by Beijing in the internal affairs of the Special Administrative Region (SAR) decreased the anxiety of foreign economic stakeholders and the local population. A recession then provided the trigger for reform.

A NEW RÉGIME AND THE ASIAN FLU: AN EPOCH FOR BOLD STROKES OR LONG MARCHES?

The "Asian flu" and the deep recession it brought about in Hong Kong in 1998 have led to two contradictory developments in public management. On the one hand, they facilitated a drive to reform the civil service along principles consistent with "New Public Management" (e.g. shrinking the civil service, privatization, introduction of market mechanisms to the sphere of the public sector). On the other hand, they have encouraged a government that was lauded by Milton Friedman as a model for minimalist government in a free market economy to take a more interventionist role in its economy.

During the financial crisis of 1998, and to counter speculative runs on the Hong Kong dollar by sophisticated hedge funds, the government decided to intervene by buying aggressively in the stock market to bolster its value and discourage speculation. The fixed exchange rate between the Hong Kong dollar and the U.S. dollar was considered an essential condition for maintaining financial stability and defending the position of Hong Kong as an international financial center. The strategy succeeded and the devaluation of the Hong Kong dollar was prevented. Indeed, the government has made significant gains from its investments.

In isolation this measure may reflect an uncharacteristic response to a severe crisis. A persistent recession, however, encouraged the government to re-examine its role in economic matters and pursue what is best described as the development of an industrial strategy.

> We have caught the Net fever said Michael Sze, Executive Director of the Hong Kong Trade Development Council. Hong Kong is aiming to lay the groundwork for a dot-com boom by building a massive high-tech complex and by creating a technology-friendly financial environment. The territory's officials say Hong Kong remains strong in financial services, telecommunications and property development, and any high-tech endeavors would complement those strengths (Jang, 2000: T1).

The government articulated a vision of Hong Kong as an information technology regional hub. To implement its vision it created a new stock market for "start-up" technology companies and initiated, in a joint venture with the private sector (the Pacific Century Group), the U.S.$1.6 billion Cyberport property development project. The project will create an intelligent building complex, a state-of-the-art broadband telecommunication and information 'backbone', and a wide range of shared facilities to attract technology companies to Hong Kong (HKSAR, 1999). Developing a new financial market and even financing physical infrastructure are, arguably, not inconsistent even with the purer versions of the New Public Management ideology which could see a role for governments in coping with market failures. However, the Hong Kong government, in articulating a particular vision of the sectoral structure of its economy has gone far beyond correcting for market failures.

While the recession brought about a more interventionist public policy it also generated the expected pressures to shrink the government. Rising demands for services and falling revenues typically trigger a quest for cost cutting and increases in efficiency. The financial crisis of 1998 was accompanied by a collapse in the real estate market, thus reducing the flexibility of a government that has made, in the past, effective use of public land sales to meet unexpected financial demands. The year 1998 was also a likely year to trigger change for another, perhaps more important reason. The transfer of authority was completed. There was no apparent disruption and loss of confidence by either domestic or foreign economic stakeholders. It was now an obvious time for the new régime to re-examine the post-colonial role of government and the nature of its system.

Several administrative blunders also contributed to increasing pressures on the government to shake the civil service and introduce reforms. These include a bird flu crisis and an airport opening chaos. The South China Morning Post (October 11, 1998), for example, has welcomed a reshuffle of top civil servants stating that ". . . during the past 15 months, policy blunders and the mishandling of crises have prompted calls for action against leading lights in Hong Kong's once-vaunted civil service". The Newspaper criticized the SAR Chief Executive Tung Chee-hwa of being fully "house-trained" by the civil service, suggesting, however, that ". . . the economic crisis means there are clouds looming on the horizon of the civil service" (South China Morning Post, October 11, 1998). The newspaper welcomed plans by the government for dealing with the financial crisis looking for an increase of 5% in productivity by all departments by 2002. The newspaper article concluded that, ". . . the iron-rice bowl of guaranteed lifetime employment is also starting to crack, with plans to instead hire civil servants on short-term contracts. And the recent blunders have created a climate in which attacks on the civil service have become more frequent" (The South China Morning Post October 18, 1998).

Reform ideas introduced but not acted upon in the transition period have surfaced. Institutions such as the Efficiency Unit established to bring about change in the early nineties were ready to champion reforms and provide the technical expertise. One of the first initiatives implemented immediately after July 1997 was the initiation of the Performance Measurement Programme (PMP). In parallel, Price Waterhouse was engaged to conduct a research project covering best practice in performance in both the public and private sectors and the Government undertook "its own stocktaking to assess the state of performance measurement within the Government. Based on this assessment, the aim was to identify gaps and improvement opportunities" (The PSR Forum, no date). As long as continuity and reduced uncertainty were important objectives of the new régime the preferred way to reforming the public sector was through what Kanter et al. (1992) called a long march strategy, i.e. reforms introduced as operational initiatives by a variety of units. Change under this strategy is affected by many small wins and "muddling through" (Lindblom, 1959; Weick, 1984), not "bold strokes" involving strategic moves by top-level officials.

The severity of the recession, however, provided both the motive and legitimacy for bold strokes involving articulation of a new vision for the Civil Service. The Chief Secretary for Administration, Ms Anson Chan observed that the government had initiated the debate on Civil Service Reform not because of pressure from the community to do so, but because with the transition accomplished it was an opportune time to take a hard look to see how the government could position itself to serve the community in the next millennium (Chan, 1999).

The release of a consultation document by the Civil Service Bureau in March 1999, entitled "Civil Service Into the 21st Century: Civil Service Reform", provided for public scrutiny a rather ambitious reform program going well beyond a cost cutting exercise. This document explained the motives for the reform. It cited the economic crisis, increasing community expectations toward the Government, the mishandling of a "number of specific incidents by the government" as reasons for reform. It articulated six principles for the reform:

(1) Change amidst stability;
(2) Step by step;
(3) Comprehensive overview;
(4) Wide consultation;
(5) Practicable means;
(6) Reasonable and lawful.

These principles were intended to ensure the maintenance of smooth operations without a major interruption in the overall operation of the civil service. The chosen implementation strategy was gradual, tackling relatively straightforward proposals first. Proposals were supposed to take a systems-wide perspective and be aligned with existing operations. Wide consultation and flexibility should help reduce friction. Proposals should be vetted to ensure that they are practicable, reasonable and lawful. The objective of the reform was to build upon the strength of the existing system, a more open and flexible Civil Service system. A system that can recruit new talent and fire non-performers at all levels. The reform was also intended to create an enabling and motivating environment for civil servants through a performance-based reward system. The reform's third objective was to enhance efficiency and quality service and nurture a "performance-based service-oriented" management culture.

The document delineated the four policy areas for review and reform. These included: (1) the entry and exit mechanisms; (2) pay and fringe benefits; (3) disciplinary procedures; and (4) performance arrangements, professional training and personal development. The first area presented the greatest challenge as it threatened the job security of existing civil servants. A permanent civil service has the advantage of creating incentives for civil servants to remain in the service and thus retain their experience and expertise even in tight labour markets. The prospects of permanency and pension created disincentives for corruption. In a cyclical economy permanent civil service means less flexibility, lower incentives to perform above the average and constraints on renewal and cross fertilisation with the private sector. The document proposed a new entry system, employing lower ranked civil servants on fixed term agreements (this will cover about two thirds of the civil service). Those who do not perform or do not show potential for advancement to higher ranks will be dismissed. Appointments to supervisory positions will be done through open competition (including recruiting outside candidates). Outside candidates will be appointed initially for a fixed term and only after proving through performance their potential, they may be allowed to switch to the new permanent term (as those promoted from the inside). Permanency will be redefined to mean a promise of a structured career and long-term employment for those who perform. The retirement system will change to allow portability of pension rights, thus reducing the barriers of moving from the public to the private sector or vice-versa. Compulsory early-retirement mechanisms will be introduced to allow replacement of permanent civil servants when human-resources management needs require it.

Starting salaries will be based upon review of salaries in the private-sector. A performance pay system will be introduced. General annual pay adjustments will follow those in the private sector. Similarly, fringe benefits will be adjusted to reflect private sector practices. The document proposes to set up a centralized independent disciplinary mechanism to ensure compliance with rules and the integrity of the service (perhaps with an aim to compensate for the reduction in the degree of disincentives for corrupt or negligent behaviour).

To ensure a merit and performance-based reward system, a performance appraisal mechanism and a performance oriented management culture will be established. Proposals to achieve these objectives include:

(1) Establishing an indicative benchmark for grading distribution;
(2) Development and promotion of a system of performance measurement linked to department goals and responsibilities (continuing the efforts of the Efficiency Unit to design performance measurement system for all departments);
(3) The development of extensive training and development programs to support the reform objectives.

The document and its far-reaching proposals was definitely a bold move but the implementation principles outlined held the promise of a very long march. The 1999/2000 Budget identified the major reform priorities, and targets of the government as follows (HKSAR, 1999):

• A review of employment terms and conditions, including starting pay, allowances and other benefits;

- An overhaul of the appointment system to provide greater flexibility in the hiring and firing of staff and to consider the introduction of performance-related pay increases;
- Strengthening the result-oriented and service-based culture;
- Maximizing room for private sector involvement in the delivery of public services;
- An Enhanced Productivity Program to deliver productivity gains of 5% of operating expenditure by 2002/3 (with gains of HK$800 million (U.S.$103 million) expected in 1999/2000.

Under the initial reform plans, some 20,000 clerical and 50,000 employees in law enforcement organizations (i.e. police, the Immigration and Customs and Excise departments) would retain their tenure as permanent employees, while about 120,000 would be employed on contract basis. As an interim measure, the government introduced a pay freeze and a freeze on hiring new staff as permanent civil servants, offering new recruits one to five year contracts.

The measures initially encountered strong opposition from civil service associations and unions. For example, the Chairman of the Hong Kong Civil Service General Union, Mr. Cheung, representing general workers within the civil service most affected by the proposed reforms, suggested that his union was studying the possibility of labour actions as well as legal actions to oppose the reform. He identified four problematic areas of reform that upset his union: (1) the elimination of lifetime job guarantees; (2) changes to disciplinary procedures; (3) performance-linked pay; and (4) work culture (*Hong Kong Standard*, March 17, 1999).

The combination of a severe recession and a "high distance" hierarchical culture on the one hand and the element of uncertainty introduced by flexible implementation schedules reduced the ability of the civil service associations to mobilize public opinion and their own members' support for dramatic actions. A month later, appearing before the Legislative Council, representatives of nine civil servant associations suggested that the reforms were premature and too severe but were bound to take place. "They said that the government had begun reforms before examining what needed to be done . . . civil servants are upset that the government did not consult them before creating plans for the reform. The government's consultation paper, released in February 1999, and the consultation period that ends in June were dismissed as a side show by the civil servants" (*Hong Kong Standard*, April 30, 1999).

In June 1999, a powerful civil servants union (The Hong Kong Chinese Civil Servants' Association) departed from its usually adversarial stance to urge the government to carry out civil service reform gradually. The Association suggested dealing first with comparatively easy items (e.g. simplifying disciplinary procedures) and deferring, though with a time limit, difficult items (e.g. performance evaluation, performance pay linkage issues). The Association expressed its willingness to work with the government in carrying out the reform provided it was carried out by stages. Its spokesman warned the government not to worsen the "already damaged relationship" as civil service stability was indispensable for good administration.

The argument for maintaining stability of the civil service of Hong Kong as a symbol of continuity and autonomy of the regional government, which was effective in stopping much of the reform during the post–1997 period of transition, lost some of its power as the business community was reassured by China's relatively non-interventionist policy toward the economic affairs of Hong Kong. The recession provided the government with another argument against a privileged civil service. The government, echoing the mass media, argued that the employment terms civil servants traditionally enjoyed could not continue unchecked in a time of recession.

On October 6, 1999, in his annual policy address, Mr. Tung, the Chief Executive of the SAR, reiterated the determination of his government to continue the reform of existing government systems and procedures to adapt to changes and demands of the new era. He identified three foci to the future efforts of the government. The first area of reform was changes that are intended to defend Hong Kong's position as a regional financial centre. This included measures to consolidate financial markets and strengthen the linked exchange rate régime, i.e. the maintenance of the fixed exchange rate between the U.S. dollar and the Hong Kong dollar. These measures were intended to remove weaknesses that surfaced during the financial turmoil brought about by the "Asian flu" and speculative runs against the Hong Kong dollar. The second area of reform was rationalization of the government's basic policies and delivery system. Specific measures proposed included the launch of education reforms and dissolution of municipal councils. The third area of reform was targeted at the modernization of the civil service structure and improved efficiency. Specific measures included entry pay adjustment and the implementation of productivity enhancement mechanisms including some adjustment in the tenure of some groups of civil servants. Cognizant of the growing militancy of civil servant associations and unions, and threats of labour actions, Mr. Tung suggested that these measures would be implemented gradually after consultation and careful deliberation with the aim to improve services and efficiency. These reforms would be introduced ". . . in different areas at varying speeds by different means". The initial plans for ambitious restructuring which included elimination of lifetime job guarantees for about

120,000 non-management employees would be introduced in a way to minimize possible interruption in the supply of services and reduction in productivity (*Xinhua News Agency*, October 6, 1999).

During the radio program "Letter to Hong Kong" on RTHK the secretary for Civil Service, Lam Woon-Kwong said that the management-initiated civil service reforms were not meant to be expedient and popular. He admitted that some departments were unnecessarily big. "In order to be more flexible, transparent and able to attract capable people, he said "we must not hide inefficiencies in the excuse of morale; we must not defend inertia in the disguise of stability and we must not shy from change in the name of continuity" (South China Morning Post, March 23, 2000) – indeed bold words.

In the 2000/2001 budget, Financial Secretary Donald Tsang announced that the total civil service establishment would be cut by 10,000, or about five percent, in the three years from 2000–01 to 2002–03, not quite a bold stroke. Although the implementation of the full reform program will indeed require a long march, the bold stroke taken with the announcement of the 1999 reform opened the door for many quick, "small wins". Only a bold stroke could have moved a retrenched Civil Service system by changing expectations. Implementation, however, requires a degree of cooperation that is difficult to achieve without a measure of stability and predictability that a radical change may threaten, or a strong resolve, authority and power that require social legitimacy.

Proposals to reform the civil service to introduce "market-like" processes into government departments and general efforts to increase efficiency and reduce the size of the government were complemented by programs focusing on privatization of public assets as well as corporatization of some government services. In 1998, the government circulated an informal proposal to privatize the Water Supplies Department, the Post-Office and part of the tasks of the Housing Department. The government developed a gradual privatization program expected to see privatization of the estate management work of the Housing Department. It was reported that the Chief Executive of the SAR announced the proposal after a public opinion survey that showed a majority in favour of the plan. Most political parties and tenants also supported the move (South China Morning Post, May 4, 1999).

In the 1999/2000 Budget, the government also announced its plan to list a minority stake in the MTRC to raise HK$30 billion over two years. It anticipated the first tranche of MTRC stock to be offered in the year 2000. It also suggested that the water-supply assets and the Cross-Habour Tunnel might also be privatized along with other government services (South China Morning

Post, April 28, 1999). Some consideration was also given to a recycled 1992 proposal to privatize the KCRC but the proposal was withdrawn when it became clear that financing requirements for planned expansions of the railway would not be attractive to potential investors. The MTRC privatization proposal encountered criticism from a variety of stakeholders, e.g. users fearing a private monopoly and unions fearing losses of jobs.

The government persisted and introduced a privatization bill. A variety of amendments were introduced in the Legislative Council reflecting the concerns of stakeholders. Some of the proposed amendments would have imposed price-cap formula based on performance or required legislative approval of all fare increases. Others would require representation of staff members on the board of directors. The Government rejected the amendments noting that the legislators' plans to change the MTRC privatization bill would undermine its operations and business rating. (South China Morning Post, January 28, 2000).

The proposal for gradual privatization of state management services encountered union criticisms and social action. The government persisted in its determination backed by public sentiment. On April 26, 1999, Anson Chan, the Chief Secretary for Administration, emphasized that contracting out is the government's "major direction" (South China Morning Post, April 27, 1999). Despite its efforts the record of the Government in privatization did not impress the public. The South China Morning Post, for example, observed:

> Mr. Tung is obviously back-pedalling from his earlier ambitious reform commitments, even though he is reluctant to admit it in so many words. Only a few months ago, the authorities were eager to create a media environment favourable for privatizing the Water Supplies Department, Post Office and several other branches. Nevertheless, opposition from the civil servants and legislators has been formidable. Officials need at least untie one of the two knots of resistance to keep the reform scheme afloat (October 16, 1999).

OVERVIEW AND ASSESSMENT OF A DECADE OF REFORM ATTEMPTS

The announced targets of a decade of reform in Hong Kong are characteristic of other attempts to implement the New Public management paradigm: (1) Shrinking the public sector, allowing the private sector through the market to serve the public instead of government providing the services; (2) Increasing efficiency of the public sector, introducing to the government market mechanisms wherever it is feasible; (3) Increasing the responsiveness of the public sector to the public it serves. A decade of attempts to shrink the government in Hong Kong (1990–2000) resulted in a net growth of the civil service. The civil service grew consistently until the past year (see Table 18.1 and Fig. 18.1). The drop evident after 1991/92 reflects reorganization of government, creating the Hospital Authority and gradually shifting personnel from the Health Department to the Authority.

Government expenditures (in real term) have increased by about 51% between fiscal year 1990–91 to fiscal year 1997–98. The share of government expenditures as part of the GDP has grown from about 13% to 15%. The government over the period increased its intervention in the economy. Indeed in the end of the period the government, perhaps to counter one of the most severe recessions in the recent history of Hong Kong, has developed what can be describe as an industrial vision if not an industrial policy.

Assessment of the reform process in Hong Kong must, however, consider two factors: (1) the size of government in Hong Kong relative to the size of government in other countries was and is still small; (2) the process of modernization and increasing wealth raised the expectations of the population for services that the private sector did not provide. Perhaps without commitment to reform one could have expected even a larger public sector.

Did the reform improve efficiency? It is difficult to provide a verdict since only a short time has passed since the introduction of the last reform. There is evidence that many departments already met the government target of 5% increase in productivity, suggesting perhaps that the target may not have been very challenging. The Trading Fund experiment showed that a noticeable increase in productivity and cost savings are possible. These resulted from increases in accountability requirements. However, without exposure to competition there is a high likelihood that such gains will dissipate.

Had the responsiveness to the public increased as a result of the reforms? Huque et al. (1999: 52) assessing the success of the Trading Funds, the operations that should have provided the benchmark for comparison, concluded that:

> On balance, it can be said that the Trading Fund experiment has been partially successful. Although the objective of developing a customer-led régime has not been attained, it can be noted that customers are now recognized as an important element in the operation of Trading Funds.

Similarly, departments providing services for the public are now monitoring public satisfaction and are concerned about their public image. Whether such concerns translate to long-term satisfaction of public needs is not certain.

There is no doubt that review of government operations, the introduction of better accounting procedures, clear mission statements, work plan pledges, increased transparency brought by the various reforms are likely to improve management in the public sector. Some of the responses of the civil service to

Table 18.1.   Hong Kong Economic and Financial Data

Year	Real GDP (in Billions of HK$)	% Change	Government Revenue (in Billions of HK$)	% Change	Government Expenditure (in Billions of HK$)	% Change	Total Population (In Millions)	% Change	Strength of the Civil Service (in Thousands)	% Change	Number of Hospital Authority Employees	% Change
68	108.4	—					3.8445	—	72.936	—		
69	120.6	11.29					3.9061	1.60	75.444	3.44		
70	131.7	9.18					3.9954	2.29	77.975	3.35		
71	141.0	7.08					4.0955	2.51	81.438	4.44		
72	155.5	10.33					4.1843	2.17	84.495	3.75		
73	174.8	12.36					4.3342	3.58	89.941	6.45		
74	178.8	2.33					4.4386	2.41	95.284	5.94		
75	179.4	0.33					4.5008	1.40	104.291	9.45		
76	208.6	16.23					4.5510	1.12	104.157	(0.13)		
77	233.0	11.73					4.6315	1.77	108.385	4.06		
78	252.8	8.50					4.7699	2.99	115.674	6.73		
79	282.0	11.52					5.0247	5.34	122.838	6.19		
80	310.5	10.12	67.06		50.25		5.1451	2.40	129.217	5.19		
81	339.0	9.19	68.13	1.59	54.45	4.70	5.2385	1.82	139.252	7.77		
82	348.4	2.75	64.21	(5.75)	62.02	8.12	5.3195	1.55	154.034	10.62		
83	368.2	5.69	60.20	(6.25)	55.49	(5.91)	5.3774	1.09	166.569	8.14		
84	404.9	9.97	60.81	1.02	57.07	2.13	5.4309	0.99	170.051	2.09		
85	406.6	0.43	65.40	7.55	60.91	4.41	5.5004	1.28	172.641	1.52		
86	450.4	10.77	70.04	7.08	61.54	1.24	5.5657	1.19	174.946	1.34		
87	508.8	12.96	80.55	15.01	64.01	3.09	5.6153	0.89	179.053	2.35		
88	549.3	7.97	87.71	8.89	64.94	1.57	5.6716	1.00	182.843	2.12		
89	563.4	2.56	88.65	1.06	76.75	12.46	5.7265	0.97	186.054	1.76		
90	582.5	3.40	89.52	0.99	85.56	9.58	5.7520	0.45	188.393	1.26		
91	612.0	5.06	105.01	17.29	84.40	(0.30)	5.8153	1.10	190.448	1.09		
92	650.3	6.26	112.92	7.53	94.57	11.02	5.8876	1.24	185.685	(2.50)		
93	690.2	6.13	128.13	13.47	113.39	19.76	5.9980	1.88	182.099	(1.93)		
94	727.5	5.40	125.94	(1.71)	118.14	5.88	6.1193	2.02	180.695	(0.77)		
95	755.8	3.89	126.34	0.31	128.52	11.57	6.2700	2.46	179.972	(0.40)	43309	
96	789.8	4.49	138.06	9.28	121.04	(6.19)	6.4213	2.41	182.675	1.50	46668	7.76
97	829.0	4.97	176.11	27.56	121.71	1.88	6.6171	3.05	184.639	1.08	47802	2.43
98	786.4	(5.14)					6.8056	2.85	186.213	0.85	49534	3.62

Source: Census and Statistics Department.

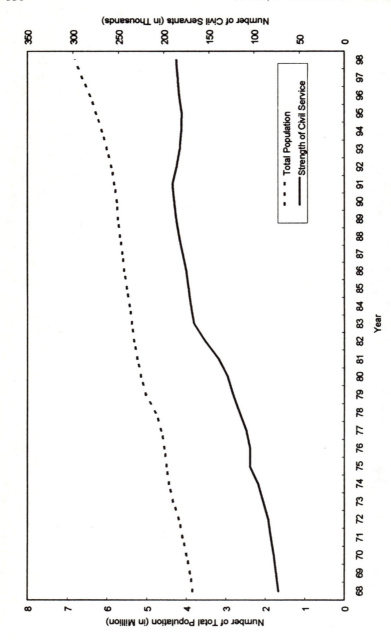

Fig. 18.1. A Comparison of Total Population and the Government Workforce 1968–98.
Sources: Census and Statistics Department and Civil Service Reform Consultation Document.

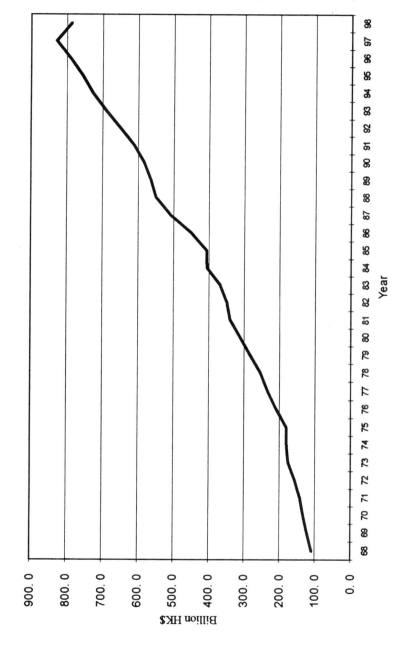

Fig. 18.2. GDP of Hong Kong 1968–1998 (at 1990 Prices).
Source: Census and Statistics Department.

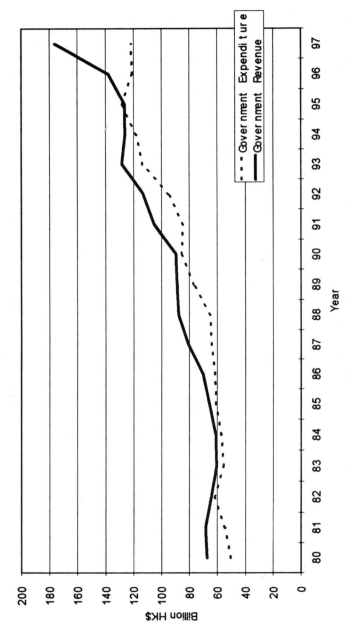

Fig. 18.3. Government Expenditure and Revenue 1980–97 (in 1990 Hong Kong Dollar).
Source: Hong Kong Annual Report 1980–97.

reform pressures may meet the new requirements in form, but not in substance. Resources may be redirected from servicing the long-term needs of the public to short-term public opinion management. The long term results of the reform will depend on the government's resolve and ability to overcome the resistance of the various stakeholders and rent seekers and its ability to mobilize and empower a Civil Service, committed to a new organizational culture, the culture of efficient management.

CONCLUSIONS

Several insights may be gleaned from Hong Kong experience with reform. Timing of reform introduction is a key strategic variable affecting its success. Shocks to the macro-system (e.g. severe economic recession, socio-political crisis) provide both a stimulus and opportunities for introducing reforms. Shocks "unhinge" systems and reduce the momentum of internal forces organized against change. Shocks to the system provide legitimacy for reforms. The riots of 1967 and the deep recession of 1998 provided examples of such opportunities for reform. The sustainability of reforms depends on the social legitimacy of reformers and their reform plans, on their resolve, vision and political skills. The Colonial Régime in the decade leading to 1997 lacked legitimacy and saw reforms as a means for getting legitimacy. It could not mobilize the population or the Civil Service as everyone waited (some feared) the transition.

The preservation of economic vital interests during the transition period required stability. The public civil service provided such stability, legitimizing no-change as the appropriate policy stance. A smooth transition that reduced the level of uncertainty and a severe economic recession provided a new opportunity for reform. It was time for bold moves. The government endorsed bold plans, but chose long marches for implementation. The legitimacy for reforms offered by the circumstances of the moment eroded, i.e. the end of the economic crisis.

The long march tends to challenge the legitimacy of the reformer as threatened stakeholders mobilize to protect their "rents". The opportunities for bold moves in Hong Kong have passed. The success of the government in implementing its vision of the New Public Management will depend on its resolve and its ability to buttress its legitimacy. Without this resolve, the latest reform will be another in a series of moves by many governments in Hong Kong's past, to get better value for money during recessions. This is not the New Public Management envisioned in the reform proposals.

REFERENCES

Chan, A. (1999). Message from the Chief Secretary for Administration, Hong Kong: Government of Hong Kong. http://www.hku.hk/hkgcsb/csreform/english/ecsm1.htm

Cheung, A. (1995). Financial, Managerial and Political Dimensions of Public Sector Reform. In: J. Lee & A. Cheung (Eds), *Public Sector Reform in Hong Kong; Key Concepts, Progress-to-date and Future Direction* (pp. 30–68). Hong Kong: The Chinese University Press.

Cheung, A. (1997). Rebureaucratization of Politics in Hong Kong, Prospects After 1997. *Asian Survey, XXXVII*(8), 720–737.

Civil Service Bureau (1999). *Civil Service into the 21st Century: Civil Service Reform.* Hong Kong: Civil Service Bureau, Government Secretariat, March.

Finance Branch (1989). *Public Sector Reform.* Hong Kong: Hong Kong Government Printer.

Government of Hong Kong (1988). *Development of Representative Government in Hong Kong.* White Paper, Hong Kong: Hong Kong Government Printer, February.

HKSAR (1999). http://www.info.gov.hk/info/sar2/budget.htm

Hong Kong Standard (1999). Action to Block Civil Service Reform is Possible Says Union. March 17.

Hong Kong Standard (1999). Reform Plans 'Premature, Severe'. April 30.

Hood, C. (1995). Contemporary Public Management: A New Global Paradigm? *Public Policy and Administration, 10*(2), 104–117.

Huang, D., Tang, D., & Chow, K. W. (1993). Public Administration in Hong Kong: Crises and Prospects. *International Journal of Public Administration, 16*(9), 1397–1430.

Huque, A. S., Hayllar, M. R., Cheung, A., Flynn, N., & Wong, H. (1999). Public Reform in Hong Kong: The Performance of Trading Funds. *Occasional Paper #2, City University of Hong Kong*, Hong Kong.

Jang, B. (2000). Asian Flu Turns to Dot-Com Fever. *The Globe and Mail*, January 27: T1.

Kanter, R. M., Stein, B., & Jick, T. (1992). *The Challenge of Organizational Change.* New York: The Free Press.

Lam, J. (1997). Transformation from Public Administration to Management, Success and Challenges of Public Sector Reform in Hong Kong. *Public Productivity and Management Review, 20*(4), 405–419.

Lee, J., & Cheung, A. (Eds) (1995). *Public Sector Reform in Hong Kong; Key Concepts, Progress-to-date and Future Direction.* Hong Kong: The Chinese University Press.

Lindblom, C. E. (1959). The Science of Muddling Through. *Public Administration Review, 19*(2), 79–88.

Pollit, C. (1996). Anti-Statist Reforms and New Administrative Directions. Public Administration in the United Kingdom. *Public Administration Review*, Jan/Feb, *56*(1), 81–90.

PSR Forum (No Date). http://www.info.gov.hk/eu/psrhk/pmp_com.htm

Scott, I. (1998). The Bureaucratic Transition. In: I. Scott (Ed.), *Institutional Change and the Political Transition in Hong Kong* (pp. 158–179). New York: St. Martin Press.

South China Morning Post (1998). Reshuffle Ends Civil Service Honeymoon, October 18, 9.

South China Morning Post (1998). Upper Hand For Civil Service, October 11, 8.

South China Morning Post (2000). Reform Need Civil Participation, March 23, 17.

South China Morning Post (1992). Mass-Transit Systems Ripe for Privatization, October 6, 2.

South China Morning Post (1992). Patten keen on privatization, August 22, 2.

South China Morning Post (1999). Scale of Property Income Presents Challenge To Privatization Ambitions; MTRC Rides Premium Risk, Sept. 23, 16.

South China Morning Post (1999). Let Us Embrace Privatization Trend, October 16, 15.
South China Morning Post (1999). Housing Staff Gear Up to Strike Over Privatization, May 4, 6.
South China Morning Post (1999). Chief Signals Further Privatization; Review Will Identify Areas to be Contracted Out in the Wake of Civil Service Shake-Up, April 27, 6.
South China Morning Post (1999). Exchange Chief Extols Privatization Benefits, April 28, 2.
South China Morning Post (2000). Attempts to Alter Bill On MTR Privatization Rejected, January 26, 6.
South China Morning Post (1992). When Privatization is Right Policy Best Policy; With Increased Demands on the Government's Financial Resources, September 20, 13.
Weick, K. E. (1984). Small Wins: Redefining the Scale of Social Problems, *American Psychologist, 39*(1), 40–49.
Xinhua News Agency (1999). Government News Release, Beijing, October 6, *10*, 39.

19. NEW PUBLIC MANAGEMENT IN TAIWAN: GOVERNMENT REINVENTION

Yu-Ying Kuo

INTRODUCTION

The New Public Management (NPM) has been developing in Taiwan for about a decade. Its highpoint is the government reinvention movement. On March 19, 1998, the Executive Yuan Premier Vincent C. Siew asserted, "The Executive Yuan is energetically planning for and promoting the national development plan for entering the next century, of which the Asia-Pacific Regional Operations Center (APROC) plan and the Taiwan Technology Island Initiative comprise the core. They will determine the direction of the island's modernization in the century to come. (The website of the Research, Development, and Evaluation Commission)". As a consequence of these plans, an across-the-board government reinvention was implemented to create a new, flexible and adaptable government and raise national competitiveness.

GOVERNMENT REINVENTION IN TAIWAN

The six crucial points set forth in the Premier's speech to guide the government reinvention effort were:

(1) the hiring of superior personnel to raise the professionalism of government service and the establishment of a bureaucratic system characterized by its excellence;

Learning from International Public Management Reform, Volume 11B, pages 337–351.
Copyright © 2001 by Elsevier Science Ltd.
All rights of reproduction in any form reserved.
ISBN: 0-7623-0760-9

(2) the introduction of entrepreneurial skills and business-like management in order to sweep away old modes of thought, see government with new eyes, and carve out new paths to follow;

(3) the involvement of the entire body of public servants in government reinvention, so that their attitudes and aspirations are focused only on the good of the nation, so that the citizens will prosper, the government will have a bright outlook, and public officials will have dignity;

(4) the emphasis on vision and creativity in promoting government reinvention;

(5) the extension of government reinvention activities so as to not depend on the strength of the executive branch alone, but to encompass other areas of government as well, including the Legislative, Judicial, Examination and Control Yuans;

(6) the creation of a client-oriented government service with agencies listening to the opinions and ideas of the public through a variety of communications channels to ensure that the will of the people becomes the wellspring of government restructuring efforts.

Pursuant to this government reinvention initiative, the Executive Yuan in 1998 proposed the "Statute of Privatization of Provincial Government Business", outlining the government reinvention concept and establishing the Government Reinvention Promotion Committee. In addition, the Government Reinvention Advisory Committee was established to offer opinions and suggestions. Three teams were set up as the primary task forces to implement the related activities: the Organization Restructuring Team, the Personnel and Service Restructuring Team, and the Regulatory Affairs Restructuring Team. Their composition and responsibilities are described by the Research, Development and Evaluation Commission (RDEC). (The website of the RDEC)

The Government Reinvention Promotion Committee
The President of the Executive Yuan will appoint committee members with the assistance of the Vice-President. Members shall be drawn from all levels of government, including heads of government agencies, as well as mid-and low-level officials. Committee responsibilities include:

(1) developing a vision for the restructuring effort;
(2) drafting policies and strategies for the government restructuring;
(3) examining and reviewing implementation plans;
(4) assessing the effectiveness of promotion efforts;
(5) coordinating and resolving conflicts between work teams and government agencies.

The Government Reinvention Advisory Committee

The President of the Executive Yuan shall appoint acommittee composed of 15 to 21 members drawn from the ranks of academic experts and enterprise managers with experience in successful enterprise restructuring. Its responsibilities include:

(1) providing recommendations for the restructuring effort.
(2) consulting and advising.

The Organization Restructuring Team

Under the auspices of the RDEC of the Executive Yuan, this team will coordinate the combined efforts of the Ministry of the Interior, the Executive Yuan personnel office, and other concerned agencies. Its responsibilities include recasting the role of government, reducing the number of administrative layers, revising the relationship between central and local governments, adjusting the abilities and structure of agencies within the Executive Yuan, drafting organizational standards, and establishing a performance-oriented oversight system.

The Personnel and Services Restructuring Team

Under the auspices of the Executive Yuan Personnel Office and the RDEC, it will coordinate affairs with the Examination Yuan, the Ministry of Justice, and other agencies. Its responsibilities include:

(1) upgrading organizational culture;
(2) eliminating corruption;
(3) raising the morale of public official;
(4) stressing participation;
(5) providing incentives for restructuring;
(6) increasing the flexibility of the official workforce;
(7) establishing a results-oriented testing system;
(8) strengthening personnel training and practical career experience;
(9) cultivating an enthusiastic service attitude;
(10) revising relevant rules and regulations;
(11) promoting rationalized, efficient and convenient administrative procedures;
(12) raising service quality;
(13) implementing "one-window service".

The Regulatory Restructuring Affairs Team

Under the auspices of the Council for Economic Planning and Development and the Rules Committee of the Executive Yuan, the Regulatory Restructuring

Affairs Team will coordinate affairs with concerned agencies throughout the government.

Its responsibilities include:

(1) making adjustments to the role of government as necessary;
(2) bringing in private sector participation in researching and drafting changes to public affairs laws;
(3) improving Ministry of Finance budgetary systems;
(4) implementing user fees and anti-fraud procedures in benefits programs;
(5) studying and revising rules and regulations which affect competitiveness and public convenience.

The primary objective of the government reinvention is to bring in the energy and commitment characteristic of enterprise management in order to raise national competitiveness through the establishment of a renewed, flexible and adaptable administrative apparatus. This course of action attempts to establish client-oriented and performance-oriented government service management systems. Underlying NPM, the central government and the local governments focus on "results" and "performance" in order to satisfy their "customers", the public. They are emulating the typical style of the New Public Management – "Entrepreneurial Government." (Chiang & Liu, 1999; Jan, 1999). Figure 19.1 outlines the structure and the procedures of Taiwan's government reinvention effort.

The Government Reinvention Advisory Committee and the Government Reinvention Promotion Committee direct the three work teams, and review the plans they propose. The work teams and the implementing agencies are to publish reports of results and performance seasonally and to submit the reports to the Government Reinvention Promotion Committee. After each team's periodic evaluation, the Government Reinvention Promotion Committee will be briefed on the actual implementation effort. Before carrying out an implementation activity, an evaluation will be performed to enable clear and concrete before-and-after comparisons of performance results, public satisfaction, and service standards, in conjunction with timely professional surveys. Each team should integrate into its own efforts the provisions of:

(1) the Statute on Administrative Reform;
(2) the Statute on Administrative Organizational Reform;
(3) the Statute on Executive Yuan Service Quality;
(4) the Government Computerization/Networking Implementation Plans;
(5) the Statute on Implementation of National "One-Window"Service; and,
(6) the Statute on Upgrading National Financial Administration.

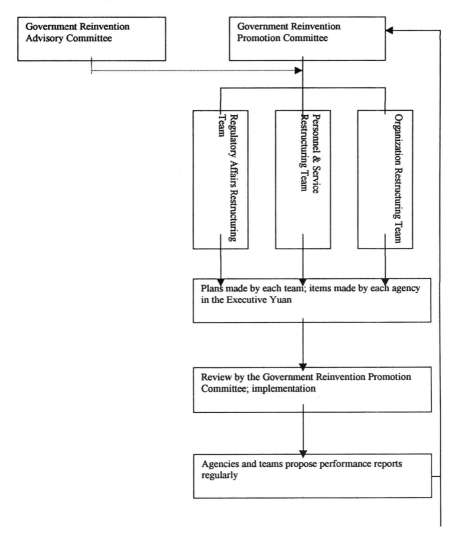

Fig. 19.1. Diagram of Government Reinvention in Taiwan.
Source: "Statute of Privatization of Provincial Government Business", The Research Development, and Evaluation Commission in the Executive Yuan, 1998.

Goals of Reinvention
The predicted outcomes of the government reinvention project include:

(1) remolding the image of public servants to raise their social status;
(2) adjusting the role of government, and expanding public participation;
(3) revitalizing organizational and personnel flexibility, and strengthening adaptability;
(4) liberalizing regulations, simplifying administrative processes, and motivating civil servants;
(5) raising service quality, and increasing public satisfaction;
(6) establishing thorough financial systems; and,
(7) raising resource management performance.

GOVERNMENT REINVENTION PRACTICES IN TAIWAN

As government reinvention in Taiwan has been promoted now for over two years, it is time to review its performance.

The Organization Restructuring Team
The most significant performance in the Organization Restructuring Team was the passage of the "Central Government Agency Organizational Basic Law" and the "Central Government Organization Total Personnel Authorization Law" (under the auspices of the Executive Yuan RDEC in coordination with the Executive Yuan Personnel Office, Legal Office, and Rules Committee). These passage of these two laws, represents an important administrative reform in the Executive Yuan. It reduces the number of administrative layers and adjusts the responsibilities and structure of agencies within the Executive Yuan.

The Personnel and Service Restructuring Team
This team's points of emphasis has been the development of electronic government, one-window service, personnel system reform, simplification of personnel regulations, and the promotion of service quality.

Electronic government or "government on-line" has been a particularly important task with in the government reinvention movement. The central government has established the government services network (GSN), using both intranet and internet, to efficiently provide information and services for agencies' staff as well as the public.

One-window service has been effectively adopted. It was intended to foster a public service-oriented administrative outlook, reinvent government through infusion with enterprise management skills, strengthen interagency contact, promote integration between central and local governments, raise government administrative efficiency, and establish these as fundamental practices of the entire government. The following includes some of the successful examples:

(1) Ministry of the Interior Central Police Bureau Criminal Investigations Office: One-window service for organized crime investigations, toll-free crime hotline and organized crime investigation suggestion box.

(2) Ministry of the Interior Central Police Bureau Criminal Investigations Office: One-window service for public reporting of cross-jurisdictional criminal cases.

(3) Ministry of the Interior: One-window service for registration of legitimization of children, registration of adoption and adoption termination, wedding and divorce registration.

(4) Ministry of Finance Taiwan Province Central District Tax Office: One-window service to implement complete taxpayer service assistance at the counter.

(5) Ministry of Justice Prosecutor's Offices at all levels: One-window service for a contact and update for victims in major criminal cases.

(6) Ministry of Economic Affairs Industrial Development Bureau: One-window service for coordination of the upgrading of investments.

(7) Ministry of Economic Affairs Industrial Development Bureau: One-window service for industrial district land leasing and selling.

(8) Executive Yuan Personnel Affairs Office: One-window service for civil service exam records for assignment and employment.

(9) Civil Service Housing and Benefits Commission: One-window service for central government employees receiving housing subsidies.

The one-window service is quite useful for handling multiple services and the operation of electronic tax administration, electronic public health, electronic public safety, and electronic commence. Furthermore, it makes easy and efficient the communication between agencies and agencies and between agencies and the public. and provides convenient, fast service to meet the public's needs.

The Regulatory Affairs Restructuring Team
In the Regulatory Affairs Restructuring Team, many plans have been effectively carried out, especially privatization and BOT (Build, Operate, Transfer).
    Regarding privatization, the following progress has been made.

(1) From 1989 to the end of 1996, seven firms were privatized: Chungchan Insurance, Chinese Petrochemicals, Chunghwa Engineering, China Steel, Yangming Shipping, Liquid Supply Office, Taiwan Machinery and Steel Products.

344   YU-YING KUO

(2) From 1997 to August 1998, eleven firms were privatized: Changhua Bank, First Bank, Huanan Bank, Taiwan Enterprise Bank, Taiwan Insurance, Retired Servicemen's Gas Factory, Taiwan Mechanical Marine Factory, Taiwan Mechanical Alloy Steel Factory, Taiwan Life, Taiwan Airlines, and Kangshan Factory.
(3) The statistical breakdown is as follows: fifteen companies and three factories with a total value of roughly $3,532,370,000 were transferred to private ownership. Additionally, Taiwan Securities was privatized by the end of August, 1998.
(4) During 1999 and through 2002: 25 companies were/will be privatized including: Tai Power Company, Taiwan Railway Company, Cigarette and Wine Company, Taipei Bank, Kaohsiung Bank, Chunghwa Telecom, among others.

Due to the prices fixed under the law and the current stock market situation, privatization as a whole has progressed somewhat slowly. But the program has gradually become more successful and the rate of privatization has been accelerating since the Council for Economic Planning and Development began meeting.

Contracting Out Services
Theoretically, contracting out government services is based on the spirits of 3Es – Empowering, Enriching, Enlightening – and 3Ps – Participation, Privatization, Partnership. For example, the Taipei City Government contracted out garbage collection, public parking lots management, car inspection, violation towing, day care, elderly care, parks management, statistical data collection and coding among other things. The Kaohsiung City Government contracted out the construction of mass rapid transit, car inspection, retardation education, government buildings clean, public safety system, etc.. This kind of combination of public and private sectors not only facilitates governmental downsizing and reengineering, but it also brings entrepreneurial management into contact with government. Therefore, to a substantial extent, it satisfies citizens' demands and dramatically improves the efficiency and effectiveness of government services.

Build, Operate, Transfer Construction
The Public Construction Commission and the Council for Economic Planning and Development jointly promoted the creation of a legal framework and strategies to provide incentives for private sector participation in public construction. In June, 1998, a BOT manual was produced, and the Public

Construction Commission also completed promotion of government procurement regulatory work. The Ministry of Justice completed law making for the
administrative procedural law reform effort in December, 1998. In Taiwan,
about ten BOT programs have emerged so far. Among them, the mass rapid
transit (MRT) of Chang Kai-Shek International Airport and the High Speed
Rail are the two cases which attracted most attention. The MRT of Chang Kai-
Shek International Airport will greatly improve the transportation between the
capital, Taipei, and the airport. The High Speed Rail will shorten the travel time
from Taipei to Kaohsiung to only 90 minutes. Although these two programs
have not yet been successfully implemented, the employment of BOT has
benefited from some other projects such as the Taipei International Finance
Building, and Taichung Mall, as well as the field of urban planning.

Impact of the Presidential Election
It will be interesting to compare the government reinvention activities before
and after the presidential election. Government reinvention has been promoted
since 1998, and the three work teams made some progress in these two years.
For example, the privatization, BOT, and one-window service areas have had
significant accomplishments. However, during the end of 1999 and the first
several months of 2000, the Organization Restructuring Team and the
Personnel and Services Restructuring Team tended to stagnate their work
schedule due to preparation for the electoral campaign and anticipated political
changes, The Regulatory Affairs Restructuring Team, on the other hand
continued the activities in their schedule. Most members in the Government
Reinvention Promotion Committee not only paid close attention to the election,
but supported the KMT's presidential candidate, Lien, Chan. On March 18,
2000, the DPP candidate, Chen, Shui-bian, won the election. The Government
Reinvention Promotion Committee ignored government reinvention-related
tasks before the election, and did nothing after the election because the political
power had shifted from KMT to DPP, and a new staff was appointed. However,
in the President's inauguration speech (Taiwan Stands Up: Advancing to an
Uplifting Era) on May 20, 2000, he asserted, "In the area of government
reforms, we need to establish a government that is clean, efficient, far-sighted,
dynamic, highly flexible and responsive, in order to ensure Taiwan's
competitiveness in the face of increasingly fierce global competition. The age
of 'large and capable' governments has now passed, replaced by one of 'small
and effective' governments, which have established partnership relations with
the people. We should accelerate the streamlining of government functions and
organization and actively expand the role of public participation. This will not

only allow the public to fully utilize its energy but also significantly reduce the government's burdens".

From President Chen, Shui-bian's inauguration speech, it may be projected that government reinvention will move steadily ahead under the auspices of the new government, but may produce different outcomes. As the new staff has not actually worked on the reinvention, and there is a lack of evaluated data on the government reinvention effort at this time, it is hard to predict if the new government's reinvention will be more or less successful or ineffective than that of the KMT.

BUREAUCRACY VS. DEMOCRACY IN NPM

Government reinvention activities cannot be successful without support from the bureaucrats. One of the important tensions discussed in NPM is that between bureaucracy and democracy. The bureaucratic imperative may at times conflict with the requirements and demands of democratic governance: autonomy vs. accountability, personal vision vs. citizen participation, secrecy vs. openness, risk-taking vs. stewardship of the public good (Bellone & Goerl, 1992). The primary tensions in the relationship between bureaucracy and democracy involve four core values in effective government:

(1) rationality;
(2) accountability;
(3) representativeness;
(4) legitimacy.

These values provide the foundation for the understanding of how the central government in Taiwan should govern and demonstrate the many complications that arise in the interaction between bureaucracy and democratic action.

Rationality, Expertise and Information
Rationality refers to the importance of incorporating expertise and information into agency decision making. For almost all bureaucrats in the world, scarce time and energy, insufficient expertise, and lack of available knowledge militate against the consideration of "all" information. Moreover, human cognitive limitation and rapidly changing policy environments place inherent limits on the rationality of decision-making. Thus, bureaucratic rationality may consist of the ability to reach closure, to come to a decision even in the absence of certainty that all data and policy options have been examined, or to reach consensus on their interpretations or on the action to be taken.

However, what is rational for the bureaucracy may not be rational for society's individuals. In other words, what the bureaucracy wants and needs to do may have little orno connection with what citizens want or need. Efficient, rational delivery of public services is somewhat under bureaucratic control, but the adequacy of the services is a political question. Bureaucratic rationality makes severe demands on political governance structures. Such structures must both encourage wide-ranging search when decisions seem to require it and to guide decision making when the search yields few definitive answers. The public may feel alienated in the decision process because decisions are being made beyond the grasp of common understanding. The fear is that bureaucrats are making substantive value decisions. Entrepreneurial bureaucrats may feel the need for secrecy in order to be competitive in the market, while democratic politics call for open information and citizen participation. Yates (1982) proposed that whenever possible, bureaucratic rationality, without for substantive values, ought to be discussed openly and explicitly. Without such an accounting, citizens have little way of knowing the criteria bureaucrats use for decisions. Bellone and Goerl (1992) argued that secrecy in new ideas is not necessarily beneficiary, that openness in new ideas may actually produce more competitive, more creative ideas, and promotes citizens' acceptance.

Accountability
Accountability refers to the capacity of elected officials (acting on behalf of the voters) or their delegates (such as personal staffers and political appointees) to monitor and, when necessary, redirect the activities of an agency. From the perspective of the agency, accountability amounts to "answerability" to elected officials and, through them, to the general public. However, entrepreneurial autonomy or discretion may at times make accountability impossible. For instance, complicated tax issues may need bureaucrats' autonomy to achieve optimum financial solutions. Usually the higher the level of autonomy, the more difficult is the accountability issue. Bureaucracies with relatively high levels of accountability and factual expertise may actually promote democratic activity. Paying attention to the demands of elected officials, for example, may provide decision makers with a better sense of the extent of financial and political support they can count on for various policy opinions. Most importantly, in representative democracy, accountability to elected officials for policy implementation also requires bureaucratic actors' attention to policy content, at least insofar as interpretating the intent of statutes. As suggested by Bellone and Goerl (1992), carefully reviewing the performance of each agency or each program can, to some extent, solve the conflicts between autonomy and accountability.

Representativeness
Representativeness directs attention, first, to the inclusiveness of the decision process, pointing to the importance of participation by those who may be affected by the decision and by those whose assent appears to be critical to the acceptability of both the policy process and the decision outcome. Entrepreneurial bureaucrats require a personal vision to create new ideas; however, this sometimes conflicts with citizen participation. Which parties should be included in a decision may vary according to whether the decision problem involves goals or technologies. Concerns with representativeness and bureaucratic rationality may be mutually reinforcing. Broadening participation in decision-making may increase the range of information and policy options available to decision makers.

Legitimacy
Legitimacy refers to the general satisfaction of citizens and other political actors with how decisions are made rather than what decisions ultimately result. In this view, the public treats decision outcomes as authoritative – even if they disagree with the policy content – when policies are formulated in acceptable ways, through justifiable procedures. For example, entrepreneurial bureaucrats may take risks to overcome obstacles and obtain short-term benefits, but this may not be consistent with prudent stewardship of the overall public good. Nonetheless, if bureaucrats are supported by the citizens who are willing to take the risk of failure, resulting conflicts can be smoothed out. This is referred to as "civic-regarding entrepreneurship". (Bellone & Goerl, 1992).

To sum up, what constitutes "acceptable" ways of formulating policy may reflect the perceived rationality, representativeness, or accountability of policy making. Proactive style bureaucrats are the ones who meet above requirements to create public interests, foster the consensus among agencies, and encourage citizen participation in the decision process (Harmon, 1986). This is just like what Jun (1986) pointed out, there are eight criteria for bureaucrats to enhance public interests:

(1) rights of citizens;
(2) ethical and moral standards;
(3) democratic processes;
(4) professional knowledge;
(5) analysis of unanticipated knowledge;
(6) considering common interests;
(7) public opinions; and,
(8) openness.

Taking public interests into account, entrepreneurial bureaucrats can:

(1) satisfy their customers' needs to achieve government of the people;
(2) keep "civic-regarding entrepreneurship" in mind to achieve government by the people;
(3) promote the performance of public services to achieve government for the people (Chiang & Liu, 1999).

CONCLUSIONS

As Premier Siew concluded in his 1998 speech, ". . . for the 21st century, the ideals of government service should be those of: providing fair, unbiased and professional government service; providing energetic, motivated, and efficient government service; and, providing convenient, timely and polite government service." The government reinvention practices in Taiwan have made some progress, though there is still room for improvement.

Government reinvention activities in Taiwan have paralleled the history of NPM development. The NPM paradigm in Taiwan can be characterized by:

(1) the devolution of authority, providing flexibility;
(2) the insurance of performance, control, accountability;
(3) the development of competition and choice;
(4) increases in the responsiveness of public services;
(5) an improvement in the management of human resources;
(6) the optimization of information technology;
(7) an improvement in the quality of regulation;
(8) a strengthening of steering functions at the centers.

In analysis of rationality, accountability, representativeness, and legitimacy we should reconsider the assertion of Dwight Waldo (1948) in the *Administrative State* that the administrative reformers of the twentieth century almost universally held democracy to be their goal, but believed democracy to be unobtainable without a government that could produce usable results. Democracy is not threatened by bureaucracy. It is aided by it, increasing rather than diminishing the realm of societal possibilities.

The difficulty of controlling bureaucratic agents can lead to complaints of bureaucratic independence and poor responsiveness to the electorate. In terms of democratic theory, the conscientious bureaucrat's best defense rests in allegiance to what Yates (1982) calls "administrative process values". When there are no easy answers or correct solutions, adherence to administrative process values—accountability, responsiveness, accessibility—helps to ensure

Table 19.1. Comparison of Competitiveness among Asia's 'Four Dragon' Nations

	IMD				WEF		
	1996	1997	1998	1999	1996	1997	1998
Taiwan	18	23	16	18	9	8	6
Singapore	2	2	2	2	1	1	1
Hong Kong	3	3	3	7	2	2	2
Korea	27	30	35	38	20	21	19

that bureaucrats act as democratically and efficiently as possible under the circumstances.

The conflicts between bureaucracy and democracy were peacefully compromised during this decade. Table 19.1, based on IMD and WEF reports, indicates Taiwan's competitiveness, compared the other Asian "Four Dragons" – Singapore, Hong Kong, and Korea. Taiwan's relative competitiveness is now at the median level, having made some progress, based on WEP reports.

There is still much room for improvement and, therefore, government reinvention should proceed and its performance should be carefully evaluated. Still, the tensions between bureaucracy and democracy should be reconsidered and reviewed during the ongoing process of government reinvention. However, this chapter has its limitations. Future research can conduct empirical studies in attempt to understand the reality of the structure as well as the practices of the government reinvention in Taiwan. Since government reinvention has only been promoted for two years, there is a lack of data and evaluation to show which agency or program has succeeded or failed. Future research also should focus on the evaluation of the overall government reinvention initiative to investigate and test its performance.

REFERENCES

Bellone, C. J., & Goerl, G. T. (1992). Reconciling Public Entrepreneurship and Democracy. *Public Administration Review, 52*(2), 130–134.

Chiang, M-C., & Liu, K.-I. (1999). *Entrepreneurial Government: Theories, Practices, and Critiques*. Taiepi: Best-Wise Co. Ltd.

Fox, C. (1996). Reinventing Government as Postmodern Symbolic Politics. *Public Administration Review, 54*(2), 112–122.

Harmon, M. M., & Meyer, R. T. (1986). *Organization Theory For Public Administration*. Little, Brown & Company.

IMD (1999). *The World Competitiveness Yearbook*. Lausanne, Switzerland.

Jan, C.-Y. (1999). *New Public Management: Theories and Practices of Government Reinvention*. Taipei: Wu-Nan.

Jun, J. S. (1986). *Public Administration: Design and Problem Solving*. New York: Macmillan.

Kaboolian, L. (1998). The New Public Management: Challenging the Boundaries of the Management vs. Administration Debate. *Public Administration Review, 58*(3), 169–182

Konig, K. (1996). *On the Critique of New Public Management*. Speyer University.

Lynn, L. E. (1996). *Public Management as Art, Science, and Profession*. NJ: Chatham House.

OECD (1995). *Governance in Transition: Public Management Reform in OECD Countries*. Paris: OECD.

Shafritz, J. M., & Hyde, A. C. (1992). *Classics of Public Administration* (3rd ed.). Pacific Grove, CA: Brooks/Cole.

The Research, Development, and Evaluation Commission in the Executive Yuan (1998). *The Outlines of Government Reinvention*. Taipei.

Waldo, D. (1948). *The Administrative State*. Novato, CA: Chandler & Sharp Publishers Inc.

Waldo, D. (1980). *The Enterprise of Public Administration*. Novato, CA: Chandler & Sharp Publishers, Inc.

WEF (1998). *The Global Competitiveness Report*. Geneva, Switzerland.

Yates, D. (1982). *Bureaucratic Democracy*. Cambridge, MA: Harvard University Press.

20. COPING WITH WICKED PROBLEMS: THE CASE OF AFGHANISTAN

Nancy Roberts

INTRODUCTION

Government officials and public managers are encountering a class of problems that defy solution, even with our most sophisticated analytical tools. These problems are called "wicked" because they have the following characteristics: (1) There is no definitive statement of the problem; in fact, there is broad disagreement on what 'the problem' is. (2) Without a definitive statement of the problem, the search for solutions is open ended. Stakeholders – those who have a stake in the problem and its solution – champion alternative solutions and compete with one another to frame 'the problem' in a way that directly connects their preferred solution and their preferred problem definition. (3) The problem-solving process is complex because constraints, such as resources and political ramifications, are constantly changing. (4) Constraints also change because they are generated by numerous interested parties who "come and go, change their minds, fail to communicate, or otherwise change the rules by which the problem must be solved" (Conklin & Weil, no date: 1).

Wicked problems can be distinguished from other types of problems in the following way. Type 1 problems, or what I call "simple problems," enjoy a consensus on a problem definition and solution. For example, a group of machinists agree that a machine has broken down and they also agree how to fix it. Problem solving is straightforward engendering little if any conflict among those involved. Given their training and experience, these problem

Learning from International Public Management Reform, Volume 11B, pages 353–375.
2001 by Elsevier Science Ltd.
ISBN: 0-7623-0760-9

solvers, within a short period of time, recognize what the problem is and activate established routines and standard procedures to deal with it.

Type 2 problems introduce conflict to the problem-solving process. I call them "complex problems". Although problem solvers agree on what the problem is, there is no consensus on how to solve it. Consider the following example. Suppose a community comes to understand that students are not learning in school as judged by their test scores. Stakeholders then become embroiled in debates on the 'best way' to improve student learning. Some suggest an increase in school funding, while others demand better teachers and new pedagogical tools. Some support programs to improve students' home environments while others call for restructuring of the educational system to allow for vouchers between public and private schools. Type 2 problems generate conflict among the stakeholders. Despite agreement on the problem definition, there are unresolved issues concerning its solution. The increase in conflict makes the problem-solving process more complex.

Type 3 problems engender a high level of conflict among the stakeholders. In this instance, there is no agreement on the problem or its solution. Consider this example. You live in a rural community. It faces water shortages, an influx of wealthy people from surrounding urban areas who are buying up housing and available land for second homes, pressure from developers who want to put in more golf courses, and complaints from a growing number of community members who drive longer and longer distances to find affordable housing and jobs. What is 'the problem'? Is it affordable housing, a lack of jobs, an underdeveloped public transportation system, too much growth, or not the 'right' kind of growth, degradation of the environment, or population growth rates? Attempts to address 'the problem' accomplish little. Political and resource constraints force constant re-definitions of the problem and its solutions as interested parties come and go and community preferences shift. Officials launch efforts to conserve water one year only to abandon them the next as short-term weather patterns change and political will evaporates. Housing surfaces as an important issue only to be replaced by jobs during the next election cycle when the economy takes a downturn. The problem-solving process is further complicated because stakeholders in a democratic society have the power to block initiatives not of their liking through lawsuits, judicial reviews, and the time-honored tradition of throwing the 'rascals' out of office. Nothing really bounds the problem-solving process – it is experienced as ambiguous, fluid, complex, political, and frustrating as hell. In short, it is wicked.

We have a long history with wicked problems, although our awareness of them only began to take shape in the 1960s and 1970s (Churchman, 1967;

Rittel & Webber, 1973). Alerts have come from specialists in many quarters – product designers, software engineers, planners, and policy makers (DeGrace & Stahl, 1990; Guindon, 1990; Verma, 1998). These experts voice warnings that traditional linear methods of problem solving (e.g. specify the problem, gather and analyze data, formulate a solution, implement solution) do not seem to be working, especially for a certain class of problems. What is worse, there appears to be no apparent alternative in sight.

We can speculate on the recognition and rise of wicked problems at this point in time. Perhaps the expansion of democracy, market economies, privatization, travel and social exchanges highlight value differences and thus promote dissensus rather than consensus in the problem-solving process. Perhaps the technological and information revolutions enable more people to become active participants in problem solving, and in so doing, increase the complexity of the process. Perhaps the ideological shifts in policy and management that encourage organizational decentralization, experimentation, flexibility, and innovation weaken traditional authority and control mechanisms that heretofore have keep a lid on conflicts. Whatever the source of wicked problems, there is little doubt that public managers and officials need immediate help in dealing with them.

The purpose of this chapter is to explore various strategies public officials and managers can employ to cope with wicked problems. Section One examines what I believe to be three generic coping strategies: authoritative, competitive, and collaborative. I briefly describe each strategy and summarize its advantages and disadvantages. The model from which these strategies derive is based on the level of conflict present in the problem-solving process, the distribution of power among stakeholders, and the degree to which power is contested.

Collaborative strategies provide the focus for the remainder of the chapter. A case on the relief and recovery efforts in Afghanistan illustrates the challenges of pursuing a collaborative strategy to cope with wicked problems. Numerous 'lessons learned' emerge from the experience. The chapter concludes with implications for using collaborative strategies to deal with wicked problems in crisis countries and other developing regions around the world.

COPING STRATEGIES

Coping strategies to deal with wicked problems derive from the basic model in Fig. 20.1. Three questions prompt strategy selection. On the far left-hand side, we ask how much conflict is present in the problem-solving process. If there is an agreement on the problem and its solution, then we have a simple or Type

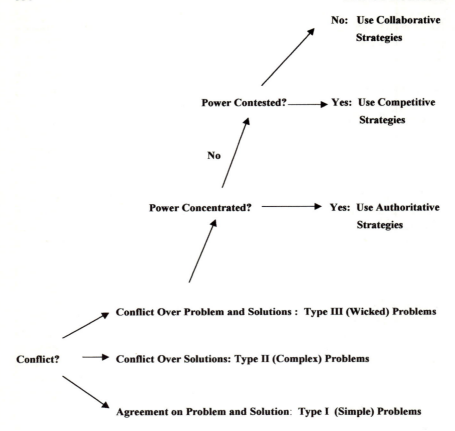

Fig. 20.1. Coping Strategies to Deal with Wicked Problems.

1 problem. If conflict exists over solutions, then we face a complex or Type 2 problem. If there is conflict over the problem definition and its solution, then we confront a wicked or Type 3 problem.

   Following the path for wicked problems, we then ask how power is dispersed among the stakeholders. If power is concentrated in the hands of a small number of stakeholders, then authoritative strategies can be employed to identify the problem and its solution. If power among the stakeholders is not concentrated but dispersed, we proceed to a third question. Is power contested among the dispersed set of stakeholders, meaning is there a struggle for power that characterizes their interactions? If power is dispersed and contested, then competitive strategies can be employed. If power is dispersed but not contested, then collaborative strategies can be utilized. Thus, we find three generic strategies for coping with wicked problems. Let us explore each in greater detail.

Authoritative Strategies

Authoritative strategies are 'taming strategies.' They diminish the level of conflict inherent in wicked problems by putting problem solving into the hands of a few stakeholders who have the authority to define a problem and come up with a solution. Identification of this small set of stakeholders may rest on their knowledge and expertise, organizational position in the hierarchy, information, or coercive power, etc. But whatever the basis for selection, other stakeholders acquiesce in the transfer of power to the 'anointed' few and agree to abide by their decisions. Thus, when an organization is engulfed in disputes over performance and future strategy, a CEO can use the power of her position to step in and decide what path the organization will pursue. When the U.S. Congress is unable to decide on what military bases to close, it forms a committee and gives it broad authority to operate and make recommendations on base closures. When disputes arise over reproductive rights, U.S citizens rely on the power of the Supreme Court to establish the definition of life. When economic indicators are confusing and difficult to interpret, the U.S. turns to a Federal Reserve Board to establish monetary policy and set interest rates. Authoritative strategies, in essence, give the problem to someone or some group, who takes on the problem-solving process while others agree to abide by their decisions.

Authoritative strategies have their advantages in coping with wicked problems. Reducing the numbers of stakeholders decreases the complexity of the problem-solving process. If a large number of people are in on 'the action,' it is hard to get anything done. Problem solving can be quicker and less contentious with fewer people involved. It is on this basis that we elect representatives to govern us rather than resort to a direct democracy and we keep some residual command and control structures in organizations even when we are flattening hierarchies. Reliance on experts also can make problem solving more 'professional' and 'objective,' especially when specialization provides them with knowledge and sophisticated problem solving tools that laymen do not posses. Taking time to update non-experts who do not understand the 'finer points' of complex issues and who are not familiar with expert procedures 'wastes' valuable time and resources. Sometimes it is more important for authorities to get on with the work they have the knowledge and skills to deal with; that is why they were given the jobs in the first place, or so the argument goes.

Yet reliance on an authoritative strategy to cope with wicked problems has its disadvantages. First and foremost, authorities and experts can be wrong – wrong about the problem and wrong about the solution. Executives at GM saw mostly American cars in parking lots and freeways in the early 1970s and concluded they had little foreign competition to worry about. Nuclear power plants are not as safe or as cheap a source of energy as the experts originally thought. 'Failsafe' procedures did not keep Three Mile Island and Chernobyl open and skyrocketing insurance and development costs in the United States made nuclear energy less competitive compared to other sources of energy. Unanswered questions about nuclear waste still haunt us – questions that breed their own series of wicked problems. Setting aside disagreements among experts in a particular problem domain, experts tend to search for solutions within their narrow bandwidth of experience, potentially missing other important issues and considerations. Analysts at the Environmental Protection Agency (EPA) developed a model to calculate the probability of deaths due to arsenic emissions from the ASARCO plant in Tacoma, Washington (Scott, 1990). Not only was the model incorrect, as members of the community later pointed out, because it was based on erroneous assumptions about the terrain, but other factors, such as lost jobs opportunities and their consequences were not addressed. For the EPA, the limited definition of the problem and its solution made sense. Its mandate and experience centers on environmental protection not jobs and community development. On the other hand, community members, struggling with tradeoffs between a plant closure and deaths from arsenic emissions, had more than environmental concerns to consider. They faced competing definitions of the problem that included pollution issues, economic issues, and political issues. A closely related disadvantage is the lost opportunity for learning. If problem solving is left to experts, especially in a democratic society, then citizens can become further and further distanced from the important issues of their time. A democracy rests on an informed citizenry and it is not clear how authoritative strategies keep them informed and engaged in the governing process (Reich, 1990).

Competitive Strategies

Competitive strategies have a long history. Whether they have been played out on the battlefield, in politics or in the market, stakeholders following this strategy assume a 'zero-sum game.' If my opponents win the right to define the problem and choose the solution, then I lose. If I win the right, my opponents lose. A win-lose mind-set thus permeates interactions. Warfare provides an extreme example of zero-sum competition when countries claim the right to define their wicked problems and their solutions (over religion, land, trade policy, etc.) in such a way that it threatens other countries. In the 1930s, Japan's need for oil and its expansion into the Pacific were considered to be a direct threat to U.S. interests. U.S. attempts to limit this expansion were viewed as a direct threat to Japan's national security. Each country's insistence on dealing with its wicked problems in its own way resulted in war.

Central to the pursuit of competitive strategies to deal with wicked problems is the search for power. To the extent a competitor can build a power base larger than his opponents, using whatever tactics his ethics and morality permit, he can increase his chances to win and define the problem and its solution in a way he sees fit. Power, after all, is the ability to get what one wants against resistance (Pfeffer, 1992). When a player wins out over the competition and can sustain those wins over time, then power is concentrated in his hands. Concentration of power, as noted earlier, enables him to resort to authoritative strategies instead of dissipating his resources in the competitive fray. Admiral Hyram Rickover serves as a good example in this regard. Developing his expertise over a number of years and surviving competition among the technical experts, he established control over nuclear technology and positioned himself as the authority in both civilian and military sectors in the U.S. His base of power was so great that few dared to question his authority (Lewis, 1980). Thus, over time, he was able to 'tame' his wicked problem by moving from competitive to authoritative strategies.

The advantages of competitive strategies to solve wicked problems are numerous. In the case of the market economy, industry competition prompts the search for new ideas. The energy sector offers a recent example. Companies have developed a new hydrogen fuel cell technology that is touted to be a cleaner, less polluting replacement for other forms of energy. What has appeared to be an intractable issue, (environmental degradation that results from using oil and gasoline), may in fact have found resolution through the invention of this technology. Without competition among the providers of energy, it is unlikely that this new technology would have been developed. One also finds advantages in the political economy. When no clear consensus emerges in a democratic system on the definition of a problem or its solution, and competition among the stakeholders is great, why should a decision be made? Without a clear path, it is preferable not to go forward in any one direction – an assumption built into the U.S. constitution and its 'shared power' system of governance. Competitive strategies also have an advantage in that they challenge the institutionalization of power. Keep power circulating among the competition, so the argument goes (Pfeffer, 1992). One day you win, the next day I win, so in total, neither of us is able to centralize and institutionalize his power. Power is not corrupting; it is the concentration and institutionalization of power that is dangerous (Pfeffer, 1992).

Yet there are disadvantages to competitive strategies. Pushed to their extreme, they can provoke violence and warfare as noted above. The scars from competition in Northern Ireland, the Middle East, and Rwanda run very deep and continue to render the social fabric. Competition also consumes resources that could be spent on problem solving. The Port of Oakland in northern California learned this lesson the hard way when stakeholders battled for years over plans to dredge the harbor to accommodate new container ships that draw 30 to 40 feet. The costs associated with the procedural delays and attempts to resolve the dispute (litigation, regulatory and judicial review, etc.) were enormous (Kagan, 1991). The Port of Los Angeles in southern California benefited from the deadlock by building a multi-agency, multi-city political forum to cooperate on their port expansion plans and by absorbing the business that the Port of Oakland could not accommodate. The stalemates and gridlock that occur when stakeholders have enough power to block one another but not enough power to get something done keeps important things from getting accomplished. The continuing closure of the Oakland freeway due to earthquake damage and stakeholders' inability to agree on how to repair it is one such example. The delays have been estimated at $23 million per year in extra transportation expenses and fuel (Pfeffer, 1992). The indecision in mobilizing political support and getting agreement among the many stakeholders to fight AIDS is another example. It cost thousands their lives (Shilts, 1987).

Collaborative Strategies

Collaborative strategies are prompting a great deal of interest judging by the increasing references to them in the literature (Bardach, 1998; Chrislip and Larson, 1994; Gray, 1989; Huxham, 1996; McLagan and Nel, 1995). Deriving meaning from the French verb *collaborer,* translated as *working together*, collaboration is premised on the principle that by joining forces parties can accomplish more as a collective than they can achieve by acting as independent agents. At the core of collaboration is a 'win-win' view of problem solving. Rather than play a 'zero-sum game' that seeks to distribute 'pie shares' based on winners and losers, they assume a 'variable sum game' that seeks to 'enlarge the pie' for all parties involved. Alliances, partnerships, and joint ventures are all variations of the theme as they find expression in government, business, and international relations.

Advantages of collaboration are numerous and evident in the following examples. Members of research consortia share the costs and benefits of developing very expensive technology rather than carrying the full risks on their own (Doz & Hamel, 1998). Military alliances add strength in numbers and share the burden of their mutual defense. Even competitors of the same product line find virtue in working together to deliver better products and services to their customers (Doz & Hamel, 1998). Redundancies are eliminated and organizational efficiencies achieved when organizations outsource tasks and functions that enable both the organization and its supplier to add value by concentrating on what they do best (Quinn, et. al., 1996).

Disadvantages of collaboration are also well known. Adding stakeholders to any problem solving effort increases 'transaction costs.' There are more meetings, more people with whom to communicate and get agreement – interactions that can take a great deal of effort. Sorting out which operating procedures and whose norms of conduct will prevail takes time. As the number of stakeholders grows, so does the difficulty of achieving synergy. Skills of collaboration are limited, too, especially among people who work in a traditional bureaucracy with a strong hierarchy that limits participation and team-based approaches to problem solving and decision making. Collaboration requires practice; it is a learned skill. If members do not have these skills, they need to acquire them and that takes additional time and resources. Then in the worst case, collaboration can end poorly. Dialogue can turn into debate and debate into protracted conflict with little to show for the hours of preparation and meetings. Positions can harden making agreement even more difficult to attain in the future. There are no guarantees that the outcomes of collaboration will be satisfactory to everyone.

COLLABORATION FOR RELIEF AND RECOVERY IN AFGHANISTAN

The challenges of using a collaborative strategy to cope with wicked problems can be illustrated in the following case concerning relief and recovery efforts in Afghanistan. The case begins in 1997 when the United Nations determined that it needed to find new ways to help countries in crisis. Aware that previous efforts had had limited success, some members of the UN community saw the potential for taking a more collaborative stance with the groups, organizations, and nations that wanted to be involved in helping the country rebuild.

Afghanistan has been wracked by war and the consequences of competitive strategies for over two decades. Some 50,000 combatants from a population estimated to be well over 20 million are actively engaged in fighting. The country lacks a legitimate government with control over its whole territory. Following the Soviet Union's withdrawal in 1989, there was a sense that the Afghan conflict would move towards resolution. This has not happened. The instability continues marked by the absence of functioning entities of governance. The crisis in Afghanistan has two facets: the absence of peace and security and the destruction of its civil infrastructure.

The country's human development indicators continue to erode. The long years of economic collapse have not halted population growth. Two decades of minimal education opportunities have seriously eroded the human capital base. Scarce employment, a decline in real wages, and the absence of formal banking structures characterize the economy. The formal economy has been criminalized with the production of over 2,500 tons of poppies annually. Afghan farmers have been drawn into poppy production due to the lack of alternatives. Large refugee populations, fluctuating numbers of internally displaced persons, and conscription of young men into fighting forces have reduced the potential workforce and placed pressure on family economies. Morbidity and mortality remain higher than before the war. Preventable diseases claim an increasing number of lives. Basic sanitation and health care are absent from most parts of the country. Human capital is depleted and the prolonged absence of a uniform and extensive system of primary and secondary education holds serious implications for the future. Gender discrimination is severe and widespread in the territory controlled by the Talliban. In health, education, and mine clearance, international assistance plays a key, if not a predominate role.

International Assistance

International assistance suffers from a number of constraints. Stakeholders are numerous and consist of international non-governmental organizations (NGOs), United Nations' field agencies and staffs from headquarters, and bilateral and multi-lateral donors. All work independently and all suffer from declining funds. There is no institutional infrastructure, inter-organizational network, or authority to coordinate their activities. Direct interaction among the stakeholders is therefore difficult, limiting the development of an authoritative strategy to guide relief and development work. Stakeholders have strong value and political conflicts over both ends and means. Some insist, for example, that relief and development should be predicated on the Talliban's change of gender policy, an unlikely event. Other stakeholders argue that without international aid, the condition of women in Afghanistan will continue to deteriorate.

As a "country in crisis," Afghanistan does not allow for 'normal development' interventions on the part of the international community. Crisis countries lack a state structure and legitimate channels for representation and empowerment of their populations. Due to the absence of representative and regional and national authorities and weakened local authorities, international entities often take on exceptional responsibilities when they intervene. Intervening unilaterally, they begin to assume ownership of projects and programs that 'belong' to them. They end up deciding what needs to be done and where, and in so doing, serve as surrogates for governmental authorities.

As a consequence of this intervention pattern, a multiplicity of assistance agencies spring up and operate independently of one another. The agencies follow different mandates, rely on multiple sources of funding each with its own constraints, and engage in similar work without acknowledgment of the significant duplication that occurs among them or its consequences. Their interventions usually result in uncoordinated relief and development activities within the country.

This picture is further complicated by little coordination between the international political actors and their relief and development partners. The peace process concentrates primarily on the search for an end to hostilities and negotiating disarmament and other related agreements between warring parties. The web of contacts and the knowledge about the countries in crisis acquired by relief and development partners are not systematically utilized in informing the political strategy. There tends to be little substantive discussion of political developments and the continued threats to human suffering, the functioning of the economy and the continuing search for opportunities to support recovery.

The challenge of coordination among international partners in a fragmented state without the basic institutions of governance, especially when surrogate government functions need to be performed is "formidable." Current arrangements – "coordination by consensus" – when the United Nations coordinator acts as advocate and facilitator, have been clearly ineffective. According to an Inter-Agency Mission Report on Afghanistan, the international attempts to alleviate the human distress and suffering have been plagued by ". . . unclear objectives, doubts and fears about impact and effectiveness . . . inefficiencies, lack of economies of scale, a multiplicity of agencies and duplication . . .". It concludes that the ". . . disparate collection of assistance institutions" has yet to form, ". . . a community with shared principles, complementary purposes and common goals," to which all can subscribe (Inter-Agency Mission Report, 1997).

Intervention for Collaboration

Aware that UN efforts have not always been effective in the past, the United
Nations Undersecretary General for Political Affairs, the focal point for peace-
building in crisis countries, offered an alternative to 'business as usual.' The
idea was to create an inter-agency mission charged with the responsibility of
building a strategic framework for the relief and development efforts in a crisis
country. The strategic framework was to set out principles, policies, and
recommendations that all of the international partners would use to guide their
relief and development interventions. The UN's Committee of Agencies (ICC)
was to oversee the initiative and select a "crisis country" that would serve as the
first pilot. The ICC selected Afghanistan.

The strategic framework was to be a common vision and a broad consensus
on what the aid collective intended to achieve. It was also to contain
mechanisms for ensuring continuing negotiations and consultations between
and among all external stakeholders, and increasingly, their Afghan counterparts when hostilities ceased. Not only was it to be an instrument for
international partners to reassess and reconfigure their collective efforts, but
ideally it would enable the political and security strategy and the emerging
humanitarian, economic and development strategy to inform, and be informed
by each other. The hope was that all stakeholders would stand to benefit from
the systematic sharing of knowledge, information and perspectives that affect
both domestic and political environments in Afghanistan. Coping with the
intractable, wicked problems in Afghanistan called for a strategy of
collaboration.

The mission team selected to work on the Afghanistan project included UN
staff from the Department of Political Affairs, Department of Human Affairs,
United Nations Development Program, and participants from the World Bank,
UNESCWA, OXFAM, and the United Nations Staff College. The UN
coordinator for Afghanistan assigned three consultants to the mission and the
manager of the World Bank's resident mission in Islamabad assigned two staff
members. In addition, a four-person UN Staff College team assisted the
mission in conducting a workshop that was to be a focal point in the
collaborative process.

The mission team leader, a veteran of the UN system, planned a series of
steps that would build momentum for the overall collaborative effort. Activities
included team building, planning and site visits to Afghanistan prior to the
workshop for members of the mission team; a workshop in Afghanistan for all
of the stakeholders; post-workshop visits throughout Afghanistan to confer
with local leaders and agencies; mission team development of the strategic

framework; validation of the strategic framework at the policy level in New York; and finally, implementation of the framework at the field level in Afghanistan by the original workshop members.

Reality Intervenes

Preparations for the stakeholder collaboration were complicated by a number of factors. The ICC's choice of Afghanistan was delayed and planning efforts at the policy level were put on hold due to the continuing war in Afghanistan. The original idea had been to select a pilot country where hostilities had ceased. But eager to get the project underway, anticipating that the war would be over soon, advocates recommended going forward in Afghanistan. Interest had been generated and commitments had been made to various agencies and contractors who were supporting the mission. A short window of opportunity remained when mission team members would be available. The mission team leader himself had plans to finalize his commitments to the UN within the year.

By the time the UN made its official decision to launch the pilot in Afghanistan, there was little time to follow through with the original design of the overall collaborative effort. The mission-team leader, embarking on an innovative project never before attempted within the UN system, had to spend most of his time building political support and approval for the overall collaborative effort at the policy level. That left him little time to concentrate on mission design, management and implementation. On paper the overall collaborative effort appeared workable, but in reality there were some serious flaws. Overall project management and integration were minimal. Anticipated mission-team country visits, organizing, planning, and team building meetings did not occur. Coordination was limited among the agencies and individuals involved. People were scattered throughout the world – in the field throughout Afghanistan and Islamabad, Pakistan, at the UN Staff College in Turin, Italy, at the UN headquarters in New York, and throughout the United States. As a consequence, roles among the mission team members were never clarified nor were members able to meet face-to-face until a few days before the workshop was due to begin. Some members did not arrive until the workshop was well under way.

The workshop itself had to be moved outside of Afghanistan to Islamabad, Pakistan to ensure participants' safety. Given the uncertainty surrounding the workshop, the designer/facilitator was unable to do much prior planning. She had little control over the arrangements: when and where the workshop would occur; the number and type of stakeholders who would attend; participants' advance preparation; clerical support during the workshop; and follow-up after the workshop. Workshop attendees were reluctant participants, at least initially. They had not received explanations, instructions, or invitations about the workshop until the week before the workshop was scheduled to begin. Travel was difficult for many, especially those who had to be evacuated from northern Afghanistan where the fighting had intensified. And key people were missing; the UN resident coordinator and some UN agency heads had prior commitments and other pressing duties. Their absence prompted some to question whether the whole effort would be worthwhile.

Workshop Process and Outcomes

Despite the start-up difficulties, more than 80 people appeared at the opening of the workshop. Members came from various UN agencies, bilateral and multi-lateral donor countries, Afghan and international NGOs and the Red Cross Movement. Working through a loosely designed set of activities asking people to assess their environment and the state of their inter-organizational relationships, participants identified some 247 strategic issues that were of concern. Grouping the issues into 25 basic categories, they identified 14 major issues on which they wanted to focus their work. Small groups then developed strategies and actions plans for each issue (Bryson, 1995).

Participants were self-managed when workshop activities required them to break into smaller groups. Each group identified its own discussion leader, timekeeper, recorder, and reporter (and members were encouraged to rotate these roles). The large group and the sub groups made decisions based on consensus. The one exception was the exercise that required participants to rank strategic issues in order of their personal priorities. Participants and the facilitator established ground rules for the event. Interaction was to be open and equal with no one group or organization dominating. Everything was to be recorded on flip charts and people were to listen, be considerate and mutually respectful of one another and not to make speeches. Scheduled times were to be observed. Participants were to seek common ground rather than dwell on their differences, self-manage their small groups, and keep comments off the record and not for attribution.

After the workshop concluded, the mission team began the next phase of the overall effort. Its charge was to write a strategic framework, based on workshop input, to guide future relief and recovery efforts. Here is where collaboration faltered. Mission team members, uncertain of their roles and responsibilities, could not agree on what to do or how to proceed. Tension intensified when they were unable to decide what a framework was or should be. Hoping to break the impasse, they created sub groups, each one taking topics on which the members were expert. The mission leader then was to take the lead in pulling the subgroup reports together in order to prepare the final document. Drafts were to be circulated for final mission-team approval. The document went through many late-night revisions both in the two-week aftermath of the workshop in-country and the following months when the mission leader returned to the U.S. Observers described its writing as a painful process to watch and members described it as an equally difficult process in which to participate. Upon last report, policy makers had yet to meet and approve the mission-team document.

Despite the breakdowns in the handoffs between the workshop and the mission team strategic framework, between the strategic framework and its approval at the policy level, there were some impressive outcomes at the field level in Afghanistan. Stakeholders continued to meet throughout the next year both at the regional and national levels. New relationships among the donors and relief and development partners were forged. The NGOs, who previously had not been part of inter-agency interactions, still retained their 'voice' and were involved in the programming exercises. Stakeholders came to agreement on a number of changes: the establishment of the Afghanistan programming board consisting of NGOs, UN personnel and donors. The programming board was to oversee five regional areas and its defacto chair would be the UN Resident Representative. A common mechanism for coordination was developed on a regional basis. Regional stakeholders would meet to develop a coherent program, decide on criteria for selection of programs, and set priorities to fund only those activities that supported the common effort. At last report, they had agreed to a joint monitoring mechanism, in principle, the details of which they expected to work out by the end of the year. According to a UN headquarters staff member, "the workshop provided the raw material for a consensus . . . and gave legitimacy to what came afterwards." The "analysis on the ground" helped policy makers recognize that the political strategy and the relief and development strategy had to be linked.

IMPLICATIONS FROM THE CASE

The UN-sponsored events surrounding relief and development in Afghanistan offer valuable lessons and insights to those who would use collaborative strategies to deal with wicked problems, especially in crisis countries. I have singled out four that merit particular attention.

Fail into Collaboration

Nobody of whom I am aware came to the Afghanistan project believing that previous efforts at relief and development in crisis countries had been very successful. In fact, when I asked what prompted their interest, many poignantly spoke of failures they had witnessed first hand. As experienced members of bureaucracies, large and small, they were also very familiar with what I have termed authoritative and competitive strategies for dealing with wicked problems, and they were well acquainted with their disadvantages. So despite their fatigue and skepticism, and the pull from the field to deal with emergencies, they came to the workshop willing to give collaboration a try. They were in search of a better way of doing things.

It is my firm conviction that people have to fail into collaboration. Experiences with authoritative and competitive strategies and personal knowledge of their disadvantages are great teachers. People have to learn what does not work before they are willing to absorb what they perceive to be the extra 'costs' associated with collaboration. This learning is especially important for people who come from cultures that place a high premium on taking charge, making decisions, being competitive, and using authorities and experts to settle whatever disputes arise. Only when people come to realize the shortcomings of competition and handing over decisions to authorities, are they willing to experiment with collaboration as an alternative way of coping with wicked problems.

Beware of Attempts to Tame Wicked Problems

Despite the start-up difficulties in getting the innovative project off the ground, once underway, the workshop enabled stakeholders from field activities in Afghanistan to identify some common ground and focus on issues of joint interest. Unfortunately, the next step in the collaborative effort – the handoff to the mission team did not go smoothly. The subject matter experts on the mission team had a great deal of difficulty in pulling together the materials and writing a strategic framework. That difficulty, in my view, was to be expected.

The mission team was composed of a wide-ranging set of experts – political scientists, economists, historians, managers, and businessmen. Not only did their educational and work experiences condition them to see the world differently, but their organizational affiliations predisposed them to have very different definitions of 'the problems' and 'the solutions' in Afghanistan, not unlike the participants of the workshop. But instead of attempting to work out these differences as full participants in the collaborative effort and learning from one another, they remained on the sidelines as observers. Some did not even attend the workshop. They assumed that as experts, they would be able to take whatever was generated from the workshop, and in a short period of time, turn it into a strategic framework, reconciling the major conflicts that had been years in the making. In essence, they fully believed it was possible to use an authoritative strategy to tame wicked problems (strategic framework written by experts) and overlay it on a collaborative strategy used by the stakeholders in the workshop.

As noted, authoritative strategies can be employed to tame wicked problems to the extent that power is concentrated and uncontested among the players. Neither condition obtained in this case. Multiple centers of power were represented at the workshop and within the mission team. The UN convened the events, but there was no one, overarching authority that all of the stakeholders deferred to or that was powerful enough to 'force a decision' on the other players. Competition among the participating groups and agencies, if activated, could be keen. They had been known to act in ways to guard their turf and independence, especially surrounding resource and policy decisions. With power dispersed among the players, and with no agreement to hand over the wicked problems of relief and recovery to anyone, including mission team leadership, an authoritative strategy was unlikely to be effective in this instance.

"Get the Whole System in the Room"

Wicked problems and their solutions are socially defined. People have to construct their meaning. The trouble with social definitions is that they vary because people's personal preferences, backgrounds, educational experiences, and organizational affiliations vary and predispose them to see the world in different ways. We have all become specialists of one kind or another. Our diverse interests and perspectives become a curse when each stakeholder believes it holds 'the truth' and expects everyone to share it, or worse, when a stakeholder wants to impose his view of truth on others and considers anyone who refuses to accept it as dumb, ignorant, or morally deficient. We end up talking past one another instead of having a "dialogue" with one another (Bohm, 1990).

One way to move people beyond their 'my truth is better than your truth' positions is to get "the whole system in the room" so stakeholders can begin to learn from one another (Bunker & Alban, 1997). What they can learn in working together is that each holds 'some truth' in dealing with wicked problems. By asking what they are hearing from others that can help them better understand the problem and its solution, they can begin to appreciate their differences and view them as an opportunity to learn more about the problem and its potential solutions. Appreciative inquiry is built on this basic premise (Barrett, 1995; Cooperrider & Srivastva, 1987).

Getting the "whole system in the room" has its challenges, however. Figuring out what the system is, who the stakeholders are and how to select them, how many can be accommodated under one roof, what the agenda will be, and how to facilitate interactions have all been mentioned elsewhere as major issues to consider (Emery & Purser, 1996; Jacobs, 1994; Weisbord, 1992; Weisbord & Janoff, 1995). Here I want to identify some issues that were particularly salient in the Afghanistan case.

Stakeholders, especially under crisis conditions, can be impatient and want to get on with things so that they can get back to their 'real work.' It helps to begin by explaining that the real work in dealing with wicked problems is learning together, not learning as independent entities. This type of learning takes time; patience is required of themselves and of others. Scaling down expectations under these circumstances is advisable. Rather than jumping immediately into what-is-the-problem-and-how-are-we-going-to-solve-it exercises, building opportunities for stakeholders to talk about themselves and their issues of concern can be time well spent. The real challenge is to help them begin to build a *community of interest* where none existed before. The fact that the stakeholders continued to meet after the workshop and developed a mechanism to ensure an ongoing dialogue about relief and development in Afghanistan speaks volumes in this regard. Once people saw the value of getting "the whole system" together, they figured out a way to keep it going so they could build on their earlier experiences.

Dealing with wicked problems requires a delicate balance. There are very real differences that separate stakeholders and ignoring them does not make their differences disappear. On the other hand, it is difficult to begin a learning process if all stakeholders do is argue about what divides them rather than focus on what unites them. What this means in practice is that there may be some areas surrounding wicked problems that are just too difficult for a group to tackle, at least formally, and at least initially. Time may be better spent in finding areas of common ground on which they can take some collective action and feel good about what they have accomplished (Weisbord, 1992; Weisbord & Janoff, 1995). The debate over gender policy in Afghanistan illustrates the point. Instead of a heated debate on the issue of gender that threatened to divide the stakeholders and disrupt the proceedings, workshop participants took the issue of gender policy "offline." Interested parties met after hours at lunch or in the evening to discuss gender issues, while workshop activities continued to search for issues on which they could work together. Getting the whole system in the room does not mean everyone will or has to agree, but it does mean that they have to find some areas of common interest, or there will be nothing on which they can collaborate to become a learning community.

Be Open to Self-Organization and Co-Evolution

The stakeholders operating in Afghanistan worked in an "under-organized" system (Brown, 1980). Few formal or informal mechanisms existed to legitimate their meeting as a group to exchange ideas and learn from one another. Complicating the picture was an inability to organize due to the crisis conditions and the difficulty of bringing together people from all over the world. In contrast to standard approaches for activities such as these that recommend months of pre intervention planning and preparation (Emery & Purser, 1996; Jacobs, 1994; Weisbord, 1992; Weisbord & Janoff, 1995), the workshop was a "come as you are event" without certainty of what would happen and how. Organizers guessed that somewhere between 30 to 40 people would attend. Well over 80 appeared on the first day.

By necessity, this meant that the workshop became a self-organizing system: it was open to and structured by naturally occurring interactions and activities (Jantsch, 1980). It literally developed on a moment-by-moment basis. People appeared and things began to happen. True, the designer/facilitator established guidelines for interactions that were agreed to by all participants (e.g. stakeholders in the workshop were co-equal members with the same rights to participate, contribute, and set direction). And the group created constraints to regulate their interactions (e.g. self-organizing small groups; no speeches; no cell phones, no smoking in common areas). But the designer/facilitator literally "made it up" as the intervention unfolded. Based on her assessment of where the group was and what it needed, she would open each day with suggestions on how to proceed, drawing on her background in planning for large groups. The workshop members were free to go forward with her ideas or opt for others that made more sense to them. As a consequence of the open-ended nature of the interactions, participants created a "complex adaptive system" – one that developed its own rules of behavior, reflected on its behavior, and self-directed its interactions based on what it was learning (Stacey, 1996). By necessity, the designer/facilitator's role had to highly flexible and adaptive – a role that constantly co-evolved in relationship to participants' needs and understandings. She was under no illusion that she or any one else was 'in control' of what was happening during the workshop. The actions of a given moment just fed into and gave direction to subsequent activities; they were not, nor could they be under the circumstances, predetermined by any particular design.

Others have written on our need to find new patterns of leadership (Block, 1993; Chrislip & Larson, 1994; Daft & Lengel, 1998; Wheatly, 1994), new ways of managing and organizing (Jantsch, 1980; Kiel, 1994; Prigogine & Stengers, 1984) and new ways of thinking and behaving (Senge, 1990; Stacey, 1992; 1996) to deal with conditions similar to the Afghanistan case. These and other references provide valuable suggestions on how to function, create, and learn under conditions of high uncertainty and ambiguity. In addition to their insights, I would offer, as the workshop's designer and facilitator, a few remaining observations of my own.

Essential to any undertaking, especially in crisis conditions, is the ability to "trust the process" and the group's ability to monitor its own progress and make self-corrections along the way. Many things would be nice to have in large-group interventions: a mission and vision that sets direction; participants well trained in group skills; leaders who can galvanize energy for collective action; time for planning and preparation. But under crisis conditions, it is unlikely that all or even some of these elements will be present. In my view, it is better to just get on with it rather than wait until everything is in place, an unlikely occurrence anyway given the circumstances. What really matters in a situation like this is each person's willingness to make a 'leap of faith' that commits him or her to working together, acting with integrity, and trusting that somehow something will come out of the collective effort without any guarantees that it will. What all this amounts to is less heroics, more humility, and a greater appreciation for experimentation, 'groping along,' and 'muddling through' than we normally permit ourselves given the weight of our rational analytic tool kit and strategic management practice. It really is an act of courage on everyone's part that starts the effort. We should not underestimate how difficult and important it is to acknowledge and take this first step.

CONCLUSIONS

Wicked problems will be with us for some time, deriving as they do from the interdependencies and complexities of living together without a shared set of values and views. One alternative is to develop better-coping strategies. Three strategies have been outlined with the greatest attention paid to collaborative strategies, the least understood and practiced of the three. A stakeholder collaboration concerning the relief and recovery efforts in Afghanistan served as an example of how wicked problems can be approached, even under crisis conditions, when power is widely distributed among the stakeholders. Although the collaborative effort surrounding Afghanistan has its unique attributes, there are some important 'lessons learned' that can be applied to other regions torn by conflict and in search of better ways to approach relief and development work.

We learn to take care in attempting to tame wicked problems by turning them over to experts or some center of power for definition and solution. If we are truly dealing with wicked problems when no one is "in control," then it is unlikely that the experts and leaders will be able be able to act unilaterally to define the problems and their solutions. In fact, their insistence in doing so may impede the problem-solving process. We learn that wicked problems are socially defined so that getting the "whole system in the room" to enable people to learn from one another is very useful. And given the constraints and complexity of crisis situations, social learning is more likely to be successful if it remains a self-organizing, complex adaptive system that co-evolves as stakeholders meet, interact, and inform one another's actions. Ultimately, we learn that to lead, facilitate and participate in such collective undertakings requires an act of faith. It begins with the hope that there is a better way of doing things, a recognition that failure is possible, and a willingness to 'trust the process' without guarantees of a particular outcome. It is sustained on personal reserves that enable people to remain calm and centered in the face of the unknown and the unknowable. These are important lessons for all of us to learn.

ACKNOWLEDGMENTS

My thanks to Dr. Raymond Bradley for suggesting the link between the collaborative efforts in Afghanistan and a complex adaptive system operating on the principles of co-evolution, self-organization, and learning.

REFERENCES

Bardach, E. (1998). *Getting Agencies to Work Together: The Practice and Theory of Managerial Craftsmanship,* Washington, D.C.: Brookings.

Barrett, F. (1995). Creating Appreciative Learning Cultures. *Organizational Dynamics, 24*(1), 36–49.

Block, P. (1993). *Stewardship*. San Francisco: Berrett-Koehler.

Bohm, D. (1990). *On Dialogue*. Cambridge, MA: Pegasus Communications.

Brown, L. D. (1980). Planned Change in Underorganized Systems. In: T. G. Cummings (Ed.), *Systems Theory for Organizational Development* (pp. 181–208). New York: Wiley.

Bryson, J. M. (1995). *Strategic Planning for Public and Non-profit Organizations*. San Francisco: Jossey-Bass.

Bunker, B., & Alban, B. T. (1997). *Large Group Interventions: Engaging the Whole System for Rapid Change*. San Francisco: Jossey-Bass.

Chrislip, D. D., & Larson, C. E, (1994). *Collaborative Leadership: How Citizens and Civic Leaders Can Make A Difference*. San Francisco: Jossey-Bass.

Churchman, C. (1967). Wicked Problems. *Management Science, 4*(14), B141–142.

Conklin, E. J., & Weil, W. (no date). Wicked Problems: Naming the Pain in Organizations. Working Paper. jconklin@gdss.com

Cooperrider, D. L., & Srivastva, S. (1987). Appreciative Inquiry in Organizational Life. In: W. A. Pasmore & R. W. Woodman (Eds), *Research in Organization Development and Change* (Vol. 1, pp. 129–169). Greenwich, CT: JAI.

Daft, R. L., & Lengel, R. H. (1998). *Fusion Leadership: Unlocking the Subtle Forces That Change People and Organizations*. San Francisco: Berrett-Koehler.

De Grace, P., & Stahl, L. H. (1990). *Wicked Problems, Righteous Solutions: A Catalogue of Software Engineering Paradigms*. Englewood Cliffs, N.J.: Prentice-Hall/YOURDON Press.

Doz, Y. L., & Hamel, G. (1998). *Alliance Advantage: The Art of Creating Value Through Partnering*. Boston: Harvard Business School Press.

Emery, M., & Purser, R. E. (1996). *The Search Conference: Theory and Practice*. San Francisco: Jossey-Bass.

Gray, B. (1989). *Collaborating: Finding Common Ground for Multiparty Problems*. San Francisco: Jossey-Bass.

Guindon, R. (1990). Designing the Design Process: Exploiting Opportunistic Thoughts. *Human Computer Interaction, 5*, 305–344.

Huxham, C. (Ed.) (1996). *Creating Collaborative Advantage*. London: Sage.

Interagency Mission Report on Afghanistan (1997). New York: United Nations.

Jacobs, R. W. (1994). *Real Time Strategic Change*. San Francisco: Berrett Koehler.

Jantsch, E. (1980). *The Self-Organizing Universe: Scientific and Human Implications of the Emerging Paradigm of Evolution*. Elmsford, N.Y.: Pergamon Press.

Kagan, R. A. (1991). Adversarial Legalism and American Government. *Journal of Policy Analysis and Management, 10*(3), 369–406.

Kiel, L. D. (1994). *Managing Chaos and Complexity in Government: A New Paradigm for Managing Change, Innovation, and Organizational Renewal*. San Francisco: Jossey-Bass.

Lewis, E. (1980). *Public Entrepreneurship: Toward a Theory of Bureaucratic Political Power*. Bloomington: Indiana University Press.

McLagan, P., & Nel, C. (1995). *The Age of Participation: New Governance for the Workplace and the World*. San Francisco: Barrett-Koehler.

Pfeffer, J. (1992). *Managing With Power*. Boston: Harvard Business School Press.

Prigogine, I., & Stengers, I. (1984). *Order Out of Chaos*. New York: Bantam.

Quinn, J. B., Anderson, P., & Finkelstein, S. (1996). Leveraging Intellect. *Academy of Management Executive, 10*(3), 7–27.

Reich, R.. B. (1990). *Public Management in a Democratic Society*. Englewood Cliffs, N.J.: Prentice Hall.

Rittel, H. W. J., & Webber, M. M. (1973). Dilemmas in a General Theory of Planning. *Policy Sciences, 4*, 155–169.

Scott, E. (1990). Managing Environmental Risks: The Case of ASARCO. In: R. B. Reich (Ed.), *Public Management in a Democratic Society*. Englewood Cliffs, N.J.: Prentice Hall.

Senge, P. M. (1990). *The Fifth Discipline: The Art and Practice of the Learning Organization*. New York: Doubleday Currency.

Shilts, R. (1987). *And the Band Played On: Politics, People, and the AIDS Epidemic*, New York: St. Martin's Press.

Stacey, R. D. (1996). *Complexity and Creativity in Organizations.* San Francisco: Berrett-Koehler.

Stacey, R. D. (1992). *Managing the Unknowable: Strategic Boundaries Between Order and Chaos in Organizations.* San Francisco: Jossey-Bass.

Verma, N. (1998). *Similarities, Connections, and Systems: The Search for a New Rationality for Planning and Management.* Lanham, MD: Lexington Books.

Weisbord, M. R. (1992). *Discovering Common Ground.* San Francisco: Berrett-Koehler.

Weisbord, M. R. (1995). *Future Search*, San Francisco: Berrett-Koehler.

Wheatley, M. J. (1992). *Leadership and the New Science: Learning About Organizations from an Orderly Universe.* San Francisco: Berrett-Koehler.

21. THE WORLD BANK AND PUBLIC SECTOR MANAGEMENT REFORM

David Shand

INTRODUCTION

The experiences of the World Bank in public sector management reform (PSMR) appear to reflect those of many individual countries, and of other international institutions and donors. In analyzing Bank's work in PSMR the following background is relevant. Firstly, the Bank's role has historically been one of lending for "development" purposes, mainly for specific projects – covering both infrastructure (roads, energy, irrigation etc) and human capital (education, health etc). The skills of Bank staff have thus traditionally been in the technical areas covered by the loans (irrigation, health), in project analysis and management and, consistent with a focus on economic growth, in macroeconomic analysis and "development economics", or strategies for economic development. PSMR issues have therefore in the past been somewhat peripheral to the Bank's work and staff with knowledge or skills in public sector reform issues are small in number – as indeed they are in many governments and other international institutions.

Secondly, and related to this point, moves to more general programmatic (as opposed to project) lending, providing general budgetary support, referred to in Bank parlance as adjustment lending, leads to greater prominence to public sector management issues. What institutional arrangements in the public sector might provide some assurance that such loans will be well spent? But other reasons may better explain the growth in Bank PSMR work, as explained later in this chapter.

Learning from International Public Management Reform, Volume 11B, pages 377–390.
2001 by Elsevier Science Ltd.
ISBN: 0-7623-0760-9

Thirdly, it is a Bank, not a general aid organization or technical support agency, Technical support provided by the Bank to a particular country is linked to its loan program with that country. Generally speaking this means no loans, no assistance, although there are exceptions for reconstruction activities (e.g. East Timor, Liberia, and natural disaster relief in a number of countries), and in addition the World Bank Institute provides training courses on a wide range of issues, including public sector management issues.

Finally, the Bank recognizes that its past performance in PSMR activities has been mixed at best. Of course this record does not make it worse than the public sector reform activities of other institutions, including the national governments of many countries. This issue is treated in more detail later.

EAST ASIAN ISSUES

Most of the public sector reform issues addressed in this chapter are reasonably generic and apply across all regions. However a discussion of World Bank public sector work in the East Asia region is an appropriate point to commence.

The Bank's major public sector work is focused on three of the "East Asia five", namely Thailand, Indonesia and Philippines (the other two of the five are Korea and Malaysia), and in the group of smaller countries on Cambodia (less on Laos and Mongolia) with more limited public sector work in the transition economies of China and Vietnam.

Before the regional financial crisis public sector institutions in the three countries were perceived to be functioning reasonably well. A perceived competent civil service was contributing to sound fiscal results (with relatively small public sectors, in relation to their per capita income levels) and impressive economic growth and poverty reduction. Although the existence of an overstaffed and frequently non-performance based civil service, generally poor public sector service delivery, inefficient regulation of the private sector, official corruption and poorly performing public enterprises were recognized, interestingly they seemed to have little impact on investor confidence and on economic growth – at that time.

The regional crisis changed all this, leading to pressures for urgent reforms to increase public sector performance. Firstly, the substantial deterioration in fiscal positions, largely caused by the budgetary costs of restructuring the banking sectors has forced governments to explicitly attempt to "do more with less", including instituting social safety nets to assist the poor most affected by the crisis. Secondly, there has been a sea change in demands by citizens for more accountable government – involving tackling corruption, decentralization and improved service delivery (World Bank, 2000).

These pressures cover all or most of the components of the Bank's public sector work, description of which follows in this chapter. The challenge for the Bank will be to use its new strategies and policies to assist governments in delivering tangible results – while at the same time persuading governments that their improving economies do not lessen the need for public sector management reform.

CHANGING PERSPECTIVE TOWARD THE PUBLIC SECTOR

In recent years the Bank's role in East Asia and elsewhere has been both restated and refined. In particular, the greater emphasis on poverty reduction reflects a greater realization that not all economic growth is pro-poor, and that both growth and poverty reduction are key objectives.

A key issue for the Bank's PSMR work is therefore the extent to which this contributes to economic growth and poverty reduction, or putting it another way what elements of public sector reform will assist economic growth and poverty reduction in particular countries. Given the limited theoretical and analytical basis of public sector reform world wide, this is indeed a challenge. While Bank publications promote the view that better government helps to explain the difference in performance between east Asia and sub-saharan Africa for example, and that countries with good economic policies and stronger institutional capacities grow faster than other countries, the challenge is to more precisely identify the key elements in each country. Considerable analytical and diagnostic work is going on in the Bank in this area. (Kaufmann et al., 1999).

The World Development Report 1997 (WDR, 1997) *The State in a Changing World* is a seminal statement of these issues as well as reflecting a sea-change in the Bank's thinking about the public sector, setting out an agenda to improve the performance of governments. Reflecting the disappointing experiences in many developing countries of a growing, often bloated and non-performing public sector, the Bank's earlier public sector work focussed on public sector downsizing through civil service reform and privatization. A good public sector was perceived as a small public sector.

However WDR 97 recognized explicitly the importance of a well functioning state in promoting economic growth and poverty reduction, or as some have put it, mainstreaming "good governance" into Bank work. While matching the role of the state to its capacity is important and the state should thus not be seen as the sole provider of many public services, this matching now also includes re-invigorating state institutions to increase their capacity. Thus, far from supporting a minimalist view of the role of the state, WDR 97 discusses the importance of an effective state, playing a "catalytic, facilitating role encouraging and complementing the activities of private business and individuals."

The origins of this new focus on the role of the state vary but as outlined by WDR 97 include.

- the important role of the state in the east Asian "miracle" economies.
- the collapse of the command and control economies of the former Soviet Union and central and eastern Europe.
- the fiscal crisis of the welfare state in many OECD countries.
- the collapse of some states through wars and other humanitarian emergencies.

This new focus may also reflect the greater agenda of public sector reform in many advanced countries, which are major Bank contributors or shareholders.

Whatever the origins, PSMR has become a new wave of activity in the Bank. Some observers have drawn a parallel between this new interest and the "greening" of the Bank, or the increased emphasis on environmental issues in Bank work from the mid 1970s. Many of the strategies to re-invigorate state institutions reflect the thinking of the new institutional economic – the importance of structures, rules and restraints and norms and practices, and the need for appropriate management, incentives both positive and negative for the system to work.

SOME BASICS OF "GOOD GOVERNANCE"

What therefore, at least in the Bank's view, constitutes a well performing public sector? While these elements can be classified in many different ways the most basic elements are listed as follows by the Bank.

- the rule of law operates. This involves adequate laws to ensure personal security and facilitate the functioning of markets, which are adequately enforced through an independent and predictable judiciary, and the absence of official corruption.
- a policy environment which facilitates economic growth and poverty reduction. This includes sound macroeconomic and fiscal policies, sound budgetary institutions and good prioritization of government expenditure, and predictable and efficient regulation of the private sector, including the financial sector.

- adequate investment in people (particularly through public expenditures on basic health and education) and in infrastructure, involving good allocation of public expenditures between and within sectors.
- protecting the vulnerable through affordable and targeted safety nets and generally ensuring an appropriate "pro-poor" emphasis in public expenditures.
- protecting the environment, including assuring that economic growth does not cause environmental degradation.

These general elements are a mixture of outcomes (e.g. adequate levels of expenditures, acceptable budget deficits) and process or institutional measures (e.g. sound budgetary institutions).

The process and institutional measures are contained in greater detail in the large number of diagnostic tools developed within the Bank to guide various aspects of PSMR. Apart from general set of governance indicators these include anti-corruption (referred to, perhaps inappropriately, as service delivery) diagnostic surveys, public expenditure management diagnostics and national institutional assessments, (the latter having separate toolkits to evaluate cabinet decision-making, civil service reform and service delivery arrangements and other issues) to name a few. There is even a draft toolkit to analyze the "reform readiness" of individual countries. Two key assessments which involve ranking of individual countries and which affect the priority to be given to them in overall Bank lending are country policy and institutional assessments (CPIAs) which attempt to assess the quality of policies and institutions, of which the quality of public sector management and institutions is a major component, and country financial accountability assessments (CFAAs) which assess the adequacy of financial management.

Between them these diagnostic tools represent an impressive attempt to develop measures of "good governance". But they have their problems. They have generally been developed in isolation from each other and there is considerable duplication. Some also do little more than state the obvious e.g. that Indonesia has high levels of official corruption and an overstaffed and underpaid civil service. Some appear to be more statistical in nature (e.g. the number of civil servants) and their role as performance criteria is not clear.

The way in which they are to be used may also be a problem. Firstly they may invite a check-list approach to measurement in which form may dominate over substance. Secondly their potential use to rank or compare countries, rather than to develop country specific public sector reform proposals, needs to allow for the inter-action between measures or the weighting to be given to individual measures. Clearly any country comparisons should be made carefully to allow for these differences, but accepting that some form of country ranking is needed, given limitations on the amount of funds the Bank has available for lending. Thirdly it is not necessarily clear what policy prescriptions flow from them. For example a country may have a high level of official corruption but what should be the strategy to reduce this ? Thus it is important that they be used carefully, with further analysis and judgment, rather than jumping to conclusions.

These diagnostic tools also replicate or complement various country ranking measures developed to guide international investors. These include International Country Risk Guides (ICRG), the World Competitiveness Yearbook (WCY) and Transparency International's Corruption Index, to name but a few.

MAJOR PUBLIC SECTOR ISSUES

Regardless of the imperfections in some of these indicators and diagnostic tools, they do reflect a general consensus in the Bank about the major public sector management issues in developing countries in Asia and elsewhere, which the Bank seeks to address through advice and technical assistance, as well as general conditions in its loans. These can be found in many Bank documents such as public expenditure reviews and in loan documents pertaining to public sector reform lending. They can be listed as follows:

- the civil service is not affordable. There are too many civil servants and individually they are poorly paid. What is required is fewer, better trained and better paid civil servants.
- the civil service is not productive. It delivers poor services or gets in the way of a productive private sector. This may be as basic as failure to ensure law and order, or as general as a failure to apply rules and policies predictably. Other elements may be lack of resources for adequate services, unnecessary administrative complexity and layers of decision making, and lack of administrative capacity – civil servants being literally incapable of performing their prescribed tasks. The latter element may in turn be affected by lack of merit based recruitment and promotion, or general lack of a performance orientation in the management of the civil service.
- policy development or coordination is poor. This may be reflected in fiscal difficulties at the aggregate level and poor prioritization of expenditure at the sectoral level. There may be little linkage between national plans and budget allocations or budget implementation. Policies may be subject to unpredictable changes. Private investment, either domestic or foreign, may be discouraged by such unpredictability.

- the rule of law is not operating adequately. In particular there may be substantial official corruption, either petty or grand. The judicial system may not function adequately, either efficiently or impartially.

The relative significance of or causes of these problems may differ between regions and countries. For example in sub-saharan Africa the major problem may be described as a general lack of administrative capacity. On the other hand the main issue in southern Asia is not lack of capacity (there are many talented civil servants) but rather over-regulation; there is too much "red tape" for citizens or businesses seeking to do business with the government, and in internal government administrative procedures. In East Asia, administrative capacity is also relatively good and fiscal policies have been generally sound and per se did not lead to the east Asian crisis; rather inadequate regulation of the financial sector coupled with some official corruption was the major cause. But the problems of lack of policy coherence and poor service delivery are general to East Asia and all regions – although their causes and thus remedies may differ between countries.

THE BANK'S PUBLIC SECTOR REFORM WORK

The scope of this work in East Asia and elsewhere reflects the potentially great number of causes of a poorly performing public sector.

- *"civil service reform"*. This work has traditionally focussed on measures to reduce the civil service wage bill and improve civil service capacity. This commonly involves reducing the size of the civil service (for example through early retirement schemes, eliminating "ghost" workers) and increasing average salaries. It also generally involves simplifying classification and pay structures, reducing layers of management and instituting merit or performance based recruitment and promotion. The Bank's own reviews of its work in this area have identified some problems; frequently inadequate attention has been paid to the capacity and incentives required to make a performance based personnel management system operate in developing countries (Nunberg & Nellis, 1995; Nunberg 1999).
- this work may be accompanied by *"functional reviews"* or *"fundamental reviews"* under which some or all ministries, departments or agencies are subject to detailed review to evaluate the need for their activities or programs, whether there is duplication between organizations and whether some activities could be contracted out to the private sector or devolved to subnational government. Internal organizational structures may also be reviewed for duplication of activities and excessive layers of management.

- *decentralization of functions to sub-national governments* is a major trend in countries as diverse as Thailand and Indonesia (or Ethiopia and Mexico). Devolution of activities within national governments to regional offices may also reflect the same objectives. In many countries this trend reflects political demands for local autonomy, as well as a desire to improve responsiveness and efficiency of service delivery. However it raises major issues of matching revenues with responsibility and of improving administrative capacity at the sub-national level (Litvack et al., 1998; World Bank, 1999).
- *strengthening institutions to improve policy development and coherence*, while a key issue in public sector performance, has been little emphasized in Bank work until recently. Bank work on reforming central agencies of government has tended to focus on budget/finance and civil service functions rather than policy making role of the prime minister's or president's office – although the budget/finance changes may be a lever for improved policy development and coordination.
- *reforming public expenditure management or budgetary systems* has been and continues to be a significant component of the Bank's PSMR work. Reforms to budgeting systems aim to develop comprehensive budgeting (limiting off-budget accounts and facilitating coordination between recurrent and investment (capital) budgets), improving the linkage between national plans and the budget, developing a medium-term fiscal framework and developing a closer link between performance issues and the budget (in some cases through "performance budgeting") so as to improve both allocative efficiency (prioritization) and operational efficiency are key objectives. Apart from this "upstream" work, "downstream" work on improving budget implementation and monitoring, including the development of financial management information systems continues to be important. Increasing emphasis is now also placed on improving fiscal transparency, both externally to taxpayers and international donors, and internally within the government (World Bank 1998; Schick 1998).
- there is a close link between the process issues of public expenditure management and the substantive issues of *public expenditure policy* – how much is being spent on what purposes and with what results, and what changes in expenditure allocation patterns might be desirable. Clearly improved processes for allocating and evaluating expenditures should lead to improved expenditure outcomes. A considerable amount of Bank public sector work, such as public expenditure reviews (PERs) combines both public expenditure management and policy issues.
- international developments in *performance management*, particularly in OECD countries, including the development of performance measures for

government programs, of various forms of performance contracting including moves to performance budgeting and of program evaluation techniques, have also influenced Bank public sector work, particularly related to public expenditure management. However the transferability of some of these concepts to governments with limited administrative capacity is open to debate, as referred to later.

- *privatization and public enterprise reform* continue to be important in the Bank's public sector work. This reflects needs to reduce the budgetary impact of loss making public enterprises and to improve efficiency and service delivery, in some cases adversely affected by official corruption (World Bank, 1995). But it is now recognized that privatization is no panacea, and can create its problems in terms of corruption and efficiency, particularly if there is inadequate regulation of private sector monopolies. But regulation itself requires the development of a public sector capacity. Public enterprise reform generally stresses the need for clear financial and service quality targets, reasonable commercial autonomy in operating decisions to achieve these targets and corresponding accountability by management for achieving this performance.

- *improving revenue collection* is an important aspect of public sector reform. Poorly functioning revenue collection agencies constrain governments' ability to deliver services and may also give rise to fiscal difficulties. Such agencies are often microcosms of the general public sector problems of low administrative capacity unnecessary complexity and official corruption. But because of their strategic importance they are often focussed on under separate or special reform initiatives. Both revenue policy and revenue management issues may be typically covered.

- *particular sectors or ministries* may be focussed on or given priority in the Bank's public sector reform work. In particular the operation of the basic health and education systems are often considered key in reducing poverty and achieving economic growth. For example the operation of hospitals and health posts may be an early area to be addressed in public sector reforms – for example in a "fundamental" or "functional review".

- *judicial and legal reforms* are also part of the Bank's public sector reform "armory", but generally undertaken by the Bank's Legal Department rather than integrated with overall public sector reform activities. They aim to improve the functioning of the legal and judicial system through raising its capacity (lack of training and skills is frequently a problem) as well as appropriate arrangements to ensure judicial independence and accountability.

- *anti-corruption work* has greatly increased in importance in the Bank's work. Some of this reflects political pressures from Bank members requiring assurances that Bank loans will be spent on the purposes for which they are given and reflecting high profile cases of official corruption in countries such as Indonesia (and Russia). There are many types of corruption and each country's pattern is distinct. Corruption is a complex phenomenon which touches many other aspects of public sector reform work, such as civil service reform, judicial and legal reform, revenue administration and public expenditure management. A key approach has been the development of diagnostic surveys to measure the extent of corruption (Kaufmann et al., 1998) e.g. the need to pay bribes to obtain government services, the need to pay bribes to obtain a government position (the amount being in part a reflection of the revenue earning potential of the position). While there has been some emphasis on more traditional "bureaucratic" responses such as enhancing the role and capacity of inspection or prosecutorial agencies , or increasing low levels of civil service pay (which may contribute to corruption) there is increasing recognition that effectively tackling corruption requires a long term approach, including enhancing the role of civil society as a watchdog partly through increasing transparency of decision making and of results (Stapenhurst & Kpundeh, 1999).

EVALUATIONS OF PUBLIC SECTOR WORK

The Bank has a strong tradition of self evaluation, and notwithstanding allegations of secrecy by uninformed critics, generally a highly visible and transparent approach to its operations. The Bank's own evaluations have concluded that, overall, the it's public sector management projects and institution building components of projects in other sectors have frequently performed poorly. A 1999 review concluded that the Bank's civil service reform work had often not achieved the objectives of reducing the civil service wage bill or increasing civil service capacity. Perhaps the Bank is too hard on itself. How many public sector reforms initiated by governments themselves or by other international agencies are fully successful. Nevertheless, it is important to use such evaluations as a learning exercise to improve the Bank's public sector work.

The following reflect the major criticisms in these reviews as well as the author's own observations.

- many Bank staff or consultants have tended to adopt a narrow technocratic view of public sector reforms. In other words new structures, systems or procedures were proposed with insufficient consideration of implementation capacities or issues. In some cases countries may get the impression that all that is needed is to "plug in" the reform, and it will commence working of itself. An example of a such a narrow technocratic approach may be proposals in some countries to introduce "performance budgeting". Countries may be given the impression that this is the magic solution to "doing more with less", whereas if done properly it firstly requires a major exercise to determine objectives and priorities in and between ministries and will expose a large number of difficult trade-off decisions to be made at the political level.

- in some cases the Bank has used inappropriate "best practice models", which did not take sufficient account of local conditions or implementation capacities. For example, the Bank may have suggested the New Zealand system of accrual output budgeting without considering the information systems and resources needed to operate such a system. It may have proposed the British system of autonomous agencies, without setting in place the accountability pre-requisites to prevent such autonomy becoming a license to do as the organization pleased.
- insufficient consultation with the country on the nature of the problem and its potential solutions has been another problem identified. In other words, the Bank tended to adopt a "supply driven" approach, rather than respond to demands articulated by the client country – leading to inevitable lack of ownership of the proposed reforms.
- some Bank interventions have focused on addressing the problem "down-stream", before an adequate "upstream" diagnosis had been carried out. For example a number of financial management reform projects proposed the development of large financial management information systems, without first addressing possible changes to the budget structure, for example to make the budget more comprehensive in its coverage.
- traditional Bank lending instruments, focusing on one project or area of activity have not encouraged a long-term and holistic view of public sector reforms. Thus Bank staff or consultants may propose remedies in particular areas without considering their impact elsewhere in the public sector. At a general level an example might be measures to introduce performance based human resource management systems into the civil service without developing parallel reforms in budgeting and expenditure management – or vice versa. At a more specific level an example might be recommendations made in some countries to upgrade the skills and staffing of the national audit institution – itself a worthy objective, by paying higher salaries to audit staff. The major impact of this might be to denude the Finance Ministry of most of its staff with accounting qualifications. Yet arguably, ensuring a proper

budgeting and accounting function may have greater priority than developing the auditing function.

- a further problem concerns coordination with other donors and competition between donors, involving both donor countries and other international institutions such as UNDP, IMF and the regional development banks. Each of these is typically also involved in lending or technical assistance activities in PSMR, and indeed there may be competition between them to sell their particular approach or country model to the government. In the absence of either prior coordination by the donors themselves, or the capacity within the government to evaluate and prioritize the differing proposals, the government may become involved in a range of uncoordinated and in some cases conflicting public sector reform activities.

Other problems identified with Bank public sector work reflect lack of staff skilled in this area, as referred to earlier, and to possible perverse incentives for Bank staff. The latter point may be controversial but reflects the role of a Bank. Bank staff may be partly evaluated on their success in developing an active loan portfolio with their particular country. This might mean for example that Bank staff would have an incentive to promote a multi-million dollar financial management information system for the government rather than propose more modest, but possibly equally effective alternatives.

Finally it should be noted that donors institutions generally may have other adverse impacts on public sector management reforms. Often they require special accounting and auditing arrangements for their funds, and such arrangements complicate budgeting, accounting and auditing. Donor willingness to fund projects, whether in public sector reform or elsewhere will reflect their priorities, which may differ from government priorities.

MOVES TO IMPROVE PUBLIC SECTOR WORK

Many of the issues and problems listed above are not confined to the Bank's public sector work, but rather are general issues and problems of Bank operations. As such the changes in the Bank's approach to its PSMR work partly reflect changes in other work – as reflected in the Bank's new Comprehensive Development Framework (CDF).

The CDF emphasizes the need for comprehensive approaches to reform, to build capacity within the client country and to develop partnerships with governments, non-governmental organizations (NGOs) and civil society in implementing its lending programs. While there is nothing particularly new about the CDF, it provides a useful framework for moving the Bank's work forward.

The CDF stresses the need to move beyond internal bureaucratic change, to incorporate "voice", (e.g. citizen surveys to determine problems, needs and satisfaction) "partnership" (e.g. working with civil society and NGOs, as well as with the government) and "competition" (e.g. government not being the sole provider of services) in all projects. Citizens and civil society in general will thus become more empowered to demand improvements in and monitor the performance of the public sector and governments will be better able to respond. A greater role is also seen for parliaments to push for improvements and to develop their oversight role.

Other changes in the Bank's approach call for

- greater selectivity of interventions. The Bank should be involved in reforms only when it has capacity and comparative advantage. It should not attempt to do too much, and should coordinate better with other donors
- more upstream diagnostic work to determine the nature and extent of the problem before developing proposed reform. This is reflected in the diagnostic instruments discussed earlier in this chapter.
- greater emphasis on "home grown" solutions and country ownership – its commitment to and capacity to drive the reform process
- more realistic targets and expectations concerning public sector reform. As in many other reforms there has been a tendency to overall their likely results and to be over-optimistic about what can be achieved within a particular time.

The general move to more programmatic or sectoral lending as opposed to project lending, is likely to continue. There are already three cases of comprehensive Bank public sector reform loans – for Thailand and the Indian states of Andraya Pradesh and Uttar Pradesh. A comprehensive "governance" strategy is being developed for Cambodia. A preliminary assessment of a possible public sector reform loan for the Philippines has been made, but no action has yet eventuated. Each of these examples demonstrates a new approach to public sector reform in World Bank policy for Asia and elsewhere.

REFERENCES

Kaufmann, D., Pradhan, S., & Ryterman, R. (1998). *New Frontiers in Diagnosing and Combating Corruption.* Washington, D.C.: The World Bank.

Kaufmann D., Kraay, A., & Zoido-Laboton, P. (1999). *Governance Matters.* Policy Research Working Paper 2196. Washington, D.C.: The World Bank.

Litvack,. J., Ahmad., J., & Bird, R. (1998). *Rethinking Decentralization in Developing Countries.* The World Bank, PREM Network.

Nunberg, B., & Nellis, J. (1995). *Civil Service Reform and the World Bank*. World Bank Discussion Paper 161.

Nunberg, B. (1999). Rethinking Civil Service Reform, The World Bank PREM Note No. 31.

Schick,. A. (1998). *A Contemporary Approach to Public Expenditure Management*. Economic Development Institute of The World Bank, Washington, D.C.: The World Bank.

Stapenhurst. R., & Kpundeh, S. (1999). *Curbing Corruption: Towards an Integrated Model for Building National Integrity*. Washington, D.C.: The World Bank, EDI Development Studies.

World Bank (1995). *Bureaucrats in Business*. Policy Research Paper. Washington, D.C.: The World Bank.

World Bank (1998). *Public Expenditure Management Handbook*. Washington, D.C.: The World Bank.

World Bank (1999). *Decentralization Briefing Note*. Washington, D.C.: The World Bank.

World Bank (2000). *East Asia – Recovery and Beyond*. Chapter 5, Washington, D.C.: The World Bank.

SECTION IV

LEARNING FROM COMPARATIVE
AND INTERNATIONAL REFORM

22. CAN NATIONS SAVE? EXPERIENCES WITH BUDGET SURPLUSES

Paul Posner and Bryon Gordon

INTRODUCTION

The United States has just completed its second consecutive fiscal year of budget surpluses. Following years of chronic deficits, this fiscal outcome provides a dose of welcome economic and fiscal news. Moreover, CBO and OMB have both projected growing surpluses over the next ten years, building to nearly 3% of GDP by 2009 (CBO, 1999; OMB 1999). For the longer term, absent any policy changes, the GAO's simulations suggest that surpluses could be with us for the next 30 years (GAO, July 1999). Other OECD nations have also entered into a period of budget surpluses.

These surplus projections rest not only on uncertain economic assumptions but also on the assumption that political leaders will maintain the requisite fiscal discipline to sustain surpluses over many years – a premise that many would regard as heroic to say the least. Notwithstanding the political challenges, a compelling economic and fiscal case can be made for increased public saving from surpluses, both in our country and in other OECD nations as well. Particularly for a nation with a low saving rate, higher public surpluses can offset low private saving and ultimately promote higher levels of investment and economic growth in the medium and long term. For instance, the GAO has estimated that national income could be nearly $20,000 higher per person in real terms by 2050 if the Social Security portion of the budget surplus is saved, in comparison with a unified budget balance position (GAO,

Learning from International Public Management Reform, Volume 11B, pages 393–423.
2001 by Elsevier Science Ltd.
ISBN: 0-7623-0760-9

November 1999). Moreover, the government's interest costs can be substantially reduced with declining levels of publicly held debt, thereby freeing up room to address emerging fiscal claims and pressures. Creating additional economic and fiscal capacity over the longer term is particularly important for advanced nations like the United States and most other OECD countries, which are about to experience a demographic shift with a smaller cohort of workers shouldering the burden of providing for the retirement of a larger elderly population. By reducing the levels of publicly held debt, budget surpluses can ultimately promote higher longer-term economic growth and thereby expand the resources available to future generations. As budgetary resources are increasingly encumbered with outlays for pension and health care programs in these nations, reduced interest costs become more essential to promoting fiscal flexibility within the budget.

Although a substantive case can be made for saving surpluses, substantial doubt remains over whether our nation, or indeed any democratic nation, can muster the political resolve to sustain surpluses over a period of time. Fiscal restraint has been marshaled both here in the United States and in other OECD nations to achieve budget balance, reflecting the compelling appeal of zero balance as a fiscal goal (GAO, 1994). However, it appears that it would be more difficult to ask for fiscal sacrifice in the service of sustaining a surplus, particularly for systems that have achieved surpluses only after years of fiscal restraint. Political leaders intent on saving surpluses face a stiff challenge indeed. If surpluses are in fact as important to our economic future as many economists suggest, it is then worth exploring in some depth what arguments, strategies, and rules might be available to leaders to promote the requisite public support for continued fiscal restraint.

This chapter reports on the results of a study recently completed by the General Accounting Office (GAO) exploring the politics of budget surpluses in six OECD nations that have achieved budget surpluses in the past decade – Australia, Canada, New Zealand, Norway, Sweden, and the United Kingdom (GAO, November 1999). At the request of Senators Domenici and Lautenberg, the GAO study addressed whether and how political support was forged for fiscal policies sustaining budget surpluses for several years in those nations and what lessons we might learn for our fiscal policy and politics.

THE POLITICS OF RUNNING A BUDGET SURPLUS

Balancing the budget is a fiscal goal that often commands broad support – at least in the abstract – from policymakers and the public alike. The idea of a government spending no more than it takes in has a near universal appeal across the political spectrum. In contrast, a budget surplus is a goal with less intuitive appeal, and a policy that often lacks a natural constituency. Periods of surplus tend to elicit proposals for new spending or tax cuts. This may reflect in part a reaction to a period of restraint and the often difficult steps taken to eliminate deficits. In the face of these calls to respond to deferred demands, it can be difficult for politicians to justify running a surplus.

The politics of surplus are very different from the politics of deficits. During a deficit reduction period the goal is clear and political decisions tend to focus on the mix and severity of spending cuts and tax increases needed to bring the budget into balance. While there may be disagreement over the detailed actions to be taken and how long it should take to achieve balance, there is generally agreement on the goal of balance. Although a thoroughly arbitrary target from an economic standpoint, budget balance in fact is the one fiscal goal with the broadest public appeal (Keech, 1995: 125). During a surplus period, the political debate focuses on whether surpluses are needed at all. If consensus is reached on the need for surpluses, then agreement can be reached on how long they are needed and how large they should be. The answers to these questions are not obvious as there is no single goal with the intuitive appeal of a balanced budget or zero deficit.

While most economists agree that there are economic and fiscal benefits of running a surplus, these benefits are longer term and must compete with current needs. It appears particularly difficult to generate public support for sustaining surpluses over a period of several years. Constituencies supporting spending increases or tax cuts generally are well organized and can point to specific, visible, and immediate benefits (Shepsle, Weingast & Johnson, 1981: 642–664).

Support for retaining a surplus can be further weakened by the fact that many countries achieve surpluses after several years of painful deficit reduction efforts. Popular programs may have already been cut and/or taxes raised to achieve surplus. Electorates willing to accept relatively tight fiscal discipline to achieve balance may be unwilling to continue to do so when there is "excess" money at the end of the year. This "fiscal fatigue" can greatly increase the pressure to "spend" the surplus. Consequently, governments that adopt a surplus goal often allow a portion of surpluses to be used for spending increases or tax cuts.

KEY DIFFERENCES AMONG THE SIX COUNTRIES

We chose six case study countries – Australia, Canada, New Zealand, Norway, Sweden, and the United Kingdom – because they have all recently experienced budget surpluses. Admittedly, the six case study countries differ from the United States in many ways. They are all smaller and more dependent on foreign trade. The role of the central government varies from country to country. Two countries – Australia and Canada – have a federal system similar to ours, while the other four countries have unitary systems, with the central government playing a key role in financing local sector activities. When all levels of government are combined, the case study countries generally have a larger public sector than the United States.

Another key difference is that all six case study countries have parliamentary systems of government. Parliamentary systems are thought to facilitate controversial political action by consolidating power in the hands of the governing party. In contrast, the U.S. system's separation of powers is thought by some to present leaders with greater obstacles to political agreement. Yet imposing sacrifice, even during a period of surplus, is a difficult task for any democratically elected government. In fact, Paul Pierson has argued that fiscal sacrifice is more politically risky for parliamentary governments because of the concentration of political accountability for the outcomes (Pierson, 1994: 168). Furthermore, coalition or minority governments can form in some case study countries resulting in confrontation and controversy between the coalition partners. Coalition or minority governments routinely must seek the support of other political parties in order to enact legislation, and as result can act in a similar fashion to our system of separate legislative and executive branches.

FISCAL HISTORY AND CONDITION OF THE CASE STUDY COUNTRIES

In its simplest definition, a surplus is an excess of revenue over spending in a given period. However, definitions of revenue and spending vary among countries, and to compare across countries we used OECD data wherever possible. OECD data are presented on a general government basis, which includes the aggregate fiscal balances of all levels of government in that nation. In analyzing the experiences of the individual nations we focused on the measure of fiscal position used by the central government, which formed the basis for policy debates. The definition of budget balance varies significantly from country to country, and can have an impact on the nature of the budget debate during a period of surplus. For example, Canada excludes surpluses in its public pension system from its primary measure of fiscal position.

As of 1998, each of the case study countries has a budget surplus. Norway and New Zealand have had surpluses since 1994, the longest periods of sustained surpluses among the case study countries. The other four countries achieved budget surpluses in either 1997 or 1998. Four of the six case study countries achieved budget surpluses in the late eighties and then returned to deficits in the early nineties (See Fig. 22.1).

Debt burden varies from country to country. As of the end of 1998, general government gross debt as a percent of gross domestic product (GDP) ranged from a high of nearly 90% in Canada to less than 35% in Australia and Norway. General government gross debt includes the debt of the central government and all sub-levels of government, such as states and provinces, counties, and cities. However, it is also instructive to look at net debt, which accounts for government owned financial assets, such as loans, stocks, and bonds, because it provides a better picture of the government's net financial impact on the economy. As of 1998, general government net debt ranged from a high of about 60% of GDP in Canada to a low of about negative 47% in Norway – meaning that Norway owns more than enough financial assets to completely pay off its debt. See Fig. 22.2 for each country's most recent general government gross and net debt figures.

FACTORS SHAPING THE SURPLUS DEBATE IN THE 1990s

The political debate surrounding a budget surplus was influenced greatly by the economic slowdowns and budget deficits of the late 1980s and early 1990s. Each country we studied experienced a significant economic slowdown during this period, generally coinciding with a broader worldwide economic slowdown (See Fig. 22.3). In several countries the slowdown became severe. Sweden, for example, experienced three consecutive years of negative growth beginning in 1991. In other countries, including New Zealand and Norway, there were prolonged periods of below-average growth.

The economic slowdowns of the late 1980s and early 1990s were a major factor leading to the reemergence of large budget deficits in the case study countries. In four countries, deficits followed a period of budget surpluses. For these countries, spending increases and/or tax cuts made during a period of surplus also contributed to the reemergence of deficits. The reemergence of large budget deficits was seen as a step backward following years of progress reducing budget deficits.

In several case study countries, a loss of investor confidence in fiscal and economic health added to the economic downturn, and fiscal and monetary policies were tightened in reaction to investors pulling money out of those countries. Contrary to the conventional wisdom which holds that fiscal policy should be expansionary during economic downturns, many of these nations

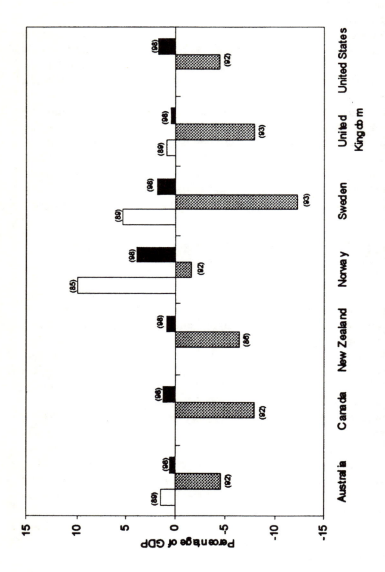

Fig. 22.1. Shifts in General Government Financial Balances. Note: Data for 1998 are estimates. General government financial balance accounts for all levels of government. Source: *OECD Economic Outlook 65*, June 1999.

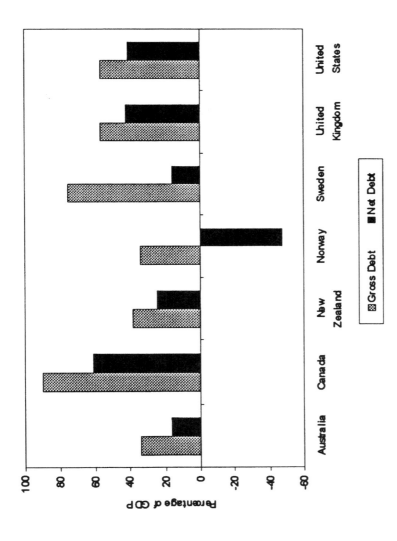

Fig. 22.2. 1998 General Government Gross and Net Debt as a Percent of GDP. Note: Data for Norway, Sweden, the United Kingdom and Australia are estimates. Net debt includes government financial assets, such as loans, stocks, and bonds. Norway's net debt is negative because it owns more financial assets than it has debt outstanding. Sources: *OECD Economic Outlook 65*, June 1999, and New Zealand Treasury.

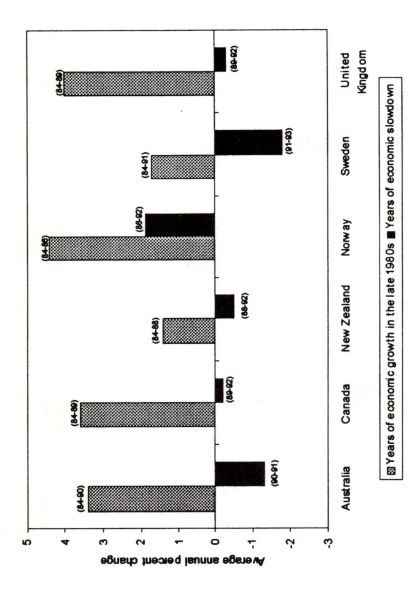

Fig. 22.3. Change in Average Annual GDP Growth During Economic Slowdown of Late 1980s and/or Early 1990s. Source: *OECD Quarterly National Accounts, Number 3,* 1998, and *OECD National Accounts, Main Aggregates Volume I,* 1960–1996.

were prompted by credit and currency markets to take procyclical actions to win back investor confidence. For example, both Norway and Sweden were pursuing a policy of fixed exchange rates when a drop in investor confidence resulted in downward pressure on currency valuations. To support the value of the currency, each country raised interest rates, which had the effect of further slowing the economy. Several countries such as New Zealand and Sweden took actions to reduce budget deficits during the economic downturn, which slowed the economies further. These decisions reflected a keen awareness in these nations of the need to sustain foreign and domestic investor confidence in these nations' economic and fiscal policies. Arguably, competitive capital markets may serve to place a limit on the ability of many nations to sustain expansionary fiscal policies during periods of recession.

In reaction to slow economic growth, large budget deficits, and a drop in investor confidence, leaders in the case study countries took actions to restore fiscal and economic health. In general, the pervasive philosophy was that in order to sustain economic growth, inflation rates had to be kept low and stable and efforts taken to reduce budget deficits. To show their commitment to reducing inflation rates, five case study countries set explicit inflation targets and increased the independence of the central bank to respond to inflationary pressures. Each country also renewed deficit reduction efforts and implemented budget process changes to reinforce their commitment. For example, in 1994, Sweden enacted a deficit reduction package amounting to 7% of GDP over 4 years. Similarly, in 1994, the Canadian government introduced a package reducing the deficit by over 3% of GDP over 4 years, while the New Zealand government reduced its budget deficit by more than 4% of GDP from 1991 through 1993.

Leaders in each country enacted difficult spending cuts and/or tax increases in their efforts to bring the budgets back into balance. The New Zealand government cut fiscal year 1991–92 net spending by 10% from the level projected in October 1990 and delayed implementation of a campaign promise to eliminate an unpopular surcharge on public pensions. Australia reduced expenditures in health, education, and employment services. Canada cut the federal workforce by 15% and cut back aid to provinces significantly, which had the effect of reducing spending on health care. Likewise, Sweden enacted a deficit reduction package that included reductions in subsidies for medical and dental care, indexation of certain taxes, and increased contribution rates for the unemployment benefit system.

A strengthening economy combined with deficit reduction efforts contributed to a significant improvement in fiscal position in each of the case study countries. By 1998, all of the case study countries had achieved a budget surplus. (See Fig. 22.4 for the fiscal position as of 1998 for each country.)

NATIONS DEVELOPED FISCAL STRATEGIES FOR A PERIOD OF SURPLUS.

As case study countries entered a period of budget surpluses, decision makers had to decide what their fiscal policy goals would be. The previous period of slow economic growth, deteriorating fiscal conditions and loss of investor confidence continued to influence fiscal policy decisions as these countries emerged from deficits. In some respects, the fiscal and economic hardships of the early 1990s still resonated within decision making circles in many of these nations, and was reflected in the subsequent fiscal policy paths pursued by most of these nations.

In general, the countries in our study have decided to continue with a fiscally cautious approach and surpluses came to be viewed not as a political albatross but rather as a means to achieve broadly supported national fiscal and economic goals. Three countries – New Zealand, Norway, and Sweden – set a goal for continued budget surpluses. The other three – Australia, Canada, and the United Kingdom – set budget balance as their main fiscal goal, but as part of a cautious fiscal strategy that has resulted in them achieving small surpluses.

Leaders in these countries found surpluses to be a means to achieve broader goals generating widespread public support within each nation. Some articulated the case for surpluses as a way to win back and sustain the confidence of investors and currency markets. Others pointed to the opportunity to reduce publicly held debt, particularly by foreign investors, thereby achieving greater budgetary flexibility and eliminating a source of volatility within their budgets when debt was denominated in foreign currencies. Still others viewed surpluses as promoting lagging national saving rates which could help increase economic growth and reduce dependence on overseas investors for capital. One nation – Norway – used surpluses as an opportunity to use current wealth to accumulate financial assets that would be available to address future pension obligations when their baby boom retires.

The decisions to use surpluses to save for current or future needs represents a significant shift in fiscal policy for many of these nations. In the past, reaching a 0 budget balance was viewed as the outer limit of fiscal policy – a broadly supported goal that was sought as the end point of fiscal policy. While many countries professed to follow a Keynesian approach to fiscal policy, they

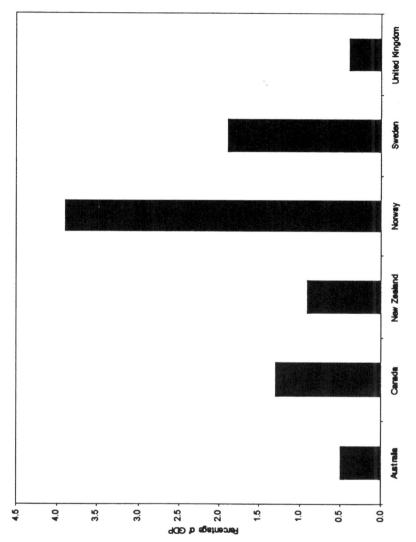

Fig. 22.4. 1998 General Government Financial Balance. Source: *OECD Economic Outlook 65*, June 1999.

often did not act to preserve and promote surpluses when economies reached the high point of the business cycle. While counter-cyclic fiscal policies can help restore a stagnant economy to equilibrium, such policies leave an overhang of debt that can have longer-term structural implications for the budget if not followed by periods of surplus sufficient to pay down debt to sustainable levels. Some nations learned that running a surplus as the fiscal policy norm provided them with the fiscal cushion of lower debt that would give them more breathing room for the next recession. Such a fiscal cushion can help limit the size of future deficits for nations like Sweden and New Zealand that have paid a high price for running large deficits during previous recessions.

Budget balance also proved to be vulnerable to a variety of contingencies that arose threatening to undermine fiscal goals during the course of the year, either jeopardizing 0 balance itself or prompting extraordinary measures to stay the course. Surpluses again provided the cushion to buffer the consequences of unforeseen events jeopardizing fiscal goals.

Finally, nations found it necessary to go beyond 0 balance to an actual surplus to address long term growth issues through budget policy. For these countries, reducing high levels of public debt or increasing national saving through the governmental sector have become goals that can best be addressed by running sustained surpluses.

Considering the conventional and theoretical wisdom regarding the purported political obstacles to sustaining surpluses, the experience of the nations we observed is counterintuitive at the very least. The leaders in the nations we have studied have generally been successful in mobilizing public support behind continued fiscal prudence and surpluses, even following years of deficit reduction. Several nations – Sweden, New Zealand and Norway – have instituted spending cuts to sustain surpluses during this period. Remarkably, New Zealand enacted budget cuts to sustain surpluses in the face of the Asian economic crisis, which was projected to prompt renewed deficits in the absence of policy actions. The legacy of the economic crisis of the early 1990s has enabled the leaders of these nations to articulate a compelling rationale to justify some continued fiscal restraint. Notably, in order to maintain continued public support for fiscal goals, these nations have also made room for additional spending initiatives and/or tax cuts, in some cases to address pent-up needs following a period of deficit reduction. As will be discussed in more length later, budget processes have played a critical role in reinforcing the commitment to continued fiscal restraint and surpluses. Following, is a discussion of how each country developed it strategy for surpluses.

NORWAY: SURPLUSES FOR LONG-TERM FISCAL AND ECONOMIC STABILITY

Norway has established a goal of sustained surpluses in order to build up savings to address long-term fiscal and economic concerns resulting primarily from an aging population and declining petroleum revenues. Norway projects both a near doubling of retirement benefits from about 7% of GDP currently to about 15% of GDP by 2030 and a parallel decline in oil revenues from about 8% of GDP to less than 1% over the same period. Also, Norway is concerned that economic growth could decline in the long run if a strong petroleum industry crowds out investment in other industries. The combined effects of an aging population and declining oil revenues are projected to result in an unsustainable fiscal path and eventual economic decline. This long-term problem has been clearly communicated to policymakers and the public and has developed as a primary rationale for their current fiscal policy of sustained surpluses.

In the mid–1990s, Norwegian decision makers reached a broad consensus on the need to save projected surpluses to pay for future budget needs and to help increase long-term economic growth. Surpluses were projected to result from increased oil revenues and a strengthening economy. To ensure that surpluses were saved, the government created the Government Petroleum Fund, in which surpluses were to be deposited to help pay for future pension costs. (The government decided not to use surpluses to pay off debt. It wished to keep a domestic debt market active in case it needed to increase borrowing, and by paying off debt it would keep petroleum money in the domestic economy, possibly adding to inflationary pressures).

The fund's assets are invested in foreign stocks and bonds to help reduce inflation and upward pressure on the exchange rate. Low inflation and a stable exchange rate help to keep Norway's exports competitive with other countries. If Norway allowed excess petroleum revenues to remain in the domestic economy, it could result in higher levels of inflation and an appreciation in the value of its currency. As a result, non-oil industries would become less competitive over time as the price of their goods and services would rise relative to foreign competitors. This is a major concern to policymakers because Norway projects that petroleum output will decline early in the 21st century, and Norway will have to rely more on its non-oil industries to generate economic growth. If those industries lose their competitiveness now, it could have a negative impact on long-term economic growth when the petroleum industry declines. Consequently, policymakers in Norway have come to view surpluses as critical to the long-term fiscal and economic health of the country. The Government Petroleum Fund has become a symbol of the importance of saving for future needs.

NEW ZEALAND AND SWEDEN: SURPLUSES TO REDUCE DEBT BURDEN AND MAINTAIN INVESTOR CONFIDENCE

Both New Zealand and Sweden have set sustained surpluses as their primary fiscal goal. Surplus goals were adopted to regain investor confidence after a loss of confidence in the early 1990s led to a credit downgrade and/or currency devaluation. Debt burdens for both nations had grown to levels that were perceived to increase these nations' vulnerabilities to shifts in international credit markets. New Zealand's general government gross debt reached a peak of nearly 65% of GDP in 1992, while Sweden's debt climbed to over 80% of GDP in 1994.

As each country neared a budget surplus, decision makers decided to set sustained surpluses as their main fiscal objective. In New Zealand, this goal took the form of an explicit goal to reduce debt burden by running surpluses. In 1994, New Zealand enacted the Fiscal Responsibility Act (FRA) which put in place a framework to guide fiscal decision-making. FRA was enacted in part to address concerns that a recently enacted electoral reform could weaken political resolve to sustain fiscal discipline. In 1996, New Zealand's electoral system was changed from a first-past-the-post system, in which the candidate with the most votes won the seat, to a mixed member proportional (MMP) system, in which seats were awarded to political parties in rough proportion to their share of the popular vote. MMP was put in place to address concerns that smaller political parties were not adequately represented in Parliament. As a result, the likelihood for coalition and/or minority governments increased greatly. FRA requires the government to set a prudent debt level, and to attempt to run budget surpluses until the goal is achieved. A debt target provides an explicit measure to justify sustaining surpluses – a measure which is viewed as a good proxy for enhancing the nation's economic capacity and reducing its vulnerability to market pressures.

FRA has played a critical role in New Zealand's ability to sustain fiscal discipline during its current period of budget surplus. Initially, in 1994, the government set a goal to reduce net debt to between 20 and 30% of GDP from over 40%. The government committed the entire budget surplus to debt reduction, but promised to cut taxes once the debt target was achieved. In 1996, when it became apparent that the 30% debt target would be achieved, the government enacted a tax cut and reset its debt target to 20% of GDP.

Sustaining surpluses through the framework set by the FRA has proven to command widespread support across party lines – ensuring that surpluses became a consensus goal over a number of years despite turnovers in political leadership. Following the 1996 election, a coalition government formed for the first time in many years. The minority partner in the coalition government was a strong advocate of new social spending, while the larger National party, which had held the previous majority government, was a major advocate of continued debt reduction and tax cuts. Nonetheless, under their coalition agreement, the new government set continued surpluses and debt reduction as its overall fiscal policy. As a compromise, they agreed to delay planned tax cuts 1 year and implement a spending package while still allowing for continued surpluses. In 1998, the minority partner left the coalition government and the National party continued as a minority government. The government has retained the previously agreed to debt target to justify continued fiscal discipline. In the fall of 1998, when budget forecasts showed that the budget would go into a deficit, largely as a result of the Asian economic crisis, the government enacted a package of spending cuts and scaled back the previously promised spending increases to prevent a deficit for FY1999–2000 and to sustain surpluses thereafter.

Similarly, the Swedish government has also set a goal of sustained surpluses to reduce debt and to maintain investor confidence. Of the case study countries, Sweden experienced the most severe economic downturn and the largest budget deficit during the 1990s. In reaction, the government ended its fixed exchange rate policy, enacted a large deficit reduction package, and reformed the budget process to better support fiscal discipline, putting in place multi-year expenditure limits for the first time. These ceilings cover both discretionary and entitlement spending in the aggregate as well as for over twenty broad expenditure areas. In 1997, when it became apparent that the budget was nearing balance, the government set a goal for surpluses of 2% of GDP in order to help retain investor confidence in its policies and to ensure continued progress toward debt reduction.

By setting an explicit goal and keeping to expenditure limits, the Swedish government has been able to maintain fiscal discipline during the early stages of its current surplus period. Specifically, the government established expenditure limits for 1998 that would allow it to gradually achieve its surplus goal. However, due to continued strong economic growth and other technical factors, Sweden achieved its surpluses earlier than expected. For example, in 1998, the government incorporated the National Pension Fund's real estate holdings, which resulted in an upward adjustment of the financial balance due to government accounting rules. As larger than expected surpluses are projected, the government has reiterated its commitment to the previously agreed to expenditure limits. At the same time, the government has been able to increase spending somewhat because of the way the expenditure ceilings work. Under Sweden's new budget process all open-ended appropriations, mostly to entitlement programs, were abolished, making all expenditures subject to annual reviews. To provide a buffer against forecasting errors in these programs, the government built a "budget margin" into the expenditure limits. Thus, to the extent economic and budget forecasts turn out to be accurate or better than expected, the government can increase spending up to the amounts allowed under the expenditure ceilings. If budget or economic forecasts turn out to be overly optimistic, then the government would presumably be forced to take action to stay within expenditure limits by cutting spending. There is some additional flexibility to borrow against future year expenditures. Since the expenditure ceilings have been in place, the economy has outperformed the forecasts, freeing up additional room for spending.

In 1999, actual spending was projected to breach the expenditure caps. The government reiterated its commitment to the expenditure caps and proposed cutting spending by about 1% to stay within the caps, including cuts to labor market programs, agriculture, and health care. Due to concerns over its international competitiveness – Sweden has among the highest overall tax levels among OECD countries – the government has also proposed a package of tax cuts aimed mostly at low and medium income workers.

AUSTRALIA: MAINTAINING NATIONAL SAVING

Australian policymakers have focused on the need to increase national saving and long-term economic growth to guide their fiscal policy decisions. The government was particularly concerned that continued deficits could act to reduce national saving, which had fallen in the early 1990s by more than 5 percentage points below the average of the prior three decades. This is of major concern to policymakers because Australia has had to rely on foreign sources of capital to finance private investment. Concerns arose about Australia's prospects for long-term economic growth if it had to depend on foreign sources to make up the saving-investment gap. As the fall in national saving closely tracked increased public sector borrowing, policymakers committed to fiscal policies aimed at restoring national saving by reducing government borrowing.

Consequently, the current government in Australia has set a fiscal goal of balanced budgets over the economic cycle to ensure that, overtime, the Commonwealth general government sector "makes no call" on national saving, and therefore does not detract from national savings. The government took "balance over the cycle" to mean that it would run surpluses during periods of economic growth to increase budgetary flexibility and allow the government to better respond to future economic shocks. For example, one of the justifications for establishing mandatory private pensions was to increase national saving. In 1992, the Commonwealth government passed the Superannuation Guarantee Act making it mandatory for employers to offer retirement benefits, in the form of employer-funded pension programs, to their employees. Under the Act, employers make contributions to individual pension accounts of the employees' choosing. By 1996, approximately 89% of public and private sector employees were covered by superannuation, with the remaining 11% of the work force falling below the income threshold where superannuation started to apply. Currently, the government is aiming for budget surpluses for the medium term to coincide with a strong economy.

Since 1996, the "Charter of Budget Honesty" (the Charter) has played a critical role in framing Australia's fiscal policy stance. The Charter set out principles for the conduct of sound fiscal policy and put in place institutional arrangements, including goals for debt burden and national savings. The framework of the Charter allows flexibility for the government to define its medium-term fiscal strategy and short-term fiscal goals in such a way as to fulfill these principles.

In fiscal year 1997–98, Australia achieved a small budget surplus, and, with the fiscal year 1999–2000 budget, the government forecasts surpluses for the next 4 years. Beginning in 1996 the Australian measurement of the surplus/deficit changed from a cash basis to an "underlying" balance basis, which excludes the net effects of advances, such as loans, and equity transactions, such as sales and purchases of capital assets, from the calculation of surplus/deficit. If a cash measurement is used, Australia achieved a small surplus in fiscal year 1996–97.

The government's medium-term fiscal strategy, developed as required by the Charter, is to balance the budget over the cycle, which means a short-term goal of running surpluses during the projected period of expansion. Also, the government currently has a goal to eliminate net debt by fiscal year 2002–03 from its 1998–99 level of about 11% of GDP.

Within this goal of surpluses for the short term, the government has made room for new spending increases and selective tax cuts. The fiscal year 1998–99 budget proposed spending initiatives totaling nearly A$10 billion through fiscal year 2001–02, with a large portion dedicated to health care. The government has also decided to use a portion of its projected surpluses to help finance a major tax reform, which was passed in 1999. The tax reform package included the introduction of a national goods and services tax (GST) along with a reduction in income tax rates for individuals. A GST has been proposed several times in Australia's recent history but has failed to pass due to concerns over its regressiveness. However, the government was able to pass the GST in 1999 due, at least in part, to the availability of budget surpluses that could be used to pay for income tax rate cuts used to offset the impact of the GST.

CANADA: "BALANCE OR BETTER"

Upon achieving a surplus, Canada set as its fiscal goal to achieve "balance or better" and has kept its "prudent" budget practices in place to better ensure that it meets its goal. These "prudent" budget practices were put in place to end what had amounted to a long period of chronic deficits beginning in the 1970s. Despite deficit reduction initiatives in the 1980s, the deficit proved to be persistent and total net public debt of all governments approached 100% of GDP in the mid–1990s. Prompted by the Mexican crisis of 1994, investors began to shift assets out of Canada as well, pushing up interest rates and threatening the value of their currency.

In response, a newly elected government in 1994 stepped up deficit reduction measures which ultimately succeeded, along with a stronger economy, in eliminating the deficit in fiscal year 1997–98. As part of this initiative, the government adopted new budget formulation processes, which entailed a shortened forecast period, the use of conservative economic forecasts and the creation of a contingency fund to be used for unforeseen events or debt reduction.

The effect of these practices has been that Canada has in fact achieved a budget surplus for two consecutive fiscal years. Under the current government's cautious approach, the Finance Department's economic assumptions have often been more pessimistic than actual outcomes. The contingency reserve is an annual amount that is built into projected spending, but is not allocated to any specific program. For example, excluding the contingency reserve, the Finance Ministry does not publicly project budget surpluses. The government's current fiscal goal is, at a minimum, a balanced budget – a strategy that it refers to as "balance or better." In fiscal year 1998–99, the government projected a balanced budget. This balanced budget estimate assumed that the CAN$3 billion contingency reserve would need to be spent to compensate for shortfalls in the projections. However, because the budgetary forecasts have been based on pessimistic assumptions, in fact the government has actually realized a surplus of about CAN$3 billion that will be used to reduce debt.

During a surplus period, the effect has been to limit the ability of the government to spend surpluses until they materialize. Thus, Canada has adopted a cautious allocation strategy, waiting until additional resources are nearly certain before introducing small-scale tax cuts and spending increases. While the government is committed to using a modest amount of budget surpluses for debt reduction through the contingency reserve, it also uses surplus revenues for new spending and tax cut initiatives. This strategy of dividing surpluses between debt reduction, tax cuts, and new spending was articulated during the government's 1997 reelection campaign. In both the fiscal year 1998–99 and 1999–2000 budgets, the government introduced a number of new spending and tax initiatives. The Finance Ministry estimates that these initiatives will cost the government about CAN$50 billion cumulatively from fiscal year 1997–98 to 2001–02. On the spending side, these initiatives have focused on health care and education. The tax changes include an increase in the amount of income that low-income earners can receive on a tax-free basis, the elimination of a 3% surtax, an increase in the Child Tax Benefit, and a reduction in employment insurance rates for both employers and employees.

UNITED KINGDOM: INCREASE INVESTMENT SPENDING

The current government has developed a new framework for fiscal policy that reflects "lessons learned" from the United Kingdom's past experiences. The fiscal strategy emphasizes a greater focus on the structural budget, a more explicit distinction between current and capital spending, and firm multi-year spending ceilings that will not be subject to annual review. The current Labour government's fiscal strategy is guided by two rules: (1) the "golden rule," under which borrowing will not be used to finance current spending (that is, total spending excluding investment), and (2) the "sustainable investment rule," which promises to keep net public debt as a share of GDP at a "stable and prudent" level (which the government currently defines as below 40%). Both rules are to be applied over the economic cycle, allowing for fiscal fluctuations based on current economic conditions.

Under the "golden rule," the government is aiming for operating balance, allowing for deficit financing of capital investment. The government defines investment as "physical investment and grants in support of capital spending by the private sector." (Fiscal Policy, undated: 7) Investment spending was significantly restrained under the previous deficit reduction efforts, and, as a result, the current government has made boosting public investment a major priority, proposing to nearly double it as a share of the economy – to 1.5% of GDP – over the course of the current Parliament. While investment spending is a priority, the "sustainable investment rule" is intended to ensure that financing such spending does not result in an imprudent rise in debt.

A sharper focus on the economic cycle is a general feature of the current government's policy that explicitly reflects the "lessons learned" from the past. A recent Treasury report explains the importance of taking the cycle into account:

> Experience has shown that serious mistakes can occur if purely cyclical improvements in the public finances are treated as if they represented structural improvements, or if a structural deterioration is thought to be merely a cyclical effect. The Government therefore pays particular attention to cyclically-adjusted indicators of the public sector accounts (Stability and Investment, 1998: 45).

As a result of the government's rules, its fiscal policy allows for small deficits to be used to finance investment spending, provided that overall debt burden as a share of the economy is kept at a stable and prudent level. Despite this allowance for small deficits, the Treasury estimates that the budget registered a surplus of 0.1% of GDP for public sector net borrowing in fiscal year 1998–99. Using the government's "current budget" measure, which excludes investment, the fiscal year 1999–2000 budget estimated that there would be a surplus of 4.1% of GDP for fiscal year 1998–99 and projected surpluses on the current budget every fiscal year until 2003–04.

BUDGET PROCESS SUPPORTS FISCAL STRATEGY FOR SURPLUS

The framework for fiscal decision making, which includes both the budget process and the way fiscal position is measured, has played an important role in the ability of our case study governments to maintain fiscal discipline. In an effort to aid deficit reduction efforts, each country made important changes to its budget process during the 1990s, which were continued and adapted to a period of surplus. As these countries moved into a period of budget surpluses, their budget processes have continued to play an important role in maintaining fiscal discipline and/or in setting fiscal policy.

As the foregoing discussion on each nation indicates, most of the nations in our study articulated a clear set of fiscal goals and targets to justify surpluses. The concept of 0 balance is generally the default in most nations, and departing from this widely accepted budgetary norm called for a high-level enunciation of new measures to sustain some degree of fiscal restraint. Several governments in the case study countries have enacted far-reaching fiscal policy "charters" that set fiscal goals not only on the bottom-line fiscal position, but also for other important fiscal and economic indicators such as debt burden, national saving, and investment spending. New Zealand was the first country to change its focus when it passed the Fiscal Responsibility Act (FRA) in 1994. Under FRA, New Zealand's decision makers must consider the impact of fiscal policy on such variables as debt burden and national wealth. New Zealand's debt burden targets have played a major role in reinforcing the need to sustain surpluses over the past several years by providing a new fiscal goal that requires continued discipline. Likewise, Australia passed the Charter of Budget Honesty Act in 1998, which requires decision makers to assess the budget's impact on national saving and debt burden. In 1998, the United Kingdom passed into law a requirement laying out the parameters within which fiscal policy must be set. Based on this statute, the current government has developed a Code for Fiscal Stability, in which the government's fiscal policy stance calls for balanced budgets, on average, while allowing for borrowing only for investment

The measure of fiscal position is important because it can be used to define a goal and to measure "success." Nations departed from strictly cash, unified budget measures to account for their fiscal position. The measures used in our case study nations were adopted often well before the surpluses arrived, but they had consequences for the surplus debate.

For example, Norway's government routinely uses a structural measure of fiscal position when formulating fiscal policy. Norway's structural measure, which excludes the cyclical effects of the economy, petroleum revenues, and interest expenditures, is the key measure used to set fiscal policy. Norway's government uses this measure to assess if its overall fiscal policy is contributing to or detracting from economic growth. During periods of high economic growth and inflation, the structural measure serves to lower the reported fiscal balance, thereby reinforcing fiscal discipline. It may serve to prevent the creation of permanent fiscal claims based on what amounts to temporary budgetary windfalls. Such a measure has been critical to Norway's efforts to stabilize the economy during the current period by reducing spending and raising taxes to dampen inflationary growth.

New Zealand has adopted an accrual budgeting framework, which uses an accrual-based measure – the operating balance – as a primary measure of deficit/surplus. In general, a cash-based system recognizes a cost when the cash outlay occurs, while an accrual-based system recognizes a cost in the period the resource is consumed. Consequently, the key difference between New Zealand's operating balance and the traditional cash balance relates to the period in which revenues and expenses are recorded. This difference can vary in magnitude and direction. For example, under the previous cash system, leave liability would be recognized when a staff member left a government organization and was paid for the cost of the leave balance. Under the accrual system, the government records an expense as the leave is earned, and recognizes a year-end liability for leave earned but not taken. Financing capital projects affects the budget measure in the opposite way. Under a cash measure, capital projects were recorded when cash was disbursed. Under accrual-based measurement, capital items are recorded in the budget over the expected life of the project, thus reducing the initial budgetary impact. Consequently, the net effect of using an accrual-based measure instead of a cash-based measure depends on the specific government activities undertaken in any given year.

In addition to the operating balance, decision makers focus on the balance sheet – assets, liabilities, and net worth – when making fiscal decisions because they feel it provides an indication of the long-term sustainability of government programs. According to officials we met with, the balance sheet has had an impact on fiscal decision-making by making policymakers more aware of some long-term liabilities that were not addressed previously. For example, the recognition of a large unfunded liability in the accident insurance program was cited as a key factor in the decision to increase insurance premiums to fully fund the program. While these decisions may not have had a large immediate impact on the current fiscal balance, they contributed to programmatic changes, which have improved New Zealand's long-term fiscal health. However, it is important to note that New Zealand does not include the commitments of its social security system in its accrual-based measures. The social security commitment is not considered to be a liability under New Zealand's accounting standards.

Two case study countries do not include the annual balances of their public pension funds in the central government's measure of fiscal position. Both Canada and Sweden account for their public pension funds separately from the general fund. The funds' assets are invested in stocks and bonds and are not available to the general fund. As a result, pension fund surpluses are not part of budget debates in Canada or Sweden. Debates regarding the need to increase pension fund assets to meet future obligations have generally occurred apart from budget debates. Both countries enacted pension reforms during the 1990s aimed at increasing the sustainability of the system as it became clear that their funds would run out of money early in the next century.

Four countries – Australia, Canada, Sweden, and the United Kingdom – enacted major pension reforms during the past two decades, which have reduced long-term budgetary pressures and put their pension systems on a more sustainable path. Australia and the United Kingdom carried out pension reforms in the 1980s and 1990s; and as they have entered a period of surpluses, long-term budgetary pressures due to increasing pension costs have not emerged as a major focus of political debates. Canada and Sweden have traditionally accounted for their pension systems separately from the government budget, and their pension fund assets have been invested outside the government. As a result, pension fund surpluses have not been included in their surplus debates. Each country was able to reform its pension system during the 1990s, placing it on a more sustainable path.

Expenditure limits as part of a top-down approach to budgeting have played a key role in attempts to control spending, both during periods of deficit and surplus. Under this approach, decision makers agree on overall spending limits prior to making specific decisions on policy initiatives. After reaching an agreement on spending and/or revenue levels, any new policy initiative must fit within these limits.

Expenditure ceilings represented a significant change for two countries in particular. Prior to budget process reforms in the 1990s, Norway and Sweden had not previously set expenditure ceilings. In fact, the general trend in each country had been for Parliament to increase spending above the government's budget proposals, and this was perceived to be a problem in each country.

The Norwegian Parliament reformed its budget process in 1997 to show its continued support for fiscal discipline and in reaction to past spending increases. For the first time, the Parliament adopted a top-down approach to budgeting, setting aggregate revenue and expenditure ceilings. Under the old procedure there was no agreement on an overall expenditure and revenue limit at the beginning of the budget process, and the final budget represented the aggregate of individual spending decisions. Under the new budget process, Parliament agrees on an overall fixed budget ceiling and ceilings for 23 spending and 2 income areas at the beginning of the budget process. All spending and revenue proposals must fit within these ceilings.

Sweden enacted a comprehensive budget process reform in the mid–1990s in reaction to several studies which found its budget process to be among the weakest in Europe in its ability to control spending and react to large budget deficits. Under this reform, Parliament is required to pass an aggregate expenditure ceiling, and expenditure ceilings covering both discretionary and mandatory programs for a 3-year period. Once enacted, the expenditure ceilings are fixed and generally cannot be changed. Parliament passes a new aggregate expenditure limit every year for the third year only.

Sweden's budget process reform has had a significant impact on fiscal policy during the current period of projected surpluses. As Sweden entered the current period of projected surpluses, the government has remained committed to the previously agreed-to expenditure ceilings. As a result of its commitment, the government has proposed spending cuts totaling nearly 17 billion kronor in fiscal years 1999 and 2000 to remain under the expenditure ceilings. This is much different than in the past when Sweden found it difficult to maintain fiscal discipline. Also, the expenditure ceilings have changed the focus of Sweden's debate. Because the government remains committed to the expenditure ceilings, the surplus debate has so far focused mainly on the need to reduce debt or cut taxes. As a result the current government has proposed a broad-based income tax cut as part of its fiscal year 2000 budget proposal.

IMPLICATIONS OF SURPLUSES

Much of the conventional wisdom, as well as much of the academic literature on public choice and fiscal policymaking, would suggest that surpluses have little chance of surviving as a politically sustainable fiscal policy. Absent the fiscal anchor provided by the 0 balance norm, those championing continued fiscal restraint would seem to be no match for the political forces promoting higher spending or lower taxes, particularly when those forces had been purportedly constrained during years of deficit reduction. Yet, this study has found that several advanced democratic nations have reached consensus on sustaining surpluses as a new fiscal equilibrium, at least for a period of several years. Moreover, the political support for this policy appears to be broad-based, tapping support from succeeding governments and political coalitions.

This is not to say that surpluses come naturally to any system. Rather, the nations sustaining surpluses were acutely aware of the fragility of this policy and the political vulnerabilities of those pressing for continued restraint after years of deficit reduction. Building on this understanding, in fact, these governments engaged in sophisticated initiatives to build a case for surpluses by tying this policy goal to broader national concerns and anxieties. Most importantly, surpluses were adroitly defined as a relevant, appropriate, and even necessary response to recent economic crises experienced by each of these nations.

Leaders in these nations recognized that sustaining surpluses called for the articulation of new goals and targets to justify going beyond 0 balance, and a variety of targets were adopted. Continued fiscal restraint was reflected in specific fiscal goals that guided the use of surpluses and helped crystallize political agreement. Such goals, however, had to be justified to publics that had already experienced several years of deficit reduction – a challenge that was met by pointing to the broad and compelling national economic and fiscal challenges that needed to be addressed. The fiscal goals articulated by the nations in our study were, accordingly, justified as ways to improve their long-term fiscal and economic outlook, reduce debt burdens, maintain investor confidence, and increase the national saving rate. As part of their strategy to maintain continued support for surpluses, the case study countries enacted spending increases or tax cuts, which were sometimes used as a reward for continued fiscal progress.

Leaders in these nations sought to develop or augment fiscal rules and institutions to bolster fiscal discipline during times of surplus. Rule-based fiscal regimes can be intentionally designed to limit the discretion of current and future decision makers, in recognition of the profound pressures such officials will invariably face (Keech, 1995: 155). Most critically, such rules can be designed to promote accountability and transparency by requiring decision makers to relate annual fiscal decisions to a set of predetermined criteria for fiscal policy (Campos & Pradhan, 1996: 1–57). Spending limits, contingency funds and even earmarked revenues all played a role in these nations in bolstering discipline. Although such constraints had been in place for some time before surpluses emerged, what was unusual was the observance of constraints during periods of growing surpluses, culminating in real cuts to programs to enforce these self-imposed limits at a time when surpluses approached 7% of GDP in the case of Norway and 2% of GDP in the case of Sweden.

The strategies used by these nations to sustain surpluses can be viewed through a variety of lenses. Some might see them through a rational choice perspective, as the manipulation of incentives facing competing actors in the system. Limits on spending, for instance, have traditionally been viewed as altering the traditional proclivity of budget-maximizing bureaucrats to achieve their expansive spending agendas (Aucoin, 1991: 191). Some have viewed rules and criteria as responding to the prisoner's dilemma by creating incentives for "shared sacrifice" and the certainty that all will bear a portion of the costs of restraint. Making the rules public and promoting reconciliation between actual spending and the fiscal goals increases the costs for those who might renege on fiscal compacts (Campos & Pradhan, 1996: 9).

The behavioral assumption behind this view is that actors are motivated by their self-interest to pursue private gain at the expense of the public interest. Buchanan attempts to demonstrate how bureaucrats and politicians alike will force government budgets to be higher than they should be to increase their own "political incomes." (Buchanan, 1977) Agents use their superior information as well as their superior political organization and intensity over principals, i.e. the electorate, to push up spending and perpetuate a larger public sector. The distribution of costs and benefits reinforce this bias. As James Wilson has observed, "clientele" politics promotes the expansion of government benefits because those enjoying concentrated benefits have a greater incentive to mobilize than do the broad publics paying for these programs. However, efforts to unwind these programs are undermined by "entrepreneurial politics" where those bearing the concentrated costs of cutbacks have greater incentive to voice their concerns than do broad publics who stand to realize diffuse gains (Wilson, 1980).

Interests and incentives of key policy making actors play the central role in these models. The prospects for different kinds of policies depend, then, on how those policies affect the presumably fixed interests and incentives of the key actors. Institutions and rules can be designed to shape and perhaps overcome these incentives and interests. Indeed, nations in our study crafted their own decision rules mindful of the public choice literature. Nonetheless, policies like surpluses would not be predicted to be long-lived even under the most enlightened set of fiscal rules and institutions.

This is not the place to review the critiques and defenses of public choice or rational choice perspectives. There is a large and growing literature addressing these issues (See for example, Cook & Levi, 1990; Kelman, 1987). The politics of budget surpluses can indeed be illuminated by concepts borrowed from this field. Although clearly useful, the rational choice perspective alone does not help us understand how sustaining surpluses catch on as a sustainable policy in some nations. We would suggest that the agenda formation literature can help illuminate these outcomes.

The agenda formation literature suggests that the outcomes of public policy decisions are critically dependent on how the issues are framed and defined at the outset of the debate. As Schattschneider wrote years ago, the winners of political conflict are those who succeed in defining or redefining what the conflict is about (Schattschneider, 1960). More contemporary treatments by Deborah Stone and Rochefort and Cobb point to how the skillful use of indicators, measures, symbols and synecdoches can play important roles in setting the agenda of public issues that are taken seriously by decision makers (Stone, 1997; Rochefort & Cobb, 1994). In his garbage can model of agenda formation, Kingdon discusses how leaders opportunistically attempt to define problems in crisis terms and to link their own solutions to the problems of the day (Kingdon, 1995).

From this perspective, fiscal goals, rules, and limits all represent attempts by leaders to wrest control over the definition of the issues at stake from others with competing frames and issue definitions. Like any other public policy issue, surpluses can be defined in terms of several competing concepts, each with broad public appeal. For instance, some suggest that surpluses present opportunities to address pressing needs for immediate public consumption, such as infrastructure replacement, health care coverage or education. Others argue that surpluses represent the overburdening of individuals and businesses by government and that tax cuts are in order to return what amounts to a "taxpayer overcharge." Those who wish to save all or a portion of the surpluses, thus, are in competition with others to frame the issue that will govern the debate. A "0" budget balance served as a strong claimant in the battle for agenda control during periods of deficits. However, during periods of surplus, the relative resonance of fiscal restraint can be expected to wither unless it is redefined in terms of other overarching goals. Thus, articulating broader economic and fiscal targets can be seen as attempts to reframe fiscal policy in terms of values with broad public appeal. Codes of fiscal responsibility and other rule-based frameworks setting forth criteria governing future budgets attempt to control agendas for the future as well, or at least make it more difficult for competing issue frames to emerge.

The agenda formation perspective differs from the rational choice perspective by placing ideas and their champions in a central role. Far from simply rationalizing interests, ideas and issue framing have the potential to transform policy outcomes by redefining what the debate is about. While interests are relatively fixed, ideas are more volatile and create the potential for greater change and greater instability as well. As Deborah Stone notes, problems and policy issues in themselves do not have fixed effects and patterns. Rather, political actors can define and redefine how the effects of particular policy proposals are perceived through the contest over framing which issues are at stake (Stone, 1997: 224). When translated into compelling policy images and categories, ideas can become powerful forces for political mobilization.

New research has documented how new policy images can succeed in overturning established policy iron triangles and lead to major policy transformations in relatively short order (Baumgartner & Jones, 1993). When accepted by policy elites and issue networks, ideas can assume hegemonic status that drives individual policy decisions in fundamental ways. Timothy Sinclair has argued, for instance, that political elites in many OECD nations have embraced fiscal discipline and the so-called "deficit discourse" as the reigning public philosophy of the day (Sinclair, 1998). The decisions of some nations to sustain surpluses can be attributed in large part to the consensus among these elites over the utility of continued fiscal discipline as a prerequisite for achieving important economic goals. Ultimately, such a process has succeeded in transforming surpluses in some nations from an occasion to address short term consumption needs to a relatively unassailable rationale to continue to defer new spending or tax cuts for what is perceived to be more important goals.

CONCLUSIONS

A nation can indeed save for the future, in our view. Compelling policy ideas and rationales can be used to reframe the debate and make continued fiscal sacrifice politically palatable, and even unassailable. Nonetheless, as the public choice literature aptly tells us, sustaining surpluses remains a major challenge for any democratic system and requires artful leadership. Other nations experiences suggest that the prospect of continued surpluses calls for a framework that links annual budget decisions to certain broader economic goals of importance to the nation. A fiscal goal anchored by a rationale that is compelling enough to make continued restraint acceptable is critical. For each country in our study the goal and the supporting rationale grew out of a unique economic experience and situation. Targets served to reframe the debate by providing an accountability framework to evaluate annual budgetary outcomes, not an ironclad set of controls prescribing outcomes. In this sense, targets are similar to budgetary points of order, where the goal is to prompt accountability for decisions, not necessarily to prevent decisions from being made where sufficient majorities exist. Budgetary limits and constraints forged for deficits were revisited and renewed to address pent-up demands.

Although policy design lessons might be drawn from these nations, significant differences remain among nations in the political challenges they face in sustaining surpluses. For instance, the rationale for sustaining surpluses is arguably more politically compelling in nations recently emerging from a period of economic and fiscal crisis. In these nations, in fact, the continued demands of international credit markets may provide a more immediate and urgent reason to continue fiscal restraint. For nations like the United States that are not as vulnerable to the short-term pressures of credit markets, the case for sustaining surpluses is different. Here, the case for surpluses involves saving for the longer-term demographic shift – much like several nations in our study including Norway. The challenge is to prompt the nation to sacrifice current consumption so the nation can better meet our future obligations by promoting a stronger budget and economy for the longer term.

This is a tall order, but it is by no means an impossible challenge. Indeed our nation has made measurable sacrifices for future goals when those goals were defined in compelling enough terms. What must be done is to develop a framework that succeeds in reframing the annual budget debate to focus more intently on the longer-term outlook for the nation. In our view, selecting appropriate targets in a time of surplus is necessary to sustain surpluses, but the task is complicated – there is no single number like zero in the surplus world. Targets can play a role in framing the budget debate, but as the U.S. experience with Gramm Rudman suggests, targets should be considered as benchmarks and criteria not necessarily as ironclad controls.

Although we have not yet achieved consensus on broad fiscal policy targets or codes of fiscal responsibility, the emergence of "saving the social security surplus" as a politically unassailable idea shows how the budget debate may be in the process of being reframed to justify sacrificing current consumption for longer-term goals. Indeed, the apparent bipartisan endorsement of saving social security surpluses illustrates how ideas, when effectively framed, may drive fiscal action in a system that is purportedly paralyzed by divided government and gridlock on most budget issues.

The emergence of a fiscal policy consensus in our current setting would again be counterintuitive – the political cohesiveness of government is said to be important for sustaining fiscal discipline (Roubini & Sachs, 1988). From this perspective, divided government would be predicted to frustrate fiscal discipline. Indeed, surpluses could serve to promote political agreement in this setting, as both parties bid up fiscal actions to satisfy all of their major constituencies (Weaver & Rockman, 1993: 445–461). However, in the United States, divided government has recently served to promote surpluses as the default position when the two parties fail to agree on tax and spending priorities. In this case, then, political inertia promotes fiscal discipline. This equilibrium, however, may be short-lived unless there is a broader agreement on substantive fiscal policy goals. Yet, as the emerging consensus on social security surpluses suggests, achieving such an agreement may not be as unlikely as some suggest, particularly if surpluses are defined in valence terms as a politically unassailable goal that neither party can be viewed as opposing. David Mayhew has shown that divided government has not prevented the emergence of major policies and has often spurred policy change as both parties compete to champion compelling new ideas with strong public support (Mayhew, 1991).

We also know that a politics of ideas is volatile and potentially unstable. It indeed appears that a new fiscal regime has emerged in many OECD nations characterized by continued fiscal caution in times of surplus. It is notable that surpluses have survived both changes in governments and economic slow-downs in several nations. However, many competing policy ideas wait in the wings to spring forth when economic and political circumstances shift. In fact, surpluses in most of these nations, like the United States, were boosted by strong economic tailwinds, which enabled political leaders both to maintain surplus goals and to provide additional spending and/or tax cuts. When the economy turns, it is unclear whether surpluses will turn to deficits or whether nations will learn from the early 1990s to continue to observe fiscal caution in limiting new commitments. Other claims may emerge to compete with fiscal caution for the allegiance of national policymakers. However, even if deficits return, we do know that those nations sustaining a portion of their surpluses will have lower debt and interest costs and, arguably, be better able to absorb additional fiscal pressures in the future.

ACKNOWLEDGMENTS

We would also like to acknowledge the assistance and hard work provided by Tom James, Tuyet Quan Thai, and Melinda F. Bowman of the General Accounting Office. This chapter is based on a paper delivered at the annual research conference of the Association for Public Policy Analysis and Management, Washington, D. C., November, 1999.

REFERENCES

Aucoin, P. (1991). The Politics and Management of Restraint Budgeting. In: A. Blais & S. Dion (Eds), *The Budget-Maximizing Bureaucrat: Appraisals and Evidence* (p. 191). Pittsburgh, Pa: University of Pittsburgh Press.

Baumgartner F. R., & Jones, B. D. (1993). *Agendas and Instability in American Politics*. Chicago, Il: University of Chicago Press.

Buchanan, J. M. (1977). Why Does Government Grow? In: T. E. Borcherding (Ed.), *Budgets and Bureaucrats: The Sources of Government Growth*. Durham, N. C., Duke University Press.

Campos, E., & Pradhan, S. (1996). Budgetary Institutions and Expenditures Outcomes: Binding Governments to Fiscal Performance (pp. 1–57). Washington, D.C.: The World Bank.

Congressional Budget Office (1999). *The Economic and Budget Outlook: An Update*. Washington D.C., July 1.

Cook, K. S., & Levi, M. (1990). *The Limits of Rationality*. Chicago, IL: University of Chicago Press.

Fiscal Policy: Current and Capital Spending (Undated). HM Treasury, United Kingdom, 7, ftn 2.

Keech, W. R. (1995). *Economic Politics: The Costs of Democracy* (p. 155). New York, N. Y., Cambridge University Press.

Kelman, S. (1987). *Making Public Policy*. New York, N.Y.: Basic Books.

Kingdon, J. (1995). *Agendas, Alternatives and Public Policies*. New York: HarperCollins College Publisher.

Mayhew, D. (1991). *Divided We Govern*. New Haven, CT: Yale University Press.

Office of Management and Budget (1999). *Mid-Session Review*. Washington D.C., June.

Pierson, P. (1994). *Dismantling the Welfare State? Reagan, Thatcher, and the Politics of Retrenchment* (p. 168). New York, N. Y., Cambridge University Press.

Rochefort, D., & Cobb, R. W. (1994). *The Politics of Problem Definition*. Lawrence, KS: University Press of Kansas.

Roubini, N., & Sachs, J. (1988). Political and Economic Determinants of Budget Deficits in the Industrial Democracies. *European Economic Review, 14*(2), 122–141.

Schattschneider, E. E. (1960). *The Semi-Sovereign People.* New York: Holt, Reinhart and Winston.

Shepsle, K., Weingast, B., & Johnsen, C. (1981). The Political Economy of Benefits and Costs: A Rational Choice Approach to Distributive Politics. *Journal of Political Economy, 89,* 642–664.

Sinclair, T. J. (1998). Budget Deficits and Policy Change: The International Dimension. Paper presented to the 94th Annual Meeting of the American Political Science Association, Boston, MA, September 3–6.

Stability and Investment for the Long Term: The Economic and Fiscal Strategy Report 1998 (1998). HM Treasury, United Kingdom, June: 45.

Stone, D. (1997). *Policy Paradox: The Art of Political Decision Making.* New York: W. W. and Norton and Company.

U.S. General Accounting Office (1999). *Federal Budget: The President's Midsession Review* (GAO/OCG–99–29, Washington D.C., July.

U.S. General Accounting Office (1999). *Budget Surpluses: Experiences of Other Nations and Implications for the United States.* GAO/AIMD–00–23, Washington D.C., November.

U.S. General Accounting Office (1994). *Deficit Reduction: Experiences of Other Nations.* (GAO/AIMD–95–30, Washington, D.C.

U.S. General Accounting Office (1999). *Budget Surpluses: Experiences of Other Nations and Implications for the United States.* GAO/AIMD–00–23, Washington, D.C. November.

Weaver, R. K., & Rockman, B. A. (1993). When and How Do Institutions Matter? In: R. K. Weaver & B. A. Rockman (Eds), *Do Institutions Matter?* Washington, D.C.: Brookings Insitution, 445–461.

Wilson, J. Q. (1980). *The Politics of Regulation.* New York, N.Y.: Basic Books.

23. LEADERSHIP AND MANAGEMENT: ROLES AND STYLES AMONG LOCAL GOVERNMENT CEOs

Kurt Klaudi Klausen

INTRODUCTION

Based on data from a comparative research project comprising fifteen western countries, this chapter analyses the perceived and preferred roles and styles among local government CEOs. An analytical framework is developed pointing at four roles (the administrator, the political advisor, the organizational integrator and the policy innovator) and four styles (authoritative, participative, quick and incremental). A hypothesis regarding the importance of national cultures and clusters of countries is confirmed primarily with regard to the role as administrator. More surprisingly, however, new conceptions of management and leadership seem to bridge classical cleavages between countries and cultures, indicating that the rhetoric of New Public Management has been widely adopted at least symbolically.

INITIAL FINDINGS

One of the conclusions from the first book of the U.Di.T.E. project[1] was that "... we need more elaborate classifications of the roles of the CEOs in order to better understand their activities and how they operate in different

Learning from International Public Management Reform, Volume 11B, pages 425–454.
ISBN: 0-7623-0760-9

425

dimensions of the position" (Klausen & Magnier, 1998: 276). In the book we made use of Putnam's now classical dichotomy between the classical and the political bureaucrat (Putnam, 1975). While the former is characterized as the neutral, professional and (politically) loyal civil servant, who is procedure and rule oriented, the latter is more policy oriented, more problem and program oriented. And while the classical bureaucrat so to speak is mentally above politics, the political bureaucrat recognizes the inherent inseparability of administration and politics. The role character of the classical bureaucrat is found in the classical writings of e.g. Weber (1921). The role character of the political bureaucrat is found in the writings of e.g. Appleby (1949). In this way, the dichotomy captures one of the major themes in public organization theory and political science (Denhardt, 1984; Harmon & Mayor, 1986), namely how the relationship between the political and the administrative systems is and should be. Should the systems be strictly separated (often referred to as the position first advocated by Wilson, 1887) making the administrative apparatus merely the neutral implementation instrument of political decision-making of the so-called democratic chain of command (Olsen, 1978), or are they and can they in reality be more intimately connected, and, if they are inseparable, how is the relationship handled in an ethically correct way by politicians as well as by civil servants (Svara, 1990)?

Nevertheless, the identification of the two roles of the classical and the political bureaucrat seemed to work in identifying specific and characteristic differences among and between the countries. As can be seen from Fig. 23.1, both roles are granted some importance in all countries, indicating that to some extent the CEOs can identify with the roles, that these, so to speak, are meaningful to them. This was to be expected, more interesting, however, is the finding of clusters of countries which have something in common: namely a Southern European group of countries comprising Belgium, Italy, Portugal and Spain (with France quite close to this group); a Northern European group encompassing Denmark, Finland, Great Britain, Sweden and The Netherlands (with Norway quite close to this group); and, finally, an Anglo-American cluster including Australia, Ireland and the USA (with Great Britain close to this group). The three clusters of countries become even more distinct when we look at the way in which CEOs perceive the ideal role of the politician (Klausen & Magnier, 1998: 272), then the countries described as "close to" fall within the clusters. The countries identified as "close to" in Fig. 23.1 may also be described as interesting exceptions to the patterns which are to be expected according to the classical hypothesis regarding state- and nation-building (Tilly, 1976), referring to old empires (the Roman Empire, the Viking expansion, the Napoleonic conquest, the British Empire), with their political, military,

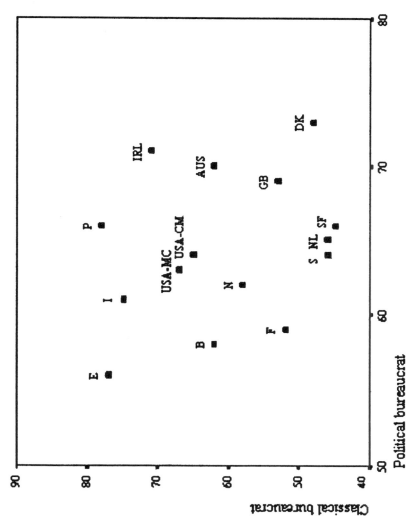

Fig. 23.1. The Two-dimensional Role of the CEO. (Klausen & Magnier (Eds) 1998: 274).

jurisdictionary and administrative systems. Both the clusters and the exceptions can be seen in the light of these old empires and their geographical distinctiveness and overlaps, all of which are echoed in more or less separate religious traditions (Catholic vs. Protestant) and underlying cultures with normative views of appropriate behaviour. The differences between north-south confirm previous studies on local government (Page & Goldsmith, 1987) as do the three clusters of studies of culture consequences in organization research (Hofstede, 1980).

LEADERSHIP AND MANAGEMENT – ROLES AND STYLES

We identified those in charge as managers, directors, executive officers. Research about them deals with the ways in which they perform effectively. When talking about what they do, it is not uncommon to distinguish between leadership and management. There are many definitions of what leadership and management is all about, and there are numerous ways of naming different aspects thereof. In a popular, but nonetheless very meaningful saying, management may thus be associated with doing the things right while leadership is about doing the right things (Yukl, 1989). A similarly well-known phrase states that leaders have followers opening up for informal leaders to enter the arena.

In any case, well performing organizations need both managers and leaders, and, preferably, those who hold formal power should adhere to some portion of both properties. Often, however, the words leadership and management are used synonymously, so although meaningful to make the distinction, I shall from here on refer to them as if they meant the same.

We may distinguish between periods in the history of leadership and management research and theory, each characterized by paradigmatically different assumptions and focuses. Typically, four such periods are pointed out in authoritative overviews. (Handy, 1987; Yukl, 1989; Bryman, 1996) The *first period* dating from the late 1940s is called the *traits approach*. The focus is on the personal qualities/traits of those in charge. The assumption is that the individual leader is more important than the situation and that it is specific qualities in leaders' personality and abilities which make them successful, for instance that they are gifted with particular intelligence, are convincing and dynamic or have particular social and communicative capabilities. According to the theory, you are supposedly born with such dispositions (born leaders), and consequently the task of the management group or the board of directors in finding the right leader for a vacant position is simply to find a person with such qualities (traits). While at first this approach proved unsuccessful, as it was not possible to find and generalize particular patterns of traits, some 50 years later, at the turn of the 20th century this approach has gained ground.

The *second period* that lasted until the late 1960s is called the *style approach.* The focus is on management and leadership style, and the assumption is now a correlation between the chosen style of the leader and the way in which the organization is performing. Thus, it was to be expected that the success of managers depended upon whether they were more or less autocratic or democratic, more or less dominating or facilitating, more or less delegating etc. Again, it proved difficult to point out one "best way." Rather there were many ways and research showed that what might work well in one situation might not do so in another.

This insight paved the way for the "third period" which has proved the dominant approach until today and has been named the *contingency approach.* This approach takes both style and roles into consideration, and, as the style approach paved the way for the contingency approach, we may say that the leadership style is the way in which leaders play their roles under the assumption that this should be dependant upon the situation, i.e., the task, the employees, the resources and the situation at large (i.e. the strategic situation of the organization in an organization-environment perspective). Finally, some (see Bryman, 1996) argue for a fourth approach called a *New Leadership Approach* characterized by a focus on the leadership of change and on charismatic leadership. However, I find it difficult to recognize that this approach should be but an elaboration and/or combination of its predecessors, and would have preferred to identify a fourth approach that would questions some of the crucial assumptions of the former theories, for instance the assumptions of (economic) rationality and centrality of the leaders and managers. The "new leadership approach" still belongs to the "modern paradigm."

We find a break with the modern paradigm in the paradigms of *late- and post-modern theories.* The late-modern theories question rational choice, rational reasoning and concrete action of individuals and emphasize limited knowledge, uncertainty, ambiguity and incidental garbage can situations and institutional constraints on action (among others late- and post-modern theories are derived from the writings of e.g. Silvermann, Weick and March and Olsen) all of which make bottom up and appropriate processes, symbolic action and underlying values more important than hierarchies and making the "right" choice. In Weick's phrasing (1969), the focus changes from organization to organizing.

Post-modern theories (Clegg, 1990) question rationality more radically and see chaos everywhere including the questioning of the boundaries of the organization and its environment. However, whereas late-modern theories still have both descriptive, explanatory and normative consequences for management and leadership, post-modern theories have less to offer. To some e.g. network-approaches and virtual organizations are properties of postmodern thinking. I, however, believe it important to underline that such aspects of organization and strategic thinking work very well with classic (modern) assumptions about leadership. Those who would argue that this is only a part of the contingency approach fail to recognize the intrinsic assumptions about rational action underlying the modern paradigm. Thus, my final conclusion is that the different perspectives should be combined, despite or perhaps because of their different assumptions about management and leadership, both in order to better understand and manage differences and different situations. Unfortunately, although we may be able to identify different roles and styles of management and leadership in this study, we cannot, however, say anything about the effect of the variations.

Both roles and styles are embedded in tradition and culture, can be seen/ found in the individual leader by others, and may be chosen and/or acted out by the individual. Analytically, a difference is to be expected: while the roles so to speak may be derived from functional aspects of the job and the situation, it is to be expected that the style is more closely attached to normative or cultural aspects of the job and the situation. On the other hand, certain roles and styles may be more or less appropriate in different settings/cultures and more or less preferred by the individual leader. So what we are looking for is whether or not it is possible to distinguish between structural and individual explanations for the patterns we are about to find.

GENERIC VERSUS CONTEXT APPROACH: ROLES AND STYLES OPERATIONALIZED

The many roles of leaders are found described in the dominant school until today i.e. the contingency approach. To name a few: based on a few case-studies, Mintzberg (1973) arrives at ten different roles, Johnsen (1975), on an analytical basis, arrives at twenty-seven, and Adizes (1989), on a normative ground, points out four major roles which should be found in the leading team if not in the CEO himself. Blake and Mouton (1964) similarly arrive at five preferred roles depending upon the managers' relative concern for people and production.

It is a shared characteristic of contingency theory, and of all its variants as in the models for design (Galbraith, 1973; Mintzberg, 1983), strategy (Chandler, 1962; Porter, 1980), and, as we have just seen, leadership, that they are intended to be "generic" or if you like universally applicable. Often derived from studies in large American private corporations they are believed to be applicable throughout the world, in any context and any situation: the situation is all, the context does not matter. What I mean by this somewhat cryptic phrasing is that in contingency theory it is the situation, with regard to the strategic situation, job content, the resources, etc., that determines what leaders and managers should do, while the larger context does not make this specifically different. Thus, it is basically the same no matter with what branch (production, service, sales, IT, etc.), what sector (public, private or third sector) or what country we are dealing. This position, which is found in most organization literature, about management, strategy, OD, etc., in all its old and new forms and techniques from MBO to TQM and BPR, holds that the public sector typically would benefit from introducing these techniques derived from private sector experience.

The most consequent stating of this position is found in political science by contenders of the so-called public choice school (Buchanan, 1986); and has lately been applied to the public sector in a narrow sense using market mechanisms in the reforming of the public sector, and, in a broader sense, using generic managerial tools from private sector experience (Osborn & Gabler, 1992; Barzeley, 1992). The new icon, although disputed and criticised, is New Public Management (Hood, 1991; Ferley et al., 1996; Lynn, 1998). This position is the same also when turned upside down as in Bozemann (1989) who holds that, ". . . all organizations are public," in so far as they are subject to public authority.

Contrary to this position, others argue that there is in fact a sector specific context i.e. the public context constitutes a special frame for organization and management (see, for example, Harmon & Mayer, 1986) who talk about a normative context) different from the private and third sector context. They argue that this frame typically sets up limitations to what managers can do and makes very precise directions as to what they should do, so that in the end, to use Wallace Sayre's aphorism: "Public and private management are fundamentally alike in all unimportant respects" (Allison, 1979: 27). The specific context among other things is constituted by the inherent political and regulated character of both goal-setting and performance (Wamsley & Zald, 1976; Denhardt, 1984; Heffron, 1989). There are many political actors and they are setting the overall goals (not the leaders and managers of public institutions even if they influence the decision making processes), these goals are subject to change whenever shifting political coalitions find it fit, and they are typically broad and ambiguous. The problems which are being dealt with are often "wicked"/complex with no one-way solutions all of which makes evaluation and comparison more difficult than in a private sector context. Furthermore, there are often strict rules and regulations as to how various tasks and jobs are to be accomplished, what is to be done and what is not to be done, e.g. the room for strategic manoeuvring is often very limited, for instance a public institution can neither change its line of production nor can it harvest and invest any profits it may gain from reducing the spending of resources or from performance pay.

As I would like to make our study (the U.Di.T.E. leadership study) a part of the latter approach I would prefer to develop and use concepts which for our purpose to a large extent will be in accordance with a number of characteristics. It is more likely that the management and leadership roles we find would be more sector specific than the styles (the way in which the leader play his role). What I am saying is that it is to be expected that some of the roles, but not all, may be specific for the public context while the styles are not. On the other hand, we would expect the management and leadership styles to differ according to hypotheses anchored in the theory of the consequences of national cultures. Thus, some roles may be sector specific, styles probably not, and on both dimensions national differences are to be expected. Accordingly, we should choose and develop roles that preferably should be context sensitive, functionally anchored, analytically coherent, empirically verifiable, and comparatively meaningful.

The role-concepts should be context sensitive in order to come to grips with what may be specific for the CEO in the public sector (here local government), not merely genetic, although there would probably also be such roles (for example such roles as those associated with POSDCORB, Gulick, 1937). The public context, of course, also differs from country to country. Nevertheless, at a certain level of abstraction it is to be expected, that there are many and crucial, shared features across countries, just as the western countries of our sample differ from e.g. South American, African and Asian groups of countries. That the roles should be functionally anchored means that there should be a connection between what the word/concept signals and the content of the actual job performed. Being analytically coherent means that the various contents of the concepts belong to and supplement each other in a meaningful way, and that they do not overlap (that the variables on which they are constructed do not belong to another category/concept). To be empirically verifiable simply means that we should be able to identify them in situ – here we find them on basis of our empirical data – in that sense they are empirical – but we should also be able to find them "out there" if we confronted anyone with them. Finally, they should be comparatively meaningful, meaning that they should be applicable to our international study, that is identifiable and given the same meaning and content in all countries (which paradoxically makes them generic for the public context).

I fully realize that all this may sound somewhat ambitious, this is no less so because the four concepts, which I am shortly to present, are concepts we constructed in retrospect after the data had been gathered. Thus, they are not, as should conventionally be the case, part of the initial research design (originally, we had Putnam's and Adizes' roles in mind while constructing our survey and case studies). On the other hand, this is no different than any other construction of concepts from systematic observation. On the positive side, we may say that it is greatly to their credit that we found them without looking specifically for them. On the other hand, the findings might have been more convincing and subtle had we known them in advance. Nevertheless, we were of course not looking blindfoldedly, we did not do our research *tabla rosa*, but rather had an intimate knowledge about local government affairs before we started our endeavours.

The four role concepts we are going to use from now on are: the Administrator, the Political Advisor, the Organizational Integrator and the Policy Innovator. We found and developed them on the basis of a combination of what we already know about the way tasks previously were categorized, what we knew beforehand (and through our qualitative interviews) about organization and management in local government, and, finally, on the grounds of statistical methods – factor analysis. The four role concepts are created from question C23.

The role as *administrator* is well known. This dimension captures the core of the management job with respect to the administrative organization. It is very similar to the classical bureaucrat but has no direct connection to the political level.

The role as *political advisor* could be considered as a classical role in the public context as between top civil servants and ministers. In local government, the relationship between the mayor and the CEO is the most important connection between the administrative and the political system. This dimension concerns tasks directed towards the political body and how the CEO tries to manage and influence political processes.

The role as *organizational integrator* is both a classical and a new role in so far as at least some would regard the stimulation of cooperation between departments to be a new aspect of previously divisioned public bureaucracies, but also because some tend to think the attention to human resource management is a fairly new interest in the public sphere. Thus, this dimension is oriented towards employees in the administrative organization and captures aspects related to new public management.

The role as *policy innovator* is also related to new public management but is more externally oriented. It captures entrepreneurial and efficiency oriented aspects. This too is a fairly new role in the public sector, this is not to say that entrepreneurs were not among top civil servants before, but that there are rising expectations implying that CEOs take on the role as leaders in the ongoing reformation, or if you like, modernization of the public sector. This role clearly captures the specific public context with its imperative of seeing the strategic situation in a holistic view including both the political situation and local society at large.

To place the categories in four fields may strengthen the argumentation regarding functional anchorage and analytical coherence. If, however, this is not feasible, it does not automatically mean that they are not separable and meaningful in their own right.

We must recognize that the role as political advisor is more upwards than outwards oriented and that the policy innovator is more outwards than upwards oriented even if entrepreneurial initiatives will eventually have to be politically confirmed. Nevertheless, both have to do with policymaking, in the broad sense of the word, applicable to the public sector context at large. While the dichotomic orientation out- and upwards versus inwards and downwards seems to work without too many problems in placing the four roles, I find the second categorization somewhat more dubious. The roles as policy innovator and integrator fit nicely also into this placing and the roles of political advisor and administrator at first sight also seem to be somewhat classical and passive. It can be argued, however, that at least the role as political advisor, depending upon how it is conducted, can be played out more modern and pro-actively. This can only be determined in each concrete case – closely related to style. Should we then abandon the idea of a four-field-illustration? I am not so certain. In any case it gives us a rough indicator of important differences between the roles.

Two issues should be mentioned specifically. First, the roles as political advisor and policy innovator are the ones most in accordance with the public context, while the roles as administrator and integrator are more generic. Second, it can be argued that the roles as policy innovator and integrator are related to ideas comprised under the concept of New Public Management. However, this is in the very broad sense of the NPM concept, and would indicate that the roles were more dynamic and offensive (the policy innovator) and caring for OD (integrator) as in private firms. It may be that being entrepreneurial to some extent is a new feature of public CEOs, I however find it rather questionable to attach the caring for employees to NPM and to private sector organizations (but this is more of a problem with the NPM concept than with the categories chosen here).

We also need to find some indicators of the preferred management and leadership styles of CEOs. We may use the attitude towards change strategies to construct such indicators. We asked the CEOs, "One aspect of the work of the chief executive is the management of organizational change. How would you weight the circumstances mentioned below as part of such a process of organizational change?" From four subquestions we constructed two sets of roles. From the subquestion "Wide-range involvement of the employees," we constructed the "participative style," and from the subquestion "Careful preparation with a small number of executives," we constructed the "autocratic style" (meaning that the CEO could be more or less authoritative or participative). From the subquestion "A quick reorganization" we constructed the "quick reorganization oriented style", and from the subquestion "Achieve incremental reorganization rather than an extensive reform" we contructed the "incremental style" approach to organizational change. We expect the two pairs to be negatively correlated and the two sets to be interconnected to an extent that it is meaningful to place them in a four-field-table.

Nevertheless, it is necessary to make some methodological reservations. First, it should be mentioned that the concepts, because of the way we asked the questions, are not necessarily perceived as a dichotomy. Second, and interconnected with this, the answers are generalizations of situations that are specific – meaning that the same CEO may choose to act differently in different situations (e.g. sometimes authoritative and in other situations participative). Despite these reservations, we are going to use the concepts. After all, they seem to be reasonably in accordance with the prerequisites earlier prescribed, and they also make sense from a purely statistical point of view. All this, however, is no promise of a clear-cut result.

THE TRIUMPH OF NPM OR OF LEADERSHIP?

When we analyse the results of the tests on management and leadership roles we arrive at both a confirmation and a more varied picture than we did in the first test of the concept of the classical and the political bureaucrat.

Looking at the role of the Administrator (Fig. 23.2) this is typically a role which is considered to be of less importance among the CEOs in Denmark,

Finland, Sweden, Great Britain and the Netherlands, while this role is considered very important in Spain, Italy, Portugal, Ireland and France. In between, we find Belgium, Norway, the USA and Australia where the CEOs only moderately identify with this role.

With the exceptions of Norway, and to a certain extent Ireland both of which we would have expected to be within a North European group, and Belgium which we might have expected to come closer to the South European group, these findings basically point in the direction of the classical clusters we have seen before. Even so, it is interesting to note that in the first of these clusters this classical role, normally considered as one of the main functions, scores low. In trying to explain the findings it is probably not without importance that the North European local authorities typically have more employees than the South European. This would give us a functional explanation of how likely it is that a given CEO could actually overlook and carry out detailed supervision and control. In the Northern group, these duties have to a large extent been delegated to lower officers. In the Southern group, it should be noted that there are many CEOs who have an educational background in law, this together with a smaller organization, a more hierarchic chain of command and notably control may help explain the findings.

This picture becomes even more varied when we look at the findings regarding the role as Political Advisor. This role is only given high priority in Denmark, while the CEOs in Finland, Norway, Sweden, Great Britain, Ireland and Australia only moderately identify with the role, however, this role also receives moderate identification by the CEOs in Spain and Portugal. Furthermore, this category, as could be expected because it is the anti-thesis to the loyal and neutral civil servant of the administrator role, receives a very low score in Belgium, France and Italy; however, also the USA and the Netherlands belong to this category. So here we find that Spain and Portugal, the USA and the Netherlands are the exceptions to the previously identified pattern. To give political advice, however, is a very delicate matter and might be considered inappropriate or politically incorrect in some countries more so than in others.

Looking at this role, it seems that there are relatively small differences among the CEOs. They all seem to identify highly with this role. Maybe this can be understood as a reflection of the ideas derived from NPM. Our country studies all point out that many of these ideas on modern management (breaking down traditional hierarchies and stimulating HRM) are gaining ground in their country (at least at a symbolic and rhetorical level). If that is the case, we should expect to find the same picture with regard to the role as policy innovator.

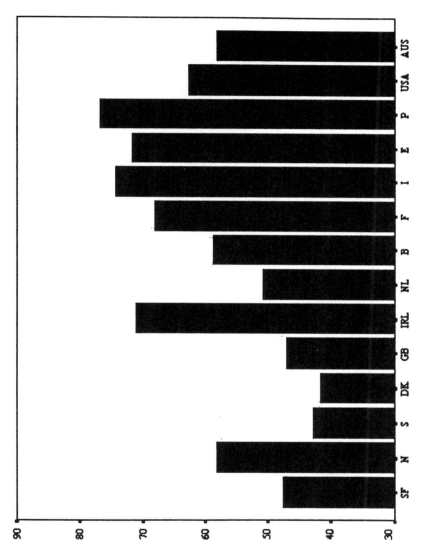

Fig. 23.2. The Administrator. (Based on Udite-data).

Fig. 23.3. The Political Advisor. (Based on Udite-data).

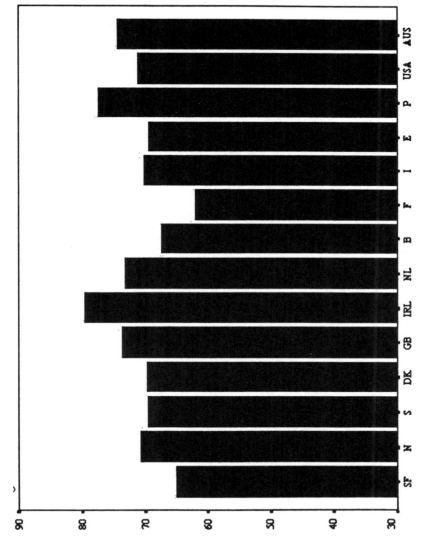

Fig. 23.4. The Organizational Integrator. (Based on Udite-data).

Fig. 23.5. The Policy Innovator. (Based on Udite-data).

Indeed, this is the case. In all cases, this role receives a high score. Thus, the ideas about the need for formulating visions, promoting new projects in the community, of being responsive to citizens' viewpoints, attracting external resources and ensuring that resources are used efficiently are echoed in the role-perceptions of the CEOs. All of these ideas are somewhat coherent with a broad definition of NPM. Finland, Ireland and Australia stand out as putting particular emphasis on this role. This may be attributed to the fact that in these three countries the CEOs hold a very highly potential authority based on the government structure. These three countries (together with the USA) also differ from the rest of the countries because (as we know from other parts of the survey) the CEOs view themselves as having a high influence on the budget and on economic development in general and vis-à-vis the mayor.

One way of interpreting these role-perceptions is to say that the classical role of the administrator reflects historical and cultural structures, whereas the new roles of the organizational integrator and policy innovator bridge previous gaps. In this sense, one may argue that certain features associated with NPM are shared cross-culturally. Again this may push management at this level in the direction of constituting a community or even a profession (this is also evidenced in some of the job posting-analyses of the U.Di.T.E. study and by some of the shared "traits" of the CEO – educational background etc.), and point in the direction of looking upon them as belonging to a profession – embryonic as this profession may be.

When looking at the four management-styles, it is confirmed that the differences between the countries are less pronounced than the cultural hypotheses would lead us to believe. All the CEOs put great emphasis on the participative management style, a little less on the authoritative and the incremental management style, and least on the quick reorganization management style. The incremental and the quick reorganization styles are negatively correlated. But the variations are difficult to account for.

If we place the four styles in two figures (Figs 23.10 and 23.11) it becomes clear that it is neither possible to demonstrate the expected correlation nor the cultural hypothesis.

Similarly, when trying to combine roles with styles, we only find a few significantly interesting patterns of relationships among all the combinations. These are exposed in Figs 23.12 through 23.15 and even if the relationships between the roles and styles are as expected this does not make it possible to confirm the hypothesis about clusters of states except for Fig. 23.15. For instance, Fig. 23.12 shows us that even if there are clusters of the administrator role, the style-dimension quick reorganization differentiates these clusters.

Fig. 23.6. The Participative Management Style. (Based on Udite-data).

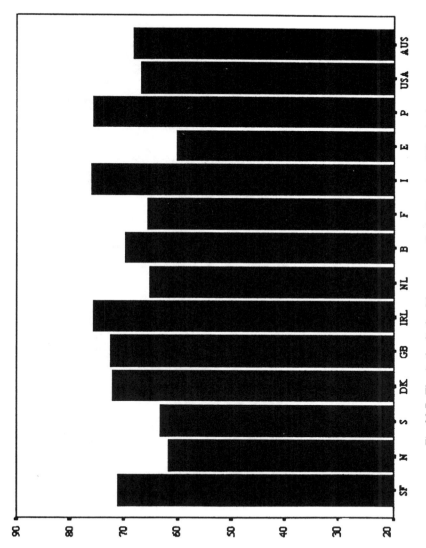

Fig. 23.7. The Authoritative Management Style. (Based on Udite-data).

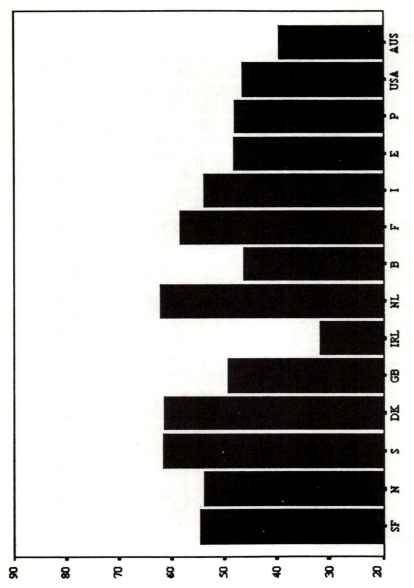

Fig. 23.8. The Quick Reorganization Management Style. (Based on Udite–data).

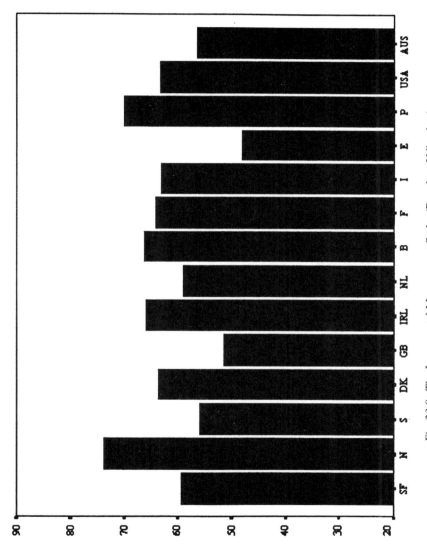

Fig. 23.9. The Incremental Management Style. (Based on Udite-data).

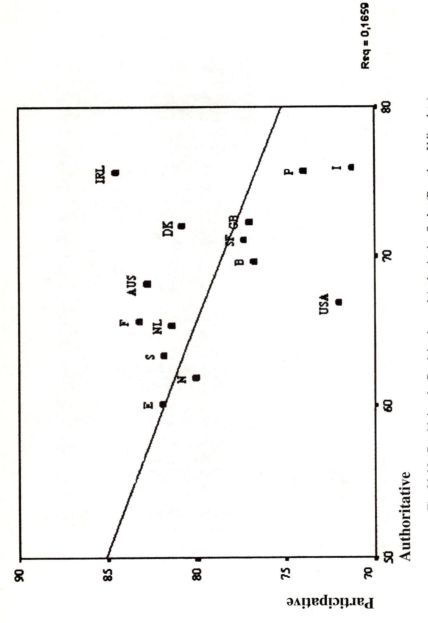

Fig. 23.10. Combining the Participative and Authoritative Style. (Based on Udite-data).

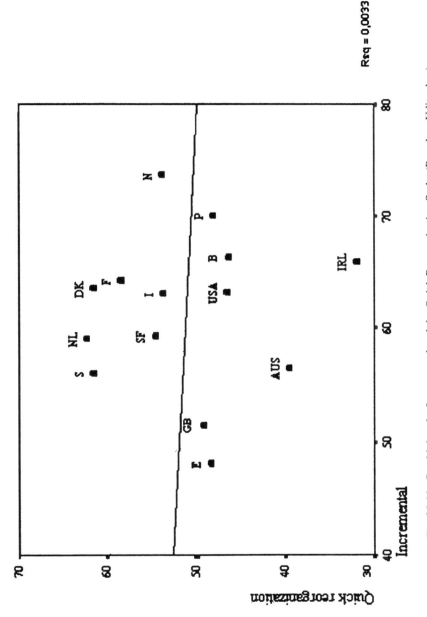

Fig. 23.11. Combining the Incremental and the Quick Reorganization Style. (Based on Udite-data).

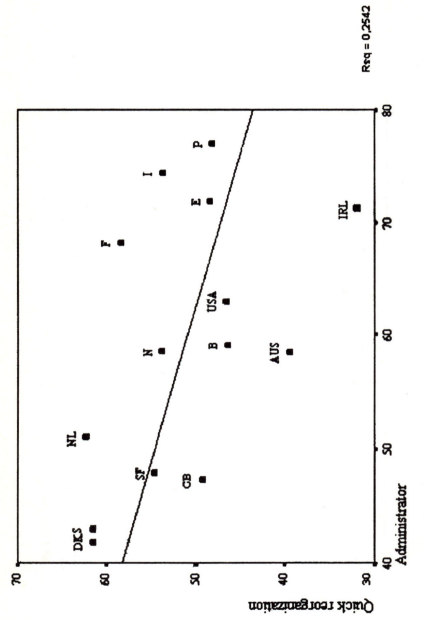

Fig. 23.12. Combining the Quick Reorganization Style and Administrator Role. (Based on Udite-data).

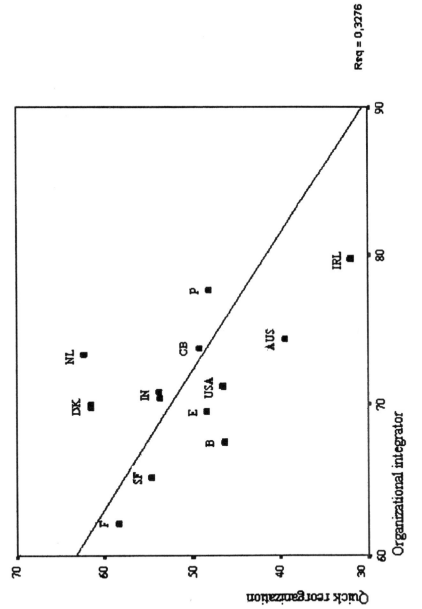

Fig. 23.13. Combining the Quick Reorganization Style and the Organizational Integrator Role. (Based on Udite-data).

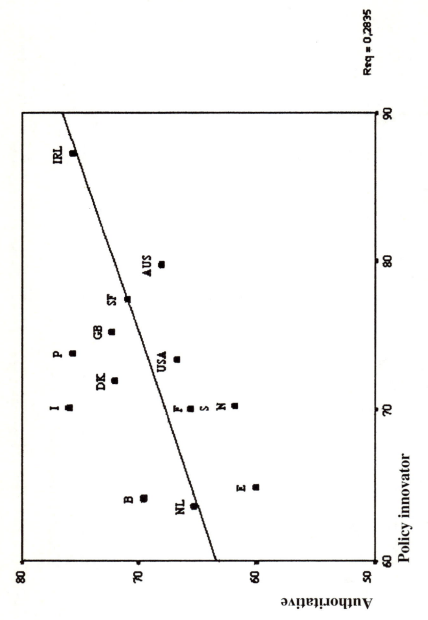

Fig. 23.14. Combining the Authoritative Style and the Policy Innovator Role. (Based on Udite-data).

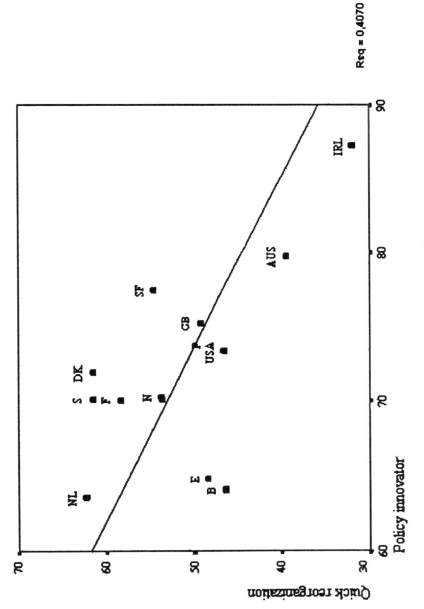

Fig. 23.15. Combining the Quick Reorganization Style and the Policy Innovator Role. (Based on Udite-data).

CONCLUSIONS

What does this all add up to? We can explain only a few of the findings from the national culture hypothesis. We find it clearly confirmed only in the perception of the role as administrator. The other roles and styles differentiate the population in other ways. We find some of the expected relationships between roles and styles, meaning that there is a tendency to play a particular role with a particular style. Nevertheless, the overall picture is one of similarity in perception of management roles and styles.

We do not have ex ante data, so although tempted, we cannot say anything about convergence and divergence. However, there may be some ground for interpreting the findings as follows: What we find is a vast group of shared attitudes regarding leadership and management, so that at least at a symbolic level there is a shared language and an interpenetration of the rhetoric of New Public Management. Another interpretation would be to say that the anonymous classical administrator-role has been supplemented, if not surpassed, by new management and leadership concepts, ideas and ideals, and that these are bridging classical cleavages between countries.

NOTE

1. U.Di.T.E. is an acronym for Union des Dirigeants Territoriaux de l'Europe, the association of local government Chief Executive Officers (CEOs) in Europe who supported the research project. The U.Di.T.E. project covered 15 western countries. Research teams in each country carried out their own study based on a shared survey, case-studies and job posting analysis. There were more than 4000 respondents.

REFERENCES

Aberbach, J. D., Putnam, R. D., & Rockman, B. A. (1981). *Bureaucrats and Politicians*. Cambridge: Harvard University Press.

Adizes, I. (1989). *Corporate Lifecycles. How and Why Corporations Grow and Die and What to Do About It*. Englewood Cliffs: Prentice Hall.

Allison, G. (1980). Public and Private Management: Are They Fundamentally Alike in All Unimportant Respects? In: J. Shafritz & A. C. Hyde (Eds), *Classics of Public Administration* (pp. 510–529). Chicago: The Dorset Press.

Appleby, P. (1945). Government is Different. In: J. Shafritz & A. C. Hyde (Eds), *Classics of Public Administration* (pp. 158–164). Chicago: The Dorset Press.

Barzelay, M. (1992). Breaking Through Bureaucracy: A New Vision for Managing in Government. Berkeley: University of California Press.

Blake, R. R., & Mouton, J. S. (1964). *The Managerial Grid*. Hougston: Gulf.

Bozeman, B. (1989). *All Organizations Are Public. Bridging Public and Private Organizational Theories*. San Francisco: Jossey-Bass Publishers.

Bryman, A. (1996). Leadership in Organizations. In: R. Stewart, C. H. Clegg & W. R. Nord (Eds), *Handbook of Organization Studies* (pp. 276–292). London: Sage.

Buchanan, J. M. (1986). *Liberty, Market and State – Political Economy in the 1980s*. London: Weatsheaf Books.

Chandler, A. D. (1962). *Strategy and Structure: Chapters in the History of the Industrial Enterprise*. Cambridge: MIT Press.

Clegg, S. R. (1990). *Modern Organizations: Organization Studies in the Postmodern World*. London: Sage.

Denhardt, R. B. (1984). *Theories of Public Organization*. Monterey: Cole Publishing Company.

Dogan, M.(Ed.) (1975). *The Mandarins of Western Europe: The Political Roles of Top Civil Servants*. Beverly Hills: Sage.

Ferlie, E., Ashburner, L., Fitzgerald, L., & Pettigrew, A. (1996). *The New Public Management in Action*. Oxford: Oxford University Press.

Galbraith, J. (1973). *Designing Complex Organizations*. Reading: Addison-Wesley Publishing Company.

Gulick, L. (1937). Notes on the Theory of Organization. In: J. Shafritz & A. C. Hyde (Eds), *Classics of Public Administration* (pp. 79–90). Chicago: The Dorset Press.

Handy, C. B. (1987). *Understanding Organizations*. New York: Penguin Books.

Harmon, M. M., & Mayer, R. T. (1986). *Organization Theory for Public Administration*. Glenview: Scott, Foresman and Company.

Heffron, F. (1989). *Organization Theory and Public Organizations. The Political Connection*. Englewood Cliffs: Prentice Hall.

Hofstede, G. (1980). *Culture's Consequences*. London: Sage.

Hood, C. (1991). A Public Management For All Seasons? *Public Administration, 69*, 3–19.

Johnsen, E. (1975). *Teorien om ledelse*. København: Nyt Nordisk Forlag.

Klausen, K. K., & Magnier, A. (Eds) (1998). *The Anonymous Leader. Appointed CEOs in Western Local Government*. Gylling: Odense University Press.

Lynn, L. E. (1998). A Critical Analysis of The New Public Management. *International Public Management Journal, 1*(1), 107–123.

Mintzberg, H. (1973). *The Nature of Managerial Work*. London: Prentice Hall.

Mintzberg, H. (1983). *Structures in Fives: Designing Effective Organizations*. Englewood Cliffs: Prentice Hall.

Olsen, J. P. (Ed.) (1978). *Politisk organisering. Organisasjonsteoretiske synspunkt på folkestyre og politisk ulikhet*. Bergen: Universitetsforlaget.

Osborne, D., & Gaebler, T. (1992). *Reinventing Government: How the Entrepreneurial Spirit is Transforming the Public Sector*. Reading: Addison-Wesley.

Page, E. C., & Goldsmith, M. (Eds) (1987). *Central and Local Government Relations: A Comparative Analysis of West European Unitary States*. London: Sage.

Porter, M. E. (1980). *Competitive Strategy. Techniques for Analyzing Industries and Competitors*. New York: The Free Press.

Putnam, R. D. (1975). The Political Attitude of Senior Civil Servants in Britain, Germany and Italy. In: M. Dogan (Ed.), *The Mandarins of Western Europe: The Political Roles of Top Civil Servants* (pp. 87–128). Beverly Hills: Sage.

Shafritz, J. M., & Hyde, A. C. (1987). *Classics of Public Administration*. Chicago: The Dorset Press.

Svara, J. (1990). *Official Leadership in the City. Patterns of Conflict and Cooperation*. New York: Oxford University Press.

Tilly, C. (Ed.) (1976). *The Formation of National States in Western Europe*. Princeton: Princeton University Press.

Yukl, G. A. (1989). *Leadership in Organizations*. London: Prentice-Hall.

Wamsley, G. L., & Zald, M. N. (1976). *The Political Economy of Public Organizations*. Bloomington: Indiana University Press.

Weber, M. (1921). *Wirtschaft und Gesellschaft*. Tübingen: Mohr.

Weick, C. (1969). *The Social Psychology of Organizing*. Reading: Addison Wesley.

Wilson, W. (1987). The Study of Administration. In: J. Shafritz & A. C. Hyde (Eds), *Classics of Public Administration* (pp. 10–25). Chicago: The Dorset Press.

24. PERFORMANCE BUDGETING IN SWITZERLAND: IMPLICATIONS FOR POLITICAL CONTROL

Kuno Schedler

INTRODUCTION

This chapter assesses recent reforms to implement performance budgeting at the national level in Switzerland with emphasis on the necessity for integrating the political dimension. The political context in Switzerland is described as a regulation-driven with fairly liberal but still detailed private and public law, and where the legal basis is the major subject of political influence. In practice, the law is the result of long-term politics while the budget reflects the short-term, actual value of tasks is determined by the legislators. Thereby, a systematic link between legal obligations and financial resources – such as is the case in U.S. programs – does not exist in the traditional form of political steering. In times of financial pressure, this can lead to laws that are not enacted due to a lack of resources. The chapter analyzes traditional budgeting and contrasts it with results-oriented public management and performance budgeting as manifest in the Swiss model.

Learning from International Public Management Reform, Volume 11B, pages 455–478.
ISBN: 0-7623-0760-9

Adapted from an article in International Public Management Journal Volume 3 Number 1, 2000
© Elsevier Science Inc.

POLITICAL CONTROL STRUCTURES IN SWITZERLAND

Political Background

The Swiss Confederation was founded in 1291. The Swiss Federal government (the Federal Council or *Bundesrat*) is a collegial authority of seven ministers. Switzerland has neither a president nor a prime minister – the seven federal councillors constitute one single decision-making body, with all members having equal rights. A typical feature of Switzerland is its special form of concordant democracy that, in contrast to the 'competitive' or 'adversarial' democracies of Anglo-Saxon countries, incorporates all the major political parties in the national government. The latter's composition does not vary in that it always includes both the major political parties and the various linguistic regions. Parliament consists of two chambers with equal rights: the Council of States, comparable to the American Senate and the National Council, comparable to the American House of Representatives. These chambers reflect the diversity of the party political landscape, although the 'governing parties' occupy 74% of the seats.

Unlike the British Westminster system, but similar to the U.S. one, Swiss parliaments see themselves as part of a system of "checks and balances". In practice, parliaments often behave like an opposition to the government that, in turn, develops its own tactics to get around parliament if necessary.

A notable feature of Swiss government is the country's system of direct democracy. Its major instruments are the 'initiative' and the 'referendum'. An initiative (requiring 100,000 signatures) enables citizens to demand that a new constitutional article be submitted to a nation-wide ballot. With 50,000 signatures, citizens can demand a nation-wide referendum against an alteration of a federal statute. Democratic awareness has deep roots in Swiss political culture, and any attempts at changing democratic possibilities of intervention in favour of more efficient processes can be expected to provoke total resistance from the population and its representatives.

Laws as a Major Means of Political Influence

As Switzerland is a regulation-driven nation with a fairly liberal but still detailed private and public law, the legal basis is the major subject of political influence. In practice, the law is considered the result of long-term politics while the budget reflects the short-term, actual value a certain task is given by the legislator. Thereby, a systematic link between legal obligations and financial resources – such as is the case in U.S. programs – does not exist in the traditional form of political steering. In times of financial pressure, this can lead to laws that are not enacted due to a lack of resources.

The law (or Act of Parliament) as the traditional means of parliamentary control is suffering from an increasing loss of effectiveness. A recent report of a committee of experts (1996) on the subject can be summarised as follows:

- It is becoming more and more difficult to solve long-term problems with general and abstract regulations.
- The law is not a suitable means of carrying out the necessary constructive tasks.
- Legislation often arrives too late because the legislative process is too slow.
- The law of the land and law as people experience it are drifting further and further apart.
- Law nowadays does not make any systematic link between tasks (services) and resources.
- The latent financial shortage is threatening to dominate legislative decisions.

Nevertheless, it must be clear that the major function of the Swiss legislature is the creation and up-date of a legal framework for the co-existence of the diverse actors within the nation. Therefore, budgeting is important but – in general – not the most important aspect of political life.

TRADITIONAL BUDGETING

Switzerland's tradition in budgeting is easily comparable to the one in other countries. Before the new public management debate started in the early nineties, line-itemized input budgets were the regular case, which was not questioned until a few years ago. There was, however, a certain difference in the degree of detail in that smaller local bodies always had a fairly 'lean' budget while the city of Zurich, for example, usually published a thick book full of figures. For the normal citizen, both forms did not transport much information that could be understood without considerable effort. So it came to the internationally, often experienced, situation that parliamentary committees spent hours discussing small spending items for unimportant matters while the administration decided on long lasting strategies without the political bodies.

Even in Switzerland, where direct democratic habits lead to a whole people voting on questions that have more or less strategic value four times a year, there was a growing dissatisfaction with the uneven partition of real power between the administration, the government and the legislature. Even when it comes to the core function of the legislator, the enactment of new laws, MP David (1998: 172) points out that the administration has a much greater influence than is usually expected, and that, ". . . not only are the bureaucrats competent, but they also have a political point of view. This is rarely discussed."

The rise of a modern managerialist view of the administration created a need for management information that went further than just the financially dominated input view. Soon it became clear that the traditional accountability patterns lacked of outputs and outcomes. Although there had always been implicit ideas about output and outcome targets behind allocation decisions, a systematic feedback and – if necessary – correction process was not in place. In the context of increasing financial pressure and several scandals of mismanagement in Swiss public institutions, a growing dissatisfaction gained ground among public officials and politicians. Some solutions were to be found in the private sector management domain which promised stronger strategic leadership with a new managerialist rationale of the whole decision making process.

RESULTS-ORIENTED PUBLIC MANAGEMENT AND PERFORMANCE BUDGETING: THE SWISS MODEL

Results-oriented public management (*Wirkungsorientierte Verwaltungsfüh-rung*) is the key term for Swiss reforms of the new public management type. It is on the one hand similar to the U.S. National Performance Review, on the other hand it differs from most NPM projects in terms of political control processes, and it emphasises outcomes rather than outputs. Although it has not yet been possible to achieve total results-orientation – the ultimate aim of the reforms – the awareness of all parties that this should be the way to go seems to be a competitive advantage for the Swiss reforms in the international context.

Swiss reforms can be titled "concept-driven" or "theory-driven" as the theoretical debate of academics and practitioners about the "right" public management model for this country has been intense since the beginning of the nineties. This is an important difference to, say, the Dutch reforms as Kickert (1999) points out that no such in-depth debate had ever taken place in the Netherlands before or during the reform process. Although the academic driving forces for the Swiss NPM reforms came from management theory, it was only until an interdisciplinary debate between lawyers, management scholars, and economists started that the Swiss NPM was too managerialist. Since 1996, a much broader approach has tried to design a Swiss NPM model that takes into consideration the peculiarities of the direct democratic system in this country. Some of the ideas were detailed earlier by Schedler (1997) to an international audience.

Political-Administrative Control Structures

The general concept that lies behind the results-oriented public management contains a new form of control:

- the general basis for all state action will always be a legal one. In contrast to the U.S. or anglo-saxon system, Switzerland has a specialised public law with a strongly conditional logical concept (if-then-relatios).
- in order to give the managers a greater freedom of action, one-line budgets replace the traditional line-itemised budgets.
- this increase in managerial freedom in order to create a minimal degree of concrete terms for the allocation of financial resources, so-called "products" are defined that are comparable to the "outputs" in U.S. terminology.
- the targets of each programme and/or public institution are made transparent with beneficiary effects for political decision making and the staff working in a certain organisation.

Products and targets are the core ingredients of so-called performance agreements, which are to be combined with a one-line budget per organization or performance unit. Up to this point, the Swiss model does not differ much from other internationally known concepts.

The most important argument for the results-oriented public management is the creation of a win-win situation in which all the actors profit from the new structures:

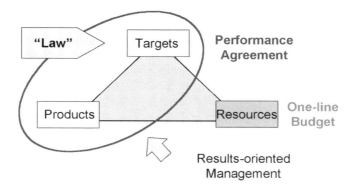

Fig. 24.1. The Logic of Results-Oriented Public Management.

- the parliament will get a new transparency about outputs and outcomes and will therefore be able to take better informed decisions
- the government will gain stronger managerial influence and also output and outcome transparency
- the administration, at last, will have more room to manoevre for managerial decisions.

In theory, these arguments were welcomed by the reform community and the Swiss model of a results-oriented public management has been implemented since 1993 in pilot projects in nearly all the Swiss cantons. Meanwhile, it has become clear that the model suits well to the administration as its managerial rationality fits to the needs of the newly created public managers. Transparency has been increased within the administration which gave rise to a great support of the new model within the administration. If it had not been for the politicians, the results-oriented public management would be fully implemented in Switzerland.

However, political rationality differs widely from its managerialist counterpart, and the benefits of the results-oriented public management for the administration are of little importance to the politicians. Here, the major topic has been the diversion of political influence (and therefore power) in the new model. A politically rational decision can not be limited to the so-called strategic level if a (for managers unimportant) detail helps to find majorities.

It is therefore necessary to draw typical border lines between the responsibilities of parliament and government at first hand and the administration at second. Thereby, several choices have to be made by the responsible political institutions about the layout of the political interaction between parliament and government:

- will the one-line budget be linked to an organisational or a performance unit? If the latter, who will be responsible for the budget?
- will parliament take its budget and results decisions on the basis of (approximately) 1000 products, 200 product groups, or 50 task areas?
- will parliaments have a direct influence on single activities within the administration, or are they restricted from managerial decisions and limited to output or outcome specifications?

Practice demonstrates that there is a variety of solutions and combinations among the different cantons, which can be traced back to a wide range of political cultures around the nation. At the University of St. Gallen, we have developed an ideal model (see Figure 23.2) that divides direct influence as follows:

Parliament decides directly on expected outcomes and impacts in up to 50 task areas and sets targets on that basis. A performance measurement system delivers the politically important information on the achievement of outcome and impact goals. For information only, output and outcome figures per product group are delivered to the parliament, which in case of dissatisfaction has its own instruments to intervene with the government.

The government's duty according to our model is the "translation" of outcomes into output targets for the administration at the product group level. The single ministry will then set up a performance agreement with the administration that goes down to output targets at the product level.

The administration will organize its activities autonomously in order to achieve its targets and measure its performance. A layered reporting system creates managerial and political information which is delivered to the government and the parliament periodically.

Performance Budgets In A Political Context

The performance budget allocates a one-line budget and a performance contract to each of the administrative departments in order to produce given groups of products. The one-line budget for administration, approved by the Parliaments in each case, now basically takes two different legal forms:

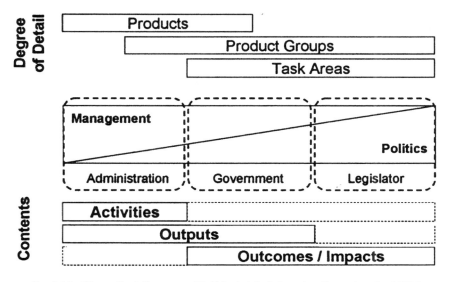

Fig. 24.2. Theoretical Concept of Political-Administrative Control under NPM.

- The *"pure" performance budget*: this allocates net costs or net expenditure to given product groups (the "product groups budget") or task areas (the "task area budget") with binding legal effect. Shifting budget amounts from one product group or field of activity to another later is only possible with a supplementary loan or amendment resolution.
- The *Institution budget* (e.g. departmental budget): this allocates net costs or net expenditure to given institutions with binding legal effect. Although financial data are shown for each product group, they have no binding legal effect and it is permissible to move financial resources between the product groups in any one department without special permission, provided the agreed services are delivered. The decisive factor is the "contract total" for each institution. This is the form that is currently being used in most projects because the administrations rarely have the basic figures for producing a binding product group budget.

Under this system, budget sovereignty still remains with Parliament, meaning that Parliament can determine how much money is devoted to which purposes; it is only the "specification", or the form in which the resources are bound, that is changed.

The product group budget is backed by the product group account as the instrument for keeping accounts. The present form of annual report, often divided into an accounts and an administrative report, thus separating the financial aspects from the services performed, will be superseded by the new reports.

Indicator Systems and Political Indicators

The projects currently running under the heading of results-orientated public management are showing that the information systems being used in the projects – interim reports, product group accounts, etc. – contain too much management information and are thus often imposing too much work on the parliamentarians. Those involved have therefore been asked to keep the information on the product groups as concise as possible in order to provide a view of the interesting aspects. It was questioned by the government of the Canton of Berne whether a plenary session of parliament can handle *interim reports* anyway. In many cases, therefore, the parliamentary committees are only being given *political deviation reports* on the interim results, which can be passed on to the government on request and if necessary. The political indicators thus take the place of the (excessively) detailed performance indicators.

Mastronardi (1998: 87), a specialist in constitutional law, describes the problems of administrative dominance in designing the new management system very clearly:

> Parliament is not doing its job if it accepts sight-unseen the performance aims and indicators put up to it by the government and the administration. It would otherwise be allowing itself to be guided far too much by the commercial point of view, which is currently the dominant one in the context of the NPM projects. Instead, it should on its own initiative check whether the information on offer is relevant to those questions that are themselves relevant to judging the political effectiveness: are the political aims being achieved by the measures that are being taken? Political effectiveness control requires politically defined effectiveness indicators.

Political indicators require properly formulated political goals. The basic principle here is: no goal without an indicator, no indicator without a goal. For Parliament, this means that the government's suggested goals must be examined critically and if necessary replaced or augmented with Parliament's own goals. Although it is desirable for these various Committees to play an active role, the situation should be avoided in which they interfere in management questions and/or place too much of a workload on the administration by demanding a disproportionately large amount of information. For this reason, it was decided in the Canton of Solothurn, for instance, that the number of (political) indicators that Parliament can require should be reduced, and this had the agreeable side-effect that the Committee now has to set priorities.

It is obvious that a considerable amount of uncertainty is still affecting the question of political indicators, in both theory and practice. The projects currently running are still too new to allow conclusive results to be expected, and there are hardly any examples of any similar schemes in other countries. Nevertheless, the idea is gaining acceptance in practice and is therefore worth mentioning.

Example 1: Political Indicators in the Canton of Solothurn
The Canton of Solothurn proposes the political indicators in its Ordinance "Experiment with results-orientated administrative management in the Canton of Solothurn". In response to an application from one of the competent Committees, the Parliament defines goals for selected product groups for which the politically significant indicators for the attainment of the goals have to be supplied with the proposal. The Parliament also lays down the period of time over which an indicator is to be monitored. The relevant Committee approves the amended political indicators as proposed by the Government.

It is envisaged that, during the experimental period, each Supervisory Committee can require three political indicators and each Technical Committee as many as the individual departments can handle. If any decide not to lay claim to a political indicator, another can claim two. As this regulation is very new it is not yet possible to say how it will develop in practice.

CONCEPTUAL CONSEQUENCES FROM PERFORMANCE BUDGETING

Instruments for Controlling Outcomes by Parliament

All Swiss members of parliament are part-timers and parliamentary secretariats are relatively weak. This fact represents a considerable restriction on the ability of Swiss parliaments to take action. Information brought into Parliament by the government can hardly be subjected to any further work unless individual parliamentarians work on them, and this inevitably results in their having a high degree of specialisation, but also to a great asymmetry of information – to the disadvantage of the parliaments.

In connection with the current series of reforms, therefore, the parliaments are constantly calling for their facilities to be strengthened. The ability of Parliament to exert any influence is currently limited to its legislative instruments, the only real exceptions being budget decisions and, particularly, its supervisory activities, even though sanctions normally have to take the legislative course.

The principle of results-orientated public management requires the parliaments to concentrate harder on *strategic and standard-setting functions* and leave operational work to the government and the administration as much as possible. This leads to the logical consequence that Parliament will have to be given the necessary facilities (instruments and resources) to be able to do its job. Mastronardi (1995: 1550) stresses correctly that removing the control of resources without replacing it with other (results-orientated) possibilities for exerting influence and control is in practice rejected for democratic reasons.

Parliamentary control in Switzerland often boils down in effect to *indirect control*, unless it is carrying out business on its own account. Since Parliament will not take on any political or management responsibility, it should not interfere directly in the executive management function. However, there are exceptions to be found in the major tasks that fall within the competence of Parliament.

In order to put all the various activities and possibilities at the interface between Parliament and government into some kind of logical order, in practice and in the literature a distinction is made between *the resources of political communication* and *instruments of parliamentary intervention*.

- Communications resources define the form in which the political intentions of the executive are communicated to Parliament and the population at large. This includes those cases that serve for obtaining the authorisation needed for later implementation, e.g. of the annual budget.
- Instruments of intervention are used to enforce or instigate given political actions. They do not of themselves define policy, but are the tools of parliamentary work.

In Switzerland, Parliaments of the larger or smaller kind have the following possibilities for intervening in government policy:

- Binding instructions: Government is not allowed to do anything other than implement them.
- Guidelines: The government can take other action than direct implementation but must give a political justification for doing so, and is required to pursue the stated aim.
- Clarification request: Parliament requests the Government to clarify whether in a given question a certain course of action should be taken.
- Political indication: Parliament indicates its considered position on an important political question on which no decision can be taken at the moment. The Government can decide not to conform with the indicated policy.
- Parliamentary wording (Bill): Parliament hands down a completely formulated draft Act (or Bill). The Government has to accept it as it stands.
- Information: The Government must provide the requested information (in the requested form).

Ultimately, however, all these instruments suffer from the fact that they are limited to the legislative function of Parliament. Directly laying down goals for performance or effectiveness is not possible within the traditional system. An instrument had therefore to be created that is capable of doing this: the *Auftrag*.

Auftrag – A Parliamentary Order to the Government

An *Auftrag* has been described as follows by the federal committee of experts that recommended it to Parliament as a new instrument:

> An *Auftrag* is a general instrument with which the Federal Assembly can control future decisions regardless of whether they are to be taken by Parliament itself or the Federal Council. The allocation of authority does not dictate the permissibility but the effect of the *Auftrag*:

- If the Federal Council and the administration are required to support the Federal Assembly in the exercise of its own powers, the Order will have the same effect as *instructions*. . .
- If the Federal Council is required to issue regulations or undertake application acts that lie within its sphere of decision-taking authority, the *Auftrag* will have the same effect as a *guideline* . . .

Article 22^{quarter} of the Parliament Business Routines Act subsequently enacted in the Federal Parliament now states:

- The *Auftrag* instructs the Federal Council to issue or amend a performance contract under Article 44 of the Federal Government and Administration Organisation Act. The *Auftrag* shall have the effect of a Guideline from which deviation shall only be permitted in well justified cases.
- The draft *Auftrag* can be amended.
- The *Auftrag* shall require the consent of the other Council. If the first Council decides on a difference during the Second Reading, the Reconciliation Conference shall be called in.
- Decisions by one Council to write off *Aufträge* shall require the consent of the other Council.

The Federal Parliament thus has a co-determination right in the form of performance contracts, which goes further than its previous overall supervisory function. Furthermore, by revision of the Federal Budget Act the basis for a management by one-line budgets was created:

The *Auftrag* enables Parliament to do almost anything. For instance, it can:

- intervene in the product groups budget,
- intervene in long-term plans and developments,
- require laws to be formulated or adapted which issue a planning Auftrag.

The instrument of the *Auftrag* has also been introduced at the Cantonal level, but here it is so new that no experience has yet been accumulated that can be evaluated. The Cantons that work with the *Auftrag* include Solothurn and Berne.

Leistungsmotion – A Performance Order

The Parliament of the Canton of Zürich has decided on a slightly more specific form of intervention, but it does have a certain similarity to an *Auftrag*. The *Leistungsmotion* that has been introduced here requires the executive to calculate the financial consequences of a stated alternative level of performance in the next budget, or to include a stated performance goal in the one-line budget for stated groups of performance.

Only the standing parliamentary committees are authorised to bring in a *Leistungsmotion*, which has to be submitted to parliament no later than the end of January. The government then states its considered view on the matter within eight weeks, and the parliament decides at its next meeting on the handing over of the performance. The Government submits to the parliament in the next one-line budget the draft that was handed over with the *Leistungsmotion* and submits its application. If the government comes to the conclusion that an extended goal cannot be reached within the envisaged period of time it is free to state with what resources and within what period of time the goals can be reached.

The *Leistungsmotion* was introduced in June 1999 when the revised Cantonal Parliament Act took effect.

Further Parliamentary Instruments

The Canton of Zürich has introduced another new instrument, the "planning postulate", with which measures for medium-term planning can be required, and the right of the business management and the standing committees to submit their own motions and planning postulates. In the Canton of Berne, the people can vote on a "basic decision" which is an order to the government that a specific programme should be planned. In general, a certain amount of money for the funding of the planning activities is linked to the decision. Other Cantons have also introduced further parliamentary instruments, but these will not be discussed in detail here.

Task and Finance Planning

In most Swiss governments, there is broad consensus that the one-year perspective of traditional budgets is too short a period to steer effectively. Therefore, new forms of mid-term steering instruments are being developed which affect the communication between government and parliament. Although the biennial budgeting models of some U.S. states and cities have been studied by Swiss parliamentary committees, it seems to be too early to make that step away from yearly budgets. It is argued by politicians that the parliament would give away its power if it does not insist on its yearly influence on the budget.

In order to emphasise a stronger focus on the mid-term development – combined with a strategic management perspective – the government's planning resources have also been re-designed. Here too, a systematic link between budgetary and performance figures has been created so that the basic idea of the performance budget is reflected in the multi-year plans.

The government will, according to our model, draw up an *integrated task and finance plan* as described by Haldemann (1997: 131). It is the instrument designed to present the medium-term consequences of political decisions in terms of costs, output, and effects over four to six years. It is a rolling plan, meaning that every change such as those caused by political decisions or external factors is registered and the plan adapted accordingly. Every decision by Parliament therefore has to be examined for its effects on the task and finance plan, and presented transparently.

The plan contains at least the following information:

(a) planned developments regarding output and effects in the various working areas;
(b) the financial ramifications for the Current account and the Investment Account;
(c) the key financial and output figures for the Cantonal budget.

It has to be submitted in a form that is digestible for Parliament together with the preliminary estimate, and Parliament takes due note of it. As the plan does not cover any fixed period of time, but "rolls on" forever, no final report is necessary.

Example 2: Government Policy Guidelines in the Canton of Berne
In 1998, the government of the Canton of Berne submitted to the public for the first time its so-called Government policy guidelines for the next four years (1999 to 2002). They can be described as follows:

> The Government policy guidelines form part of political planning. They contain a declaration of intent. The Government gives an overview of the main government tasks and the aims that it intends to achieve in the next four years. . . . The planning of tasks and the financial plan are thus linked together. Planning has much to do with early warning, co-ordination, and the search for consensus (Chancellery of State of the Canton of Berne).

Parliament takes due note of the guidelines, and can express its considered opinion by issuing a declaration of its own. The citizens also are to be consulted, but because the style of presentation is decidedly technical this might prove to be a problem.

The guidelines cover task and financial planning for the coming four years, and consist of the following elements:

• a description of the initial situation in 28 different fields of activity defined by the government
• aims and activities, with priorities, relating to these fields of activity
• the legislative programme for each field of activity
• the legislature financial plan.

The guidelines thus form a combination of legislature, task, and finance planning. They have both a programmatic and a prognostic character.

Legislature Planning

While the integrated task and finance plan is more of a management-type mid-term instrument, legislature planning is the government's priority political programme, of which Parliament takes due note at the beginning of each legislature. In its traditional form, the legislature plan mainly contains information about new laws that are to be created; the results-oriented aspect of the new form of legislature planning is the list of political programmes which the executive would like to draw the most attention to during the coming legislature. For each priority it contains a reference to the consequences to be expected in the medium term. Its degree of detail must be such that it is possible to check on progress (politically) by means of the definition of "milestones" every year.

As with every planning instrument, the legislature plan has to have the appropriate report providing information at the end of the period on whether the output or effects have been achieved or how much progress has been made in this direction.

It is normally the job of the government to formulate the legislature plan. It gains in significance when Parliament takes note of it and when *indirect* influence is exerted on the legislature plan by means of various instruments. The main problem, however, is the fact that the plan is not given any formal statutory force. It is not binding, and as a result hardly any real notice has been taken of it up to now.

Political Resources in their Overall Context

Looked at in their entirety, the new resources can be seen as forming a consistent whole. Behind the model presented here is a fundamental question which matters greatly at least for medium-term control: how tightly can and should Parliament allow itself to be bound in the medium term? Discussions with parliamentarians and experts indicate that some Swiss parliaments would even accept the necessity for making short-term changes *more difficult*. On the other hand, it is at the moment an open question whether a parliament would allow itself to be bound strictly over a period of several years, for instance by accepting that an outline resolution that had once taken effect could never be altered. Up to that point, however, the Federal Parliament had regularly dispensed with any such self-limitation (see Committee of Experts: *Division of authority*: 488).

Figure 24.3 shows in diagrammatic form how the various different control possibilities are meant to fit together with one another in Parliament. This will

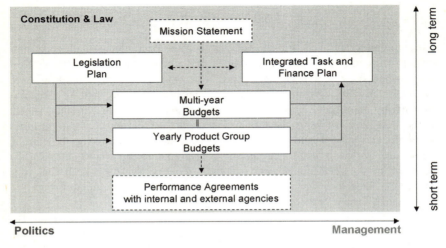

Fig. 24.3. Theoretical Structure of Results-Oriented Steering Instruments.

make it clear that the interplay between them is very greatly influenced by their different time scales and the characteristics of the communications resources.

All the elements are embedded in the constitution and the law. The objective shows the long-term vision for public policy, which in an ideal situation will be reflected in the legislature plan, in the Integrated Tasks and Finance Plan, and in the outline resolutions and product group budgets. The relationship between the legislature plan and the Integrated Plan can be described this way: in the legislature plan, the government sets the political priorities for the coming legislature, but is subject here to the financial restrictions imposed by the income side that can be seen in the Integrated Plan. At the same time, every priority in the legislature plan consequently alters the Integrated Plan on the expenditure side and in the finances.

Outline resolutions defined development priorities in certain areas of activity, and should therefore of course be in harmony with the legislature plan. In the product groups' budget, finally, the consequences of all these preliminary political decisions become visible and are broken down into the year under consideration. Any change, be it made in the form of an outline resolution or in the product groups budget, must have its impact on the Integrated Plan and must make it *immediately transparent*. Although this all-embracing model is accepted as such, it is hardly ever implemented in any specific application.

New Parliamentary Structures

Results-orientated public management in combination with performance budgeting in some respects requires new parliamentary structures in Switzerland. In particular, the tasks of the parliamentary committees are becoming more and more demanding, and in some cases – in the Canton of Zurich, for instance – the parliament's offices are being expanded. Instead of the traditional ad hoc committees, a certain amount of standing specialist committees are going to be needed in order to be able to meet the new requirements of outcome target setting, interpretation of government reports on tasks, and working with indicator systems. Various different standing committees already exist at federal level, although they hardly ever deal with NPM questions.

Example 3: Standing Committees in the Canton of Zürich
The Canton of Zürich now has specialist committees for every individual aspect of its business. During the course of the amendments to the Cantonal Council Act, standing "subject" committees take the place of the special committees. They take over and work on drafts from a given specialist area, e.g. education and culture, or economics and taxes.

Example 4: Standing Specialist Committees in the Canton of Basle City
An efficient organisation and infrastructure has to be created if Parliament is to retain its *Miliz* (or part-time service) character. Parliament also is to be given a staff organisation reporting to it alone, which will take on the existing financial control functions in the service of Parliament and also other tasks in the field of political monitoring and control. Standing specialist committees are intended to ensure that the specialist knowledge necessary for parliamentary work can be put to good use. Another point to be covered is access by members of the parliamentary committees to the internal administrative information relevant to their work. It must be possible to use all modern means of communications in parliamentary work as well.

PRACTICAL EXPERIENCE WITH PERFORMANCE BUDGETING

The Federal Level

At the Swiss federal level, the performance contract is designed to act as a management instrument for the Federal Council (government). It is not legally binding on Parliament. The definitive performance contract is fleshed out in precise detail by the National Department responsible for it in the form of a performance agreement with the department concerned.

After the end of the financial year, the department submits a business report to the Federal Council and Parliament. The latter formulates its opinion on the execution of the performance contract and its annual implementation. The business report contains a management summary, a management report, a performance report describing the output for the year by product group, and a financial report describing the financial results with a full set of figures appended as required by public-sector accounting systems. At the end of the performance contract period, a separate performance contract report can also be requested.

One-line budgets at federal level are made up of the following elements:

• applications for payment loans by product group
• justification
• information
• any supplementary documentation.

Parliament evaluates income and expenditure in each product group and in each organisation during the transition phase to one-line budgets and performance contracts. The one-line budgets are binding under credit law.

Article 44: Performance contracts:

(1) The Federal Council can issue performance contracts for certain groups and departments, and determine the degree of independence necessary for each one.
(2) It shall consult the competent parliamentary Committee of each Council in advance.

Article 44 of the 1997 Government and Administration Organization Act forms the first major basis for the partial introduction of administrative management forms based on the NPM principles. The time horizon for these contracts is always four years. The requirements laid down in the executive's performance contracts and parliament's one-line budgets are filled out in detail in the performance agreements between the Federal Departments and the individual organisations. The time horizon here is one year.

In practice, Parliament has been following the development at federal level on the basis of the experiments already at hand, and has expressed a critical opinion of the progress made towards implementation. Particular criticism has been levelled against the absence of reliable cost and performance information, and the fact that Parliament has too little possibility for intervening on the basis of the information that is available. Better examples are to be found at the Cantonal level.

The Case of the Swiss Meteorological Institute (SMI)

The Swiss Meteorological Institute (SMI) started on 1st of January 1997 to be managed on the principle of results-oriented public management, with a performance contract and a one-line budget. The SMI, together with the State Topographical Survey Office, is a pilot scheme under the Federal NPM project designed to accumulate initial experience relevant to government and administrative reform.

The job of the SMI has been defined in a number of statutory decrees published by the Swiss Federal Council (1996: 2), and can be described as follows:

- acquisition of meteorological and climatalogical data covering the whole country completely
- national and international exchange of data
- public meteorological service
- information and advisory service
- aviation weather service
- technical support for military meteorological services
- climate monitoring
- international collaboration and representation of Switzerland to the outside world within the area of authority allotted to it.

Performance contract (outline contract)
The Federal Council awarded the SMI a performance contract on 6 November 1996. This can be roughly broken down into:

(1) legal principles
(2) general performance specification
(3) specific goals and strategies for the performance contract period (1997–99)
(4) services to be performed (product group)
(5) general operational provisions
(6) special regulations
(7) performance management and quality assurance
(8) provisions for amending or terminating the contract.

Section 3 is concerned with the goals and strategy for the 1997–99 performance contract period. The five product groups are listed first. In addition to quality requirements, the performance contract also contains a prescribed cost-savings target – a 5% reduction by the end of 2000. Another important innovation is the maintenance of operating cost accounts, which will now also mean that it is possible to calculate the degree to which costs are being covered.

Section 4 outlines each product group in detail. The group is described briefly and its subordinate goals are defined. This is followed by the financial framework for 1997 to 1999. the main products are mentioned, and the "customers" – government departments or outside companies receiving the services provided – are named. Specific goals are set at the end of each product group.

The next section of this chapter covers the outline operating provisions, including the target that expanded commercial services must not exceed 5 to 10% of the total output. Cross-subsidies are strictly forbidden. The action is defined that has to be taken if expenditure falls short of or exceeds the amounts approved in the one-line budget. The outlines of personnel management also are described; e.g. the staff is subject until further notice to federal personnel

Table 24.1. Example of a product group: Aviation meteorological service

Description	An Ordinance from the Federal Council has allocated this responsibility to the SMI, and it will require about 30 percent of the SMI's total effort. The Ordinance covers the provision of meteorological information for all flights over Swiss sovereign territory (at all altitudes), the operation of manned aviation meteorological advisory centres at Geneva and Zurich airports, and the supply of Swiss aviation weather observations and forecasts in accordance with ICAO standards.
Overall goals	Weather warnings, information, and advice will lead to safe, efficient flying in Switzerland and neighbouring countries. Aviation services are to be sold to customers at prices which cover their costs.
Financial framework	Total expenditure 39,5 Total income 55,0 Net financial requirement 0,0 Total costs 58,0 Total revenue 58,0 Average cost-cover requirement 100%
Main products	• Warning of weather phenomena which could entail any danger to aviation • Services for air traffic control • Services to pilots flying by instrument flight rules • Services to pilots flying by sight rules and for military aviation
Customers	All users of Swiss airspace, airports, and airfields.
Goal and performance specification	(1) Limitation of costs to the 1996 level; handling additional demand for aviation weather resulting from the greater number of air movements without incurring greater costs; 100 percent adherence to the rate of issue of information required by ICAO recommendations. (2) Number of missed warnings: maximum of 1 in the 1997–99 period.

law, with the exception of the central job structure. It is also worth mentioning that provision is made for creating a performance-related pay component. The contribution for this is budgeted by the Swiss Federal Office of Human Resources. Starting from this performance contract, the Swiss Federal Ministry of Internal Affairs signs a performance agreement with the SMI every year.

Performance agreement (annual contract)
The performance agreement contains quantifiable annual goals for the SMI's individual products and outline operating provisions for the year covered by the agreement.

Any deviations from the performance agreement have to be disclosed in the business report and the reasons stated.

To return to the example above, the product group "Aviation meteorological services" is used as the basis for presenting the product "Services for pilots flying by sight rules and for military aviation:

Formalities such as the frequency of reporting are regulated at the end of the agreement.

Internal management
The director of the SMI has developed a vision and strategies for it covering the years 1996 to 1999. This planning horizon matches the legislative period. The strategies have been implemented by the SMI management as specific target fields and projects. "Planning and Management Conferences" review the annual plans every four months; this procedure was first carried out operationally in 1996.

Results
The SMI has been managed under the principles of results-orientated administrative management since 1 January 1997. Initial experience with results-oriented public management has been evaluated briefly by those concerned as successful, challenging, and demanding a great deal of work. The interim report on the evaluation states the following (SMI, 1997):

Table 24.2.   Goals and performance specification for 1998

Costs, revenue, and quantities	• Cost reduction of 10 percent from the 1996 level • Maintain cost-coverage at the 1997 level despite increasing international demands
Quality	• Maintain quality at the 1996/97 level
Projects	• Rationalise existing product range, in collaboration with customers, and reduce to the minimum necessary, without any loss of air safety

The performance contracts are currently at the middle "specificity" level, and describe the limits of the SMI's activities mainly in qualitative terms regarding resources, areas of activity, and reporting. For the government departments concerned, the annual performance agreements are of the greatest importance; it makes specific goals visible and checkable. The way the performance contract was prepared at the SMI was not perfect; the lack of knowledge of key internal figures slowed the process down, and greater willingness to make changes would have been desirable. Both instruments require a discussion between the parties concerned, as this enables management tasks to be handled better.

The 1997 SMI business report presents the main results of the first pilot year in the Report of the Ministry of Internal Affairs (1997):

The management of the SMI enjoyed greater operational room to manoeuvre and thus more flexibility in the area of resources (management of jobs and loans). The national and international environment and market situation are dominated by the rapid developments in the field of communications (e.g. the expansion of the Internet) and the trend in all meteorological offices to commercialisation in the sense of moving from a seller's to a buyer's market. The specifications laid down in the performance contract were attained, both in the financial sense and with regard to production/output. The operation work, as the main part of the SMI's duties, was handled without any major limitations, and various new, quality-raising services were offered as well. Operating accounts show an increase in the level of cost coverage compared with the preceding period (1995), from 32 to about 36%.

It proved possible to meet the cost-cutting target of 2.5% in the first year of operation, and to keep within the one-line budget approved by Parliament. At the same time, new services were offered such as those in the areas of motoring weather, tourism, forest fires, and rain and snow forecasts for emergency services. In the personnel field, use was made of the possibilities for flexible contracts of employment, which enabled requirements on the demand side to be met better. Cost-consciousness and customer orientation underwent a considerable improvement. Internally, not only were the new management instruments such as cost accounts and output time registration that were developed further but also management and operating procedures were reorganised on the basis of a process analysis. The anxiety suffered by staff as a result of the process of change was countered by an increase in the flow of information and by involving them more closely.

In general terms, the introduction of performance budgeting has resulted in a large amount of new knowledge being gained relating to the organisation, cost structure, and management philosophy of government departments, and this provides a good basis for further improvements in the SMI's strategy and management. On the minus side, the additional workload is enormous, and the changes are still causing nervousness in the staff.

CONCLUSIONS

The Swiss reform movement has started at the cantonal level, which has remained one of the major driving forces for the new public management in Switzerland. Since 1994, some cantons have experimented with different formats of performance budgets, with more or less success. Shining examples such as the cantons of Zurich or Lucerne have succeeded in including parliamentarians into the process of development of the performance budgets. The modes of sharing power between parliament and the governments of most cantons still differ from the "ideal" model developed in St. Gallen and from each others' model. However, the notion of separating outcomes and outputs and installing indicator systems that provide information about the two levels respectively seems to have found ground in Switzerland.

Although at the Federal level, only few projects with performance budgeting are currently running, there is a irreversible trend at the cantonal and the local level towards the NPM-type budgeting. First evaluations such as in the City and the Canton of Berne as well as in other cantons demonstrate a wide support for performance budgeting within the administration. Not surprisingly, it is primarily the politicians who fear a loss of influence over the administration and/or a shift of power from government to parliament or vice versa.

Performance budgeting has succeeded in changing political debates within parliamentary committees in that the new transparency on outputs and outcomes combined with a loss of detailed financial information leads to substantial political discussions about outputs and outcomes. There remains, however, the necessity to transport the "NPM knowledge" from parliamentary reform committees to the plenaries. It is also unclear how far the new forms of steering and budgeting affect the work of political parties and fractions.

The most burning problem at the time is certainly the provision of useful outcome information for political decision makers. In the City of Zurich in 1999, the city parliament decided not to implement performance budgeting before the administration is ready and able to produce valuable performance information. As a strong emphasis was put on outcomes in Switzerland, there is a certain obligation to provide for outcome information, which could turn out to be nearly impossible for certain task areas such as defense. International comparison shows that this is not a problem of the Swiss alone (see Boston, and Jones and Mussari in this volume). Bureaucratic use of performance indicators is a difficult task encountered internationally.

As held generally in Switzerland and elsewhere (see, for example, Jones and Thompson, 1999), that the new public management affects not only administration but leads also to reform of political systems, expectations by both the media and the politicians supporting the NPM are high. Performance budgeting is an integral part of the Swiss NPM, and many hope that it will change the political culture both in governments and in parliaments. Experience in several cantons shows that results-oriented public management can meet only some of these expectations. Although the first signs of a cultural changes in political institutions are clearly observable, it is doubtful whether some public officials' dreams of more management rationality in politics will ever come true. In fact, this might not even be democratically wise as it may be argued that the two systems – management and politics – should be better integrated rather than separate.

ACKNOWLEDGMENTS

The author wishes to express his thanks to Mathias Brun for the assistance in collecting data about the Swiss Federal Administration, and to Larry Jones for his encouragement of this work.

REFERENCES

Committee of Experts set up by the State Political Committees of the Swiss National Councils (1996). *Division of authority between the Federal Assembly and the Federal Council.* BBl: 485.
Haldemann, T. (1997). *New Public Budgeting.* In: H. Schmid & T. Slembeck (Eds), *Finanz- und Wirtschaftspolitik in Theorie und Praxis* (pp. 117–146). Berne/Stuttgart/Vienna; Paul Haupt.
Jones, L. R., & Thompson, F. (1999). Public Management: Institutional Renewal for the 21st Century. Stamford, CT: JAI-Elsevier.
Kickert, W. (1999). New Public Management in Zwitserland (unpublished; in Dutch).
Mastronardi, P. (1995). *Staatsrecht und Verwaltungsorganisation. Reflexionen am Beispiel des New Public Managements.* In: AJP 12/95:1550 *et. seq.*
Mastronardi, P. (1998). New Public Management im Kontext unserer Staatsordnung. In: P. Mastronardi & K. Schedler (Eds), *New Public Management in Staat und Recht* (pp. 47–119). Berne/Stuttgart/Vienna: Paul Haupt.
Schedler, K. (1997). Legitimization as granted by the client. In: L. R. Jones, K. Schedler & S. W. Wade (Eds), *International Perspectives on the New Public Management* (pp. 145–168). Greenwich: JAI.
Swiss Federal Council (1996). *Performance Contract for the Swiss Meteorological Institution,* 1997–1999.Federal Council resolution of 6th November.
Swiss Federal Ministry for Internal Affairs (1997). *Report on the business management of the Swiss Meteorological Institute.* Berne, Switzerland.

25. CONSTRUCTING THE IMAGE OF ACCOUNTABILITY IN DANISH PUBLIC SECTOR REFORM

Lotte Jensen

INTRODUCTION

This chapter explores the question why a relatively "healthy" governance system like Denmark embarks on and continually develops NPM inspired public sector reforms. Expanding Roberts' categorization of problems as "simple", "complex" and "wicked", the chapter interprets Hood's paradox of the "malade imaginaire" as "solution driven problems" in strong economies.

It is argued that accountability problems pervade western democracies, but that accountability itself remains a contested concept. NPM provides a battery of fiscal accountability solutions that frame the understanding of the nature of late modern governance problems and enhance the position of actors who are able to develop, institutionalize and legitimize fiscal accountability mechanisms as the most overarching and fundamental in a democratic governance system. The past 20 years of Danish public sector reform illustrate how the Danish Ministry of Finance has succeeded with normatively constructing and institutionally underpinning fiscal accountability as a prime source of democratic accountability and by the same token enhance its position in the continual governance game in the Danish polity.

Learning from International Public Management Reform, Volume 11B, pages 479–497.
2001 by Elsevier Science Ltd.
ISBN: 0-7623-0760-9

PUBLIC SECTOR REFORM IN DENMARK – WHOSE PROJECT?

In his keynote speech at the International Public Management Network conference in Sydney (Hood, 2000), Hood addressed three apparent paradoxes in the way NPM inspired reforms have or have not proliferated in the western world. One of those paradoxes was termed the "malade imaginaire" paradox: it seemed to be the "healthiest" patients (countries) who had visited the NPM hospital most eagerly and taken the doctors prescriptions most seriously. This apparent paradox was, along with two others, explained by type of "public service bargain" (PBS) between politicians and senior public servants. When politicians anticipated a better bargain (lower agency or uncertainty costs – or alternatively an increase in the senior bureaucrats ' commitment to politicians' policy programs) they would *ceteris paribus* opt for reform strategies even in administratively "healthy" systems. In the introduction to the lecture Hood made the point that:

> In a fuller analysis the preferences of public servants over bureaucratic structures and control systems would need to be given equal attention since attempts at bureau shaping or resistance to more rigorous control frameworks seem to be common in the politics of public-service managerialism (Hood, 2000: 15; see also Dunleavy, 1991).

This point is well taken for the case of Danish public sector reform. In Denmark, administrative politics is hardly seen as high politics. In fact – as Christensen (1994) points out – it is hard to sustain political interest in the matter over any longer period of time. Also, the assumption of macho politicians able and keen to steer the public sector should be treated as a hypothesis rather than a fact. It is therefore worthwhile exploring some alternative reasons as to why Denmark, which belongs to the countries that were "relatively honest and effective" in the first place has been "first in line" (Hood, 2000: 19) with and continues to develop administrative reforms inspired by prescriptions from the NPM drawer. First, however, it is useful to clarify what is meant by NPM in this context.

What is Meant by NPM?

It has been widely recognized that NPM is an umbrella label or indeed a 'shopping basket' (Pollitt, 1995) containing a variety of public sector reform elements so diverse that academics have been tempted to conclude that if NPM is everything – maybe it is nothing, and as a minimum the expression of NPM is so dependent of national governmental traditions and administrative cultures that it is pointless to talk about a general global phenomenon (Rhodes, 1999).

However, varied as it may be, a "reform agenda" discursively underpinned by the OECD has floated around and lent inspiration and conceptualization to national reform movements in the western world (Naschold, 1995). The NPM agenda is summarized by Pollitt (1995: 134) as: Cost cutting, dis-aggregation, decentralization, purchaser-provider splits, introduction of markets or quasi markets, performance measurement, performance related pay and increased service quality. Although Denmark can never be accused of being excessive, the Danish reform "basket" contains elements of – at least – attempts to:

(1) Decrease public involvement (corporatization of public enterprises, sale of state assets and contracting out) and spending (continual attempts to modernize budget systems)
(2) Restructure the public sector more principal-agent oriented manners (budget frame steering, agency contracts, individual contracts and enterprise accounts)
(3) Introduce performance measurement at both individual and institutional levels to reassure effective use of public funds, e.g. bench marking, enterprise accounts, knowledge accounts, performance related pay systems. (For a comprehensive account of public sector reform trends, see: Greve & Jensen, 1999; see also Jones & Thompson, 1999).

In this chapter, what is referred to as "NPM-inspired reforms" will cover items 2 and 3 in the list above – reform initiatives that aim at enhanced economic steering capacity and enhanced efficiency. The current situation in Denmark is summarized broadly by the permanent secretary of the Ministry of Finance:

> In the eighties we established capable economic steering mechanisms. The nineties became the decade where 'target- and performance' -steering was put on track. The task for the coming decade is to get still more employees in still larger parts of the public sector to make sense of target- and performance steering (Eldrup, 1999: 32).

It is hence safe to conclude that although Denmark has been nowhere near as radical as for example New Zealand, Britain or Victoria a battery of NPM inspired concepts have been employed and continue to be developed and articulated.

PROBLEMS SEEKING SOLUTIONS – SOLUTIONS LOOKING FOR PROBLEMS?

Hood (2000) points out that the Scandinavian countries were amongst "the first in line" when it comes to NPM inspired reform, in spite of the fact that they are all relatively efficient and honest. In the terminology Denmark can therefore be seen as a case of "malade imaginaire". Why is this so? What problems do those reform solutions address?

Roberts, in her presentation at the Sydney conference (see Roberts in this volume) distinguished between three types of "problems" depending on whether the problem definition and the solution were contested. Defined problems with defined solutions were termed "simple problems"; defined problems with contested solutions were termed "complex problems" and, finally, the delicate situation where both problem definition and solution were contested was termed "wicked problems". Following the political scientist predilection for two-by-two tables, we miss a fourth category, namely the situation with a defined solution, but where the problem definition is not obvious or recognized: "Consider, for example solution-driven problem solving. Although there seems to be ample evidence that when performance fail to meet aspirations, institutions search for new solutions, changes often seem to be driven less by problems than by solutions." (March & Olsen, 1989: 62) In this vein we can term the fourth category of problems "solution driven" to capture the situation where stake holders in given solutions look for opportunities to define problems to attach them to. The types of problems are shown in Table 25.1.

This observation introduces another possible interpretation of the 'malade imaginaire' paradox. Public sector reforms are political interventions that create winners and losers, enhance the power of some players and weaken the power of others. It is therefore a continual battlefield in its own right. It should be considered that certain elements of the NPM inspired reform agenda (solutions) may have strong national stake holders, not *only* (albeit also) because they may improve public sector performance, legitimacy and accountability. But *also* because their employment enhances their power position in the total system in the same go.

Consequently, political-administrative systems are not only "susceptible" (as Hood expressed it) to reform "pressures" from the international advocacy coalition of the OECD. Systems may as well be "inhabited" by actors who see a point in actively adopting certain reform solutions for a variety of reasons, one of which can be that those solutions contribute to defining the public sector

Table 25.1.   Types of Problems

The Problem/solution mix	Defined Problem	Contested Problem
Defined Solution	1. Simple	4. Solution-driven
Contested Solution	2. Complex	3. Wicked

Sources: Roberts (2000), March and Olsen (1989)

problem we face in a way that favors their interests. I argue that this is among the things that the Danish Ministry of Finance has successfully managed to do. We will now turn to the issue of defining "the public sector problem".

DEFINING "THE PUBLIC SECTOR PROBLEM"

"By the mid-1980s, it became clear that there was a remarkable degree of consensus among the political leadership of various countries about what was wrong about the civil service." (Peters & Savoie, 1994: 419) The macho version of this consensus fell into Roberts' category of "simple", concerning both the boundaries and the structure of the public sector. The problems were viewed as:

(1) The public sector is too encompassing, and
(2) It builds on an input logic, which defeats rather than exploits the "natural" incentive structures within human beings.

Similarly, the solutions were viewed as

(1) Roll back the boundaries of the public sector, and
(2) Reshape its internal mechanisms in accordance with the utility maximizing animals that inhabit it.

Simplicity has its appeal and the reforms of Victoria (Hughes & O'Neill, 2000) and New Zealand (Boston et al., 1996) to varying degrees illustrate that this is not just a caricature, but live guidelines for administrative reform. Certainly, for the Danish case, the reform initiatives in the early 1980s were prompted by considerable economic deficits, as expressed by the minister of Finance in a famous TV speech in 1979:

> Some people say that we are driving at the edge of the abyss. We're not, but we're heading towards it . . . and when I talk about the abyss, I refer to a situation where – directly or indirectly – our economic policy becomes dictated form elsewhere (Østergaard, 1998: 292).

The overspending problem was easily defined. "Solutions" – that is reform programs – had to address that problem. In year 2000, we are envisaging a different situation: "A key element in the medium term strategy continues to be maintaining a significant public sector surplus" (Ministry of Finance, 2000: 1). What used to be the simple problem is no longer so. However, as we shall see, solutions that address economic steering problems continually multiply and proliferate.

Over the past decade 'simplicity' in Roberts' sense has blurred somewhat even in the most rigorous reform experiments. For example, it is uncertain what the reform effects are, if indeed they can be measured. (Boston, 2000; Gregory, 2000) Countries that adopt a more pragmatic stance towards reform have come up with a variety of different solutions, so there is no longer such a thing as "the best country." (Wolf, 2000a) Also, it is no surprise that administrative reform has its opponents and deprived groups will always try to combat and change the reform agenda (Hughes & O'Neill, 2000). In sum, there have been widespread controversies both in academia and practice about the transplantation of the compelling simplicity of economic theory to the politico-administrative domain.

Al Gore's neat catch phrase of "a government that works better and costs less" (Gore, 1993) has come to mean something much more indeterminate because one thing is cost cutting but what does "work better" entail? The public sector "problem" has begun to seem not only "complex" in Roberts' terminology, but even "wicked" as interpretations of the nature of the actual governance problems multiply. An influential strand in Public Administration (See for example Rhodes, 1997; Kooiman, 1993) has highlighted the fact that public sector organizations are increasingly complex systems that link interdependent organized actors within and across national boundaries, policy areas and public, private and voluntary sectors. The central governance systems are seen as "hollowed out" (Weller, Bakvis & Rhodes, 1997) because competence is given over to supranational bodies (in Europe, notably the EU) or devolved to de-central entities, be it the local authorities, state agencies, state owned or voluntary bodies. Democratic decisions thus "explode" into confetti as they are made in a multitude of forums, and yet those forums "implode" and become difficult to access and overview. (Pedersen, 1994). In such complex systems, there is no *one* "command bunker" from where commands are hierarchically sprinkled out over a deferring environment. Some authors refer to this as "the center-less society" others as "polycentrism" (Andersen, 1995: 91). Societal governance is a multi-actor, multi-level game in which actors must define themselves, the problems and the solutions together in ever permuting coalitions to accommodate and try to partly shape and steer the social, technical and physical environment (Mayntz, 1997; Kooiman,1997; Dunsire,1997). Late modern governance thus may be viewed as a "wicked" activity.

There is a considerable gap between this "wickedness" and the general increasing human aspirations to control (Mayntz, 1997: 12), as well as the quest for accountability built into the parliamentary chain of governance that normatively frames western democracies:

> We can all probably agree that our societies are no longer characterized by simple and transparent structures. And we all realize that modern political and administrative

institutions are extremely complex. At the same time, however, most of us subscribe to the classical principles of political institution building (Wolf, 1999: 1).

The gap has two distinct, but simultaneous consequences. First, it poses new challenges to any actor who aspires to control others. As fixed hierarchies erode, power becomes less a matter of position, more a matter of successful game playing. (Jensen, 2000).

Second, the gap mentally accentuates the urge to make the world "steerable", to hold somebody to account for the multiple decisions that form our lives. There is a pressure to get to grips with development in society. Public sector reform is a continual contribution to the reassurance of faith in modern democratic systems based on human agency, will and choice: "Efforts at administrative reform, like other political efforts, express – and thereby confirm – a fundamental confidence in the possibility of directing and controlling human existence, or, more specifically, the government" (March & Olsen, 1989: 91). It is an attempt to give the parliamentary chain of governance more than just symbolic meaning by institutionalizing structures through which it – against all odds – makes sense to place responsibility on the shoulders of actors who are held accountable by the electorate. Therefore, the normative thrust of much public sector reform is that the aim is to improve *accountability*:

> Trust in government is what makes democratic government effective. Without trust no living democracy and no real citizenship, without trust no compliance with rules and regulations and no willingness to pay taxes, without trust no civil service of high standards and without accountability no trust in government (Wolf, 1999: 3).

WHAT DOES ACCOUNTABILITY MEAN?

Unfortunately, accountability is in itself a contested concept, although is it possible to generically define it as the ". . . ability to answer and respond when asked" (Wolf: 1999: 9). How should the accountability problem be defined? Who is supposed to give accounts to whom and for what? Wolf (1999: 10) suggests five dimensions of accountability: *Legal:* To what extent do actors comply with normative prescriptions? *Fiscal:* To what extent do actors spend public money the most effective way? *Performance:* To what extent do actors meet the goals articulated by elected politicians and the expectations that they have created in the public domain? *Democratic:* To what extent do actors respect democratic values and enhance democratic processes? *Ethic:* To what extent do actors behave in accordance with codes of ethics and general moral standards?

Each dimension has distinct normative foundations and technical or/and political prerequisites. The normative argument for *legal accountability* is closely related to the Rechtsstaat tradition and the core idea that action taken must be grounded in legislation which must not be retrospective, must be generalizable and allow citizens to calculate the effects of their actions and their rights vis-à-vis the state. The technical prerequisites for legal accountability are that there are accurate regulations to follow. This prerequisite increasingly breaks down in late modern governance because of the need for flexibility, for judgments made by professionals and because the scope of regulation is now so far ranging that it is down right impossible to legally pin down all regulations (Rothstein, 1997).

Compared to legal accountability the normative argument for *fiscal accountability* lacks formality. It has to be continually constructed. That generally takes to forms. One is the need to "make ends meet" as in a normal household budget. The other is the prospect that it is possible to "make the cake bigger" so there is a bigger welfare slice to everybody. The technical prerequisites for budget control (necessary for the first reason) are multiple: information about spending patterns has to be available, interpretable and comparable. Structural economic politics (which is necessary for the second reason) require that political programs in a variety of sub-areas (e.g. tax, labor market, infrastructure) are fiscally "vetted" and coordinated. This – in turn – requires a political platform from where this can happen.

As for *political performance accountability* the whole idea that elected politicians are held accountable for policy outputs and civil service performance lies at the heart of the image of parliamentary democracy. The prerequisites for policy- and performance accountability is, in short, a compliant civil service, otherwise the parliamentary system looses its normative meaning and politicians are held accountable for actions and decisions they are not in control of. The technical prerequisite for performance accountability is that politicians know the details of policy implementation, the output of public sector organizations and the final outcome of their decisions.

The underlying normative idea of *democratic accountability* is that there is no democracy without democrats. Therefore it is a value in itself that a decision is made in accordance with democratic principles and includes citizens directly in the process. The technical prerequisite here is public access to knowledge about civil service behavior and decisions and institutional arrangements suitable for participation.

Ethical accountability implies that actions and decisions are accounted for with regards to general moral standards or specific professional ethics. Ethical standards are not fixed. Even though basic human rights are held high, the concrete interpretations hereof vary. The prerequisites for ethical accountability are, again, public access to knowledge about civil service behavior and decisions and relevant files and records.

Regarding the five dimensions suggested by Wolf, it is easily illustrated that the "accountability problem" is ill defined. What reasons for individual or organizational behavior will sate our quest for accountability? That rules were followed? That the money was spent most effectively? That it was in line with the overall policy goals? That it represented the views of the parties involved and stimulated their involvement and commitment? That it represented accepted and treasured values in society? What is it that we want decision-makers to account for?

One answer could be 'everything – but in its proper place'. In this 'advanced technician's dream' we are dealing with a multi-facetted, but coherent system of accountabilities where each dimension of accountability applies to different relations and are irrelevant for others. Why don't we then just call in a consulting firm and get them to design a coherent and transparent system where the appropriate form of accountability can be evoked under the appropriate conditions? This is because reality intervenes.

First, on the daily political scene (notably in a multi party, minority-coalition government system like the Danish), anybody can be held accountable for almost anything anytime as questions can be raised, often unexpectedly in one or several dimensions. Different forms of accountability are evoked under different circumstances by different actors: the public, the press, the Parliament, the Ombudsman, the Audit Office, the minister or private companies/voluntary associations competing with public sector bodies in a context of outsourcing. As giving accounts is inherently related to legitimacy, what counts is not if a certain account is technically correct, what counts is if it persuades the right people at the right time. However, it is not possible to prepare for all instances and produce readymade documentation for everything – just in case.

Moreover, as outlined above – giving accounts in particular ways has specific technical prerequisites, need specific organization of information and institutionalization of accounting procedures in order to work. In order to judge if a decision was illegal, there needs to be legal documents, in order to judge if money was spent properly, there needs to be proper financial accounts and a standard of comparison etc. Developing accounting systems in practice is far from cost free. Therefore priorities become necessary. Finally, although there is no *necessary* conflict between the different dimensions of accountability it can easily be debated which one is the prime source of legitimacy and which ones are subordinate in case more than one can be evoked. (e.g. is it more important to treat refugees applying for asylum in an ethically defensible manner than it is to optimize the use of organizational resources – i.e. put the complicated cases in the bottom of the pile to meet the performance targets?). The preference for one dimension of accountability over others easily becomes a political game of its own.

In a situation where all dimensions of accountability can potentially be evoked; where attention is scarce but unpredictable; where development of accountability procedures, conventions and techniques must be prioritized and where there may be potential conflicts between the different dimensions of accountability, mobilizing attention and procedures around one solution to the accountability problem helps to grasp what is more and less important. (Lægreid & Roness, 1999). So, "(s)olutions and opportunities stimulate awareness of previously non-salient or unnoticed problems or preferences." (March & Olsen, 1989: 62) The solutions at hand help us to understand what the problem 'really' is. Hence, ". . . accounting does not represent reality – it creates it." (Pallot, 1999). Further,

> . . . although it is difficult to guess when an opportunity to attach a favorite solution to some problem will arise, a solution that is persistently available is likely to find an occasion . . . Any specific re-organization project is likely to fail, but persistent repetition of similar ideas and similar arguments over a relatively long period of time appears to make some difference. Bureaucratic reform seems to require long-run commitment, patience and perseverance (March & Olsen, 1989: 86).

Consequently, ". . . governance becomes less a matter of engineering than of gardening, less a matter of hunting than of gathering" (March & Olsen, 1989: 94). The conclusion is then, so far, first, that the accountability problem is likely to be defined in political games between actors with stakes in different perspectives on the public sector problems. Second, those actors who can master and organize a long-term commitment to certain solutions have the best chances of institutionalizing their preferred perspective. The question is then who keeps the "solution-pot" on the stove. As pointed out above, it goes for the Danish case that "reorganization efforts have difficulty in sustaining the attention of major political actors " (March & Olsen, 1989: 81). We, therefore, turn our attention to "the institutional gardener," i.e. the stake holders that, solidly, over a long time span create, broadcast and maintain specific types of accountability mechanisms – solutions – that subsequently help to frame our minds to discover and understand the basic nature of the governance problem.

THE HISTORICAL PROBLEM-SOLUTION CIRCUIT: THE ART OF KEEPING THE SOLUTION POT ON THE STOVE

The Ministry of Finance has historically been a heavy weight ministry both because it plays what Aaron Wildavsky characterized as the "guardian" role (see Kelly and Wanna in this volume), and because Finance ministers are traditionally forceful individuals with considerable influence in government. Institutionally and politically, the Ministry of Finance has generally found it self close to the political core arena. However, in the late 1970s – during the Social democratic government period, it lost terrain. The tension between a sound economy and low unemployment was solved in the favor of the latter. The prime minister's priorities went in the direction of the Minister of Labor, state debt was growing which led the minister of Finance to the above mentioned comments on "the abyss". The Ministry of Finance found itself in a "humiliatingly weak position" and the ministry was marked by "worry and frustration" about the economic development (Østergaard, 1998: 292–3). The problem was for the ministry two-faced. One face was the economic deficit the other was the organizational power decline. The strategy employed addressed both.

Despite frustration, the ministry, among other things, began to develop a new budget system, inspired by the PUMA project "The Capacity to Budget". The core ideas were frame budgets, – not line item budgets, effective incentive structures, simplifications and enhanced use of IT. "In and around the ministry of Finance there was a clear feeling that one was not dealing with a particularly Danish problem" (Østergaard, 1998: 312) By 1982 the government changed color and a coalition led by the Conservative party took office. Eventually, the seeds that were sown by the gardeners in the Ministry of Finance over the past couple of years got some ideological manure and were taken out in the open as 'the Modernization Program'. The Modernization Program was the first coherent administrative policy document (Østergaard, 1998: 314):

> The political agenda expressed a changing paradigm. It became legitimate and interesting to talk about contracting out, markets and privatization. In the ministry of Finance years of frustration followed by and new self-confidence bordering on 'Besserwissen'. The minister of Finance was also deputy Prime Minister and there was a feeling that anything the ministry ever wanted was now possible. (Østergaard, 1998: 313).

However, as with most other broad policy programs, administrative politics proved a short run failure. In spite of the big noise – the "publicity boosting" (*Administrativ Debat*, (2000), 1/87: 2), not a lot happened and the ideological hey-days came to an end quickly. Indeed, the government learnt the lesson that it was necessary to ". . . de-emphasize the political and ideological aspects of administrative reform." (March & Olsen 1989: 102) For example, privatization caught ideological fire to the extent that the Prime Minister responded to a privatization report from the minister of Finance by slipping it down his desk drawer with the comment that "I am now doing you, our political party and the country a huge favor" (Qvortrup, 1999). However, the Ministry of Finance continued to work on the ideas of the 'Modernization program' under shifting ideological labels. Consequently, many of the ideas launched back in the early 1980s during the Conservatives have been implemented by the Social democrats during the 1990s:

> In the summer of 1993 the ministry of Finance published a report "Reinterpreting the public sector". It was stressed that the quality of society and competition depended on a well-functioning public sector. The public sector was not the problem, but a part of the solution to the challenges facing Denmark. But the concrete initiatives for renewal of the public sector hardly differed from the previous activities (Østergaard, 1998: 354).

Some of the initiatives launched by the one government and carried out by the opposition encompass for example contract agencies (1992), enterprise accounting (1995), individualizing the pay system (1997) introducing performance contracts (1995) and selling out public assets (1994–1997).

The Conservative coalition government of the 1980s could be characterized by the Yorkshire expression of "all mouth and no trousers" as far as the NPM reforms were concerned, whereas the current Social democratic coalition government is characterized by a lot of action, but less ideological talk. This is not illogical. It is a case of short run failure – long run success (March and Olsen, 1989: 87) and not of a particular party ideological program, but of an organizational strategy, where gardeners tender, adjust and articulate ideas continually for a longer period of time. So, the preoccupation with economic steering that solved the problems in the first place now helps to define the new problems to deal with. In a public lecture in September 1999 the permanent secretary of the Ministry of Finance remarked that, "The ministry has had two political 'scoops' . . . one, when the Conservatives wanted to show they could steer the economy in 1982 and two, when the Social democrats wanted to prove they could do this better than the Conservatives in 1993." To deliver solutions to the initial problem of acute economic deficits, the Ministry of Finance has managed to institutionalize a point of view in the mechanics of public sector accountability that not only produces solutions, but also frames the interpretation of the problems. The problem is no longer to overcome severe deficits but to avoid future problems:

> The fiscal consolidation process has gradually increased the general government surplus to 3% of GDP in 1999. The main strategy behind the fiscal consolidation process has been to

use the improvement in the public sector surplus caused by the interaction between automatic stabilizers and structural reform to reduce government debt. On top of this some net fiscal tightening has taken place, in particular in recent years. This has put government debt on a downward trend, which is to be continued for a long period in order to prepare for the aging population. Reducing public debt and thus interest payments has top priority compared to cutting taxes or increasing expenditures (Danish Economy, 2000).

Thus, the nature of the problem that the Conservative government faced in the early 1980s has changed, and the current government prides itself of being in charge of the economy. Where this is indisputably good news, optimism also has its down sides seen from the ministry's point of view, since ". . . expenditure politics is impossible in Denmark, when everything goes too well." (Jensen, 2000: 47) The Ministry of Finance has a paradoxical interest in solving and re-inventing the economic 'public sector problem'. In attempt to solve the initial problem, accountability mechanisms were institutionalized that – in the second round – serves to frame the interpretations of the potential future problems that we must already treat as "real". Currently, the problem is constructed of three elements: the tax level, the demographic development and the state debt.

Compared with other OECD countries Denmark has generally high tax level directly and indirectly and a steep progression in the tax system. (Ministry of Finance, 1998: chapter 12). The tax base needs fundamental legitimacy. Lacking legitimacy in taxation leads to fiscal constraint. This lack of legitimacy is relatively easy to evoke politically. This is regularly done, if not by government, then by the opposition. On the other hand, the trust in government and the willingness to pay taxes is very high. (Ministry of Finance, 1999a: 24), so the constraint stemming from the tax burden has to be evoked. This is done by explicitly evoking the "taxpayer-identity" within the public by stating that the public sector is spending taxpayer money and, therefore, the public service has a duty to spend it most effectively (Ministry of Finance, 1999a).

Second, in the coming years Denmark will have less labor working and more children and elderly; fewer people will have to provide money for more. Rising service expectations in the public compounds this problem. The "new elderly" grew up in the welfare state and do not suffer from gratitude toward the public sector. This, in turn, creates pressure on public sector efficiency.

Third, the need to pay off debt will be a major burden on our children if not paid off now. Fiscal accountability here achieves a moral/ethical dimension, resembling environmentalism, e.g. as captured by graffiti observed on Webb Street in Wellington, New Zealand, "We did not inherit the world from our ancestors, we borrowed it from our children." This perspective makes us accountable beyond the current population, the current electorates and service users.

These future problem elements are already seen as "real" in the sense that solutions are designed to cope with them even better than we have already done. In one sense it is always possible to do better and this becomes and argument in its own right, because if we know how to do things more effectively, what is then the argument for not doing it? So mechanisms of fiscal accountability help us to grasp the problem: Because accounting for economic performance is possible we start to ask why people or organizations are not performing even better. Because comparative techniques are available, we start to ask why some are performing less efficiently than others are. And we want them to account for the difference.

HOW DOES THE INSTITUTIONALIZATION OF FISCAL ACCOUNTABILITY EMPOWER THE MINISTRY OF FINANCE?

Refering back to the point about late modern governance as permanently "wicked," the observation was made that in a system of increasing governance complexity, no *one* actor, individual or collective can rest in a position of power on the top of "the hierarchy" – because there is no *one* hierarchy:

> In the OECD world, the unilateral exercise of state authority is internally limited by the fragmentation of political power and by the success of the deregulation movement, and it is externally constrained by the rise of transnational economic and ecological interdependence, which, even in Western Europe, far exceeds the slow progress toward more effective supranational policy coordination (Scharpf, 1993:125).

Any actor, even the ones that are by convention and folk wisdom seen as most powerful, must continually re-install, re-invent, re-new their capacity to remain central in the game-traffic of late modern governance systems (Jensen, 2000). Different organization analysis have competing analytical points of departure (see for example Morgan, 1988), but the variety of interpretations is beyond the scope of this chapter. (See Jensen, 2000). I therefore follow the conventional assumption that most organizations find themselves as more or less open entities in an environment in which they seek to survive (Morgan, 1988: 72). In the case of Finance ministries, the theoretical point of organizational "survival" should not be taken too literally. It is unlikely to run a modern state without a Finance ministry. Finance ministries throughout the world vary in structure, competence, power, history and culture, but unlike many other ministries they don't suffer from an ever-present threat of being abandoned. However, their actual influence on the economic situation, the political scene and administrative system must continually be fought for. As the current minister of Finance expresses it in the foreword of the 150th anniversary publication (Østergaard, 1998: 4), "As long as the Danish state has existed, somebody has had keep the finances together. This has indisputably been done with varying success".

Although invariably seen as a prestigious "top ministry", the position of the Ministry of Finance is continually fought for – and regularly won – in recurring games with the environment. In a complex environment with no hierarchy set in stone, organizational "survival" entails continual management of relations to other actors. In these relations the Ministry of Finance strives to maximize influence on the relevant environment and minimize foreign influence on itself. Maximizing influence on the relevant environment can be done either by controlling the specific decisions in that environment or by deciding the premises on which decisions in the environment are reached or agreement between the Ministry of Finance itself and the other actors are made. Given the sheer scale of public sector activity, the amount of decisions made and the fluid interdependence of multiple relations, the first option is not permanently realistic or economic for any actor. As important as winning a game towards other actors in the sense of making them decide what you want them to decide, is the capacity to play the next game as well, preferably even better. Preserving and developing the gaming capacity becomes an important criterion for organizational "survival".

In this light public sector reforms may help the Ministry of Finance to create and institutionalize a set of overarching principles that other actors have to consult and comply with when they make all their individual decisions in a diversity of areas. If it succeeds it gets to play the role of 'the central bank' issuing the communal currency with which all actors must trade: "There are two general media of communication across ministries. One is legality – another is money". (Interview with a senior executive in the Ministry of Finance, January, 2000)

Reforms that build on fiscal accountability as a value and as institutionalized mechanisms enhance the position of the ministry of Finance ideologically, organizationally and politically. *Ideologically* they help to frame the mind of citizens and decision-makers that "first we look at the money, then we look at the rest." The ideological impact of public sector out of the Ministry of Finance has been a vigorously debated issue in the Danish academia and press over the past 2 to 3 years. Fiscal accountability is seen as, "becoming a mantra" because the whole of the public sector is absorbed in counting and accounting for their use of public funds and their own performance. (Jensen, 2000) The critics' assumption is summarized neatly by Gregory's (2000) catchphrase, "If it can't be counted, it does not count."

Organizationally, public sector reforms have enabled the ministry to "bureau shape" in Dunleavy's (1991) use of the term as it has off loaded numerous of its initial control functions to agencies or other institutions and institutionalized mechanisms by which the former controlled are now controlling themselves within broad budget frames for each ministry. The aim of this exercise was to get rid of "dead flesh" to get "closer to the political hurricane center" so, "there is a truth in the saying that small is beautiful." (Eldrup, 1994) The dictum of the functionalist architect, Mies van der Rohe: "less is more" seems to capture the organizational strategy of the ministry. Free from its "dead flesh" the "shaped bureau" is thus investing its organizational resources in broader structural/economical analysis (tax systems, pension systems, labor market, education systems) on the back of which it enables itself to substantially coordinate policy initiatives for the government as a whole. As stated by the Permanent Secretary of Finance, the idea is that the ministry of Finance is:

> (n)o longer waiting for the other ministries coming to us with their propositions. The ministry of Finance . . . must be able to predict problem areas and regularly take the first initiative, so that the Finance minister sets the scene . . . from being a brake block were are becoming the initiators (Østergaard,1998: 350).

This – in turn – means a substantial *political* empowerment of the ministry, not in the sense of controlling specific political decisions (although there are such examples), but more in the way of framing the political agenda. Whether, how and to what extent this is in itself a democratic problem is a separate debate beyond the scope of this chapter (See Jensen, 2000).

CONCLUSIONS

Complex, multilevel governance systems with many players are a fact of life in late modernity, a fact that only by a considerable stretch of imagination fits the normative idea of a transparently controllable bureaucracy, i.e. one that gives meaning to the parliamentary chain of governance. The gap between the need to control and an uncontrollable system is continually being bridged by institutionalizing different types of accountability that – by the same token – serve to enhance the position of certain players over others in a continual political-administrative power game.

The debate on NPM-inspired public sector reforms tends to separate into two distinct debate communities: a normative community, where it is debated whether reforms are "good" or not, and a technical one where it is debated whether reforms are "smart" or not. It is argued that we get reforms because they represent better values (such as legitimacy, accountability, parsimony, etc.) or because they enable "getting the job done" in a technically smarter way. We should, however, not jump to the conclusion that the reason why we get the reforms is that they are "better" or "smarter". We should consider that the reasons given for reforms are relevant, but not preemptive; we should see public sector reforms through the spectacles of Nietzsche's (1987: 77) observation that:

> . . . the cause of origin of a thing and its eventual utility, its actual employment and place in a system of purpose lie worlds apart; whatever exists, having somehow come into being, is again and again reinterpreted to new ends, taken over, transformed, and redirected by some power superior to it.

We should, therefore, also look at how public sector reforms are adopted or rejected, reinterpreted or accommodated to political strategies within the specific systems where they take place. The construction of fiscal accountability as a prime source of governmental legitimacy is highly in the interest of the Ministry of Finance, not only because good arguments can be brought to bear, and not only because it is always necessary to develop new steering techniques to control how public money is spent. Both the normative and the technical takes on the debate are relevant. But, it is also necessary to recognize that the normative plea for fiscal accountability as a cornerstone in democratic governance, and the preoccupation with institutionalizing economic steering techniques also place the Ministry of Finance in the center of the political game, and this position is always actively fought for in it own right.

REFERENCES

Administrativ Debat (2000). Interview med Søren Christensen, *1*(87), 2–4.

Andersen, N. Å. (1995). *Selvskabt Forvaltning.* København: Nyt fra Samfundsvidenskaberne.

Beck J. T., & Mouritzen, P. E. (1997). *Udgiftspolitik og Budgetlægning.* Viborg: Systime.

Boston, J., Martin, J., Pallott, J., & Walsh, P. (1996). *Public Management. The New Zealand Model.* Auckland: Oxford University Press.

Boston, J. (2000). The Challenge of Evaluating Systemic Change: The Case of Public Management Reform. Paper for the IPMN Conference, Sydney: 3.

Christensen. J. G. (1994). Efter Bogen. *Administrativ Debat*, 2(94), 1–2.

Danish Economy, The (2000). http://www.fm.dk/uk/pubuk/ /frmChapter01.htm

Dunleavy, P. (1991). Democracy, Bureaucracy and Public Choice. Economic Explanations in Political Science. New York: Harvester

Dunsire, A. (1997). Modes of Governance. In: J. Kooiman (Ed.), *Modern Governance – New Government-Society Interactions* (pp. 21–34). London: Sage.

Eldrup, A. (1994). Speech manuscript from the annual congregation of the Nordic Administrative Association (NAF).

Eldrup, A. (1999). Resultatkontrakter og Ledelse i Staten. In: *En ny tids ledelse* (pp. 19–35). Copenhagen: Ministry of Finance.

Flyvbjerg, B. (1991). *Rationalitet og Magt. København*. Akademisk: Forlag.

Gregory, R. (2000). Getting Better But Feeling Worse? Public Sector Reform in New Zealand. Paper for the IPMN Workshop, 10 March, Wellington: Victoria University of Wellington.

Greve, C., & Jensen, L. (1999). *Central Government Reforms and Best Practice: The Case of Denmark*. Wissenshcaftzentrum Berlin and University of Potsdam, Germany.

Hood, C. (2000). Paradoxes of Public Sector Managerialism. Old Public Management and Public Service Bargains. Paper presented at the IPMN Conference, Sydney, 4 March.

Hughes, O., & O'Neill, D. (2000). The Limits Of New Public Management: Reflections On The Kennett 'Revolution' in Victoria. Paper for the IPMN Conference, Sydney 5 March.

Knudsen, T. (1997). Politiceres/Policieres Centraladministrationen? Inaugural lecture manuscript, Institute of Political Science, University of Copenhagen.

Jensen, L. (2000). Finansministeriet. In: T. Knudsen (Ed.), *Regering og Centraladministration*. Århus: Systime.

Kooiman, J. (1997). Governance and Governability: Using Complexity, Dynamics and Diversity. In: J. Kooiman (Ed.), *Modern Governance – New Government-Society Interactions* (pp. 35–50). London: Sage.

Lægreid, P., & Roness, P. (1999). Administrative Reform as Organized Attention. In: *Organizing Political Institutions. Essays for Johan P. Olsen* (pp. 301–331). Oslo: Scandinavian University Press.

March, J., & Olsen, J. P. (1989). *Rediscovering Institutions. The Organizational Basis of Politics*. New York: The Free Press.

Mayntz, R. (1997). Governing Failures and the Problem of Governability: Some Comments on a Theoretical Paradigm. In: J. Kooiman (Ed.), *Modern Governance – New Government-Society Interactions (pp. 9–20). London: Sage*.

Ministry of Finance (1996). *Budgetredegørelse*, Copenhagen.

Ministry of Finance (1998). *International Benchmarking of Denmark*, Copenhagen

Ministry of Finance (1999a). *En offentlig sektor på borgernes præmisser*, Copenhagen

Ministry of Finance (1999b). *Budgetredegørelse*. Copenhagen.

Ministry of Finance (2000). *The Danish Economy. Medium Term Economic Survey*, Copenhagen.

Morgan, G. (1988). *Images of Organization*. London: Sage.

Naschold, F. (1995). *The Modernization of the Public Sector in Europe: A Comparative Perspective on Scandinavia*. Helsinki: Ministry of Labour.

Nietzsche, F. (1987). *On the Genealogy of Morals*. New York: Vintage Books.

Pallot, J. (1999). Presentation at Wissenschaftzentrum Berlin, 20th September.

Pedersen, O. K. (1994). *Demokratiets lette Tilstand*. København: Spektrum.

Peters, G. B., & Savoie, D. (1994). Civil Service Reform: Misdiagnosing the patient. *Public Administration Review, 54*(5), 418–425.

Peters, B. G. (1999). Institutional Theory and Administrative Reform,. In: *Organizing Political Institutions. Essays for Johan P. Olsen* (pp. 331–357). Oslo: Scandinavian University Press.

Pollitt, C. (1995). Justification by Works or by Faith? Evaluating the New Public Management. *Evaluation, 2*, 133–153.

Qvortrup, M. (1999). Interview with Previous Finance Minister Henning Dyremose. IS THIS A PUBLICATION? IF SO, PROVIDE REQUIRED INFORMATION.

Rhodes, R. A. W. (1997). *Understanding Governance*. Buckingham: Open University Press.

Rhodes, R. A. W. (1999). Comparing Public Sector Reform in Britain and Denmark. *Scandinavian Political Studies, 22*(4), 341–370.

Roberts, N. (2000). Coping with Wicked Problems. Paper for the IPMN Conference, Sydney, 5 March.

Rothstein, B. (1997). Demokrati, Implementering og Legitimitet. In: B. Rothstein (Ed.), *Politik Som Organisation. Forvaltningsteoriens Grundproblemer.* Stockholm: SNS Forlag.

Scharpf, F. (1993). Coordination in Hierarchies and Networks. In: F. Scharpf (Ed.), *Games In Hierarchies And Networks: Analytical And Empirical Approaches To The Study Of Governance Institutions* (pp. 125–167). Frankfurt am Main: Campus.

Wanna, J., & Kelly, J. (1999). Once More into Surplus: Reforming Expenditure Management in Australia and Canada. *International Public Management Journal, 2*(1), 127–146.

Weller, P., Rhodes, R. A. W., & Bakvis, H. (1997). *The Hollow Crown. Countervailing Trends in the Core Executive.* London: Macmillan.

Wolf, A. (1999). Acountability in Public Administration: General Conference Report. Sunningdale Conference on Accountability, United Kingdom, 12–15 July.

Wolf, A. (2000). Trends and Themes in Public Management Today. Keynote Speech Manuscript for PUMA, Portugal, 9 May.

Østergaard, H. H. H. (1998). At Tjene og Forme Den Nye Tid. Copenhagen: Ministry of Finance.

26. MANAGEMENT CONTROL REFORM WITHIN A RESPONSIBILITY FRAMEWORK IN THE U.S. AND ITALY

L. R. Jones and Riccardo Mussari

INTRODUCTION

This chapter focuses primarily on efforts to improve management control systems and processes, including budgeting, accounting and reporting, within the context of a responsibility framework in the United States and Italy. In public management theory, management control is assumed to be a process for motivating and inspiring people to perform more effectively in the context of working in complex organizations (Jones & Thompson, 1999: 130). From this perspective, management control attempts to motivate public managers to serve the policies and purposes of the organizations to which they belong, and to meet the demands and preferences of the citizens and customers they serve. Additionally, management control is a means for correcting performance problems and including inefficient use of resources. Among the initiatives taken to implement management control systems and to control costs is the design of new or reconfigured budgeting, accounting and reporting systems. One approach to redesign is responsibility budgeting and accounting, now widely practiced internationally.

The discipline of management control is based on the presumption that managerial and all behavior of individuals working in organizations is largely

Learning from International Public Management Reform, Volume 11B, pages 499–529.
Copyright © 2001 by Elsevier Science Ltd.
All rights of reproduction in any form reserved.
ISBN: 0-7623-0760-9

self-interested, also a tenet in economics. Goals of management control include increased efficiency and effectiveness, and minimization of agency costs. Three interconnected techniques typically are employed in implementing improved management control systems: (a) performance measurement using internal accounting systems, (b) incentives and disincentives intended to reward or deter particular types of behavior and performance, and (c) methodologies that delineate decision making authority and responsibility within the organization. Bureaucratic organizations define decision authority and responsibility by separating decision control from decision management through the creation of hierarchical structure.

RESPONSIBILITY BUDGETING AND ACCOUNTING

A primary instrument of management control is responsibility budgeting and accounting, implemented through performance related techniques incorporated into budget formulation and execution. Typically, under responsibility budget formulation, organizational policies are formulated into performance and financial targets that correspond to the domains of administrative units and managers (Anthony & Young, 1996: 19). In responsibility budget execution, operations are monitored and managers are evaluated, rewarded and sanctioned relative to achievement of performance targets. Responsibility budgeting thus involves organizational engineering in addition to cost accounting (Jones & Thompson, 1999).

Under responsibility budgeting, work is monitored and controlled in administrative units according to mission, function and performance targets. Administrative units and their relationships to each other constitute the administrative structure of the organization. Responsibility budgeting requires decision authority and performance responsibility resulting from decisions to be allocated to individuals who manage units within the organization. This allocation constitutes the organization's responsibility structure, i.e. where responsibility for mission accomplishment is centered. Responsibility budgeting also requires an accounting system to record, measure and evaluate performance information including inputs, costs, transfers, activities, and outputs. This system constitutes the spine of the organization's control structure. Under a fully developed responsibility budgeting and accounting system, administrative units and responsibility centers are coterminous and fully aligned with the organization's accounting and control structure, since the information it provides can be used to coordinate unit activities as well as to influence the decisions of responsibility center managers.

Several basic rules govern organizational design in the responsibility structure formulation. First, organizational strategy should determine structure. Strategy means the pattern of purposes and policies that defines the organization and its missions and that positions it relative to its environment. Single mission organizations thus are intended to be organized along functional lines; multi-mission organizations should be organized along mission lines; multi-mission, multifunction organizations may be organized along mission lines or in matrix structure. Where a matrix organization is large enough to justify an extensive division of labor, responsibility centers should be designated as either mission or support centers, with the latter linked to the former by a system of internal markets and transfer prices.

A second rule is that the organization should be as decentralized as possible. Management theory supports the thesis that the effectiveness of large, complex organizations improves when authority and responsibility are delegated out through the organization (Jones & Thompson, 1999).

Thirdly, authority should not be delegated arbitrarily. Decentralization requires prior clarification of the purpose or function of each administrative unit and responsibility center, procedures for setting objectives and for monitoring and rewarding performance, and an accounting structure that links each responsibility and service center to the goals of the organization as a whole.

As explained elsewhere (Thompson & Jones, 1986),[1] the most significant difference between traditional government budgets and responsibility budgets is that government budgets tend to be highly detailed spending or resource acquisition plans that generally are required to be executed as they are approved. In contrast, operating budgets in the private sector are usually spare of detail, often consisting of no more than a summary of financial targets. One of the originators of responsibility budgeting, General Motors' Alfred P. Sloan, believed that it was inappropriate and unnecessary for top managers at the corporate level to know much about the details of responsibility center operations (Womack, Jones & Roos, 1990: 40–1). If the reporting showed that performance was poor, that meant it was time to induce change in responsibility center management. Responsibility center managers showing consistently good results were promoted and rewarded in other ways.

This notion that responsibility centers should be managed objectively by the numbers from a small corporate headquarters reflects the effort to delegate authority and responsibility outward into the organization. As explained in the OECD report, *Budgeting for Results: Perspectives on Public Expenditure Management* (1995), delegation of authority means giving agency managers the maximum feasible authority needed to make their units productive or, in the alternative, subjecting them to a minimum of constraints. Hence, delegation of authority requires operating budgets to be stripped to the minimum needed to motivate and inspire subordinates. Under responsibility budgeting, the ideal operating budget for each administrative unit/responsibility center contains only one or several performance targets related to corresponding costs to achieve the performance indicated. (e.g. a production quota, a unit cost standard, or a profit or return on investment target). It is very important that targets be stated in monetary terms, both to compare the performance of unlike responsibility centers and to keep higher levels of administration away from operating details, thereby discouraging them from "micromanaging" the decisions of responsibility center managers.

Types Of Responsibility Centers

Responsibility centers are classified according to two dimensions:

• The integration dimension – i.e. the relationship between responsibility center objectives and the overall purposes and policies of the organization;
• The decentralization dimension – i.e. the amount of authority delegated to responsibility managers, measured in terms of their discretion to acquire and use assets.

On the first dimension, a responsibility center can be either a mission center or a support center, as noted. The output of a mission center contributes directly to organizational objectives or purpose. The output of a support center is an input to another responsibility center in the organization, either another support center or a mission center. On the decentralization dimension, accountants distinguish among four types of responsibility centers based on the authority delegated to responsibility managers to acquire and use assets (Anthony & Young, 1995).[2] Discretionary expense centers, the governmental norm, are found at one extreme and profit and investment centers at the other. A support center may be either an expense center or a profit center. If the latter, its profit is the differences between its costs and its 'revenue' from 'selling' its services to other responsibility centers. Both profit and investment centers are usually free to make decisions about issues that are significant to the long run performance of the organization.

Discretionary expense centers incur costs. The difference between them and other kinds of responsibility centers is that their managers have no independent authority to acquire assets. Each acquisition must be authorized by the manager's superiors. In the U.S. federal government system, under detailed line item budgets, acquisitions must be authorized by Congress and signed into law by the President. However, all discretionary expense center managers are accountable for compliance with an asset acquisition plan (an expense budget), whether or not written into law. Once acquisitions have been authorized, discretionary expense center managers are usually given considerable latitude in their deployment and use. In some cases, expense center managers are evaluated in terms of the number and type of activities performed by their center. Where each of the activities performed by the center earns revenue or is assigned notational revenue (transfer price) by the organization's controller, these centers are referred to as *revenue centers*. University development offices are frequently revenue centers. Managerial accountants generally believe that unit should be set up as a discretionary expense center only where there is no satisfactory way to match its expenses to final cost objects, as in an accounting department.

In a cost center, the manager is held responsible for producing a stated quantity and/or quality of output at the lowest feasible cost. Someone else within the organization determines the output of a cost center – usually including various quality attributes, especially delivery schedules. Cost center managers are usually free to acquire short term assets (those that are wholly consumed within a performance measurement cycle), to hire temporary or contract personnel, and to manage inventories. In a standard cost center, output levels are determined by requests from other responsibility centers and the manager's budget for each performance measurement cycle may be determined by multiplying actual output by standard cost per unit. Performance is measured against this figure – the difference between actual costs and the standard. In a quasi-profit center, performance is measured by the difference between the notational revenue earned by the center and its costs.

In profit centers, managers are responsible for both revenues and costs. Profit is the difference between revenue and cost. Thus, profit center managers are evaluated in terms of both the revenues their centers earn and the costs they incur. In addition to the authority to acquire short term assets, to hire temporary or contract personnel, and to manage inventories, profit center managers are usually given the authority to make long term hires, set salary and promotion schedules (subject to organization wide standards), organize their units, and acquire long lived assets costing less than some specified amount. In investment centers, managers are responsible for both profit and the assets used in generating the profit. Thus, an investment center adds more to a manager's scope of responsibility than does a profit center, just as a profit center involves more than a cost center. Investment center managers in the private sector are typically evaluated in terms of return on assets (ROA), i.e. the ratio of profit to assets employed, where the former is expressed as a percentage of the latter. In recent years many have turned to economic value added (EVA), net operating "profit" less an appropriate capital charge, which is a dollar amount rather than a ratio. This change has clear implications for public sector budgeting and accounting to move toward performance reporting, measurement and management, as argued in this chapter.

Finally, under responsibility budgeting, support centers provide services or intermediate goods to other responsibility centers and charge a notational or an actual transfer price, e.g. in the U.S. defense department (see Jones & Thompson, 1999: insert pages). Reasons for transfer pricing within organizations include determining the costs of services provided by one unit to another, establishing and manipulating incentives, and measuring the performance of responsibility centers. Transfer pricing also reveals the internal costs of service decentralization where costs are born to transfer decision rights to others within an organization. When one sub-unit transfers goods, knowledge, skills, etc. to another, both units calculate the cost as a means of revealing their liquid and tangible asset use internally and in external provision of service.

RESPONSIBILITY STRUCTURE REFORM IN THE U.S. GOVERNMENT

The federal government of the U.S. accounts for purchases, outlays, and obligations, but it still does not account for consumption.[3] Full value from the application of responsibility budgeting can be obtained only where government adopts a meaningful form of consumption or accrual accounting (measuring the cost of the assets actually consumed producing goods or services). Because the U.S. government does not account for resource consumption, its cost figures are necessarily statistical in nature (i.e. they are not tied to its basic debit and credit bookkeeping/accounting records). Without the discipline that debit and credit provides, these figures are likely to be satisfactory only for illustrative purposes or where a decision maker must make a specific decision and a cost model has been tailored to the decision maker's needs. Another aspect that contrasts current U.S. practice and responsibility budgeting and accounting is that the appropriations process does not employ a separate capital budget. Finally, the existing process segregates every operating cycle to fit the federal fiscal year. Under the fully applied responsibility budgeting and accounting concept, budgeting for operating expenses and capital asset acquisition is separated, and all budgeting is continuous across a multiple year period of time. However, in matrix or networked (versus hierarchical) organizations, the distinction between capital and operating budgets is less necessary, as is the distinction between cost estimation and cost measurement (Tani, 1995; Otley, Broadbent & Berry, 1995).

Responsibility budgeting and accounting has been implemented on a broad scale internationally, e.g. in the United Kingdom in 1982 and modified in 1988 (Pollitt, 1993; Lapsley, 1994), in Australia, Canada, Denmark, Finland, and Sweden. All of these nations have adopted responsibility budgeting and accounting in one form or another. No nation, however, moved as far or as fast with this reform as did New Zealand. Moreover, New Zealand's reformers explicitly recognized their debt to the framework of agency theory outlined at the beginning of this chapter (Boston et al., 1996).

Responsibility budgeting and accounting has been attempted in the United States and influenced reform in both the Bush Administration in the period 1988–1992 and the initiatives of the Clinton Administration from 1993 to 2000. Additionally, the content of both the Chief Financial Officers Act of 1990 (CFO Act) and Vice-President Gore's National Performance Review called for performance-oriented organizations and mission driven, results oriented budgets (Jones & McCaffery, 1992, 1997; OECD, 1995: 230). Further, in 1993 Congress passed the Government Performance and Results Act (GPRA) that requires experimentation with responsibility budgeting and accounting and reporting by all departments and agencies of the federal government under the supervision of the Office of Management and Budget and oversight committees of Congress. In particular, the Defense Management Report Initiatives under Bush and Secretary of Defense Dick Cheney, and the Gore NPR stimulated considerable effort at accounting and financial management reform in the U.S. Department of Defense. Clearly, greater progress was made under Bush (e.g. introduction of reimbursable transaction accounting and budgeting) than during the Clinton – Gore administration, but both successes and failures have resulted from these initiatives (Thompson & Jones, 1994, 1999). It is clear that government-wide progress has not been rapid. As with most large governments, the U.S. federal government has been slow to change (Jones & McCaffery, 1997; Jones & Thompson, 1999). The impetus to change presently emanates from a combination of the CFO Act and the GPRA (see Stewart elsewhere in this volume).

The CFO Act requires double-entry bookkeeping and accrual accounting, neither of which are standard practice in the U.S. federal government. To receive a clear audit report from the Inspectors General who perform CFO audits, these accounting changes need to be implemented in federal department and agency accounting systems. However, few federal agencies can comply with either the double-entry or accrual requirements, and there is resistance to investing to do so given that the federal budget and appropriation accounting are done primarily on a single entry and cash basis. Changes in federal appropriation law and congressional appropriation procedures, at minimum, appear to be required to push federal agencies further toward CFO Act compliance.

The GPRA requires strategic planning (SP) and development of performance measures, which has been implemented throughout the government, and linkage between SP and resource planning and budgets, which has been done with varying success. Further, GPRA invited agency experimentation with performance budgets on a voluntary basis, to be evaluated by Congress. To date, the results from these experiments have not persuaded Congress or the President's Office of Management and Budget (OMB) that broad application of performance budgeting, using an agency theory oriented contracting system of the type employed in New Zealand and elsewhere, is worth the effort. Agencies report that their own ability to plan and execute programs, and to justify budgets has been in some instances enhanced as a result of SP and performance measure development (as required by OMB). However, few agencies and no departments in total have the capacities in their accounting systems and procedures that permit accurate and reliable (or in some cases any) linkage between performance or results data and costs or budgets. Consequently, whether reporting costs related to organizational units, functions, accounts and sub-accounts or workload for the CFO Act, or cost performance (e.g. for results) for GPRA, there is little hope for broad-scale success in the medium term for most of the U.S. federal government.

There are additional explanations for this fact. The first is that many participants and observers of the U.S. expenditure process reject the notion that responsibility budgeting and accounting can be reconciled with the American legislative budgetary process. Some even assert that it can be practiced only by unitary governments under the Westminster model, although that claim seems to be contradicted by Swiss and Swedish examples of successful implementation (Schedler, 1995; Arwidi & Samuelson, 1993). While acknowledging that it would not be easy to reconcile responsibility budgeting and accounting with the American legislative process, we do not believe that they are necessarily incompatible (Thompson, 1994; Harr, 1989; Harr & Godfrey, 1991, 1992). If operating budgets were multiple year and funded on the base of what departments and agencies received in their previous year's base, which is how federal budgeting operates for the most part presently only on a one year cycle (Wildavsky, 1964; Wildavsky & Caiden, 2000), then budgets could be linked to whatever performance standards congressional appropriators (and authorizers) would prefer. Good performance would be rewarded and poor performance sanctioned – again, much as it is done presently. Departments and agencies would benefit from a more predictable revenue base, and presumably this stability would be reflected in better service to citizens, although this advantage cannot be predicted accurately.

Capital budgeting under responsibility budgeting would be separate from operating budgets, continuous and responsive to department needs and justification as per the current system. However, persuading members of congress to pass up opportunities for annual "pork rushes" to push pet projects in favor of a more stable, longer-term resource allocation methodology would not be easy, because it is through the annual budget that rewards are provided to loyal and, in some cases, needy constituents. Perhaps the Senate would be more likely to adopt multiple year appropriation because senators are elected for terms of six years, and are often reelected for several terms. On the other hand, members of the House of Representatives serve in two year terms, which means that they have much shorter time horizons within which to provide benefits to supporters. Clearly, multiple year budgeting would be a much harder sell in the House. Still, the reelection rate of members of the House is high, so there is moderate continuity in the business of the lower house of Congress. However, the high rate of reelection is in part attributable to the ability of representatives to demonstrate results from their election quickly. Of course, none of this mitigates against the use of performance measures in budgeting. It only affect incentives toward longer-term or continuous budgeting. And, obviously, little that Congress does with its budget process has anything to do with improving department and agency performance accounting, as demonstrated by the limited results achieved under the CFO Act.

Another, perhaps weaker, explanation for failure of responsibility budgeting and accounting to influence government accounting and budget practices in the United States significantly is that, unlike most other countries, America has large, well-organized associations of government accountants, auditors, budgeters, program analysts, and teachers of government accounting and budgeting. All of these groups have to varying degrees a vested interest in differentiating public from private practice, because that difference gives value to their expertise. Anyone inclined to doubt the significance of this explanation should look carefully at the politics of the Financial Accounting Standards Advisory Board (FASAB), responsible for developing accounting standards for the U.S. federal government, where accountant members did not understand the perspective of appropriation law and the budgetary process and those with experience with appropriations process were frustrated at having to confront a wide range of issues that seemed unresolvable unless appropriation law and procedures were modified, as noted.. The standards were completed in 1997, but their success is now under evaluation as departments and agencies attempt to implement the CFO Act, with mixed results. What agencies complain about most, in addition to the absence of financial support for implementation, are the inconsistencies between the standards and the capabilities of the accounting systems, data bases and procedures used by their agencies to perform required tasks in budget formulation and execution, i.e. the same things that irritated "budget-wise" members of FASAB during development of the standards.

RESPONSIBILITY STRUCTURE REFORM IN ITALY

The introduction of responsibility budgeting in Italian government is a recent phenomenon. This introduction is only a part, even if particularly important, of a larger process aimed at the modernization of all Italian government. Many sectors of Italian government have been reformed during the 1990s. The sectors generally considered more advanced in this process are local governments, and health service organizations. Central government was also interested in reforms that attempted to introduce New Public Management philosophy and the related managerial tools but, national government seems more resistant to change in comparison with other parts of Italian public administration. Since the aim of this chapter is examining responsibility budgeting in government, local government is the focus of this exploration on Italian practice. This choice is to the fact that, in the last six years, it has been the object of the most interesting reforms in Italian government. Initially, it must be clear that local government in Italy is not a homogenous and standardized phenomenon. Furthermore, the socio-economic status of our Italy is far from uniform and this is unavoidably reflected in the behavior of administrators and those administered, in the different parts of the country.

In addition to Provinces there are more than 8,000 municipalities, the greatest portion of which have very small numbers of inhabitants (in 1995 only 1325 Municipalities had more than 8,000 inhabitants). This implies that, in practice, a large majority of public entities do not have human and financial resources at their disposal which are capable of implementing a demanding process of reforms. However, the National Legislature has already changed the rules of the accounting and budgeting practice for the nation through laws passed in the early 1990s, and this is the sure sign that the process of modernization of government can no longer be prevented. In the Italian situation, and especially in the institutional context of local government, it is not necessary to use the adjective "new" in the sense that the mode that Italy is trying to change cannot be labeled presently as managerial. Any implementation with a public management orientation will be new. The aim of this portion of the chapter is to provide reflections on the relationship between autonomy, responsibility and the introduction of a new conception of public management and management control in Italy. The effort here is to verify whether, and to what extent, the conquest of autonomy and the assignment of responsibility for results can contribute to stimulating a new public sector managerial culture in Italy.

There is extensive literature in Italy that explains the reasons for the prevailing of bureaucratic and formalist culture in our public administration and the difference between the managerial culture and control (see for example Borgonovi, 1988; Borgonovi, 1991; Anselmi, 1993; Mussari, 1994). It is necessary to emphasize the significant role that the law has in Italy. The life of our national and local communities is ruled by an enormous number of norms (laws, decrees, legislative decrees, circulars, regulations, and so on), continuously renewed or updated, that oblige public administrators to be experts more in law than in management. Current reform of local governments is based on a significant number of laws and decrees and entails the updating of municipal statutes and regulations.

The overproduction of rules often generates strong contradictions between norms so that, sometimes, the behavior of public administrators differs according to the law they consider as prevailing. It is not accidental that the leaders of public organizations and a large majority of politicians have been educated in the disciplines of law or political science rather than public administration, management or business administration. In the 1990s, the evils of poor of no management control and poor choice of which laws to enforce and to ignore was made more evident by financial scandals and corruption (Tangentopoli) that shook the country. The fear of error and of the legal consequences of error has been so strong that many local and national public services have been virtually paralyzed or significantly decelerated, e.g. public works. Scandals have ended up reinforcing the traditional prevailing model in Italian public administration that is excessively bureaucratic and one of relatively arbitrary rule enforcement relative to political motives and expedience.

Management control systems in Italy are not based on a results orientation in terms of efficiency, effectiveness, quality, equity or other criteria, but on the stiff observance of highly defined rules – rules typically decided upon and written very far from local communities. This kind of control, generally labeled as legalistic and bureaucratic, is the expression of an administrative culture and of a general culture designed to prove the validity of predominating rules and models. So, the basic problem in Italy is not to overcome or to update a managerial model that is "old" in order to change it for a new and more effective one, but to introduce, de novo, a managerial orientation that does not have historical or cultural roots in Italian government.

Given this fact, the first question to be answered is why did the debate about the necessity for exchanging the bureaucratic model for a managerial model begin in Italy? The most fundamental answer is that the existing model no longer works. Secondly, the reasons for the development of pressure for transformation can be traced to the need to supply a reasonable, non-utopian reply to the signals emerging from the contemporary economic and social scenario. Redesign of local government and the manifest legislative rules of law demonstrates a will to re-establish stronger links between local governments and the administered community. This effort is an attempt to fill the gap which, over the decades, has been created between the capacity to fulfill social needs and the actual capacity of local authorities to respond to demand for better service. Local officials need to learn to heed these signals, to decode, and to interpret them in order to translate them into effective solutions. In fact, the crisis of local governments is widely verifiable by observing that the administered community is neither adequately served nor satisfied with service availability and quality.

For too long a time, local governments have been estranged from the Italian public, functioning in effect as quasi-closed systems providing services to politicians and government officials. Consequently, with a some exceptions, in Italy there is little match between the values upon which decisions and actions of local administrators (politicians and officials) are based and the values held by different local communities, i.e. the values of people, families, businesses that pay taxes and use public services and legitimate the existence of local government. This is the "government failure" portion of the demand for managerial reform. Other variables include an increase in the service expectations of local communities as a result of better education, ever growing municipal problems that require attention and more rapid replies to continually changing circumstances, a reborn faith in market mechanisms as a means to guarantee social equilibrium, a national crisis of public finance, the disappearance of traditional political parties, and changes in the electoral system.

Some of the consequences emerging from the variables noted above include:

(1) More affluent people turning to private services as an alternative to public services, i.e. public services are only for poor people;
(2) Difficulty for taxpayers to understand the relationship between taxes paid and the qualitative and quantitative level of the services offered;

(3) The progressive return to market mechanisms for a growing number of public services (health, education, etc.);
(4) The weakening of the institutional conditions that artificially guarantee the survival of local government organizations.

Local governments face the need to respond to a different articulation of the scale of needs that follows modification of the cultural characteristics of the community (Catturi, 1995: 21; see also Di Toro, 1993; Farneti, 1995). They must do so not only by varying the mix of products and the services rendered but by changing managerial objectives to coherently correspond to the evolution of the socio-economic scenario in which they operate. Given these reasons for change, Italian local governments will be successful only if the subjects who have the duty to run them (politicians and officials) promote new values: learning capacity, organizational flexibility, orientation to quality, centrality of the citizen-user-tax-payer in the economic processes, clear identification of goals, objectives, attribution of resources, responsibility for results and overall performance of the system.

Autonomy as a Necessary Condition for Responsibility

Metcalfe and Richards (Metcalfe & Richards, 1987, 217) state that management means taking responsibility for the performance of a system. There is a consensus among public management scholars (see for example Jones & Thompson, 1999) that autonomy is a precondition, necessary but not sufficient, for effective management. It is not feasible to judge managers responsible for the results of an organization, function or a service without having made them autonomous. This condition is summarized in the expression, "the right to manage." Yet, we should clarify some aspects of this view.

Is it possible to have autonomous management and a management responsible for the results inside a public organization that is not autonomous? If we look at the Italian historical experience we come up with a negative conclusion. When local governments are not autonomous, the agents they serve are not in the local community but the central government of Italy that guarantees organizational survival. Because of cultural hindrances and also to guarantee equal treatment between different provinces and regions, in this situation the law becomes the only rule by which to measure results.

Thus, the first step to be taken to arrive at a managerial orientation is full recognition of the autonomy of local governments. In this analysis we distinguish two types of autonomy: autonomy of local government, and autonomy inside local government.

Autonomy of Local Government

What does autonomy of local government mean? From who has local government to be autonomous? Autonomy means the possibility, capacity and will to make decisions, to direct decisions, resources and actions towards defined and proper objectives that reflect the values shared by the local community. Autonomy, then, means to have the freedom to make independent decisions and to establish strategic and operative objectives along with the ways to fulfill them. Autonomy also includes the capacity of survival without artificial intervention based upon economic and social evaluation made by the taxpayers and users of public goods and services. An organization is autonomous when its components are coordinated to allow – by means of their dynamism – the fulfillment of the aims for which it exists (on autonomy of Italian local government, see Zangrandi, 1994).

Local governments were declared autonomous in the Italian Constitution (Articles 5 and 128) but, up to the promulgation of new law in 1990, autonomy was essentially fictitious. The autonomy of Italian local government is a recent, but still not completely realized, convention. Since the 1970s the expansion of local government service responsibility in the areas of social welfare and education has been very rapid, but there has not been a corresponding expansion of the tax base or managerial competence. This disparity, coupled with the decision to centralize Italian tax collection, increased dependence on the central government and caused a crisis of results and, slowly, of legitimization. The gap between the cost of local services and the insufficient taxes raised locally has been filled by central government transfers. This has contributed to raising the Italian national debt and deficit. The acknowledgment of local government autonomy is, on the one hand, a late answer to a social embarrassment and, on the other hand, an attempt to reduce the financial burden caused by the centralized fiscal system. And, the absence of autonomy was not limited to tax or financial matters, as noted below.

Previous to the approval of reforms in the 1990s, the following conditions applied. Public finance was strongly centralized. The central government raised money from taxation and distributed money, year by year, directly or through another public entity (regional government for instance) to local governments to perform many public functions and services. However, only a very small part of disposable national resources that derived from local communities was returned. It is important to note that, in the past, resources were transferred according to several criteria (in particular past expenditure) but none of these reflected the capacity of local governments to economically satisfy the needs of local users. The quantity of transferred resources depended essentially on the political leverage and negotiation abilities of the local government lobby in Parliament and, above all, on the fiscal and financial situation of the Italian state more than on performance. And the capacity of local governments seemed to be dependent more on the money available than on the capacity for using it wisely.

The administration was regulated by several Consolidation Acts promulgated before or during the years of fascism, i.e. before the present Italian Constitution was approved in 1948. This meant that organization of services, the way of rendering them, and the functioning rules were centrally fixed and, essentially, the same for all local governments without regard for their specific characteristics. The Local Government Model was uniform and predetermined by the State. Budget, accounting and financial reporting were modeled on those of the State. The system was very traditional without accrual accounting or management accounting. This was consistent with the centralized model of the State. Accounting language had to be the same since the system was only used to allocate resources rather than according to the socio-economic effects of decisions. There was no a performance measurement system.

Auditing was internal and, in conformity with the law of 1934, the accounts of local governments were audited by three councilors chosen by the Municipal Council among those who were not members of the Town Executive Board. The role of the auditors consisted of verifying the "formal correctness" of decisions made by the Town Executive Board and the correspondence between values reported in the accounting books and the figures in the Statement of Accounts. Therefore, this consisted of only a legitimacy control without any regard for the results of local government activity. Moreover, even if in most cases the audit function was assigned to honest people this, unfortunately, did not determine professional competence in performing the job.

Since the spending power was in the hands of the Town Executive Board and not senior officials, politicians ended up managing without requisite competence and, in so doing, neglected the role of managers. The consequent want of coordination among the various functions of the local government organizations made it impossible to making anyone responsible for the results of programs and services. In turn, the relationship between planning, execution and performance could not be clearly specified and this caused a lack of feedback of information for managerial and political decision-making and reporting to citizens.

The process of New Public Management (NPM) oriented reform started in 1990 (Law n.142, of 8 June 1990) and other reform laws passed since have contributed to modifying the features described above. Two fundamental principles have been prominent since 1990:

(1) Financial autonomy of local governments was guaranteed based on the certainty of receiving their own and transferred resources;
(2) Local governments gained the power to levy new taxes. Local government finance remained a mixed type with the State continuing to finance local institutions by means of transfers.

The reform law stated that the State will continue to contribute to the financing of local services which are considered indispensable, the State assigns specific contributions to cope with exceptional situations; the State contributes to local government investment in financing public works of primary social and economic interest. All the other services that local governments wanted to render to their communities have to be financed by levying taxes or imposing prices at a level sufficient to recover the full incurred costs. New local taxes have been introduced (in particular a local property tax intended to constitute the central pivot for fiscal autonomy). Other taxes have been reformed and now local governments can issue bonds.

Since 1990, municipalities can be established to render social services, and each local government has its own Statute (Charter) and regulations. Old laws have been abrogated. Now, the State establishes only the main criteria, the principles, and it is the local government that has to establish its own rules. The Statute is a sort of constitution for local government where each authority can determine the norms which before were imposed by national law. It contains the fundamental norms for the entire organization, for the tasks of the entire single organs and their co-ordination. Municipalities are free to decide the number of staff needed to perform each function and service following principles of autonomy and economy, and according to criteria of profession-alism and responsibility. Particular emphasis has been placed by the Italian Legislature on public participation and encouragement of local government to engage in dialogue with their communities to take into consideration all public information in decision making processes.

The financial accounting system was modernized and managerial accounting was introduced. In 1995, a reform was approved that significantly changed the previous system. Below are summarized some of the most important innovations from this change.

(1) Guidance for programming activity is strongly reinforced and the fiscal authorization function is designated to a multi-annual budget;
(2) The classification of expenditure in the budget is now less detailed than in the past to enhance the intelligibility of the document and reduce the necessity to update the budget too often during the fiscal year;
(3) The cash budget was abrogated;

(4) The operative budget was introduced, aimed at making officials responsible for results of the organizational units (services) they manage;
(5) A management control system is mandatory;
(6) Accrual accounting will be gradually implemented by local governments;
(7) Financial reporting has the obligation to prepare not only a financial accounting but also a reliable balance sheet and a profit and loss account.

Notwithstanding the necessity to guarantee formal and substantial uniformity to public accounts to allow their consolidation, the law gives local governments a certain degree of autonomy also in the accounting field, especially with regard to financial reporting. For instance, it is possible to add indicators of efficiency and effectiveness, to draw up a consolidated balance sheet, and to present a balance sheet at the beginning and at the end of the electoral mandate.

However, the real obstacle to overcome is not simply the production of this or other more sophisticated data but the understanding of their usefulness and, consequently, the will and capacity of communicating them. It is clear that the success of the reform will depend not only on the production of new accounting information, but also on the understanding that this effort is useful only if it produces effects. Since in the area of communication style each local government is widely autonomous, these organizations should be concerned with exploiting this opportunity.

What can be said for sure is that the old way of producing and communicating accounting data no longer will work (see Caperchione & Garlatti, 1994; Matteuzzi Mazzoni, 1983; Mulazzani, 1992; Puddu, 1984). The informative objectives, the quality and the quantity of public needs to be satisfied, the role of public organizations in the present scenario have definitively changed. But, above all, the interlocutors of local governments have changed: management control responsibility no longer resides with the Central Government but with the local communities. Importantly, the new accounting system has been implemented starting in 1999. And, unfortunately, there have been legislative interventions aimed at modifying some important aspects of the reform.

A new audit system also was introduced in 1990. The introduction of professional auditing is an attempt to satisfy the growing demand for transparency in the managing of public money and should act as a deterrent against impudent local administration. However, in addition to traditional financial auditing, the Board of Auditors, made up of three professional Auditors, must evaluate results achieved in terms of performance (efficiency, productivity and overall performance) so that the Council can judge managerial performance, and make political choices using economic information which, before the reform, was practically non-existent (on the need for accounting to relate economic information, see Stewart, 1986, 1988; Giovannelli,1995; Mussari and Scalera, 1994).

The Board of Auditors, in conformity with the law, the Statute, and the regulations of the municipality, must:

(2) Ensure that funds have been spent in accordance with what was approved in the budget and verify the formal correctness of the decisions made by the Town Executive Board;
(2) Cooperate with the Town Council in its function of control and policy;
(3) Prepare a report, enclosed with the statement of accounts, in which it expresses remarks and proposals aiming to achieve greater efficiency, productivity and overall performance.

Considerable importance is now attributed to the auditors' duty to express substantiated judgement on the clarity, coherence and reliability of the budget and relative projects and programs. The auditors are bound to suggest to the Council all measures necessary to guarantee a credible framework. In turn, the Council is required to carry out all such measures or to adequately substantiate any lack of compliance with the auditing body. Thus, the Board of Auditors becomes, in addition to its traditional role, a kind of consultant directly connected to the supreme decision makers of the organization, the Council, in the performance of its functions of management control and policy (Marchi, 1997; Mussari, 1997; Persiani, 1996).

Autonomy Inside Local Government

The apparent achievement of greater local government autonomy can be judged a necessary but not sufficient condition for improved management control of local government. We must address the question: autonomy from whom? In this circumstance the answer is far more complex since it presupposes a clarification of the meaning of management of local government. If it is really necessary to identify specific subjects in order to give them the qualification of public managers, probably we should admit that this term refers to public officials who are irresponsible for local services rather than to elected representatives. This would mean looking at local government managers in the strict sense. If we accept this limitation, the answer to the previous question (autonomy from whom?) is autonomy from politicians.

Without entering into political detail that is not important for our analysis, it is evident that a primary goal of the National Legislator was to permit municipalities and citizens to regain the decision power that in the past was largely held by long-standing political parties that have been involved in scandals related to widespread corruption. Thus, the mayor is no longer chosen by the majority parties but is elected in open elections. Further, the mayor is no longer the "hostage" of the Town Council, given direct by the citizens on the basis of a detailed program that, during the electoral campaign, must be communicated and in which candidates have to compete against each other for office.

With these and other political changes, public managers are given latitude to focus more succinctly on the administrative activities that occur within government agencies. Instead of emphasizing the political considerations that permeate the policy process and pervade the external relations of government organizations, public management is primarily concerned with the policy implementation. On the contrary, if we were to refer to local government management as a process, without any specific interest in identifying the managers of local government, then we cannot limit the responsibility for management only to those predominantly involved in administrative functions.

Management, therefore, is a process, the starting point for strategic choice of priority among purposes and the best means of achieving them (Borgonovi, 1988: 133). This process of strategic decision-making defines the way in which a number of tasks, inherent in management, are to be interpreted, together with the conditions that are essential for these tasks to be delivered effectively. These processes of management are, moreover, always located within and have to respond to a particular institutional and environmental context. Management is not just an executive process separate from policy making: effective public management requires strong links between policy-making and implementation. In the real world, there is no clear division between management and politics.

However we have to recognize that a similar approach demands a maturity of political class that cannot be easily verified in Italy especially given the disappearance of some traditional political parties. Yet, if we agree with the broader definition of local government management (management as a process that involves both the politicians and officials responsible for services), management autonomy should be referenced to the whole organization and, consequently, autonomy should be from central government, and responsibility for results should be with respect to the administered community and citizen users of local services.

On the other hand, we cannot overlook the fact that within any public organization it is necessary to establish roles, competencies and consequent responsibilities to avoid overlapping confusion. We cannot overlook that the absence of clear delineation of the roles of politicians, senior officials and staff is common and, after corruption, the most important reason for the crisis in Italian government. A qualifying element of the Italian reforms was the new distinction between politicians and officials responsibility for services. The solution offered by the National Legislature to solve the problem was to clearly establish and separate the tasks and the responsibilities of managers and politicians.

A rigid definition of roles and competencies will only work from a theoretical point of view since the solution ignores that local government is, first of all, an organization, a system in which the parts have to communicate and cooperate to achieve goals and objectives. It would be naive not to take into consideration the fact that public organizations will have try hard to find practical solutions to ensure harmonious coordination between the political and the managerial.

Given these crucial considerations, according to the law, managers must now:

(1) Manage offices and services according to the criteria and the norms established in the Statute and regulations of the municipality;
(3) Perform all the tasks, including the adoption of acts to bind the administration to other entities, which the State law and the local Statute do not reserve specifically to other organs of the municipality.

The approval of the accounting reform introduced important innovations. Each year, following the approval of the municipal budget by the Council that is following the decision on the amount of funds that can be spent for each program, function and service, the executive board assigns an operative budget to each manager responsible for a service.

In this document, the short-term objectives to be fulfilled, for each service, is known in advance (this should be consistent with those defined in the documents in which the programs are drawn up) and the financial, human and technical resources available during the next year. So, an important process of decentralization has been promoted, the consequences of which should be:

(1) The necessity for managers to have more specialized information and skills;
(2) The increase of managerial autonomy from the Town Executive Board in decision-making – it is important to note that in the future the spending power will be in the hands of managers and not Town Executive Board members;
(3) Increase of authority and prestige for managers.

The Town Executive Board is made up of the elected mayor and assessors (councilors) whose number is fixed by statute to link the maximum number relative to municipal population. The mayor gives each assessor a delegation for a specific sector of municipal administration. Then, whereas in the previous system the assessors were independent from the mayor, since they were appointed by the Town Council, under the new reform they are qualified by the law as appointees responsible to the mayor.

These norms entail a redistribution of decision power between political actors and managers of local governments. The clear identification of objectives and performance targets to be assigned to managers, along with the other variables mentioned in the previous paragraphs, signal a change for managers. They are also intended to impose widespread use of management techniques (including management accounting) indispensable for performing new tasks and making managers responsible for results.

Definition of the Management Control Structure

To clarify the definition of Italian local government management control and responsibility reform it is necessary to define the persons now to be held responsible for results. This, in turn, entails clarification of our conception of management. In this effort we limit our analysis to top public officials whom, according to the will of the legislature, are considered managers responsible for both internal and external services. The organizational structure of the municipality is articulated by services, grouped in functions, and each service becomes a responsibility center led by a manager responsible for the use of the resources assigned by the approval of the municipal budget. Three issues to be resolved in defining management control responsibilities and relationships are:

(1) Who demonstrates results and who has the right to make decisions based on results?
(2) How are the objectives set and what do we mean by results?
(3) What techniques should be used to demonstrate results?

Results Responsibility and Decision Rights
Under the new approach, local government managers are accountable to the Town Executive Board, and in particular to the mayor. The mayor, who is directly elected by local voters, has significant powers. The mayor appoints the members of the Town Executive Board, the representatives of the municipality

to public entities, and officials responsible for offices and services. In addition, the mayor attributes tasks including those for external cooperation. The power of appointing and, in some cases, of dismissing, gives the mayor the possibility to that programs introduced are operative. Decision power and responsibility for the results are now concentrated on more recognizable subjects than in the previous system. In particular, the mayor's power to appoint members of the Town Executive Board, the town managers, and the management of public entities related to the municipality, should create greater stability, cohesion and coherence in the actions of the government. Greater efficiency in the organization of the public services also should occur. Following the most recent reforms of 1998, officials responsible for services are essentially accountable to the mayor since they are appointed by him or her and because each year the Town Executive Board assigns to each manager the resources necessary for fulfilling the objectives for the following year by approving operating budgets.

Objective Setting and Definition of Results
Managers have the right to manage but the area of their responsibility has increased significantly. Since the power to spend is in their hands and no longer in those of politicians who only to approve budgets, the concept of responsibility has broadened considerably and now it includes not only formal and legal responsibility, but also the evaluation of results achieved in terms of economy, efficiency and effectiveness. This implies that it is no longer only the law that dictates the standards by which the performance of public officials is measured. In addition, new and more subjective evaluation criteria of managerial activity must be introduced. Separate from the technical implications of this necessity, it should be noted that an important consequence will be the change in the role of public officials (now public managers).

As noted, there should be a redistribution of power inside municipal organizations. In the past, public officials learned that correct behavior was judged by conformity to rules regardless of results and they tended to avoid the exercise of discretion because such an act could easily be deemed an infraction of law. Now, public managers should be able to be more innovative, experimental and, to some extent, prepared to take risks (Blease, Graham & Hays, 1986: 14; Hopwood, 1984: 171). Contrary to the past, there is no longer a pre-packaged answer dictated by the law, experience or political convenience. Instead, it is necessary, within the limits of the resources available, to make autonomous decisions and run the consequent risks to obtain the results desired by the mayor and Town Executive Board.

Techniques to Demonstrate Results

The tools for acquiring information on results achieved by officials responsible for services to evaluate performance are limited, even if not exclusively, to the area of accounting and Value for Money Auditing. Limiting our analysis to relations between managers and the mayor and Town Executive Board, the organizational structure should be divided up into responsibility centers, that is the services, and responsibility accounting should be the main tool to be used to measure managerial performance. Unfortunately, in this field Italian municipalities are only beginning to experiment. On one hand, there are cultural barriers to evaluation in the use of any technique in a context that has not considered efficiency and effectiveness as measurable or valuable. Secondly, in many municipalities there is a lack of financial resources and technical competence to define and measure results and to perform evaluation.

However, independent of the ability to introduce new systems of evaluation, the value placed on accounting and auditing information is bound to increase and the evaluative role will not be limited to the assessment of managerial performance but will also influence priorities, policy determination and decision-making (Borgonovi, 1991: 185–186). In this respect, if distribution of power within local governments changes, it is possible, paradoxically, politicians may pressure for the introduction of new techniques to control and evaluate managerial performance.

In coherence with these developments and in line with the precepts of national labor contracts, local governments are bound to evaluate the performance and duties of their managers. This evaluation is to be repeated yearly and is based on the principle of participatory evaluation. The task is entrusted to an internal evaluation organ whose formation was provided for in law in 1993 and modified in 1999. Therefore, the data collected not only makes it possible to remunerate managers with variable salaries, but also puts the mayor and the Town Executive Board in a better position to make decisions concerning reconfirmation of the posts assigned to executives in the organizational units.

There are two separate but interconnected remuneration parameters (role and performance) of the evaluation system. Role evaluation requires setting relative values for each professional role through the adoption of globally accepted criteria. Role evaluation is in no way dependent on judgement of the individual assigned to the role under evaluation. It takes into consideration the necessary qualifications, responsibilities, organizational relations and complexities associated with each role.

Performance evaluation is based on the extent to which specific objectives or pre-defined performance goals are attained. This requires detailed and timely programming of operations. Performance evaluation also involves analysis of any organizational practices considered relevant for a particular role. As such, it takes into consideration aspects including capacity to motivate, leading and evaluating collaborators, promotion of technological innovation and efforts to integrate the organization and its services (Busco & Riccaboni, 1999).

The National Legislature seems to have indicated in the reforms that level of citizen satisfaction should influence policy and organizational decisions of the officials responsible for services. If so, it is in the interest of the elected representatives and, in particular, of the mayor to control the activity of the managers. This is because they have no managerial powers themselves, but instead have powers to control managers. However, politicians have to answer to the local citizens on the quality, effectiveness, equity and efficiency of local public services. Consequently, they should be come more results oriented in their demands on managers.

This underlines the direct relationship between the local government elected by the people and the demonstrated ability to manage public resources. If political consensus is increasingly influenced by the quality and quantity of the services supplied, as well as by ideological factors including values, common interests and opportunity (Catturi, 1995: 20; Costa, 1991: 362), then political consensus will be determined more by the ability of local government officials to do the things for which they are elected or appointed. As the values and expectations of society create pressure in terms of quantitative and qualitative increase of things to be done, the ability to find the best combination in the use of scarce resources becomes a more visible and important element for acquiring and maintaining political consensus. The following appears to be occurring in Italian municipal politics:

(1) Because the number of people who believe political promises appears to be decreasing, as citizens are tired and disappointed by inconsequential ideologies, politicians may be obliged to make their messages and promises more personal and results-oriented to reach all citizens and not just specific political interest groups;

(2) The form used to communicate the political message generally no longer is holding citizen attention because it has been perceived to be inadequate in content. Therefore, the form of the message may change, i.e. more toward a results-orientation;

(3) Many citizens now have a better-informed view of public services and the responsibilities of government. They have learned to decode political messages and refuse to receive stimuli passively;

(4) The increasingly presence of reference values favoring more effective government among citizens and citizen groups, and increased public awareness of financial and managerial scandal and fraud in government makes difficult all relationships of trust in the polity. What citizens expect from public officials and managers is shifting to clarity on objectives, honesty about results, and more effective delivery of services.

Obstacles to Italian Reform of Management Control

There are two primary obstacles to the transformation of administrative culture taking place in Italy:

(1) Part of the political class does not willingly accept losing its spending power and, consequently, its ability to influence the effects of public activity. Therefore, some use all means possible to restrain the increased autonomy of public officials;

(2) Many public officials realize that they do not have the technical know-how for carrying out their assigned functions autonomously and are afraid of being judged on the basis of results that they are not certain can be achieved. They are tempted to maintain the status-quo to avoid being judged on the basis of parameters completely alien to their culture and, above all, that they are unable to control. For some, it seems better not to be autonomous and not to have the worries that come with responsibility. Furthermore, this tendency has been increased by a lack of trust in auditors. From the beginning of the reform period in the late 1990s, auditors did not seem to favor the change in management control to greater autonomy and voiced concern over what they perceived as an absence of effective managerial incentive to stimulate good performance.

CONCLUSIONS

There are distinct similarities between the management control reform initiatives in the United States and Italy. In both nations, the driving force for implementation of responsibility budgeting and accounting is the legislative branch – the U.S. Congress and the Italian Parliament. In both systems, increased emphasis on delegation of responsibility to managers is a cornerstone of reform and has met with political resistance. In both cases, there is an absence of capacity, in managerial preparation and in the capabilities of accounting systems, to fully implement the changes authorized. In both nations, traditional budget process roles are or will be changed with implementation of reform. In both nations there are technical problems in learning how to define and use performance and results measures to influence decision making. In both the U.S. and Italy, parts of the administrative culture prefer a safer existence with less rather than more responsibility for results. In both nations, the legislative branch has directed elected officials and managers to become more responsive to citizen demands and preferences and to report financial and service results with increased transparency.

The changes in management control in the U.S. and Italy detailed in this chapter provide some new perspectives on the implementation of responsibility budgeting and accounting. Although problems faced in these nations have been encountered and resolved to varying degrees in a number of other nations, the means for overcoming barriers to implementation tend to be particular to each nation to a great extent in our view (Jones & Thompson, 1999: 169–171). However, some generalizations seem to be evident.

It is now apparent, as not before, that responsibility budgeting and accounting systems restrict the upward flow of operating information within public organizations – making decentralization and autonomy a necessity and not just an ideal. Responsibility budgeting is essentially a form of internal and external contracting wherein costs of services to meet mission requirements are negotiated. Decision units are then held accountable for execution of their budgets to fulfill the commitments agreed to in the negotiation process. Responsibility budgeting employs explicit contracting between units for the provision of specific services or goods in exchange for financial resources for operation and capital acquisition necessary for production. The distinguishing elements of responsibility budgeting are: (a) the evaluation of units and managers relative to the contract obligations they accept, (b) the use of financial and performance measures to reward accomplishment and sanction failure, and (c) identification and attribution of financial success or failure entirely to managerial decisions and employee performance.

From the perspective of the environments within which public organizations function, in networks and alliances people work in information rich environments. However, access to information is not necessarily symmetrical (equally available to all). Decentralization works in such an environment only where elected officials (e.g. in Congress and the Italian Parliament, and municipal politicians in Italian local governments) and senior management in public organizations attend to executive decision and management functions including strategic planning, organizing, staffing, investment in the intellectual and cultural development of the organization, but refrain from attempts to manage the conduct of operations. This takes practice, self-restraint and a willingness on the part of legislators and senior management to accept the risks of being held accountable by citizens for results that are, to a great extent, determined by public managers and those working for them providing services distanced and insulated by management control delegation from the immediate influence of politics. This is asking a lot, as noted.

For this reason, it may make sense for governments to experiment with responsibility budgeting using pilot projects of the type authorized under the Government Performance and Results Act rather than going quickly to other, more radical, new modes of organization and control. The same may be recommended for Italian local governments. Slow adaptation probably is better that attempts to convert to the new model quickly. One impediment that makes slower transformation almost a necessity is the fact that few managers in government to whom greater delegation of authority and responsibility is to be given under reform have had much experience with this approach, or with New Public Management-oriented devolution of decision making, or decentralization generally. Further, few elected officials and senior executives outside of New Zealand and other nations that have implemented reforms of this nature have much experience with self-restraint and management by results.

The incentives and disincentives implicit in NPM-oriented responsibility budgeting, accounting and management control must be experienced and evaluated in individual institutional contexts. The methods outlined in this chapter must be adapted to the levels of budgeting, accounting and management control sophistication of each organization and level of government in which they are applied. In addition, attention must be paid to the fit of this approach to the political culture of the organization and government in which it is implemented. Leadership and politics make a significant difference in overcoming bureaucratic resistance to change (Jones & McCaffery, 1997; Johansen, Jones & Thompson, 1997; Reschanthaler & Thompson, 1997). Experience with NPM in other nations teaches that slow, careful and incremental implementation, in contrast to rapid and comprehensive change, is more likely to lead to success in attempts to reform public sector budgeting, accounting and management control practices. Provision of empirical support for this observation is not the purpose of this chapter. However, this has been found to be the case in the United Kingdom, Australia, New Zealand, Sweden, other European nations and elsewhere (Jones & Schedler, 1997). Why should we expect it to be any different for the U.S. and Italy?

NOTES

1. This article also distinguished between ex ante and ex post controls, a notion central to the exposition of budgeting for results.
2. This section is based on Anthony and Young, 1995.

3. One proposal to fix this problem is with a set of accounts similar to fund accounting systems used by non-profits. Departments would have one or more capital asset acquisition accounts. Outlays to acquire capital assets would be charged to these accounts that would hold assets but perform no operations. Assets held would be rented/leased to programs; each program account would show the cost of using assets, and rent would net out of department totals. Under this system, programs would buy their support competitively from their own department, other departments, or the private sector. Program outlays would approximate program costs and could be related to program outputs (see Rodriguez, 1996).

ACKNOWLEDGMENTS

The authors wish to acknowledge contributions to this chapter from work coauthored with Fred Thompson, Goudy Professor of Public Management and Policy, Atkinson Graduate School of Management, Willamette University. Assistance to this research also was provided by the Space and Naval Warfare Systems Command through sponsorship of the Wagner Chair in Public Management at the Naval Postgraduate School, and by the Navy Special Warfare Command.

REFERENCES

Anselmi, L. (1993). L'azienda "Comune" Dopo La Legge, 142(90). Rimini, Maggioli.

Anthony, R. (1962). New Frontiers in Defense Financial Management. The Federal Accountant. XI, June: 13–32.

Anthony, R., & Young, D. (1995). Management Control in Nonprofit Organizations (5th ed.). Homewood, IL: Richard D. Irwin.

Arwidi, O., & Samuelson, L. A. (1993). The Development of Budgetary Control in Sweden: A Research Note. Management Accounting Research, 4(2), 93–107.

Bailey, M. J. (1967). Defense Decentralization through Internal Prices. In: S. Enke (Ed.), Defense Management. Englewood Cliffs NJ: Prentice-Hall.

Borgonovi, E. (1984). La Pubblica Amministrazione Come Sistema Di Aziende Composte. In: E. Borgonovi (a cura di), Introduzione All'economia Delle Amministrazioni Pubbliche. Milano, Giuffre.

Borgonovi, E. (1988). Il Controllo Di Gestione Nella Pubblica Amministrazione. In: G. Farneti, M. Marchi, A. M. Luciano (a cura di), Nuove Prospettive Per Le Aziende Municipalizzate: Revisione Contabile E Gestionale. Rimini, Maggioli.

Borgonovi, E. (1991). La logica aziendale per realizzare l'autonomia istituzionale. In: Azienda Pubblica, IV(2), 179–199.

Bruggeman, W. (1995). The Impact of Technological Change on Management Accounting. Management Accounting Research, 6(3), 241–252.

Bunce, P., Fraser, R., & Woodcock, L. (1995). Advanced Budgeting: A Journey to Advanced Management Systems. Management Accounting Research, 6(3), 253–265.

Busco, C., & Riccaboni, A. (1999). Dal Controllo Di Gestione All'incentivazione Manageriale. Padova, CEDAM.

Catturi, G. (1994). *La Teoria Dei Flussi E Degli Stocks Ed Il "Sistema Dei Valori" D'impresa.* Padova, CEDAM.

Catturi, G. (1995). Comunicazione ed informazione aziendale: riflessioni, Quaderni di Strategia e Politica Aziendale, n° 4, Facoltà di Economia, Viterbo, Università degli Studi della Tuscia.

Chandler, A. (1962). *Strategy and Structure: Chapters in the History of Industrial Enterprise.* Cambridge, MA: MIT Press.

Costa, G. (1991). La Legge 142 E Lo Sviluppo Di Una Nuova Cultura Organizzativa Negli Enti Locali. In: *Azienda Pubblica, IV*(3), 359–384.

Demski, J., & Feltham, G. (1976). *Cost Determination.* Ames: Iowa State University Press.

Di Toro, P. (1993). *L'etica Nella Gestione D'impresa.* Padova, CEDAM. Software Engineering: Made to Measure (1993). *The Economist,* January 23: 79. A Guide to Better Buying (1986). *The Economist,* October 18: 71.

Evans, P. B., & Wurster, T. S. (1997). Strategy and the New Economics of Information. *Harvard Business Review,* (September–October), 71–82.

Farneti, G. (1995). Introduzione All'economia Dell'azienda Pubblica. Torino, Giappichelli.

Garlatti, A., & Caperchione, E. (1994). Trends in Evolution of Accounting Systems in Italian Local Governments. In: E. Buschor & K. Schedler (Eds), *Perspectives on Performance Measurement and Public Sector Accounting.* Berne, Paul Haupt.

Giovannelli, L. (1995). *La Comunicazione Economica Nell'ente Locale.* Milano, Giuffrè.

Graham, C. B. Jr., & Hays, S. W. (1986). *Managing the Public Organization.* Washington, D.C., CQ Press.

Hammer, M. (1990). Reengineering Work: Don't Automate, Obliterate. *Harvard Business Review,* (July–August), 104–112.

Harr, D. J. (1989). Productive Unit Resourcing: A Business Perspective on Government Financial Management. *Government Accountants Journal,* (Summer), 51–57

Harr, D. J., & Godfrey, J. T. (1992). The Total Unit Cost Approach to Government Financial Management. *Government Accountants Journal,* (Winter), 15–24.

Harr, D. J. (1990). How Activity Accounting Works in Government. *Management Accounting, 72,* 36–40.

Harr, D. J., & Godfrey, J. T. (1991). *Private Sector Financial Performance Measures and Their Applicability to Government Operations,* Montvale, NJ: National Association of Accountants.

Hay, D. (1992). Public Sector Accounting in New Zealand: An Update and a Clarification. *Financial Accountability & Management, 8*(1), 1–6.

Hopwood, A. (1984). Accounting and the Pursuit of Efficiency. In: A. Hopwood and C. Tomkins (Eds), *Issues in Public Sector Accounting* (pp. 167–187). Oxford: Philip Allan.

Horngren, C. T., & Foster, G. (1991). *Cost Accounting: A Managerial Emphasis* (7th ed.). Englewood Cliffs, New Jersey: Prentice-Hall.

Hyde, A. (1997). Cornerstones of Quality: Special Section. *Government Executive, 29*(7), 47–68.

Jones, L. R., & McCaffery, J. L. (1992). Federal Financial Management Reform and the Chief Financial Officers Act. *Public Budgeting and Finance, 12*(4), 75–86.

Jones, L. R., & McCaffery, J. L. (1997). Implementing the Chief Financial Officers Act and the Government Performance and Results Act in the Federal Government. *Public Budgeting and Finance, 17*(1), 35–55.

Jones, L. R., & Schedler, K. (Eds) (1997). *International Perspectives on the New Public Management.* Stamford, CT: JAI Press.

Jones, L. R., & Thompson, F. (1999). *Public Management: Institutional Renewal for the 21st Century*. Stamford, CT: JAI-Elsevier Press.

Johansen, C., Jones, L. R., & Thompson, F. (1997). Management and Control of Budget Execution. In: R. Golembiewski & J. Rabin (Eds), *Public Budgeting and Finance* (4th ed., pp. 577–584). New York: Marcel Dekker.

Juola, P. (1993). Unit Cost Resourcing: A Conceptual Framework for Financial Management. *Navy Comptroller, 3*(3), 42–48.

Kaplan, R. S. (1992). In Defense of Activity-Based Cost Management. *Management Accounting*, (November), 58–63.

Keohoe, J. W., Dodson, R., Reeve, R., & Plato, G. (1995). *Activity-Based Management in Government*. Washington, D.C., Coopers & Lybrand.

Lapsley, I. (1994). Responsibility Accounting Revived? Market Reforms and Budgetary Control. *Management Accounting Research, 5*(3,4), 337–352.

Masten, S. E. (1984). The Organization of Production. *The Journal of Law and Economics, 27*(4), 403–417.

Masten, S. E., Meehan, J. W., & Snyder, E. A. (1991). The Costs of Organization. *The Journal of Law, Economics, and Organization, 7*(1), 1–25.

Matteuzzi M. L. (1983). *Il Sistema Dei Bilanci Elle Aziende Pubbliche Territoriali*. Bologna, CLUEB.

Metcalfe, L., & Richards, S. (1987). *Improving Public Management*. London. Sage.

Milgrom, P., & Roberts, J. (1992). *Economics, Organization, and Management*. Englewood Cliffs, NJ: Prentice Hall.

Monteverde, K., & Teece, D. J. (1982). Appropriable Rents and Quasi-Vertical Integration. *The Journal of Law and Economics, 25*(3), 403–418.

Mulazzani, M. (1992). *Ragioneria Pubblica* (terza edizione). Padova, CEDAM.

Mussari, R. (1994). *Il Management Delle Aziende Pubbliche – Profili Teorici*. Padova, CEDAM.

Mussari, R. (1997). La Revisione Gestionale Negli Enti Locali. In: L. M. Marchi (a cura di), *La Revisione Nelle Aziende Pubbliche*.Rimini, Maggioli.

Mussari, R., & Scalera, G. (1994). The Communication of Economic Information: A Problem to be Solved for a Really Accountable Local Government. *Quaderni di Economia delle aziende e delle amministrazioni pubbliche*, n. 3, Facoltà di Economia, Viterbo, Università della Tuscia di Viterbo.

OECD (1995). *Budgeting for Results: Perspectives on Public Expenditure Management*. Paris: Organization for Economic Co-operation and Development.

Office of Technology Assessment (1984). *Computerized Manufacturing Automation: Employment, Education, and the Workplace*. Washington, D.C.: Government Printing Office.

Otley, D. (1994). Management Control in Contemporary Organizations: Towards a Wider Framework. *Management Accounting Research, 5*(3,4), 289–299.

Otley, D., Broadbent, J., & Berry, A. (1995). Research in Management Control: An Overview of its Development. *British Journal of Management, 6*, 31–44.

Persiani, N. (1996). *Revisione Contabile E Gestionale Negli Enti Locali*. Padova, CEDAM.

Pollitt, C. (1993). *Managerialism and the Public Services: Cuts or Cultural Change in the 1990s?* (2nd ed.). Cambridge, MA: Basil Blackwell.

Puddu, L. (1984). *Il Bilancio Degli Enti Locali*. Milano, Giuffrè.

Quinn, J. B. (1992). *Intelligent Enterprise: A Knowledge and Service Based Paradigm for Industry*. New York: Free Press.

Reschenthaler, G. B., & Thompson, F. (1996). The Information Revolution and the New Public Management. *Journal of Public Administration Research and Theory, 6*(1), 125–144.

Roberts, A. (1997). Performance Based Organozations: Assessing the Gore Plan. *Public Administration Review, 57*(6), 465–481.

Rodriquez, J. F. (1996). Budgetary Accounting and Accrual Accounting: Reconciling the Differences. Unpublished paper, presented at the Association for Budgeting and Financial Management Annual Conference. Washington D. C., October 29.

Rosenberg, N., & Birdsall, L. E. (1986). *How the West Grew Rich: The Economic Transformation of the Industrial World*. New York: Basic Books.

Schedler, K. (1995). *Ansatze einer Wirkungsorientirten Verwaltungsfuhrung: Von der Idee des New Public Managements (NPM), zum konkreten Gestaltungsmodell*. Bern: Verlag Paul Haupt.

Scott, G., Bushnell, P., & Sallee, N. (1990). Reform of the Core Public Sector: The New Zealand Experience. *Public Sector, 13*(3), 11–24.

Shank, J. K., & Govindarajan, V. (1988). Transaction-Based Costing for the Complex Product Line: A Field Study. *Journal of Cost Management*, 31–38.

Shank, J. K., & Govindarajan, V. (1998). The Perils of Cost Allocation Based on Production Volumes. *Accounting Horizons, 2*(4), 71–79

Simons, R. (1995). *Levers of Control: How Managers Use Innovative Control Systems to Drive Strategic Renewal*. Boston: Harvard Business School Press.

Stewart, J. (1986). *The New Management of Local Government*. London, Allen&Unwin.

Stewart, J. (1988). *Understanding the Management of Local Government*. London, Longman.

Stewart, R., & Stewart, J. (1994). *Management for the Public Domain*. New York: St. Martin's Press.

Tani, T. (1995). Interactive Control in Target Cost Management. *Management Accounting Research, 6*(4), 401–414.

Thompson, F. (1997). Capital Budgeting. In: *International Encyclopedia of Public Policy and Administration*. Boulder, CO: Westview Press.

Thompson, F. (1995). Business Strategy and The Boyd Cycle. *Journal of Contingencies and Crisis Management, 3*(2), 81–90.

Thompson, F. (1994). Mission-Driven, Results-Oriented Budgeting: Financial Administration and the New Public Management. *Public Budgeting & Finance, 14*(3), 90–105.

Thompson, F., & Jones, L. R. (1994). Reinventing the Pentagon: How the New Public Management Can Promote Institutional Renewal. San Francisco: Jossey-Bass Publishers.

Thompson, F., & Jones, L. R. (1986). Controllership in the Public Sector. *Journal of Policy Analysis and Management, 5*(3), 547–571.

Whittington, G. (1988). The Usefulness of Accounting Data in Measuring the Economic Performance of Firms. *Journal of Accounting & Public Policy, 7*(4), 261–266.

Williamson, O. E. (1988). Corporate Finance and Corporate Governance. *Journal of Finance, 43*(3), 567–591.

Williamson, O. E. (1985). *The Economic Institutions of Capitalism*. New York: The Free Press.

Zangrandi, A. (1994). *Autonomia Ed Economicità Nelle Aziende Pubbliche*. Milano, Giuffrè.

27. SPECIFYING OUTPUTS AND OUTCOMES: IMPLICATIONS FOR RESOURCE ALLOCATION IN AUSTRALIA AND THE USA

Randal G. Stewart

INTRODUCTION

Policy may be defined as taking 'action'. Action involves, at its simplest, a process whereby inputs (money and people) produce outputs (the 'products' of government) that aim to achieve outcomes (on impact, hopefully positive, on the community). However, this is not a mechanical task, undertaken with scientific predicability and technical accuracy. Instead, big 'P' politics and small 'p' politics impregnate policy action at every turn. It would be nice to aim for strategic and medium term coherence (as the OECD calls for), but in this highly complex and unstable environment a strategic framework is a goal to which the policy practitioner may aspire.

Much depends on the policy capacity of governments operating at big 'P' and small 'p' political levels. Different governments, such as the unitary responsible governments systems of New Zealand, the United Kingdom, the federal government of the United States of America and the hybrid federal and responsible government system of the Commonwealth government of Australia, have different strategic maps (determined by the flow of accountability and advice) at big 'P' politics level. The mere charting of these maps would suggest that every system is different. The policy practitioner's task is to learn all the different details of their own combination of big 'P' and small 'p'

Learning from International Public Management Reform, Volume 11B, pages 531–558.
2001 by Elsevier Science Ltd.
ISBN: 0-7623-0760-9

politics as unique manifestations, both in their articulation of these levels as well as the way these levels are combined, and that there is little one can learn to apply from one system to another. This seems true except for the evidence compiled by the OECD (1995).

The evidence compiled by the OECD (1995) *Governance in Transition* report is that despite all the vast differences in political culture in different systems – between very different liberal democracies like U.K., NZ, USA and Australia – the intellectual frameworks used to reform the public sector (the small 'p' – politics level) are remarkably similar. No doubt all OECD countries face similar pressures from globalization (global pressures to cooperate and compete in new ways), budget austerity (the need to reduce deficits) and a nagging dissatisfaction from citizens (who are more articulate and have higher expectations of government performance). However, similarity in the reform process, does not mean, of course, that public sectors across all the 29 OECD countries of the OECD will end up looking alike. It cannot be assumed that these small 'p' – politics reforms are going to harmonise with their Big 'P' – politics framework to make all the systems look and operate the same. Rather, it means there are common threads to follow in many countries as they change and build new frameworks.

As the OECD (1995: 15) comments: "Two vital elements of public service reform strategies stand out: a closer focus on results in terms of efficiency effectiveness and quality of service and replacement of highly centralised, hierarchical structures with decentralised management environments." I will call the first, a shift to an *outcomes-focus,* and the second a commitment to *devolution*.

In this chapter I examine the significance of an outcomes-focus for building a strategic framework and especially the skill involved in crafting outcomes objectives for policy. I show how the move to an outcomes-focus causes a redirection of programs at agency level. However, I argue that the key to success of strategic outcomes reforms is at the resource allocation level. In particular, reforms must incorporate 'strategic policy controls' that cause the budgetary process to be subordinated to specified outcomes. I illustrate these arguments by drawing on two different systems, the executive/budgetary system of Australia and the budgetary /legislative system of the USA.

THE STRATEGIC APPROACH TO POLICY

The strategic approach to business is a comprehensive management tool used to deliver results. It rests on four broad components – strategic planning, defined as the use of strategic concepts to develop a plan of action; formulation

Fig. 27.1. Components of the Strategic Management Cycle.

of strategic objectives and resource allocating including assessment of corporate and business-level strategic alternatives; strategy implementation or the deployment of resources; and evaluation of both strategic alternatives and strategy implementation.

Even before strategic planning begins, the strategic approach to business invests a great deal of time in getting the managerial context of strategy clear especially by explaining change dynamics, leadership skills and external and internal strengths and weaknesses of the organization.

The goal of the strategic approach to business is to create 'private value'. Private value is created by taking action during the commoditization cycle either at the first mover stage, at catch up stages or in the development of new features stage of the product life cycle.

The strategic approach to business relies heavily on the rise and fall of customer-demand as a product goes through a life cycle. Firms make moves at different stages of commoditization, some move first, some play catch up, others provide mass consumption.. All these moves are dynamic requiring the organization to have clarity about its strategic objectives, as well as an ability to line up its corporate and business unit levels with that strategic direction, in order to undertake rapid evaluation and implementation adjustments. This should create an organizational culture that allows the organization to quickly adapt to rapid market changes.

Strategy is an action word and the strategic approach to business is the art of managing action systems. Policy is also an action word. A strategic approach

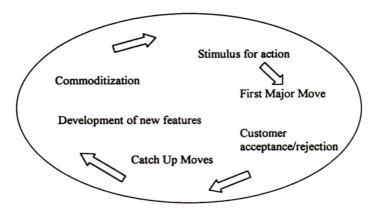

Fig. 27.2. The Commodization Cycle.

to policy would be the act of managing a policy system. There are many analogues to building a strategic framework for policy to the building of a strategic framework for business. For a start, the division of the strategic framework into four broad functions works perfectly well for policy action systems as shown below.

The idea of the private sector creating value is analogous to public sector action, as Mark Moore (1995) argues although it is much harder for policy practitioners to envision the creation of public value. This is because there is no analogue to commoditization in the public sector.

However, policy practitioners are often in a situation analogous to the commoditization cycle itself, especially in so far as they have to identify the stage the policy is at (an analogue to first mover, catch up, development of new features in the commoditization cycle). For example, Viljoen (1997: 28) shows a first mover chart as follows:

This is analogous to the moves made by policy practitioners with both new policies or adjustments to existing policies.

The analogy works up to a point. Instead of competitive and cost pressures (the commoditization part) during the strategy, the policy practitioners have their policy objectives. Moore calls this the act of making ". . . a substantive judgement of what would be valuable and effective" (Moore 1995: 22). Instead of technology or internal factors feeding into customer needs the policy practitioner has the Big 'P' – politics expectation and implementation constraints feeding into the policy context, creating and re-creating policy capabilities. Moore calls this ". . . a diagnosis of political expectations" (Moore

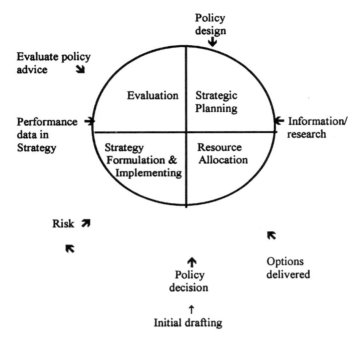

Fig. 27.3. The Strategic Framework.

1995: 22). And instead of market stimulus for action, the policy practitioner has existing and projected policy instruments and tools which can be used but which require "hard headed calculations of what is operationally feasible" (Moore 1995: 22).

Analogous to the strategic approach to business the strategic approach to policy must line up the corporate and business unit levels with the strategic direction. For the policy practitioners this is known as a co-ordination problem. It usually means aligning up the central agencies with line agencies although it can, analogous to a firm, mean aligning corporate services with line and branch management around a strategy. Either way, a problem exists in the public sector similar to that which exists in the private sector but more so. In the public sector there is no "commoditization" to align them, there is no profit motive, no easily measurable, clearly demonstrable basis upon which to line up. As well, devolution threatens to undermine the existing 'command and control' reasons for aligning. Further, central agencies and corporate services in the 'command and control' agencies need to be free of input control so that they can devote

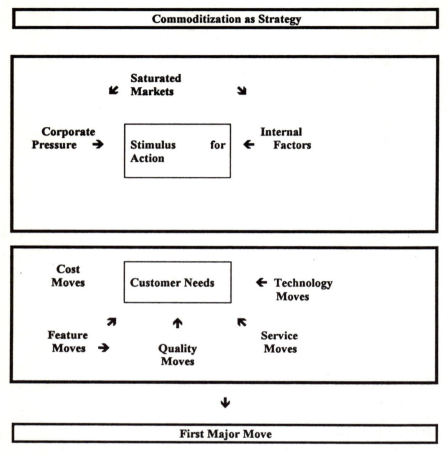

Source: Viljoen, 1997: 28.

Fig. 27.4. "First Mover" Cycle.

more time to strategic policy issues (OECD, 1995: 74). Public sector organizations are similar to private firms in that they need to get their management context clear, develop leadership skills and gain knowledge about their own strengths and weaknesses as an oganization.

The biggest problem with analogy though is that 'policy' is not an analogue to a 'product'. A product is an output, an output that succeeds or fails according

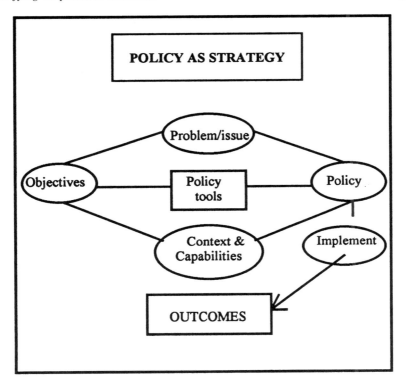

Fig. 27.5. Policy as Strategy.

to the commoditization cycle and customer demand. But a policy is an outcome, an attempt to have a positive impact on a community. There is no commoditization analogue for this in an outcomes-focus. 'Positive impacts' ("outcomes") do not necessarily fade and lose appeal, nor do they get overtaken by technology, nor do they rationally align central and line agencies. This is not to say that money and resources are not important in the public sector, they are, but it is to say that a 'policy' is not a commodity and a policy system does not have an analogue for the rational and elegant coordination the market provides.

The absence of an analogue to commoditization in the strategic approach to policy is not a cause for despair. The strategic approach is very useful and many, many analogues can be found for key concepts for a strategic approach to do a lot of good. The solution is not however, to force the policy practitioner into searching for commoditization analogues – they are not there. It is not the case that if it wasn't for red tape or bureaucracy, conservative superiors or ministers, lack of funding and lack of organizational capability/skills that the public sector could operate like the private sector. The creation of public value, as a strategic objective, is much more complicated than that.

Outcomes – Focus

There is no analogue to commoditization in the public policy process but there is a commitment to the creation of public value that will have a positive impact on the lives of citizens. Moore (1995) explains:

> An alternative approach to controlling managerial influence would be to recognise its potential utility, as well as inevitability, and to provide more formal channels through which managerial ideas about opportunities to create public value could be properly expressed. It would also be important to teach public managers how to search for and define public value more properly and effectively than they now do. Such efforts would help society make a virtue of necessity. They would allow society to have the benefit of the experience and imagination of public sector managers without having to yield to their particular conceptions of the public interest. And it is this piece of work that has not yet been done. Having forever undermined the traditional doctrines of public administration, we have not yet carefully constructed an alternative idea about how public managers should think to act (Moore, 1995: 212).

To lock in this commitment as tightly as possible, public services around the world have been re-engineered to become outcomes-focus. By outcomes-focus, it is meant that public sectors should strive to have a (positive) impact on the community. As health professionals would put it, outcomes are ". . . states or conditions of individuals or populations (the 'community' part) attributed or attributable to antecedent health care (the 'impact' part)" (Noyce & Schofield, 1997: 8). It is the 'judgement' of the policy practitioner that is vital in making sure the outcome is positive not negative.

An outcomes-focus can be contrasted with an outputs-focus (a focus on the products, annual reports, policy statements, passage of legislation etc) or an inputs-focus (a focus on resources, mainly people and money going into the public sector). An outcomes-focus forces public sectors to consider the needs, concerns and views of their communities. Public services must measure the satisfaction levels of their communities just as business must measure its sales to see if its customers are satisfied. In the absence of commoditization, public services can measure community satisfaction by extensive community consultation, monitoring implementation and performance and designing an evaluation of the impact to determine whether action should be continued, changed or stopped.

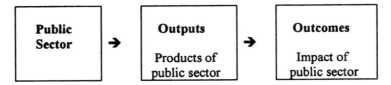

Fig. 27.6. Outputs and Outcomes of the Public Sector.

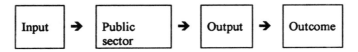

Fig. 27.7. Production Function Relationships.

If the public sector is a black box, outputs come out of the black box whereas outcomes situate these outputs in the context of consumer satisfaction and customer demand.

Public sectors can have a third focus. They may be input focused. Inputs are the resources – money, people, etc. – that go into the public sector.

It may come as a surprise to those outside the public sector that it has been necessary to explicitly re-engineer public services for an outcomes-focus. Surely, it would seem, public services have always aimed to have a (positive) impact on the community. Not so! Indeed, many public services around the world were input-focused until the 1960s and early 1970s. By input-focus it is meant that the public sector aimed to increase the resources (people and money) coming into the public sector and developed a small 'p' politics in and around increasing the inputs into powerful departments and agencies.

The British television program 'Yes, Minister' features a bureaucrat called Sir Humphrey who is input-focused. The minister, Jim Hacker, is output-focused wanting the public service to produce products for the community. The standard joke of 'Yes, Minister', is that while the community would expect both Minister and Public Servant to be outcomes-focused, in fact, neither are. The key point is 'focus'. In fact, it is necessary to have inputs, outputs and outcomes to get an action ('policy'). All these are part of the broad definition of policy process.

INPUTS + OUTPUTS + OUTCOMES = POLICY PROCESS

Fig. 27.8. Inputs to the Policy Process.

However, only an outcomes-focus forces a test or measure of community satisfaction through consultation, performance management and implementation and evaluation.

To develop a strategic approach to policy, the policy practitioners must begin with an outcomes-focus. This is not easy work. For a start, there are many possible outcomes, whose outcome should be favored? As well, there are resource and other constraints on what outcomes can be achieved. How does the policy practitioner deal with this? And there is interference from politicians to consider. Why should the policy practitioner commit to outcomes if the next election may sweep them all away? These doubts can be countered if 'outcomes' are viewed as 'action strategies' themselves.

'Outcomes' provide ways of exploiting what is happening in the environment and criteria for continually adapting to the consequences of these 'action strategies' for further deciding what to do in the future. Policy practitioners taking an outcomes-focus need not victimise themselves about success or failure, but should treat outcomes (and outcomes measures and indicators) as a means for organizing (and continually reorganizing) the effectiveness of their actions; that is, whether they have decided to take the right action, for the right group, to be done in the right way which will achieve the right (positive) outcome.

An outcomes-focused policy action must begin with the policy practitioner drafting some objectives. These objectives begin to set down what, in the view of the practitioner, is the right thing to do. Usually such judgements are based on experience and expertise as well as participation in various forums such as staff and steering committee meetings, case presentation, feedback on services delivered and professional input. After defining the right thing to do it is necessary to identify the group in the community for whom this is the right thing to do. This is where the objectives must address the question of whose outcome is favoured. Next the objectives will have to incorporate service input and output or process considerations (the 'constraints' question) because taking the right action for the right group involves doing things in the right way. Finally, objectives might include consideration of the expected outcomes within the framework of the government's platform (the 'election' consideration) and the acceptable set of outcomes within the agency itself. This last set of objectives (the 'outcomes' objectives) are the most important for although the policy objectives may include input, output and outcomes objectives, it is the 'outcomes' objectives which, link all of these and which connect the policy practitioner to the community.

Designing outcomes objectives is not easy. The skill involves projecting objectives out into the houses and streets in the community and measuring the impact 'out there', rather than measuring it in terms of activity around the Department or agency.

Strategy and Accountability within a Public Sector Agency

The structure of public sector agencies before the development of an outcomes-focus reinforced the input or output-focus. This structural distortion occurred, not through an intentionality to avoid outcomes, but rather as a by-product of a commitment to hierarchy. Hierarchical structures, both in the public and the private sectors, serve some of the basic needs of large organizations. In particular, hierarchy, allows for specialization. This is important so that the large organization can fill necessary roles and functions within the organization, reducing its dependence on individual staff though retaining its dependence on the function being undertaken. Specialization also allows large organizations to promote performance criteria less rather than patronage. Hierarchy also helps to establish routines. Routines based on fairness and equity as well as due process can be established and maintained in a working hierarchy. More importantly, for the public sector, hierarchy ensures the maintenance of organizational memories especially through the routine maintenance of files. In large organizations, the files attached to a function, rather than the memory of the individual officer that demonstrates what the organization has and has not done and, very often, gives guidance to what it can and can not do.

This internal structural distortion had implications for the way skills were used and resources allocated. For example, hierarchical organizations broke operations into those which could be easily controlled internally. In some agencies, the internal resources allocation tracked inputs (money and people) through the organization, setting up operations sections related to payments such as permanent and casual staff, telephones, office services, advertising (the 'people' line) while another section tracked inputs into Major and Minor capital works such as building, vehicles, office provision etc. (the 'money' line). The emphasis was not on results but on resources going into the organization. It is no surprise that this commitment to hierarchy and tracking of inputs created a self-serving organization, oblivious of impact and more concerned with expanding bureaucratic size.

By contrast, modern resource allocation within agencies aims to identify the part of the organization which impacts directly on the community – called programs in most public sectors – and resource these programs according to their objectives in meeting community needs. For example, a program in an agency may deal with 'migrants' and break sub-programs into temporary residents and those who have been granted permanent entry. Note how programs mix inputs together (people and money) with outputs into units called programs. Programs are bundles of inputs and outputs which claim to be delivering outcomes, that is a positive impact on the community. Programs are at the heart of the Corporate Planning and Management in the Public Sector.

Strategy and Accountability Across Government

It is very difficult to strategically manage outcomes across the 'whole-of-government'. It would be ideal for the policy practitioner if strategic priorities were designed and adhered to by the political executive. Ideal, because the policy practitioner would be able to judge exactly whether desired agency outcomes would 'fit' with political priorities. It is the job of the political leadership to *pretend* such priorities exist and it is the belief among news media and citizens that such priorities *must* exist. The policy practitioner usually understands that the coordination function is crafted and re-crafted by those close to the political executives (the ministerial advisers) and those close to the agency (the central agencies).

A principal instrument for bringing all these participants together is the most decisive formal process used to allocate funds to agencies and programs – the government's annual budget. The budget is important because the aim of delivering policy outcomes in a strategic context is thwarted if resource allocation cannot or does not reward outcomes or strategies. The Budget is:

- a statement of how much revenue the Government will raise and how it will do so, and
- a statement of how much the Government will spend in aggregate, and how this amount will be allocated between different purposes.

Budget formulations vary from year to year depending on the economic and fiscal outlook. However, throughout the OECD, there has developed a general acceptance that budget deficits have an adverse impact on the real economy. Fiscal consolidation is the term used to indicate a budget strategy that aims to reduce the deficit. Deficit reduction strategies have begun to focus less on the cyclical deficit (the year to year gap between revenues and outlays) and more on the structural deficit (the deeper trends in revenue flow through taxation and outlay commitments that create a permanent deficit). Because of budget formulation decisions such as deficit reduction, as well as the year by year impact, the government's Budget is an important political, social and economic document. In most systems, the annual budget may or may not reward policy practitioners pursuing outcomes and strategies. The policy practitioner must, as a minimum, understand the budgetary cycle and process, to protect, if not advance, an outcomes-focus in a strategic context.

Most parliamentary systems have a budgetary cycle that is fairly centralised around the Council of Ministers ("the Cabinet"). This is because the budget, in these systems, does two things that could impact on Big 'P' politics. Firstly, it awards appropriations needed to run public programs. Secondly, it provides the political executive an opportunity to set its plans before the country. The budgetary cycle is designed to facilitate input from policy practitioners (advising which programs should run) and politicians (getting their Big 'P' politics priorities right) to manage these relations and to produce the Budget papers on the night when the Treasurer, Chancellor or Minister for Finance makes the Budget speech in Parliament in the form of an Appropriation Bill.

The Executive/Budgetary Cycle in Australia

Since 1984, resource allocation, taxing and spending and the stabilization function in the budget have been determined by the economic setting and the budget framework. The economic settings have led to an emphasis on deficit reduction. For example, the 1996/86 Budget process was formulated against the backdrop of "implementation of the Governments election commitments; and Government's objective to announce in the 1996–97 Budget all the measures necessary to achieve an improvement of the budget balance of around $4 billion in 1996–97 and a further $4 billion in 1997–98". (Commonwealth of Australia Department of Finance, 1996)

The Budget framework from 1984 to 1997 was known as the Financial Management Improvement Program (FMIP) that was superseded in 1997 by the Financial Management and Accountability (FMA) Act 1997. In this section, we will introduce the budgetary cycle Australia, examining the FMIP, a vertical coordination system. In the last part of the chapter, we will examine the new FMA system that claims to be a more horizontal system of resource allocation.

The Department of Finance began implementing the Financial Management Improvement Program in 1984. Program Management and Budgeting was gradually introduced, beginning in 1985. Implementation was completed in the 1988–89 Budget. This was supplemented in 1987 with a requirement for departmental evaluation plans and for evaluation to be included in new budget proposals. The FMIP is directed at:

- streamlining the budget formulation process and simplifying and updating the body of rules regulating public financial management
- improving the system by which departments and agencies make decisions, and manage and evaluate achievements
- enhancing public accountability and scrutiny.

To achieve this, the FMIP presents a number of central principles by which coordination shall occur. These include devolution of control from central agencies and within departments to increase managerial flexibility – 'letting the managers manage and making them manage'; the user pays principle; public accountability; and effective performance. However, it is the 'results orientation' and 'risk management' principles which really highlight the nature of the FMIP.

The 'managing-for-results' system by which managers make decisions and review achievements is the raison d'etre of the reforms. It focuses management attention on the purposes of programs and the cost-effective achievement of outcomes. This is in contrast with the earlier emphasis on inputs and processes, which was a result of bureaucracies being top heavy, with a system of controls promoting the administration of rules and regulations rather than management for results. In the FMIP, departments were encouraged to move through stages of reforms leading to a 'results orientation'. These five stages included developing a corporate plan and management structure related to agency goals, a reorganization of divisions into a program structure so that these become the units of expenditure control, redesigning the organization at the top around the corporate goals and at the bottom into programs, development of a Management Information System (MIS) so that management can review program performance, and an evaluation strategy to determine if programs and subprograms should be renewed each year. In this way, agencies and their programs could demonstrate results, make savings and monitor expenditure.

Moving to a 'results orientation' puts a great deal of pressure on managers to perform, giving them the autonomy to do well but also bringing with it a new range of risks. One other important principle of the FMIP is teaching managers how to manage risks. The idea was to relax standard controls that were imposed on expenditure service-wide such as government charges and to give agencies the freedom to set their own charges for service, to engage in 'whole cost' or accrual accounting, to have great flexibility in procurement practices and to develop better cash management practices. With greater autonomy in these areas comes greater risk. Agencies could set inappropriate charges or buy the wrong things. If they did, they would carry bottom line costs (or savings). 'Risk management', like 'results orientation', is tricky in the public sector. The issue is surrounded by matters of political, social and ethical judgment. The FMIP aimed to give agencies and managers this freedom but also to remind them that while they take risks, their decisions will be reviewed this review might require management to adjust practices in the light of the reviews and new experiences.

The FMIP gives agency and departmental managers the freedom to make savings and losses at two different levels:

- the expenditure control level through a revision of the budget process
- the program level through program management budget

The expenditure control component has four parts to it:

- the forward estimate system
- portfolio budgeting
- the running cost system
- the efficiency dividend

These were the operational level reforms known as Program Management and Budgeting (PMB). These were thought to be simply the reorganizations necessary to establish programs as the public service equivalent of strategic business units, which would allow agencies to budget for their own staff and works and be evaluated accordingly underneath the overall umbrella of the expenditure control system. The PMB operational reforms of the FMIP were not considered successful (although they did cause the universal acceptance if operational units called 'programs'). Of the 'Program Management and Budgeting' part of the FMIP, The House of Representatives Standing Committee or Finance and Public Administration 1990 report criticised the FMIP for inter alia not providing ". . . better linkage of financial flexibility under the running costs system with outputs and outcomes; better public accountability" (Quoted in Barrett et al.: 65–66) two things essential to a Strategic Framework.

The Budgetary/Legislative Cycle in the USA

The budget is dominated by the executive branch in parliamentary systems. If the legislature rejects the budget then the executive falls. In the United States, budget decision making is by the legislative and executive branches. Each has its own policy/administrative apparatus, the Congressional Budget Office (CBO) serves the legislature and the Office of Management and Budget (OMB) serves the executive. The centrality of the legislature in the budget cycle places the committees in the two houses of Congress – (House of Representatives and the Senate) in a key role. There are two Appropriations and two Budget Committees, one in each house.

The Budget process begins in the OMB up to eighteen months before the beginning of the fiscal year. OMB's aim is to transmit the President's budget to Congress on the first Monday of February for the start of the fiscal year in October. The OMB begins in April by getting a four-year planning cycle in place and by liaising with Treasury to get an understanding of tax policy and tax revenue which will come in. The Treasury estimates are matches with fiscal and economic forecasts coming form the Council of Economic Advisers as well as from within OMB itself. A four-year planning cycle does give some strategic prioritising to budgetary deliberations within the executive.

The OMB is like a powerful central agency in a Parliamentary system but with an explicit political mission to win the President's budget through the system. It is divided into divisions that match up with operating agencies and it has parallel expertise with operating agencies in many program areas. Policy analysis goes on at every level within the OMB, and in other executive branches, but is at its most vigorous when OMB and operating agencies are discussing budget issues and options in the summer. This is where policy practitioners in operating agencies can penetrate the divisions of the OMB itself to ensure their outcomes. Agency strategies are reflected in the recommendations the division of OMB sends to the Budget Director of OMB.

The Executive Branch finalises the President's Budget between September and December for transmittal to Congress by 1st Monday in February. Congress receives the budget and in February the CBO submits a report on the President's budget to the Budget committees of the House of Representatives and the Senate. Congress can approve, modify or disapprove the President's budget proposals. Congress does not enact a budget as such. Instead it enacts different types of legislation that together make up a budget. The different types of legislation are known as appropriations (not direct spending measures but authority to spend. Many of these are permanent authority such as Social Security and Health and trust funds), and appropriations (the actual amount which will be spent) and concurrent budget resolutions which consider budget totals before completing action on individual appropriations and receipts measures. The committee and sub-committee structure reflects the division of the legislature and the need to address and deliberate on the separate legislative processes.

Important Events in the U.S. Budget Cycle are represented in Fig. 27.9:

Months before start of FY(t) (Year t-2)	Main events and activities
10-9 18 (April)	OMB issues planning guidance to the agencies for FY (t) to FY (t+4)
14-16 (summer)	OMB and agencies discuss budget issues and options in preparation for FY (t) budget review and decision making
13-10 (September to December)	Executive Branch develops the President's Budget
8 (not later than the 1st Monday in February)	Transmittal of President's budget to Congress
8 (15th February)	CBO submits report to Budget Committees
8-7 (within 6 weeks of transmittal)	Each Committee reports its views and budget estimates to the House and Senate Budget Committees
6 (1st April to September)	Senate Budget Committee reports concurrent resolution on the budget
6 (15th April to July)	Congress completes action on concurrent budget resolution
5 (15th May to September)	Annual appropriations bills considered in the House in the absence of a concurrent resolution
4 (10th June to September)	House and Senate Appropriations Committees report the annual appropriations bills
4 (15th June to September)	Congress completes action on reconciliation legislation
3 (15th July)	Transmittal of Mid-Session Review, updating the budget estimates

Fig. 27.9. U.S. Budget Cycle.

VERTICAL AND HORIZONTAL MANAGEMENT
PROBLEMS IN GOVERNMENT

The problem of aligning strategy ('outcomes') with resource allocation ('budgets') is well known in the private sector. Daft (1998: 216) shows that greater turbulence and uncertainty in organizational environments is creating a shift toward flatter more horizontal structures. The need for this shift is evident in government also and 'outcomes' represent a commitment to horizontal forms of linkage such as teams, networks, direct contact with the community and a core of full time 'outcomes' integrators inside agencies and at the whole of government level. We may call this horizontal emphasis a commitment to 'coherence' defined as ". . . an overall state of mutual consistency among different policies" (OECD, 1994: 4).

But the linkage mechanisms in place in most government systems are budgets and budgets contain vertical control mechanisms such as hierarchical referral, rules and plans, vertical information systems and final compromise decisions as aresult of position at the top of the hierarchy rather than on strategic goal setting. These vertical linkages are linkages of coordination, defined as ". . . appropriately linked processes and action among different policies."

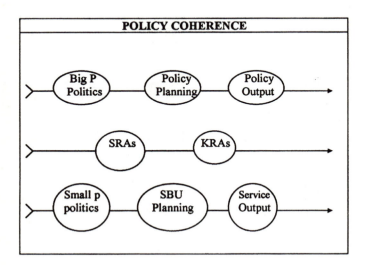

Fig. 27.10. Policy Coherence.

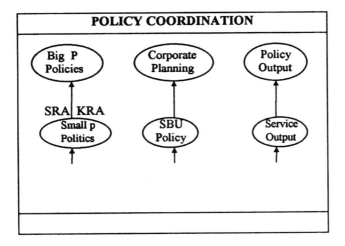

Fig. 27.11. Policy Coordination.

The crucial issue for the 'outcomes-focused' policy-maker is how to ensure, especially in a period of fiscal constraint, that vertical budget processes do not dominate and overwhelm strategic coherence. There needs to be put into Budget Coordination what may be called 'strategy policy controls'. Structures must be designed to ensure that someone will protect the strategic outcomes focus in the hurly burly of Budget formulation? Who is going to integrate budgeting considerations into the outcomes focus – will it be the polictical executive, the policy or fiscal central agencies, a powerful department outside the central agencies, or as in the USA, legislators and congressional staffers? What machanisms, if any, can be developed to ensure budget considerations are integrated into the strategic framework and not the other way around? How can we ensure we do not get 'policy making by budget', where the budget strategy, such as deficit reduction dominates other policy frameworks.

In the following two sections, we examine again the USA and Australia, to identify the possible location of 'strategy policy controls' in the decision making system. Our task is assisted by the legislative initiatives taken in both systems to advance strategy through an outcomes focus. In the USA, the Government Performance and Results Act 1993 has mandated strategic planning and the specification of outcomes for all but exempt agencies from 2000. In Australia, the FMIP has been displaced by the FMA that requires agencies to specify agency outputs and outcomes in their annual Portfolio

Budget Statements (PBS). It is too early to judge with certainty the success or otherwise of each system in delivering outcomes although some early findings are possible. In particular, as the following sections indicate, the USA GPRA Act is good at redirecting programs along outcome lines but it relies on the shifting sands of legislative coalitions for its 'strategic policy controls' to work. By contrast, the FMA is linked to the executives budget, perhaps ensuring the maintanence of more permanent 'strategy policy controls', but weakening the innovative redirection of programs at agency level.

The Government Performance and Results Act 1993 (USA)

The initiative for the change to an outcomes focus in the USA has come from both the political executive and among the policy practitioners in agencies but it is the lagislators who are responsible for receiving and monitoring strategic plans and who control 'strategic policy controls'. The principal instrument for outcomes is the Government Performance and Results Act of 1993 that is similar in many respects to elements of the National Performance Review launched by Vice-President Gore in 1993 (Gore, 1993: 161). The GPRA builds on three steps. Each federal agency must develop (a) a five year strategic plan that lays out its mission, (b) performance measures to gauge their success in meeting these plans, and (c) identify strategies to be set down in annual reports, based on those performance measures to show how well they have met their performance goals.

The Act provides for the Office of Management and Budget (OMB) to choose ten pilot projects in performance measurement and five in managerial accountability and flexibility who will develop the GPRA methodology. These reports were submitted to the Director of OMB on May 1, 1997. In September 30, 1997 agencies submitted their plans to Congress. The Act requires that the agencies consult with Congress and solicit the views of other stakeholders as they develop their strategic plans.

The GPRA has generated a lot of energy in three critical areas: (a) the development and disaggregation of outcomes-focused data, (b) the incorporation of performance objectives into budget and management functions, and (c) the attempt to put outcomes into programs which are run by different agencies but which, nevertheless, contain cross-cutting functions.

The first area can be highlighted by looking at one of the pilot programs run by the United States Coast Guard. Kowalewski (1996) explains how the agency had to learn to move beyond inputs and outputs to outcomes. He writes:

> To a large extent, these outcome measures (reproduced below) replace output and efficiency measures for our organisation. We still have data on activities, but we don't

regularly track them or hold people accountable for them. While outputs are clearly important in achieving outcomes, our overriding concern was that we change the way we do business and change what people focus on. Given the inertia to continue what we've been doing (what we know best), we felt we needed a major course correction. Besides, we didn't want to collect more data, we wanted to replace old systems and reduce our data collection overall (Kowalewski, 1996: 9).

When the outcome measures arrive, they disaggregate it. For example, the data on 'marine safety' is disaggregated into 'risk' categories such as risk, regionally, globally, in terms of systems, vessel service, flag, classification society, owner/operator operational circumstances. Time of day or season, geography, or other factors that enable targeting our efforts are identified (Kowalewski, 1996: 9).

GPRA is already having an impact on inter-agency communication. As early as 1994 the Office of Personnel Management started a monthly GPRA Interest Group to discuss GPRA requirements. Later, the Department of Health and Human Services began a Research Roundtable to discuss R & D under GPRA. GPRA may prove to be a vehicle for bringing agencies together with cross cutting issues such as education (a $120 billion/year spent through 760 programs in 39 agencies), food safety (with 12 agencies involved, drug controls affecting more than 50 agencies), international affairs, regulatory reinvention and benchmarking areas where GPRA interagency interest groups are already in existence.

Kettl (1995) sees some problems with a top down strategy instrument like GPRA. At the agency level he notes that 'strategic planning' objectives require a consensus within an agency and a good communication process within the agency. This need for consensus is acknowledged in the strategic planning literature. (Viljoen, 1994: 503). Three traps must be avoided. Firstly, that managers take the bold steps that GPRA calls for and not retreat into existing planing processes. Secondly, that they do not plan for what can be most easily measured and thirdly that they do not plan for results they cannot easily control. Kettl (1995) cautions that political executives must continue to find it politically useful to support policy practitioners conducting GPRA reviews. As well, the OMB needs to develop lead agency status with executive and legislative support and policy practitioners will have to work with Congress to ensure the translation of strategies from the political executive and the agencies themselves to Congress (Kettl, 1995: 172).

This is where the GPRA may have failed to devise adequate 'strategic policy controls' because while the GPRA itself is a top down strategy the budget itself, as we have seen, is a highly partisan negotiated compromise. Most of the 'strategy policy controls' in the GPRA are inside agencies. For example, the

THE OUTCOME INDICATORS THAT WE USE

Our strategic goal for marine safety is to eliminate deaths, injuries and economic loss associated with commercial marine transportation and the shipment of military cargo. Over five years, our programs aim to achieve these major goals:

Performance Goals	Performance Indicators
Reduce accidental deaths and injuries from maritime casualties by 20%	(1) Workers fatalities per 100,000 workers (2) Non-worker fatalities/billion tons of commerce
Reduce the risk of passenger vessel casualty with major loss of life by 20%	Vessel accidents per thousand passenger vessels
Reduce fatality rates aboard uninspected fishing and towing vessels halfway toward the average of the U.S. inspected fleet.	(1) Fishing fatalities per 100,000 workers (2) Towing fatalities per 100,000 workers
Eliminate substandard commercial vessels from U.S. waters.	Interventions per 100,000 port calls
Reduce the vulnerability of U.S. ports and waterways to intentional damage/injury	Compliance rate with IMO guidelines (Preliminary indicator, still under development)

Strategic goal for Marine Environmental Protection is to eliminate environmental damage associated with marine transportation. Over five years, our programs aim to achieve these major goals in marine environmental protection:

Performance Goals	Performance Indicators
Reduce the amount of oil and chemicals going into the water from maritime sources by 20%	Gallons spilled per million gallons shipped
Reduce the discharge of plastics/Garbage going into the water from Maritime sources by 20%	Pounds of marine debris recovered per mile of shoreline cleaned, in annual coastal clean ups
Number of major /medium spills per billion tons shipped	Increase the removal of spilled oil from the water by 10%

(Source: Kowaleski 1996:6)

Fig. 27.12. Outcome Indicators for the U.S. Coast Guard.

GPRA impact on the incorporation of performance objectives into budget and management functions can be seen inside agencies where the development and disaggregation of outcomes-focused data is having a direct impact on resource allocation and the way things are done. But the budget brokering may introduce fiscal controls that sweep away these internal srategy policy controls. Although the central role of OMB in the reporting process suggests GPRA may eventually have an impact on the annual budget, we have shown above how the OMB's budget control si shared with the CBO in practice.

The Financial Management and Accountability Act (FMA) in Australia

The FMA system is an accrual-based resource management framework in which accrual accounting is one element of the framework. This is a system of accounting in which items are brought to account as they are earned or incurred. It is based on the accountancy equation, Assets = Liabilities + equity. Accrual accounting that records assets and liabilities can be contrasted with cash accounting methods which records cash outlays and receipts. Accrual accounting records depreciation and other invisibles to deliver a balance sheet comparable to those in the private sector.

The FMA claims that the cash system (which was used in the FMIP) did not require output or outcomes goals but tended to focus, as we have seen, on cash inputs. The position taken in the FMA is that if accrual accounting is introduced the full cost of outputs (policy advice, goods and services) can be calculated. This full cost of outputs can then be linked to outcomes to clearly demonstrate the contribution of the public sector to policy formulation and service delivery undertaken on behalf of the Political Executive.

The FMA claims to be shifting the focus of the budget from inputs to outputs and ultimately to outcomes through accrual management. This is, of course, the Strategic Framework approach. The claim is that a 'cash' system encouraged a focus on inputs. The accrual accounting system encourages a focus on outputs, which are 'necessarily linked' to outcomes.

The FMA also claims to be devolving authority to program managers in a way the FMIP did not do. This claim is made because the management of information (assets, liabilities, equity) remains at agency level through an agency-based Financial Management System (FMS). The central information, the Accrual Information Management System (AIMS) is merely a quality instrument requiring only month by month reporting of data by agencies. As well, the FMA claims to be enhancing public accountability because Parliament, the political executive and stakeholders will know the exact cost of delivering policy advice and services. There is no doubt that the FMA is preparing the public service in Australia for competition with private sector providers to the Government.

The FMA, like the FMIP and other budgetary frameworks, operates at two levels: the level of the financial management environment in which agencies have to operate (the equivalent of the expenditure control system in the FMIP), and the way financial management is practiced within an agency (the equivalent to Program Management and Budgeting). In terms of the financial management environment, the FMA aims to devalue "estimates construction". In the FMIP, agencies were responsible for providing estimates advice to DOFA but DOFA had to generate, enter and authorise all estimates. This led to double handling and reduced agency commitment to meeting estimates. The AIMS system will push the previous expenditure control down to agency level. Agencies will be in control but the Government gets real cost estimates for three to four years to give it a more complete picture upon which to base its decisions.

At the agency level, the FMA is highly critical of the earlier 'Program Management and Budgeting' approach. FMA claims that while PMB gave agencies some power to build objectives it did not force them into applying real costing to these objectives nor did it explain to them how to build outputs and outcomes back into their program management and budgeting. Lennon (1998: 5) from DOFA explains:

> Traditionally with program management and budgeting, there has been an emphasis on defining planned outcomes (or objectives) and attempting to measure actual outcomes for programs. Under the new accruals framework this emphasis will be retained. However, there will be a new focus for performance management in the Commonwealth public sector – namely, the outputs on goods and services produced by agencies and how these contribute to outcomes – that is, their impact on the community. Such outputs will be described in terms of their key attributes, such as cost, quantity and quality (Lennon, 1998: 5).

The focus on outputs (and ultimately on outcomes) should help agencies with their strategic planning: "At agency level the new accrual framework gives the Government the capacity to identify and agree what goods and services will be produced and delivered by agencies (that is, their outputs); at what quality they will be produced, the prices to be paid for them; and the intended outcomes sought. It is envisaged that agencies will provide this kind of information as part of the budget process; and that they will be held responsible for delivering on planned performance in relation to their outputs". (Lennon, 1998: 8,9) Lennon insists the link between outputs and outcomes will be preserved by ensuring, ". . . the delivery of outputs assists the achievement of outcomes. If particular outputs cannot be linked to planned agency outcomes, their provision should be discontinued" (Lennon, 1998: 5).

But will this happen? Allan Hawke (1998), Secretary of the Commonwealth Department of Transport and Regional Development and chair of the Management Advisory Board project team who drafted the FMA documentation, agreed that:

> There are also significant practical and conceptual difficulties in holding (or trying to hold) agencies and senior public servants accountable for outcomes. In most cases, agencies, or at least individual agencies, have little or no control over the full range of factors, including the sum of various agencies' outputs which influence any specific outcomes ... For governments to fully achieve the benefits in service delivery they are quite clearly seeking, agencies and their senior executives, must focus their efforts on, and be responsible for, outputs. Governments, not agencies must take responsibility for determining strategies to achieve its desired outcomes for the community, and for selecting the right mix of outputs, and for that matter, the output providers, to meet the strategy (Hawke, 1998).

The FMA posits a changing role for central agencies. The skill set of DOFA budget officers will move away from an input focus to determine and agree fair output prices with agencies. They will still maintain a focus on aggregate fiscal discipline but must put that in the context of output and outcomes goals of agencies. The role of DOFA is said to move to strategy and quality and away from command and control (Commonwealth of Australia Management Advisory Board 1997: 103).

The FMA promises to aggregate vertical coordination to an outcomes focus. It does this by getting a full costing of service and policy advice outputs, by consolidating strategic business unit plans and linking them back up to Governments planned outcomes and by putting the big 'P' politics back in control through the selection of outcomes by the political executive. But these agency outputs and outcomes still have to survive the Budget process and, despite DOFA's promise to become more 'strategic' and not 'inputs' focused, its officers have to preserve the FMA in the "hurley-burley" of budget coordination and negotiation.

In Australia, the outcomes and outputs move through the CERCIS (Cabinet Expenditure Review Committee Information System). This consists of the Expenditure Review Committee (ERC), a cabinet committee comprising the Prime Minister, the Treasurer, the Ministers of Finance, Health and Family Services, Primary Industries and Energy and the Assistant Treasurer. ERC meetings may also be attended by officials, including those from the DOFA. The meetings are structured and focus on 'spending'. Ministers to speak to their proposal for outlays and are then questioned by committee members who form a view whether the proposal should be supported, rejected or sent away for further work. The Expenditure Policy Branch (EPD) of DOFA is the secretariat for ERC. It provides aggregate data by which a proposal may be assessed and presents a score sheet listing the assessment for various proposals.

It has been possible to develop a unified theme through the ERC. A Labor Party employment strategy called 'Working Nation' was developed this way, but usually proposals are treated as separate one-off claims. It is clear that much depends on the quality of the information systems. A score is completed on existing information so any move to outputs and outcomes would require more sophisticated data retrieval systems than currently exists. Whatever happens, there is no reason to suppose that the DOFA role in the CERCIS process will diminish even with the establishment of the FMA.

The 1999/2000 Budget is the first to be brought down under the FMA. It is too early to tell if resource allocation is to be subordinated to 'strategy policy controls' or the other way around. Agencies were required to present their specification of outputs and outcomes in the form of Portfolio Budget Statements (PBS). Some agencies such as the Department of Family and Community Service (FACS) took the opportunity to devise original outcomes and in the process redirected their programs in a manner similar to the U.S. Coast Guard case highlighted above. Other agencies such as the Department of Education, Training and Youth Affairs (DETYA) were more output than outcome driven, taking the view that outcomes could more or less sit on top of existing programs. At least DETYA's outcomes were at least plausible unlike other agencies such as Defence whose PBS suggests a deep lack of commitment to the whole process. In DETYA, the PBS was developed by that departments finance branch as an accounting exercise rather than a strategic redirection developed through staff and stakeholder focus groups as undertaken in FACS. The whole process is very uneven as noted in Senate committees. Agencies are not sure how much they should commit to specifying outputs and outcomes, because they are still unsure whether the 'strategic policy controls' or fiscal controls will win out.

CONCLUSIONS

Many governmental systems are experimenting with strategy in the form of outcomes. This chapter demonstrates that the success of strategic management in the public sector depends on the challenge of adding public value to operations in the form of 'outcomes'. This is much more complicated than strategic management in the private sector that relies on adding private value to operations as determined by commoditization and market realities. In the public sector there is no analogue for commoditization and the accountability demanded by communities from governments is by no means as clear cut as market signals are in the private sector.

As well, it is more difficult for the public sector to retain a coherent strategic focus because of existing public sector arrangements at the two levels at which 'value' is added – the level of 'strategy and accountability within public sector agencies' and the level of 'strategy and accountability across government'. For example, inside public sector agencies, a commitment to hierarchy may distort the strategic focus toward inputs and the program structure may privilege outputs debilitating against an outcomes focus. Strategy and accountability across government may also debilitate against outcomes that are horizontal goals not vertical functions because most whole-of-government arrangements focus on vertical aggregation ('coordination') rather than horizontal coherence.

Identifying barriers to outcomes at the two main levels at which value is added highlight the critical importance of the design of the resource allocation system if strategic value is to be added in the form of outcomes in the public sector. Simply, if the dollars do not follow the outcomes specified then all the strategic management in the world will not make the slightest difference in the public sector.

This chapter has examined two systems, the U.S.A and the Commonwealth Government of Australia, for evidence of 'strategy policy controls' that may be put in place to ensure the success of specified outputs and outcomes. Although, it is early days in strategy development in both systems, this chapter is concerned that the vertical, control system of the budgetary process may overwhelm the attempt at strategic horizontal management in the outputs/ outcomes framework. The strategic framework adopted in both systems has the capacity to redirect programs inside agencies but may change little at the 'whole of government' level.

REFERENCES

Barrett, G., Murphy, S., & Miller, R. Financial Management Reform. In: J. Stewart (Ed.), *From Hawke to Keating: Australian Commonwealth Administration 1990–1993*. Canberra: Centre for Research in Public Sector Management University of Canberra and Royal Institute of Public Administration Australia.

Commonwealth of Australia Department of Finance (1996). *Overview of the Budget Process.* (http://www.dofa.gov.au/pubs/budgproc/bp96.html)

Commonwealth of Australia Management Advisory Board (1997). *Beyond Bean Counting: Effective Financial Management in the APS – 1998 and Beyond.* Canberra, Public Services and Merit Protection Commission.

Daft, R. (1998). *Organization Theory and Design* (6th ed.). Cincinnati, Ohio: South-Western College Publishing.

Gore, A. (1993). *From Red Tape to Results: Creating a Government that Works Better and Costs Less*. Report of the National Performance Review, Washington D.C.: U.S. Government Printing Office.

Hawke, A. (1998). *Beyond Bean Counting: The Emerging Role for Senior Executives*. Paper by the Secretary of the Commonwealth Department of Transport and Regional Development on behalf of the Institute of Public Administration Australia. April.

Kettl, D. (1995). Measuring Performance When there is No Bottom Line. In: J. Boston (Ed.), *The State under Contract*. Wellington: Bridget Williams Books.

Kowalewski, R. (1996). *Using Outcome Information to Redirect Programs: A Case Study of the Coast Guards Pilot Project Under the Government Performance and Results Act of 1993*. United States Coast Guard, Office of Marine Safety, Security and Environmental Protection, April.

Lennon, B. (1998). *Contemporary Financial Management – Outcomes and Outputs: The New Resource Management Framework*. Institute of Public Administration Australia Seminar. Sydney. 30 April.

Moore, M. (1995). *Creating Public Value – Strategic Management in Government*. Cambridge: Harvard University Press.

Noyce, J. A., & Schofield, J. (1997). *Health Outcomes for Health Care Practitioners – The Australian Perspective*. Sydney: The Australian Council on Healthcare Standards.

OECD (1994). *Coherence in Policy Making*. Draft Report, (note by the Secretariat). Paris: 10th Session of the Committee, Maison de la Chumie, November.

OECD (1995). *Governance in Transition: Public Management Reforms in OECD Countries*. Paris, OECD.

Viljoen, J. (1994). *Strategic Management* (2nd ed.). South Melbourne: Addison Wesley Longman.

28. REVITALIZING HEALTH-CARE SYSTEMS WITH NEW PUBLIC MANAGEMENT IN QUEBEC AND CANADA: A CASE AGAINST THE CLASSICAL APPROACH

Yvon Dufour and Lise Lamothe

INTRODUCTION

The last twenty years have seen waves of change aimed at revitalizing health-care systems with a New Public Management (NPM) orientation in Canada. Economic and technological pressures, in conjunction with conflicting ideological pressures and taxpayer perception that governments are too expensive, ineffective and unresponsive, have created throughout the country a receptive context for the implementation of NPM ideas in the public sector. All levels of government have increased focus on management, emphasized greater adoption of private sector methods, reduced the size and scope of public services, and focused on further control. In this study, we present a brief overview of NPM in Canada. Then in order to analyze how NPM has been used, we describe some of the experience conducted in the health-care system in Quebec. In conclusion we suggest that a combined political and contingency approach best suits the specific context of health-care systems and the specific internal dynamics of such organizations.

Learning from International Public Management Reform, Volume 11B, pages 559–568.
2001 by Elsevier Science Ltd.
ISBN: 0-7623-0760-9

NPM IN CANADA: A BRIEF OVERVIEW

The public sector in Canada has come a long way on the path of reform in the last two decades. During those years the Canadians have elected two different kinds of governments. One was business-oriented; focusing on balancing budgets while introducing tax cuts to high-income earners and wealth taxes. The second type had a more social democratic approach and focused on maintaining programmes as much as possible while reducing their resources and increasing their efficiency (Glor, 2000). Despite their differences both types of government have worked toward reducing the role of the state.

Canada is ranked with the U.K., Australia and New Zealand as a leading country in implementing NPM (Hood, 1995). All Canadian provinces have been moving away from an emphasis on administration and policy, and progressing towards an emphasis on managerialism. The extent to which they have embraced NPM varies from one province to the other and its implementation also differs greatly. Provincial governments travelling down the same NPM pathway have progressed at very varying rates. The movement towards NPM in Canada has been far from uniform and cohesive. The variations in pace and rate among the Canadian provinces reiforces the idea developed by Olson et. al. (1998) that the rhetoric of NPM should not be accepted without an empirical understanding of the contextual issues of implementation.

Of all the Canadian provinces, Alberta has exhibited the most managerialist traits and Quebec the least. In that respect Alberta and Quebec can be compared to the states of Victoria and Queensland (respectively) in Australia (Hughes & O'Neill, 2000; Guthrie & English, 2000, Halligan & Power, 1992). In this way comparisons can be made on the process of introducing NPM between the Commonwealth government of Australia and the federal government of Canada. Variations in the pace and rate of reform between Canadian provinces and territories are neither atypical nor unheard of. It mimics the overall pattern of public administration reforms undertaken by the various levels of government since World War II. For instance, Alberta was the first of all Canadian provinces to reform its health services towards Medicare whereas Quebec was the last to do so. According to Dufour and Paquet (1997) there are numerous reasons for such an early adoption of NPM principles in Alberta. Among many others includes a small growing and therefore younger population in Alberta than in Quebec, the highest debt per capita in the country and a stronger ideological and political American influence in Alberta than in Quebec. These factors would have contributed to ideal conditions for a faster NPM implementation in Alberta than elsewhere in the Canada.

Health-care services have been among the most affected by the NPM reform in both provinces. In order to achieve rationalization and better integration of services, structural reforms were conducted: thousands of hospital beds were closed, numerous small peripheral hospitals were shut down and many mergers of organizations were enforced. Also, regional authorities were put into place with the hope to have better control. Although objectives were similar and structural changes in the same line of thought, the pace with which reforms were conducted was slower in Quebec. Using the Quebec situation as an example, we make a diagnostic analysis of the reform process undertaken and infer what change approaches seem more appropriate to NPM.

NPM CHANGE PROCESS IN THE QUEBEC HEALTH-CARE SYSTEM

A close look at how reforms in the Quebec health-care system have been conducted reveals that policy makers tend to adopt a classical approach in decision making, associated with a contingency approach in working out implementation conditions. In short, the classical approach is based on the idea that change and reform can be completely controlled by a small number of individuals who possess the legitimate right to exercise authority. The contingency approach assumes that change and reform result from designing structures and developing management systems in line with the objectives.

During the 1980s, there was considerable disappointment that many of the problems meant to be corrected by the structural reforms of the 1970s still existed. The external and internal environments were analyzed by the Rochon Commission (1986–1988) that established a list of the main problems to be addressed. During this period, a discourse emerged that expressed the desire for greater decentralization that would allow organizations and those working in the network to play a more active role. However, with the adoption of amendments to the *Act Respecting Health Services and Social Services* (LSSS–1992) the government showed a very clear desire to tighten its control over health-care institutions. Thus, the (Department) Ministry of Health and Social Services continued to maintain all of its political and administrative authority.

At the beginning of the 1990s, there was general agreement that accessibility and efficiency of services had greatly improved during the previous thirty years. However, the persistence of social and economic constraints (in the environment) made adjustments necessary, although these were carried out slowly due to the decision-making mechanisms and processes used. The feeling of urgency created by economic pressures, associated with an increasing perception among the public that the state was not managing health services efficiently, led to the adoption of further amendments to the LSSS in 1991 and a vast reorganization of services as a whole. In particular, solving problems related to the coordination and rationalization of services was achieved through various forms of amalgamations throughout Quebec and by massive reduction in the supply of care provided by hospitals. These changes were not implemented without opposition.

Relocation of the Hotel-Dieu of Montreal

Our first example concerns the events surrounding the planned relocation of a teaching hospital in the Montreal region (Dufour & Nadeau, 1993). As the relocation project entered its third year of discussions between the Department of Health and hospital authorities, a coalition of organizations opposed to the project suddenly mobilized in an alliance with the Chamber of Commerce of Metropolitan Montreal. The project's opponents attributed a much broader and more significant meaning to the relocation project, arguing that in reality, the project was all about a major development pole for Montreal as a metropolis.

The principal aim of the opposition campaign was to destable the Minister of Health's legitimacy and to question the "true" motives underlying his relocation proposal. Opponents were able to sow seeds of doubt in the public mind regarding conflicts of interest over the choice of the new site. After organizing ten public hearings (in which the Ministry of Health refused to participate) and consulting a variety of experts (who discredited the evaluation of the Ministry) the opponents launched an intensive public appeal. Opposition such as this finally defeated the project.

Opposition to Bill 120

The confrontation that occurred in 1991 between the Ministry of Health and Social Services and the Regroupement des médecins du Québec (RMQ – the Quebec physicians' coalition) during discussions (about) on Bill 120 (Dufour and Codjia, 1992) provides yet another example of opposition in reforming health care services. The aim of Bill 120 was to control medical practice. It was meant to respond to one of the Rochon Commission's observations that described the decision-making dynamics of the system as captive: "Everything is happening as if the system has become a prisoner of the countless interest groups that are involved in it" (407). An extensive campaign by the medical associations, aimed at raising awareness among the general public, finally resulted in the defeat of the project.

The unusual and unprecedented strength of the political and symbolic language used by the RMQ in its advertising campaigns is a forceful example of the processes of escalation of antagonism and the "management of meaning" (Pettigrew, 1985) in change. The management of meaning refers to a process of symbol and value use designed both to create legitimacy for one's actions, ideas and demands, and to delegitimize the demands of one's opponents.

Taken together, the two examples above illustrate the complexity of the political agenda of change reform in the field of health. Although at first glance the two events seem separate, they were in fact related. Indeed, it appears that opposition to the plan to move the teaching hospital benefited from the movement opposed to Bill 120. Hardy (1982, 1985), Dufour (1991) and Pettigrew et al. (1992) among others, have demonstrated the decisive impact of physicians' participation, and of the existence of a network of opposition that can be mobilized within the community, on how change in health-care organizations is received.

Quality Management Programs

Throughout the various stages of reforms and adjustments within the Quebec health-care system, employees have been encouraged to participate in a series of measures and programs. This was done on the assumption that the implementation of reforms and change depends not only on managerial structures, processes and mechanisms, but also on the involvement of individuals. The most important elements are those that influence the motivation, cooperation and involvement of individuals. Moreover, the programs in Quebec have been tangibly influenced by the "search for excellence" and Japanese-style management movements. The main examples of this trend include: management-by-objectives, human resources development planning, total quality programs, followed by continuous quality improvement programs and, more recently, process reengineering. In fact, generally speaking, the majority of recent efforts to improve the quality of health care and services draw directly on this approach.

In a study aimed at determining the real impact of quality management programs in thirteen Quebec hospitals, Daniel Lozeau (1997) pointed to the limits of the approach in this type of organization. His study showed that environment and management could have an influence on how the implementation of these programs evolves. However, the processes inherent in social dynamics group dynamics and individual personality dynamics interact and influence each other. The particular social dynamics of this type of institution give considerable leeway to middle managers and dominant professional groups with regard to their actual degree of involvement. Lozeau found that neither doctors nor nurses wanted to give up their leadership on this issue to management. Although the two groups used different strategies, doctors and nurses shared the common objective of protecting their professional autonomy rather than participating in a process to integrate the contribution of actors in service production. Thus, "... far from having been able to change the organizational dynamics, the quality management approach, and the programs that followed from it in hospitals, have tended to fade away in these dynamics, to the point of contradicting a number of the fundamental aspects that are usually associated with the concept of quality management" (Lozeau, 1997: 326–327).

Lozeau's conclusions are consistent with those of other researchers who suggest that certain characteristics specific to health-care institutions are responsible for the limited effectiveness of this approach (Weisbord, 1981; Edmonstone, 1982; Pettigrew et al., 1992). In this regard, Weisbord explains that there are three main reasons why Organizational Development works better in private industry than in health-care institutions: (1) health-care institutions have few of the characteristics of private commercial enterprises where OD, like other management tools, was developed; (2) physicians and scientists are trained to adopt an expert, rational, autonomous and specialized behaviour, which runs counter to the organization of projects that are not strictly personalized; and thus, (3) health-care institutions require three social systems, not a single one as in private commercial enterprises. However, the links between the task system administered by senior managers, the identity system that supports professional status and the management system that establishes objectives remain blurred and indirect. (Weisbord, 1981: 267)

CONCLUSIONS

Our analysis suggests that a combined political and contingency approach is more appropriate in conducting major change processes to revitalize health-care systems. This is particularly so in the context of organizational downsizing characterized by closures and reallocation of resources. The political approach rests essentially on two assumptions. First, the leader elaborates change in a deliberate way. Second, the presence of change on the agenda is the result of a complex process in which three currents converge – problems, priorities and solutions (Kingdon, 1984; Lemieux, 1995). In any case, the change agent adopts a framework in which individuals and coalitions negotiate and compete with each other in order to win in a political arena. There are three main explanations for why such a combined approach appears to be more appropriate: (1) the nature of the outer and inner contexts of health-care institutions; (2) the attributes of the change process; and (3) the characteristics of the changes themselves.

The first source of explanation concerns the general operating context of health-care organizations. Because of their public character, they have a more diversified environment, thus making them accountable to a greater number of parties and more transparent than private enterprises. This situation gives rise to a greater awareness of political behaviours. Public organizations are more exposed to media attention than private enterprises. A greater number of interest groups gravitate around a public organization. They include, for example, organized groups that must make use of political action to achieve their objectives. Public policies are often the product of a difficult compromise and the coalitions on which they are based can be unstable. This leads to strategies that are being constantly renegotiated. The management of interest groups is therefore a more critical variable for public organizations than for private enterprises. (Paquin, 1992)

Yet another explanation relates to the nature of the internal context of health-care institutions. In fact, in health-care organizations, numerous individuals and groups with very different backgrounds, skills and abilities interact on an ongoing basis, all within a structure that demands a high level of functional interdependence. In this respect, Lamothe's (1996) analysis of the formation of the structure of action in a hospital showed that the production units formed within the institution depend on an arrangement of occupational spaces. This arrangement forms an occupational structure in which the respective positioning of groups is subject to constant negotiations and depends on the organizational status of each group. The occupational structure is therefore the organization's true fundamental structure because it is directly responsible for the control of production. Its existence explains the production system's relative immunity from the administration while confirming the latter's supportive role. Thus, while health-care organizations are commonly presented as professional bureaucracies (Blain, 1975; Mintzberg, 1982, 1990; Denis & Champagne, 1990), "bureaucracies of professionals" may be a more subtle way to describe them (Bégin, 1992; Lamothe, 1996). As Bégin, (1992) points out, professional heterogeneity is their distinguishing feature while, paradoxically, professional complementarity is the principal reason that they are found within the same organizational locations. This, therefore, gives these organizations their eminently political character. The very strong presence of political games is associated with just as strong a presence of emergent change. Indeed, actions undertaken at the level of both the general and internal contexts influence the structural form. Thus, the professional bureaucracy itself becomes an emergent product of political interactions between the system's leaders and actors.

A second reason why a combined political and contingency approach may be more appropriate relates to the particular features of NPM change processes in health-care organizations. These processes are complex and are based on the interactions, learning and autonomous behaviour of the organization's members rather than on the top-level leadership, vision or mission. In these conditions, planned, intentional change is difficult. NPM change is achieved through intrapreneurship and continuous dialogue between the stakeholders. Feedback and learning require the creation of interfunctional channels of communication as well as the establishment of new exchange networks among the key actors (Hart, 1992, 1994). The role of leaders is thus to encourage experimentation, exploration and risk, to facilitate transactions, to cultivate ideas and to connect the results of these processes over time so as to provide a sense of direction in change. As Denis et. al. (1996) indicated, through experimentation, the manager provokes reactions within the existing system. Experimentation seems to be a central process since it provides a means to distinguish clearly between what is acceptable and unacceptable and to identify which groups are opposed and which are in favor of the changes.

The third explanation relates to the features of the content of NPM changes. The lack of consensus, the divisibility of benefits, the scope and depth of the required change in behaviour, the rather long-term nature of and confusion over the goals being pursued, the number and dispersion of decision points (Grindle, 1980; Hafsi & Fabi, 1996) are among the potentially important characteristics. In addition, considering the rather threatening nature of some NPM changes, particularly when health-care institutions are closed, merely alluding to the possibility of changes is enough to generate a certain amount of political energy. As Hardy (1985) pointed out, political behaviour often features in situations in which the existing pattern of resource sharing is threatened and one such example is major innovation when opportunities to seize new resources are opened up (Pettigrew, 1973; Mumford & Pettigrew, 1976; Mintzberg, 1973). Another example is that where resources decrease, positions are threatened, and political behavior may become necessary in order to safeguard interest.

Although separating these three sources of explanation may make them appear to be independent entities, they should instead be seen as three elements that are dynamically interrelated during a period of time. While a political-contingency approach appears to be desirable in the specific context of health-care organizations, the classical approach is still generally dominant, at least in the discourse of politicians and practitioners. The classical approach espouses a view that politics and administration can be simply divided. This is a myth that reinforces the belief that managers and elected officials are in full control of the New Public Management process from conception through to implementation.

REFERENCES

Bégin, C. (1992). Le Nouveau Défi Du Directeur Général Dans Les Établissements De Santé Et De Services Sociaux: Faire Éclater Le Partenariat. Document De Travail 92–56. *Équipe De Recherche En Organisation Et En Évaluation De Services De Santé*. Faculté des sciences de l'administration, Université Laval, Québec.

Blain, G. (1975). The Hospital as a Professional Bureaucracy. *Trustee*, October: 13–16.

Denis, J. L., & Champagne, F. (1990). Pour Comprendre Le Changement Dans Les Organisations. *Gestion, 15*(1), 44–56.

Denis, J. L., Langley, A., & Pineault, M. (1996). Devenir Leader Dans Une Organisation Complexe. *Gestion, 21*(4), 15–24.

Dufour, C., & Paquet, R. (1997). La Reforme De L'administration Publique: Grande Bretagne at Alberta. In: M. Charish & R. Landry (Eds), *La Gestion Publique Sous le Microscope*. Ste-Foy Quebec: Presse de l'Universite du Quebec.

Dufour, Y. (1991). *The Implementation of GP Maternity Unit Closure Proposals in Hospitals*. Unpublished Doctoral Dissertation, University of Warwick.

Dufour, Y., & Codjia, L. (1992). *La Réforme De La Santé (Loi 120): L'affrontement Entre Le Ministre De La Santé Et Des Services Sociaux Et Le Regroupement Des Médecins Du Québec*. Formation Continue En Gestion, Département D'administration De La Santé, Faculté De Médecine, Université de Montréal.

Dufour, Y., & Nadeau, C. (1993). *Le projet de "Déménagement" de l'Hôtel-Dieu-de-Montréal à Rivière-des-Prairies*. Centrale De Cas Et De Documents Pédagogiques, École des HEC Montréal.

Edmonstone, J. (1982). From Organisational Social Work to Organisational Design. *Leadership and Organisation Development Journal, 3*(1), 24–26.

Glor, E. (2000). Past, Present and Future of Public Administration: Where Are We Headed? http://home.thirdage.com/Environment/fsn/glor.html

Grindle, M. S. (1980). Policy Content and Context in Implementation. In: M. S. Grindle (Ed.), *Politics and the Policy Implementation in the Third World*. New Jersey, Princeton University Press.

Guthrie J., & English, L. (2000). Public Sector Management in the State of Victoria 1992–1999: Genesis of the Transformation. Paper at IPMN Conference, 4–6 March, Sydney.

Hafsi, T., & Fabi, B. (1997). *Les Fondements Du Changement Stratégique*. Montréal, Éditions Transcontinental.

Halligan J., & Power, J. (1992). *Political Management in the 1990s*. Melbourne: Oxford University Press.

Hardy, C. (1982). *Organisational Closure: A Political Perspective*. Unpublished Doctoral Dissertation, University of Warwick.

Hardy, C. (1985). *Managing Organisational Closure*. Aldershot, U.K: Gower.

Hardy, C., & Pettigrew, A. M. (1985). The Use of Power in Managerial Strategies for Change. *Research on Technological Innovation, Management and Policy, 2*(1), 11–45.

Hart, S. L. (1992). An Integrative Framework for Strategy-Making Processes. *Academy of Management Review, 17*(2), 327–351.

Hood, C. (1995). Contemporary Public Management: A New Global Paradigms. *Public Policy and Administration*, *10*(2), 104–117.

Kingdon, J. W. (1984). *Agendas, Alternatives and Public Policies*. Boston: Little Brown.

Lamothe, L. (1996). *La Structure Professionnelle Clinique D'un Hpiltal De Soins Ultra-Spécialisés*. Unpublished Doctoral Dissertation, McGill University.

Lemieux, V. (1995). L'émergence Des Politiques Publiques. In: *Dans L'étude Des Politiques Publiques – Les Acteurs Et Leur Pouvoir*. Ste-Foy: Presses de l'Université Laval.

Lozeau, D. (1997). *Étude Critique De La Pratique De La Gestion De La Qualité Dans Les Hôpitaux Au Québec*. Unpublished Doctoral Dissertation, Montréal: UQAM.

Mintzberg, H. (1973). *The Nature of Managerial Work*. New York, Harper and Row.

Mintzberg, H. (1982). *Structure Et Dynamique Des Organisations*. Paris: Editions d'Organisation.

Mintzberg, H. (1990). *Le Management – Voyage Au Centre Des Organisations*. Paris: Editions d'Organisation.

Mumford, E., & Pettigrew, A. M. (1976). *Implementing Strategic Decisions*. London: Longman.

Olson, O., Guthrie, J., & Humphrey, C. (1998). *Global Warning! Debating International Development in NPFM*. Oslo: Cappelen.

O'Neill, D., & Hughes, O. (2000). The Limits Of New Public Management: Reflections On The Kennett 'Revolution' In Victoria. Paper presented at the IPMN Conference, 4 March, Sydney.

Paquin, M. (1992). La Planification Stratégique Dans Le Secteur Public. In: R. Parenteau et. al. (Eds), *Management Public – Comprendre et Gérer les Institution de l'État*. Ste-Foy: Presses de l'Université du Québec.

Pettigrew, A. M. (1973). *The Politics of Organisational Decision Making*. London: Tavistock.

Pettigrew, A. M. (1985). *The Awakening Giant: Continuity and Change in ICI*. Oxford: Basil Blackwell.

Pettigrew, A. M., Ferlie, E., & McKee, L. (1992). *Shaping Strategic Change: Making Change in Large Organisations – The Case of the NHS*. London: Sage Publications.

Weisbord, M. R. (1981). Why Organisation Development Hasn't Worked (so far) in Medical Centres. In: G. F. Wieland (Ed.), *Improving Health Care Management – Organisation Development and Organisation Change*. Ann Arbor, Michigan: Health Administration Press.

SECTION V

LEARNING FROM PUBLIC MANAGEMENT REFORM: CRITICAL PERSPECTIVES ON NEW PUBLIC MANAGEMENT

29. PUBLIC CHOICE THEORY AND ECONOMIC RATIONALISM: THE BASIS OF NEW PUBLIC MANAGEMENT

Allan Barton

INTRODUCTION

This chapter examines Public Choice Theory (PCT) and its associated brand of economic rationalism (ER) as the basis for the most recent tranche of managerial reforms in the public sector, collectively referred to in the literature as the New Public Management (NPM) (Olson, et al., 1998). The various reforms instituted in Australia by the Commonwealth Government since about 1990 are examined as applications of this theory. The reforms were heavily influenced by those implemented in New Zealand and the United Kingdom a little earlier. Similar reforms have also been implemented by most Australian state governments, particularly in Victoria over the period 1993–1999 (See English and Guthrie in this volume).

In Australia, the NPM reforms based on PCT succeeded the managerialist reforms of the 1980s, which were originated by the Royal Commission on Australian Government Administration (the Coombs Commission, 1976; Guthrie, 1993). This is similar to the New Zealand developments (Pallot, 1998). The managerialist reforms of the 1980s were based on management by objectives, adoption of accrual accounting as a means of expanding the management information base, and some devolution of authority over budget

Learning from International Public Management Reform, Volume 11B, pages 571–588.
ISBN: 0-7623-0760-9

management. The more recent NPM reforms have extended these managerialist reforms by the adoption wherever possible of competitive market principles in public sector management and a review of the role of government so as to curtail its activities. Both major political parties appear to support the reforms – in Australia, they were introduced by a Labour Government and then extended by the present conservative Coalition Government.

The chapter comprises the following four sections. Section two provides some statements about the adoption of PCT as the basis of recent public sector management reforms. Section 3 gives an explanation of PCT, its development from neoclassical perfect competition theory, the key assumptions on which it is based, and its implications for the role of government in society. Section 4 discusses the application of PCT by Australian governments, firstly as a means of slimming the state through privatizations and curtailment of the welfare state, and secondly through marketization of the remaining government activities. Section 5 presents conclusions drawn from the above analysis.

PUBLIC CHOICE THEORY AND ECONOMIC RATIONALISM: THE BASIS OF THE NEW PUBLIC MANAGEMENT

While there has not been any Government pronouncement about the adoption of PCT and ER as the basis for the NPM reforms, its adoption has been noted by several scholars of public administration. For example, after reviewing the United Kingdom, New Zealand and other nations' reforms, Self (1993: cover page) concluded that:

> Economic or public choice theories of politics have contributed powerfully to a new paradigm of 'government by the market' – meaning not only that public responsibilities should be reduced and public policies adjusted to the pressure of economic markets, but also that government itself should be remodelled and reformed according to market concepts of competition and efficiency.

Holtham and Kay (1994: 3–4) also noted the adoption of PCT as the basis of market-oriented reforms of government in their review of the U.K. situation. Similarly, Corbett (1996, pp. 68–9) states that:

> The influence of the public choice school of thought . . . has been profound in the 1980s and 1990s. The Thatcher government in the United Kingdom, the Lange government in New Zealand and the government of several Australian states and the Commonwealth have all been advised by keen disciples of the public choice school.

Finally, in her review of the marketization phase (1986–91) of the New Zealand reforms, Pallot (1998: 162) states: "The most influential bodies of theory on which they [i.e., Treasury economists] drew were 'public choice', 'agency theory' and 'transactions cost analysis'".

PUBLIC CHOICE THEORY, ECONOMIC RATIONALISM AND GOVERNMENT

Public choice theory (PCT) is based on the neoclassical theory of perfect competition, even though actual market systems are not of this type. As a consequence, NPM reforms have been modelled on the operations of private competitive markets in the belief that the market system is more efficient in resource management and effective in responding to citizens needs than is a bureaucratic government administration. Moreover, it is believed that government itself should be remodelled and transformed according to market concepts of competition and efficiency (Self, 1993, cover page, Holtham & Kay: 3–4). Thus, the notion of 'government by the market' arose; and at the political level, public choice theory was adapted from economics to political science theory to provide a framework for the new style of government.

According to Corbett (1996: 69), public choice theory:

> is the application of classical economic methods of analysis to political and administrative systems. The object is to discover underlying patterns of behavior and then to prescribe policies that will increase the public's power to choose policies which serve their interests as consumers.

Furthermore, Self (1993: 3) states that in public choice theory:

> Voters are likened to consumers; political parties become entrepreneurs who offer competing packages of services and taxes in exchange for votes, political propaganda parallels commercial advertising; government departments are public firms dependent on receiving adequate political support to cover their costs; and interest groups are cooperative associations of consumers or producers of public goods, ie. all those goods supplied through a political instead of a market process.

Classical economics is shaped by the self-seeking behavior of individuals aiming to maximise their own economic welfare. In Adam Smith's theory of the 'invisible hand' of laissez-faire market competition, which is frequently referred to in the public choice literature, the self-interest of the butcher and baker in pursuing profit promotes general economic welfare (Smith, 1776: 13). Public choice theory argues that voters, politicians and bureaucrats are motivated by self-interest, similarly to Smith's butcher and baker. It leads to a view of the self-seeking behavior of parties involved in the political process, and an adverse view of the capacity of governments to satisfy those wants (i.e. government failure). This 'government failure' is claimed to arise from two factors (Self, 1993: 32–36; Corbett, 1996: 70; Holtham & Kay, 1994: 3). The first factor is the incentive for bureaucrats to pursue their own self-interest through empire building of their departments and spheres of influence, and through maximizing their own budgets. As well, there is an absence of incentives to control costs sparingly. These factors lead to an increase in the size of government generally. The second factor is the weak control of the bureaucracy arising from the private interests of bureaucrats in distorting information supplied to ministers and parliament to suit their own interests, and from weak or inexperienced ministers and the turnover of ministers.

Although Smith is generally regarded as the father of modern economics, he was in fact a professor of moral philosophy and the altruism of his competitive markets theory was based on a comprehensive set of ethical values in business. Fleming (1999: 162) for example states that:

> The relationship between social norms, economic behavior and the prevailing legal framework occupied a central position in Adam Smith's writings on social philosophy and political economy. . . . Smith incorporated an ethical system in his political economy.

Smith emphasised the many abuses to which the market system was subject as a consequence of practices in restraint of trade and the emergence of monopoly power. In contrast, there are no moral norms or altruism in public choice theory.

As well, it should be noted that the nature of Smith's treatise in the *Wealth of Nations* is only of a very general nature, and it was left to later economists to develop the technical aspects of competition theory – in particular: Marshall (1890) for the development of supply and demand theory, marginal analysis, and firm and industry equilibrium according to various market structures including perfect competition; Pareto (1909) for the development of micro-economic general equilibrium theory; and Pigou (1920) for the development of the concept of externalities.

The theory of perfect competition in economics that underpins public choice theory is not intended to be a description of firms and industries as they exist – indeed it is highly unrealistic. Rather, its use in economics is to theorize about the market structure and conduct conditions necessary to induce 'good performance'. Such performance occurs where, firstly, consumers are free to purchase the goods and services they desire at the minimum possible price; and secondly, when efficient producers are able to recover all their costs of production and provide a sufficient reward to owners or investors to attract their funds. Consumers are able to maximise their satisfactions and firms their profits in such a way that no one consumer or firm can be made better off from a redistribution of resources without making another worse off. This result is known in economic theory as the 'Pareto optimum' (Stiglitz, 1988: chapters 3 and 4).

To achieve these results from the self-seeking behavior of individuals aiming to maximise their own economic welfare, a rigorous set of market conditions is required for the model. They are:

- Large numbers of firms actively competing against each other, and consumers competing to buy the products. Hence each firm and consumer is small relative to the market and no one can influence price.
- Homogeneous products. Hence buyers have no preference for the product of any one seller over others and price is the only determinant of an individual firm's sale.
- Complete mobility of all resources and of consumers in the market. Hence firms and consumers can readily move to positions where they can maximise their benefits.
- Complete knowledge of all market opportunities and technologies for all firms and consumers so that they know how they can maximise their benefits. There is no uncertainty and hence no risks are incurred, and there is no information asymmetry as between firms and consumers. Economic rationality is easy to define in conditions of perfect knowledge.

Thus, the theory can only be approximated in those industries characterised by small business and low entry barriers, such as in agriculture and some service industries. However, large corporations dominate all capital-intensive industries where entry barriers are high, such as most manufacturing, retailing, finance and infrastructure industries; consequently the theory has very little application to them. Furthermore, the existence of uncertainty and risk taking make the concepts of rationality and an optimum allocation of resources difficult to specify and implement.

In addition, the model has two further requirements to bring about the identity of private economic welfare with the social welfare of the nation so that the 'invisible hand' works in the public interest. These conditions are of particular importance in public sector markets. They are:

- Identity between private and social costs and benefits throughout, so that the pursuit of private benefits automatically enhances social benefits.
- Rivalrous and excludable consequences of purchase transactions. Hence purchases by one consumer exclude others from buying the goods, and the consumer obtains exclusive property rights to the goods without having to share them with others.

The absence of these two conditions results in 'externalities' occurring in markets, which refer to the existence of non-rivalrous and non-excludable consumption, and differences between private and social costs and benefits. The traditional roles of government can be largely explained in terms of these two conditions (Musgrave, 1989: chapter 4). In non-rivalrous and non-excludable markets (e.g. provision of defence, law and order services, good government, street lighting and so on), consumers cannot obtain individual property rights enabling exclusive use of the services, so they cannot be sold to them. Rather, the only option is for these services to be provided freely by the government to citizens as pure public goods. Similarly, to promote social equity and perceived social benefits, governments provide a range of mixed public/private goods such as education and health services, and access to community recreational and cultural facilities such as art galleries and museums, on a free or heavily subsidised basis to all citizens who desire them. These types of public goods are often referred to as merit goods.

Where externalities in markets of the above type are important, it can be demonstrated that the private market provision of goods is both inefficient and insufficient, and that a preferable solution is for governments to supply them on a collective basis and to fund their provision primarily from taxation (Musgrave, 1989: chapters 1 and 4; Stiglitz, 1988: chapters 1, 3 and 5). 'Market failure' by private goods firms attributable to these externalities provides the basic justification for the government provision of pure public goods and of mixed public/private goods or merit goods. Private markets fail under these conditions because firms cannot charge a price to recoup full average cost as buyers do not obtain exclusive rights to use of the good and they are accessible to all citizens (leading to the 'free-rider problem'); and secondly an optimum use of resources requires charging a price equal to marginal cost (however most costs are fixed and marginal costs tend towards zero). Hence in private markets, production of such goods would be insufficient and inefficient. In addition, Australian governments have historically developed infrastructure industries because the huge amounts of capital required were beyond the abilities of private firms to fund, and because of the natural monopoly status of those industries. Until the recent spate of privatizations, governments owned 90% of the infrastructure facilities in Australia (National Commission of Audit, 1996, PXVIII). Thus, the roles of the public and private sectors of the economy are largely complementary. The government provides public goods and infra-structure facilities because of the failure in private goods markets, and commercial firms supply all other goods where there is no need for their provision by government.

It can be noted that the application of PCT to the public sector takes the opposite tack to the traditional roles based on public goods theory. Whereas public goods theory is based on the claimed failure of private goods markets to supply public goods, PCT is justified on the basis of the claimed failures of government to function efficiently and effectively in the supply of those goods. Ultimately the resolution of these counter claims can only be determined empirically.

On the basis of the above analysis, it is evident that the theory of perfect competition suffers from severe limitations in its application to most private goods markets as they exist in the real world; and it has additional limitations when applied to public goods markets. PCT not only ignores the realities of most private goods markets, but also endeavors to apply competitive market theory to public goods markets wherein the basic characteristics make it largely irrelevant. The linkage between PCT and the neoclassical theory of competition is very tenuous indeed. One is left with the suspicion that the basic reason for applying PCT to the public sector is the ideological one that, in the view of two of its leading proponents, Milton Friedman and James Buchanan, "economic intervention by the state is generally not only inefficient but immoral" (Holtham & Kay, 1994: 2).

APPLICATION OF PUBLIC CHOICE THEORY BY AUSTRALIAN GOVERNMENTS

The recent NPM reforms in the Australian public sector comprise two broad sets. The first set is that concerned primarily with slimming the state. The second set is concerned with the use of market mechanisms in the provision of those goods and services for which the government retains responsibility (i.e. marketization). They are both extensions of the earlier managerialist reforms. However the NPM reforms combine managerialist ideas with public choice theory. Likewise the two sets are inter-related in that the marketization reforms can lead to a contraction in the size of the state.

A detailed explanation of the reforms is given in Guthrie and Parker (1998: chapter 2, English and Guthrie in this volume). Only some of the major NPM reforms are considered here, with special emphasis on two of these: (a) slimming the state; (b) the adoption of market principles in public administration.

Slimming the State

Advocates of PCT aim to reduce substantially the role of the state and its responsibilities, back to what they regard as core activities, though not necessarily to the extent stated by Hotham and Kay (1994: 2) who state that, "Its aspiration is the nightwatchman state, whose functions are mainly restricted to the maintenance of law and order and the enforcement of contract."

In Australia the newly elected conservative Government established a National Commission of Audit in 1996 to review its scope of responsibilities. The Commission concluded that (NCA, 1996: 7):

> In a market-based economy controlled by a democratically elected government there are only two primary reasons for government involvement in the activities of the community:
> - Social equity. Governments have a role where the market system is incapable of delivering the social outcomes that the elected government had been given a mandate to achieve. Such outcomes are usually related to welfare issues involving the general standard of community health, education and standards of living.
> - Market failure. This is often associated with the monopoly power or undue influence through market power or where supply of a product is excessive or inadequate. Where it does occur, it is usually because of inadequate assignment and policing of property rights – both physical and intellectual. Policing such property rights is a primary role of government.

In the light of these two principles, the NCA (1996, Chapter 3) recommended a widespread curtailment of government activities including the sale of government business enterprises and other public sector assets where there appears to be no public interest for continued government ownership.

Two major public policy methods of 'slimming the state' to give effect to the reduction in responsibilities identified by the NCA were the privatization of Government Business Enterprises (GBE) and the curtailment of the welfare state. The following provides a brief summary of the NCA position and of developments since then.

The NCA believed, firstly, that GBEs operating in the competitive markets have no role in the slimmed-down state. They operate according to commercial principles, selling their products to customers on a user-pays basis and they are required to be financially self-supporting, except for capital investment. They are in competition with private firms, and their behavior and performance are subject to normal business laws and the forces of competition. In line with this policy the Commonwealth Government sold, for example, the Commonwealth Bank and Qantas in the early rounds of privatization.

Secondly, GBEs operating in infrastructure industries (e.g. Telstra, power companies, airports, railways) should be privatized wherever possible. However, as these GBEs have natural monopoly power, they have community service obligations imposed on them by government. Many also have major environmental protection obligations. As a consequence, their activities are subject to government regulation after privatization. Wherever possible, governments may restructure the industry prior to privatization to introduce some competition through breaking up the monopoly into several separate firms and/or the introduction of private firms. (Newbery, 1996, 1997). For example, new firms (C&W Optus, AAPT) have entered the telecommunications industry to compete against Telstra; the Victorian electricity industry was vertically de-integrated and several firms were introduced at each level of operations – power generation, transmission and distribution to customers; and similar types of proposals are being implemented in the privatization of Melbourne public transport.

Australia has implemented one of the largest privatization projects in the world. The extent of privatization in Australia has varied among governments. The Commonwealth Government has privatised the most assets ($30 billion by 1997), followed by the Victorian Government ($24 billion). Total government privatizations amounted to over $61 billion by December 1997 (Reserve Bank, 1997). Several more privatizations have occurred since then, including the second tranche of Telstra for $16 billion in 1999 (Walker and Walker, 2000, 21).

The second major public policy method was the curtailment of the Welfare State. Expenditure on welfare services constitutes by far the largest item in the budget, being circa 40% of the 1999/2000 Commonwealth Budget (Statement No. 4: 4–7), and it is rising each year. As well, much of the Commonwealth Government's transfers to the States (another 10% of the budget) are for those welfare items that are State Government responsibilities. Welfare expenditures are claimed to be crowding out other areas of government expenditure and creating budgetary problems for governments wishing to slim the size of the state. Some of the reasons for the growth in welfare expenditures include the high level of unemployment occurring over the past 20 years, growth in education participation, and increasing costs of health care due to new technologies and ageing of the population. In this regard, the proportion of the population in Australia aged 65 and over is projected to increase from 10.1% in 1992 to 15.9% by 2025, an increase of 57% (Duval, 1994: 6). Senior citizens draw upon social welfare services more heavily than younger people because of age pensions and health care needs.

Several mechanisms have been adopted to limit government responsibility for provision of welfare services. (NCA 1996, chapter 6) They include attempts to target their provision to more precisely defined 'needy' categories of beneficiaries so as to reduce the number of eligible recipients; the outsourcing of welfare service provision to church and other private welfare agencies to generate cost savings; the introduction of partial user-pays charges such as for health and tertiary education services; and the provision of taxation incentives to users to provide for themselves, such as for health care insurance and superannuation. Public choice theory emphasises the inefficiency of government provision of welfare services and the superiority of self-help by citizens.

The division of activities between the private and public sectors is ultimately a political decision to be made by the citizens of the nation. In practice it varies widely from country to country. Economic analysis alone cannot provide the answer. Citizens must make the choice between smaller and larger governments in the knowledge that the public provision of goods and services must somehow be paid for (Broadbent, 1998: chapter 15).

Adoption of Market Principles in Public Administration

The NCA recommended the application of private business management principles to government administration to enhance its efficiency and effectiveness. This involves the remodelling and transformation of government administration according to market concepts of competition and efficiency, which are referred to collectively as the marketization of government. In so far as they are effective, they also enable further slimming of the state.

The major commercial principles recommended by the NCA for government administration comprised: adoption of commercial accrual accounting systems; imposition of user charges; corporatization and commercialization of public trading enterprises; employment of staff on a contract basis; separation of policy formulation from service delivery; and contestability, competition and outsourcing of services. The following subsection will explore these principles.

Adoption of Commercial Accrual Accounting Systems

The NCA (1996, chapter 8) recommended that governments require departments to adopt accrual accounting systems to facilitate efficient management of resources (Department of Finance, 1994; Barton, 1999c). Governments frequently have enormous portfolios of assets and liabilities, and cash accounting systems provide no information about them except for cash itself. Only accrual accounting information systems can measure assets and liabilities of the government, its revenues, and the costs incurred on provision of public services.

For example in June 1998, the financial assets of the Commonwealth Government were $104.5 billion and its physical assets were $83.3 billion, while its liabilities comprised borrowings of $115.7 billion and unfunded provisions (superannuation etc) of $134.8 billion. (Commonwealth Financial Statements, 1998: 23).

The Accounting Standards Board, which promulgates the standards for use in Australia, believes that commercial accounting standards can and ought to be applied to the public sector (McGregor, 1999; MacIntosh, 1999). The set of accrual accounting standards developed for the public sector (AAS27, AAS29 and AAS31) are all based on existing commercial accounting standards and Statements of Accounting Concepts, with only minor modifications for institutional differences.

However, any accounting information system must be adapted to the conditions of the environment in which it is applied if it is to provide useful and relevant information for management planning, control, performance measurement and accountability purposes. Thus, commercial accrual accounting practices were developed over the past two hundred or so years to suit the needs of industry. They are based on the commercial realities of the private business environment – the need to recover all costs from revenue and to earn sufficient profit to survive, the user-pays principle, the need to raise sufficient capital from investors to fund purchase of assets and working capital, and the need to maintain a sound financial position.

Many of these conditions do not apply to government operations because the basic role and mode of public sector activities differ fundamentally from those of private, profit seeking firms (Barton, 1999a). For example:

- the bulk of public goods and services are provided to citizens on a free or heavily subsidised basis and not a full user-pays basis, for social and community welfare reasons;
- decisions are made by governments on a collective basis concerning the provision of public goods and services, and funded primarily from taxation revenue rather than an individual consumer sovereignty basis;
- many of the assets used for public purposes are natural capital assets inherited by governments at no cost – they were not purchased. They are managed for public use by the government effectively as trustee manager (Barton 1999b); and
- many public sector assets are environmental and heritage assets which are to be protected and preserved in good condition for the use of future generations of citizens. They are not to be used up in a productive process like most private sector assets;
- many public sector assets are by law open for use by all citizens, their consumption is non-rivalrous and non-excludable and they confer no private property rights to users, unlike private goods;

- the benefits of many public sector assets flow directly to the public as users and not to the government as owner/manager, for example, all community assets and public roads; and
- governments do not depend on capital contributions from investors to fund their asset purchases; rather they rely on the power to tax and to inherit natural capital assets as well as on borrowing.

None of the above characteristics occurs in the private sector and they all have significant implications for accounting information systems, yet they are ignored in the present set of public sector accounting standards.

Imposition of User Charges
Wherever possible, public choice advocates and the NCA (1996, 25) argue that governments should impose user charges to recover part of the costs of providing mixed public/private goods or merit goods, such as for health and education, and for access to public heritage and environmental facilities such as art galleries, national parks and so on (Carnegie & Wolnizer, 1995; Barton, 2000). These charges are not only intended to reduce the size of the state, but also to force the individual user to think more seriously about their use, as they are no longer a free public good. The charges move the goods in the direction of private goods markets wherein consumers must consider the costs and benefits of purchase decisions and thereby encourage greater efficiency in the allocation of resources. However they can have negative social welfare effects.

Corporatization and Commercialization of Public Trading Enterprises
Even where Public Trading Enterprises (PTEs) are not to be privatised, they are likely to be corporatized and their operations placed on a commercial basis, eg. Australia Post, State Railways and Water Authorities. Frequently in the past, these activities were performed by government departments. Although these enterprises generate their own revenues through sales of their products, they have significant community service obligations imposed on them and they are often unable to recover their full costs of operations from product sales. Hence, they normally require subsidization by government. In order to enhance their efficiency, these entities are corporatized and given some commercial independence from departments and ministers. They have their own boards of directors, appointed by government, who are responsible for their management. Normally many of the directors will be drawn from the business sector, and the enterprises are required to be as commercial as their operating charters allow.

The major concern with the corporatization of PTEs is that governments can become less accountable to parliament and the electorate for their operations.

Giving PTEs greater independence to enhance their efficiency can be at the expense of accountability of government as the arrangements are generally on a commercial-in-confidence basis. Governments can hide behind commercial confidentiality to deny responsibility and accountability.

Employment of Staff on a Contract Basis

Public choice theory and the NCA (1996, chapter 5) believe that in the traditional Westminster style of the public service, bureaucrats are not sufficiently responsive to public needs, are too protected from the market environment, and are subject to conflicts of interest, as outlined above. To overcome these claimed defects, it is proposed that senior bureaucrats should be appointed by the chief executive (i.e. prime minister or premier) under contract for fixed terms. Duties and performance targets for the bureaucrats are spelt out in the contracts, and performance bonuses are paid as an incentive. The contracts should be designed to align the self-interest of the bureaucrat as agent to achieve high performance levels, with those of the minister as the principal. However, the traditional attributes of the fearless provision of independent advice to the minister, and loyalty and a strong zeal to work in 'the public interest', are not normally part of the contract, and no emphasis appears to be placed on the role of the principal. In Australia the former Public Service Boards, which used to handle such appointments, have been abolished. The practice is being extended through departments to all levels of staff ('workplace agreements').

This new system of contract employment, colloquially called the 'Washminster System', has several major limitations. It can expose the public service to the risk of politicization. The provision of informed, independent and fearless advice to the minister where it is not appreciated could expose the bureaucrat to risk of dismissal. This occurred recently when a senior bureaucrat was dismissed by the minister who claimed he had lost confidence in him, even though the bureaucrat reputedly had recently been awarded a performance bonus, (Canberra Times, 2000: 3). In a recent study of management changes in the Department of Finance and Administration (DOFA), Geiselhart (2000: 10) noted the opinion that, ". . . the quality of policy advice had gone from 'frank and fearless' to 'fear and favour'." Furthermore, it may not be possible to prescribe all the requirements of jobs in contracts except in general terms, but this may not provide an adequate basis for measuring and assessing performance (Holtham & Kay, 1994: 4; Di Francesco, 2000). This is particularly the case for senior appointments where the major function is to provide sound policy advice and where there are complex and multiple policy objectives. Finally, the system may have some negative effects on staff morale and loyalty in parts of the public service (Geiselhart, 2000).

Separation of Policy Formulation from Service Delivery
In the NPM reforms, policy advisory and formulation functions are frequently separated from the delivery of public services to the users (NCA, 1996: 15–16). The segregation is attributable to the concept of the slimmed-down state as a service facilitator rather than a service provider, and secondly to the alleged conflict of interest for senior bureaucrats in performing the two roles, viz. in their pursuing personal interest in empire building, enhancement of power, budget maximization and so on. The separation of functions allows senior bureaucrats more time to focus on policy issues and not be encumbered or distracted by everyday problems of implementation and administration.

However, the divorce between policy formulation and service delivery raises problems at the higher levels of the bureaucracy. For example, central coordinating departments such as Prime Minister and Cabinet (PM&C), Finance and Administration (DOFA) and Treasury need to be involved in both aspects because policy formulation and its implementation must be carefully integrated for it to be effective. Also, senior executives who specialise in policy formulation and advice are likely to lose touch with the area of implementation and have no feel for the success of the policies or the problems raised by them.

Contestability, Competition and Outsourcing of Service Provision
Associated with the notion that the state should be a service facilitator rather than a provider, it is proposed that service provision be opened up to market competition wherever possible (NCA, 1996, 15–16). Government departments are often required to compete with the private sector, or even with other departments, for the provision of public services. It is generally administered through a tendering process. However, departments must base their bids on 'full cost' as calculated on commercial accrual accounting principles to ensure a 'level playing field'. Thus, departmental bid costs must include all overheads, capital consumption charges (depreciation, etc), superannuation expense, and a profit margin (currently 12% on capital investment). Purchaser-provider models have been developed to assist departments in contracting for the provision of services. By opening up public sector markets to contestability and market competition, ie. outsourcing, it is hoped to improve upon efficiency and effectiveness in the provision of public services.

Outsourcing has always been used by governments for some areas of their activities, for example in public works. However, in the NPM theories, there is a presumption in favor of outsourcing wherever possible for ideological as well as efficiency reasons. The extent of outsourcing of government activities in Australia has grown substantially in recent years, and this has facilitated major reductions in public sector staffing. The number of core public sector staff was reduced by 27% over the period 1989–1998, with the rate of reduction accelerating markedly from 1995. Almost half of the reduction resulted from outsourcing and privatization of government activities, and was mainly achieved through retrenchments (ANAO, 1998–1999: chapter 2).

While a strong case can be made for contestability and competition in the supply of public services where efficiency and effectiveness are enhanced, the use of outsourcing for ideological purposes must be questioned. It can result in higher costs in the long run where departments are crippled by unfair competition to compete in the future. Private tenderers are not required to charge 'full cost' and they may submit 'loss leader' bids. There can be a loss of in-house expertise to negotiate tenders and monitor the performance of the service provided, particularly with respect to the quality of the service. An ANAO audit (1999–2000: 14–15) found many weaknesses in the control framework for several outsourced internal services (finance function, payroll processing and internal audit), including absence of appropriate monitoring of the quality of services delivered. However, the timeliness and cost of service delivery were considered to be satisfactory. Most importantly, with out-sourcing, the contracts for service delivery are invariably labelled as 'commercial-in-confidence', and this restricts the accountability of depart-ments and governments for expenditure of taxpayer money.

CONCLUSIONS

In so far as public sector management reforms bring about improvements in the efficiency and effectiveness of government operations, they enhance the quality of government and should be supported. However, the first reason for concern arises when such reforms appear to be implemented primarily for ideological reasons. In such cases, they will not necessarily result in long-term efficiency and effectiveness improvements. Olson et al. (1998: 20) summarize the situation succinctly in their observation that: "NPFM reforms have the capacity to change the ruling language and priorities in organizations, often in relatively quiet and unnoticed ways – or as Hall suggests, 'without a shot being fired'."

The NPM reforms are not neutral with respect to the scope and mode of government operations – they have the effect of curtailing the activities of government. In a democratic society, decisions with respect to boundaries of the government sector and methods of funding it must remain with citizens exercising their electoral choices. In so far as there is a political desire by some members of society to advance the concept of minimalist government activities, they ought to promote it openly as a political policy. The scope and mode of operation of government must not be changed by stealth through management reforms that are ostensibly promoted as a means of enhancing 'efficiency' and better delivery of essential services.

A second cause for concern with the reforms is the marked decline in the accountability of governments and public servants to parliament and the public (Parker & Guthrie, 1993). This occurs through the stealthy nature of many of the reforms, the privatization of GBEs and most of the marketization processes adopted in the retained government sector. The adoption of corporatization and commercialization of PTEs, the outsourcing of service provision, the employment of staff on a contract basis associated with confidential performance agreements, and so on, all involve commercial-in-confidence arrangements. Senior bureaucrats can avoid accountability to ministers, as can ministers to parliament and governments to the public. Transparency in public sector operations is seriously curtailed. Yet accountability is a basic requirement for democratic nations. The Management Advisory Board of the Commonwealth Government in its report on accountability states (MAB, 1993: 3), "Accountability is fundamental to good governance in modern open societies . . . accountability of public officials is one of the essential guarantees and underpinnings . . . of efficient, impartial and ethical public administration."

Moreover, service provision contracts with external suppliers and staff always include performance clauses. Where the service to be provided is a complex, multi-faceted one with multiple objectives, such as the provision of policy advice and coordination, performance is difficult to specify and measure. Yet contract rewards are based on performance in the quality of the services provided notwithstanding acute measurement difficulties.

Finally, PCT is based on ideas taken from neoclassical models of perfect competition developed for an entirely different purpose. The relevance of the theory for the political objectives of PCT must be questioned. PCT theory should be seen as a political ideology aimed at promoting minimalist government rather than disguised as a means of promoting efficiency and effectiveness in public sector operations.

REFERENCES

ASCPA/ICAA (1995). AAS27, *Financial Reporting by Local Government*.
ASCPA/ICAA (1996). AAS29, *Financial Reporting by Government Departments*.

ASCPA/ICAA (1996). AAS31, *Financial Reporting by Governments*.

ANAO (1998–99). Staff Reductions in the Australian Public Service. *Performance Audit Report No. 49*.

ANAO (1999–2000). Management of Contracted Business Support Services. *Financial Control and Administration Audit Report No. 12*.

Barton, A. D. (1999a). Public and Private Sector Accounting: The Non-Identical Twins. *Australian Accounting Review, 9*(2), July.

Barton, A. D. (1999b). A Trusteeship Theory of Accounting for Natural Capital Assets. *Abacus, 35*(2), June.

Barton, A. D. (1999c). The Usefulness of Accrual Accounting for Government Resource Management. AAANZ Conference, Cairns, July.

Barton, A. D. (2000). Public Heritage Facilities – Assets or Liabilities of the Government? *Accounting Auditing and Accountability Journal, 13*(2), May.

Broadbent, J. (1998). NPFM and Issues of Policy: Where Do We Go From Here? In: Olson et. al., *Global Warning: Debating International Developments in New Public Financial Management*. Bergen, Norway: Cappelen Akademisk Forlag.

Carnegie, G., & Wolnizer, F. (1995). The Financial Value of Cultural, Heritage & Scientific Collections: An Accounting Fiction. *Australian Accounting Review, 15*(1), March.

Canberra Times (2000). Fearless Advice at Risk after Barratt Decision. 12 March.

Corbettt, D. (1996). *Australian Public Sector Management*, 2nd edition. Sydney: Allen and Unwin.

Department of Finance (1994). *Resource Management in the Australian Public Sector*. Commonwealth of Australia.

Department of Treasury (1998). *Consolidated Financial Statements for the Year Ended 30 June*. Commonwealth of Australia.

Department of Treasury (1999). *Budget 1999/2000*. Commonwealth of Australia, May.

Duval, D. B. (1994). *The Financing and Costing of Government Superannuation Schemes*. Australian Government Actuaries Office, mimeo.

Di Francesco. (2000). Performance Management and Policy Advice: Learning for Policy Coherence, paper presented at the IPMN Conference. Sydney: Macquarie University, 5 March.

English, L., & Guthrie. J. (2000), Public Sector Management in the State of Victoria 1992–1999: Genesis of the Transformation. In: Jones et al., *Learning from International Public Management Reform*.

Fleming, G. (1999). Social Norms, Economic Behaviour, and the Law: A Theoretical Introduction. *Australian Economic History Review, 39*(3), November.

Geiselhart, K. (2000). Everybody Counts: Computers, Conversations and Change in the Australian Department of Finance and Administration, paper presented at the IPMN Conference. Sydney: Macquarie University, 5 March.

Guthrie, J. (1993). Australian Public Business Enterprises: Analysis of Changing Accounting, Auditing and Accountability Regimes. *Financial Accountability and Management, 9*(3).

Guthrie, J., & Parker, L. (1998). Managerialism and Marketisation in Financial Management Change in Australia. In: Olson et al., *Global Warning: Debating International Developments in New Public Financial Management*. Bergen, Norway: Cappelen Akademisk Forlag.

Holtham, G., & Kay, J. (1994). The Assessment: Institutions of Policy. *Oxford Review of Economic Policy, 10*(3).

Humphrey, C., Miller, P., & Smith, H. (1998). Financial Management in the UK Public Sector: Ambiguities, Paradoxes and Limits. In: Olson et al., *Global Warming: Debating International Developments in New Public Financial Management*. Bergen, Norway: Capelen Akademisk Forlag.

Mackintosh, I. (1999). Public Sector Accounting Standard Setting in the Next Century. *The Standard*, No. 3, AARF and AASB.

McGregor, W. (1999). The Pivotal Role of Accounting Concepts in the Development of Public Sector Accounting Standards. *Australian Accounting Review*, 9(1), March.

Marshall, A. (1890). *Principles of Economics*. London: Macmillan.

Management Advisory Board (1993). *Accountability in the Commonwealth Public Sector*. Commonwealth of Australia, June.

Musgrave, R. A., & Musgrave, P. B. (1989). *Public Finance in Theory and Practice*, 5th edition. New York: McGraw-Hill.

National Commission of Audit. (1996). *Report to the Commonwealth Government*, AGPS, June.

Newbery, D. (1996). Privatisation and Liberalisation of Network Facilities. *DAE Working Paper, No. 9620*. Cambridge: University of Cambridge, August.

Newbery, D. (1997). Pool Reform and Competition in Electricity. *DAE Working Paper, No. 9734*. Cambridge: University of Cambridge, December.

Olson, O., Guthrie, J., & Humphrey, C. (Eds). (1998). *Global Warning: Debating International Developments in New Public Financial Management*. Bergen, Norway: Cappelen Akademisk Forlag.

Pallot, J. (1998). The New Zealand Revolution. In: Olson et. al., *Global Warning: Debating International Developments in New Public Financial Management*. Bergen, Norway: Cappelen Akademisk Forlag.

Pareto, V. (1909). *Manuel D'Economie Politique*.

Parker, L., & Guthrie, J. (1993). The Australian Public Sector in the 1990's: New Accountability Regimes in Motion. *Journal of International Accounting, Auditing and Taxation*, 2(1).

Pigou, A. C. (1920). *The Economics of Welfare*. London: Macmillan.

Reserve Bank of Australia (1997). Privatisation in Australia. *Bulletin*, December.

Self, P. (1993). *Government by the Market? The Politics of Public Choice*. London: MacMillan.

Smith, A. (1776). *The Wealth of Nations*, 1957 edition: Everymans Library.

Stiglitz. J. (1988). *Economics of the Public Sector*, 2nd edition. New York: Norton.

Walker, B., & Walker, B. C. (2000). *Privatisation: Sell off or Sell out? The Australian Experience*. Sydney, ABC Books.

30. ARE WILDAVSKY'S GUARDIANS AND SPENDERS STILL RELEVANT? NEW PUBLIC MANAGEMENT AND THE POLITICS OF GOVERNMENT BUDGETING

Joanne Kelly and John Wanna

INTRODUCTION

The 'guardian-spender' framework formulated by Aaron Wildavsky has defined the way in which most political scientists think about government budgeting since it first appeared in 1964 (Wildavsky, 1975; Green & Thompson, 1999). Wildavsky argued that budgetary outcomes could be explained (or at least analyzed) by focusing on the interplay of budget actors performing the highly stylized institutional roles of guardian (of the public purse) and spender. This behavioral framework proved sufficiently flexible to account for the differences in budgetary performance across different political systems (see studies by Savoie, 1990; Heclo & Wildavsky, 1974; Wildavsky, 1986); as well as explaining the impact of budgetary reform and divergent economic environments on budget politics (Caiden & Wildavsky, 1974; Wildavsky, 1975). Reference to 'guardians' and 'spenders' still pervades discussions of government budgeting in the academic literature of political

Learning from International Public Management Reform, Volume 11B, pages 589–614.
ISBN: 0-7623-0760-9

science and economics (Campos & Pradhan, 1997), and has become accepted as conventional descriptions by practitioners in national governments and international bodies (such as the OECD, World Bank and the IMF).

This chapter applies Wildavsky's guardian-spender framework to analyze the impact of New Public Management (NPM) reforms on budgetary politics, and to test the framework's continued *explanatory value*. It is widely held that NPM reforms are explicitly designed to transform the existing norms, rules, processes and objectives of budgetary and financial management (NZ Treasury, 1987; Hood, 1991; Boston et al., 1991; Pollitt, 1993; OECD, 1995; Thompson, 1998). We want to study how these reforms are likely to impact on the balance of power between guardians and spenders in a given budgetary setting. This initial study focuses on three widely recurring themes that typify the NPM budgetary and financial reform agenda: reformulated budgetary objectives and culture, centralized aggregate expenditure controls, and devolved financial management. In pursuing these reforms, NPM seeks to establish new budget conventions that are based on principal-agent relationships, outcome-based accrual accounting and budgeting techniques, and contract-price budgeting (variously called competitive tendering). We ask whether these NPM reforms re-model or transform budgetary systems to such an extent that the guardian-spender framework has declined in explanatory value.

Our analysis proceeds in four sections. The first re-examines central elements of Wildavsky's model of budgetary politics focusing specifically on the guardian-spender dichotomy, tools and strategies of the 'budget game' and the impact of budgetary reform. Next we identify the main categories of budget and financial management reforms introduced under NPM (OECD 1995: 94–197; 1998). The third section of this chapter examines the impact of these reforms on budgetary politics; specifically, on institutional roles and functions; on the tools and strategies available to both sets of budget actors; and on the balance of power within a budgetary system. Finally, we conclude by posing questions on the continued sustainability of the guardian-spender framework given new problems posed by changes in the budgetary environment (such as the recent arrival of surplus budgets and the political difficulties associated with managing surpluses while maintaining fiscal restraint).

The conclusion of the analysis suggests that *where NPM reforms have been extensively adopted and far-reaching* they alter the terrain of budgetary systems, establishing more complex budgetary arrangements than suggested by the guardian-spender model. NPM reforms tend to change budgetary behaviors and, in doing so, alter the balance of power in favor of guardians. The reforms also change the budgetary role of spenders as budget actors. Hence, the traditional dichotomy between rationing guardians and maximising spenders is difficult to sustain as more complex budgetary relationships emerge that do not accord with the guardian-spender model. Furthermore, NPM reforms also have the potential to shift both the locus of budgetary conflict and the areas of agreement. Budgetary relationships are likely to become more fragmented, more uncertain and less routine if contractual service deliverers are included in the process. Conflict is likely to be dissipated away from central budget agencies with spenders assuming guardian roles over resources they themselves may chose to deploy in purchasing contractual services from other actors. The advent of multi-year budgets (providing 2 or 3 year authorizations) also has the potential to contain budgetary conflicts. Finally, we ask whether the 'transformations' to budgetary systems under NPM are likely to require further amendment as governments regularly have to manage budget surpluses.

STRATEGIES AND TOOLS OF BUDGET POLITICS

In *The Politics of the Budgetary Process* Aaron Wildavsky established new methods of inquiry into the processes of government budgeting (Jones & McCaffery, 1994). Rather than proceeding from a normative basis that sought to pronounce how governments *should* budget, Wildavsky focused on explaining 'how the budgetary process actually works' (1974: xxv). He revealed the highly competitive but uncertain nature of budgetary formulation, the inherent complexity of budgetary decisions, and how budget actors need to specialize, 'satisfice' and rely on 'decisional heuristics' to contain conflict. Behavioral norms tended to characterise government budgeting in the absence of formal procedures for financial control. In other words, Wildavsky constructed a framework for studying the *politics* of government budgeting which highlighted three primary elements of budgetary politics:

- the dichotomous relations between guardians and spenders became pronounced in the absence of formal rules and procedures of financial control;
- actor strategies and practices provided some sort of 'routine' to budgetary politics; and
- the impact of reform on budget politics tended to be limited.

Government budgetary politics are depicted as a game between two sets of actors playing the institutional roles of guardians and spenders.[1] Wildavsky classified budgetary players according to loosely defined and highly stylized criteria based on 'the *expectation of behavior* attached to institutional positions' (1975: 11). These roles are performed at each stage of the budget process and at all levels of the political and bureaucratic spheres. Wildavsky summarised his argument as follows:

> One of the constants of budgeting is the division of roles into spenders and savers, a result of the universal scarcity of resources. Claims and demands always outweigh the resources to satisfy them. Hence there are always people who want more than they have and those who show them they can't have as much as they would like. Officials in charge of carrying out the government's functions are oriented toward needs. They are always confronted with things that are not done but should be done. They fulfil their task best by advocating these needs. For this reason the government's purse needs guardians who would ensure spending does not go beyond available resources and that all spending advocates get a share of what is available (Wildavsky, 1975: 187).

While Wildavsky recognized the dichotomy between spenders and guardians resulted in adversarial conflict, he did not define this conflict as problematic. Successful budgeting is portrayed as a product of ongoing guardian and spender relations: both roles are legitimate and necessary in resolving budget decisions. Dividing functions and responsibilities between spenders and guardians enables specialization, increases predictability and, therefore, reduces complexity in budget decision-making. Programs are generated by those with expert knowledge; expenditure and revenue limits are set by those responsible for the government's economic and fiscal performance. Interaction between the two sides forces compromise and requires both sides to justify and defend their position: specialization and institutional conflict between spenders and guardians produces better budgets.

Second, guardians and spenders employ an array of strategies, practices and processes to further their objectives in budgetary negotiations and these 'techniques of competition' are knowable. All budgetary systems provide actors with limited options, and in response they devise a set of strategies and practices used to play the 'budget game'. In attempting to 'protect the public purse' against the spenders, guardians may draw on their legislative and administrative authority, attempt to exercise 'moral' suasion, or manage budget decision-making processes. Guardians in parliament or congress have the legal authority to reduce or simply deny the funding requested of a particular agency. Central budget agencies adapt the systems of financial accountability to control expenditures. Guardian ministers may threaten to increase tax levels or impose across the board cuts. They often will seek agreement on expenditure targets or rationing strategies before proceeding with more detailed budget negotiations.

For their part, the spenders draw on their position as policy or program experts to legitimize claims to protect existing expenditure, increase their relative share of public expenditure, or add new programs and expand existing ones. Not only do spenders need to produce 'good work' and 'play it straight', but they should be able to recognize and exploit available opportunities at the appropriate time. Policy expertise is based on relations with the program clientele or service delivery knowledge, yet spenders must be careful not to project the image of being 'captured' by those clients. In protecting their on-going base, spenders may threaten to burn the 'Washington Monument'. Both sets of actors seek to exert political influence for their desired position by garnering congressional or ministerial support, by mobilizing interest groups or influential staffers.

Yet, budgeting is not a 'free-for-all fight' between guardians and spenders: budget actors cooperate as well as compete. The complexity of budget decision-making requires areas of stability and techniques of conflict limitation or confinement. For example, in determining how much additional funding to request or how much funding to grant, budget actors rely on various 'aids to calculation'. Under the system described by Wildavsky, both parties rely on past experience as a guide either to the reliability of a department's claims or the likelihood of spending being approved. They simplify the issues under consideration by limiting the focus of discussion to inputs rather than policy, or excluding certain agreed tracts of expenditure – such as those included in 'the base' or the non-discretionary expenditures – from budget negotiations. As a result, budget decision-makers tend to 'satisfice' rather than comprehensively review each and every possible option. The incremental method of budgeting implies regular, annual expenditure changes (typically increases) across all expenditure areas in each department. Spenders know they will get a 'fair share' increase, guardians know that increases will not be too high. Losses in one year can be gained in another; problems in one year can be deferred until the next. Wildavsky concludes: 'the men who make the budget are concerned with relatively small increments to an existing base. Their attention is focused on a small number of items over which the budgetary battle is fought' (1974: 15).

Third, budgetary reform is likely to upset the balance of power between guardians and spenders, and so affect budget outcomes. This is because the *actual* strategies available to budget actors vary according to the political, economic and budgetary system within which the budget 'game' proceeds. The balance of power over time is largely dependent on the extent to which guardians vis-à-vis spenders are able to take advantage of these strategies. Under stable institutional, political and economic conditions, the game of budget politics becomes routine: each player knows what to expect from the other and 'participants have counter-roles that necessitate a strong push from the departmental side' (Wildavsky, 1974: 19). Budgetary reform upsets this balance and previously agreed areas of budget politics become highly contested. This is one of the major reasons why budgetary reform is highly political, threatening and hotly contested.

It is within this context that we analyze the budgetary reforms introduced under the auspices of NPM. The principal reforms associated with NPM were often designed precisely to change the way public resources were allocated and were managed. As such NPM has attempted to reconstruct many of the traditional 'tools of budgetary politics'. To the extent it is successful in this regard NPM is likely to impact on the roles and capacities of the major budgetary actors. The remaining sections of this chapter present a preliminary study of what NPM seeks to achieve in budget reform; what the basic paradigm defines as 'good' budget practice; how these new budget and resource management practices impact on guardians and spenders; and how NPM reforms impact on budget conflict.

NPM AND THE VISION OF 'BETTER BUDGETING'

The central core of NPM reforms has to date been directed toward reconstructing the nature of public provision mainly using improved resourcing and financial management. By the mid–1970s, much had been written about the problems of traditional line-item budgeting (Wilenski, 1986: 225). Studies of both the American and British budgeting systems suggested classical budgetary processes favored spenders over guardians, and were the cause of ever increasing taxes, debt and deficits. These criticisms were echoed by commissions of inquiry into traditional systems of public administration established by governments around the globe. These included the Glassco (1962) and Lambert commissions (1976–9) in Canada, the Coombs (1974–6) and Reid (1982–3) reports in Australia, and Reagan's Grace commission established in 1982. In the U.K., Thatcher established the Efficiency Scrutiny Unit in the early 1980s to conduct regular 'scrutinies' of the efficiency and economy in departmental administration. Each of these investigations presented a litany of complaints against traditional budgetary systems and the outmoded financial techniques used within government. They recommending instead the adoption of far-reaching reforms typically directed toward 'letting the managers manage' – encouraging managerial flexibility within a framework of defined objectives, tight resource controls and performance monitoring.

Yet, each inquiry advocated various forms of budgetary and financial management reform, and many of their detailed recommendations appeared to be contradictory. On the one hand, critics argued that the traditional budget provided guardians with insufficient authority or incentive to limit claims for increased spending by line departments. Central agencies appeared largely incapable of overcoming the incremental bias inherent in the traditional budgetary process, and lacked the incentives that would encourage them to find new ways of doing so. If governments were to limit their size and the growth of public expenditure then reforms were needed that *strengthened* the position of budget guardians. On the other hand, traditional budget rules and financial controls were criticized as being too restrictive and control-oriented to facilitate efficient and effective financial management (see Schick, 1994, 1997). Budgetary processes were oriented toward measuring inputs, encouraging administrators to focus on probity rules and 'bean-counting' rather than on results, efficiency or the effectiveness of government programs. According to NPM reformers, new budgetary systems should be designed to provide flexibility and increase the responsibility of 'empowered managers' in both rationing resources and operating within those limits (Dawkins, 1983: 3).

To a large extent these contradictions stemmed from differences between new institutional economics (NIE) and 'managerialism' – the primary intellectual frames of reference informing these analyses (Aucoin, 1990; Hood, 1991; Pollitt, 1993; Hughes, 1994; Keraudren & van Mierlo, 1998: 39). New institutional economists applying their ideas to the public sector identified 'perverse' behavior in traditional budget institutions causing inefficiency at both the aggregate and departmental levels (for detailed review see Thompson, 1998). Traditional budgets aggregated the individual choices of self-interested budget actors. This produced 'sub-optimal' expenditure decisions (that result in higher than optimal expenditure levels, and unwanted deficits and debt) because the costs of increasing government programs can be externalized in a system in which revenues are generated from broad-based taxation and distributed through consolidated revenue funds. In other words, the beneficiaries of government programs do not bear the full taxation or political costs of expenditure increases. Benefits are likely to be concentrated while the costs will be defrayed amongst the tax paying population. Further, government program 'costing' systems paid little attention to the transaction or agency costs of conducting internal government business or delivering services. Thus, in NIE the collective actions of individual budget actors behaving rationally in the budget process will result in total expenditure levels higher than that posited as the optimal collective outcome.

In response, NIE promoted institutional reform to establish different incentive patterns in the management of government resources. Budgetary reforms, they argued, should establish rules and institutions that promote 'collectively rational' objectives to be articulated and pursued in budgetary formulation. To that end, total expenditure levels should be centrally determined and then used to discipline subsequent budget negotiations (von Hagen, 1992; Alesina & Perrotti, 1997). Such determinations are difficult under the collegial decision-making systems that characterised the traditional budgetary processes and so should be replaced by high-level hierarchical decision-making. Financial management reforms should redesign the incentive structures to align the self-interest of managers with collective intentions. Instituting competitive, market-based service delivery and pricing techniques can lower service delivery costs. And the insistence on the distinction between the operational and policy functions of government (principal-agent/purchaser-provider split) reduces the transactional costs associated with departmental rent-seeking and capture (New Zealand Treasury, 1987: 44–8, 72–95).

By contrast, managerialism identified the existing *rules and practices* of public administration as a source of government inefficiency (Pollitt, 1993). It was argued that the ethos of traditional public administration emphasised probity and compliance over efficiency and economy. As a consequence, bureaucrats in both spending and guardian agencies 'administered' rules and regulations, rather than 'managed' their program and policy resources. Managerialism proposed that these problems could be resolved by adopting private sector management techniques, and improving the quality, status and accountability of operational management. Responsibility for detailed budget-ing and financial management should be devolved to those responsible for delivering government programs. Detailed lines of input-based appropriations should be replaced by broadband appropriations defined by program objectives. Closely associated with the devolution of authority is risk management and *deregulation* of financial management techniques and processes based control systems. Line managers should be free of 'pettifogging rules or constraints' (Pollitt, 1997: 467) and therefore able to transfer resources as they see fit. Rules about the modes of service delivery should also be decreased to allow programs managers the fullest discretion in achieving 'more for less'. Program objectives should be clearly articulated, linkages made between program evaluation and budgetary allocations. In sum, reforms seek to construct a public sector in which 'managers are not limited, as in the line-item budget, to expenditures on a particular input but can, as circumstances change, judge the correct mix of resources or inputs which will best promote the success of the program' (Wilenski, 1986: 231).

Governments in the OECD variously adopted these recommendations. Three main categories of reform were introduced: reformulating the budgetary environment, centralising aggregate expenditure controls and devolving responsibility for detailed resource management (OECD, 1995, 1997). Each can be justified by either of the frameworks underpinning the NPM paradigm. Reformulating the budgetary environment redirects the self-interest of bureaucrats and politicians, and provides managers with clear objectives within which to direct their attention. Centralised aggregate expenditure controls provide managers with a stable planning environment, and a means of limiting consumption of public resources. Devolving responsibility for detailed resource management increases managerial flexibility and forces managers to assume responsibility for their government expenditures (and thereby internalise the costs of public expenditure). In the following section we explore both the expected and unanticipated impacts of these categories of reform on the role and the capacity of spenders and guardians in the budgetary process.

Before proceeding with this analysis, it is important to recognise variation and the continuing evolution of NPM reform agendas in different countries (Aucoin, 1990; Forster & Wanna, 1990; Hood, 1994; Kettle, 1997; Pallott, 1998; Peters & Savoie, 1998; Verheijen & Coombes, 1998). Comparative and individual country studies illustrate considerable variation in the extent to which these two theoretical frameworks inform NPM. By way of brief summary, Table 30.1 identifies some of the foremost statements and articulations of NPM in the five Anglo-American countries and (drawing on existing literature) notes which of the NPM 'partners' dominate the reform agenda in each country. In many instances, the theoretical underpinning remained implicit. New Zealand's self-identification with NIE is the exception (NZ Treasury, 1987; Boston, 1993). There is, of course, much overlap between the two frameworks, and this simple classification ignores the processes of cross-national learning and iteration by which the NPM paradigm evolved (for examples see Canadian Auditor General, 1995; Nagel, 1997). Nonetheless, these differences highlight an important qualification to the arguments presented below: the impact of NPM on budgetary politics will vary across countries. The following sections should be read with that qualification in mind.

REFORMULATED BUDGETARY OBJECTIVES AND CULTURE

One of the driving forces behind the NPM agenda is an effort to change the objectives and culture of government budgeting. The emergence of NPM in most countries during the early 1980s coincided with the beginning of an era emphasising fiscal restraint and rectitude. Most of the NPM 'manifestos and markers' identified in Table 30.1, present financial management reforms as a solution to problems of public sector inefficiency, an overly large public sector, unsustainable levels of government debt or all three. The traditional budget, it is claimed, contributed to ever increasing government expenditures by emphasising planning rather than restraint and its reliance on incremental decision-making. Similarly, the control based financial management systems

Table 30.1. Selected Markers and Manifestos of NPM

Country	Manifesto(s) and 'Markers' (Year)	Dominant influence
U.K.	Rayner Scrutinies 1979; Financial Management Improvement (1982 CMND 9058, 1983); Improving Management in Government: the Next Steps (Efficiency Unit 1988). Modernizing Government (1998).	Managerialism (Kemp 1990; Hood 1991; Pollitt 1993). Co-ordinated – joined up government.
Australia	Royal Commission on Australian Government Administration (1976); The 'Reid Report' (1983); Reforming the Australian Public Service (1983); FMIP (1984); Budget Reform (1984); The Australian Public Sector Reformed (1992). Beyond Bean-Counting: Effective Financial Management in the APS 1998 & Beyond (1997); Clarifying the Exchange: A Review of Purchaser/Provider Arrangements. National Commission of Audit (1996).	Managerialism (Keating 1989; Hood 1991; Corbett 1992; Davis et al 1999). New Institutional Economics – contractualism, contestability.
New Zealand	Economic Management (1984); Statement of Government Expenditure Review (1986); Government Management: Brief to the Incoming Government 1987 (1987);	New Institutional Economics – esp. Public Choice Theory (Boston et al 1991: 2–26; Pallot 1997).
U.S.A	President's Private Sector Survey on Cost Control (Grace Committee 1982) Reinventing Government (1992); National Performance Review (1993)	Managerialism (Pollitt 1993; Kettl 1997; Thompson 1998; Fredrickson 1996).
Canada	Auditor General's report on Financial Management (1978); Royal Commission on Financial Management & Accountability' – The 'Lambert' Report (1979); Increased Ministerial Authority & Accountability (1988); Public Service 2000 (1992). Getting Government Right (1995); Modern Comptrollership; Breaking Barriers in the Federal Public Service (199) Toward Better Governance: Public Service Reform in New Zealand (1984–94) and its Relevance to Canada (Auditor-General 1995).	Managerialism (Aucoin 1990; Peters and Savoie 1998). New Institutional Economics.

were designed to ensure probity in government spending and often hindered the pursuit of economy, efficiency, and effectiveness in service delivery. In contrast, NPM reforms sought to establish the values of economy and parsimony (Hood, 1991); encourage mangers to 'do more with less'; to 'restrain leviathan'; and offered a way of 'preventing the public sector from claiming an ever-increasing share of national resources' (OECD, 1995: 94). In other words, NPM reforms seek to introduce a cultural change that emphasises the objectives typically associated with guardianship over those of spending.

This change in emphasis affected budgetary politics at a number of different levels. First, it de-legitimised debate over how to *spend* government money by emphasising the importance of expenditure cuts and restraint. The emphasis of budget debate turned away from policy development to questions of 'the bottom line' financial results. In doing so it reduced the legitimacy of spenders in budget reformulation networks. Second, it provided guardians with additional strategies in budgetary debates: arguments. Third it limited spenders capacity to argue for their 'fair-share' of expenditure growth. In a climate of expenditure growth, spenders could present claims for increased expenditure based on principles of 'reciprocity' and public demand. In the climate of restraint, spenders making these assertions risked being labelled 'rent-seekers' or the captive agents of vested interests. Fourth, demands for collective expenditure restraint required spenders to assume some of the responsibility for identifying possible areas for expenditure cuts and restraint. Budget actors in spending institutions were required to 'ration' and 'save' instead of functioning exclusively as claimants. Finally, these new budgetary objectives established an environment receptive to further reform directed toward expenditure restraint. It strengthened guardians' position to shape and design on-going reforms to the system of government budgeting and financial management.

BUDGETARY POLITICS UNDER CENTRALIZED EXPENDITURE CONTROLS

In 1995 the OECD reported that most member countries had established some type of centralised control over aggregate expenditure levels (OECD, 1995: 95). This report focuses primarily on highly visible statements of budgetary targets, but aggregate expenditure controls range from statements of 'high-level budgetary targets'; more specific annual policy or portfolio specific expenditure targets and limits; to the adoption of cash limited multiple year agency budgets. As well as varying in the level of detail, these statements also vary in intent. Some are directed toward planning the rate of growth in government expenditures (examples of these planning totals were undertaken in Canada

(PEMS) and the U.K. (PESC) (Wright, 1980)); others seek to introduce a trend toward expenditure restraint; while others are the starting point for internal budget negotiations. These types of statements impact directly and indirectly on the relationships between guardians and spenders and their budgetary roles.

Public statements of budgetary objectives – especially those with specific multi-year expenditure limits – restrict both the extent to which either spenders and guardians can set the budget agenda. On the one hand, it limits capacity to argue for higher expenditure levels, or the ability to increase total spending levels through bottom-up, additive processes. But a statement of budgetary targets can also limit the flexibility of guardians to set overall budgetary parameters, and also limit the capacity to respond to short term demands whether economic or political. Experience to date suggests that many of the high-level statements of budgetary objectives are set outside the formal budgetary process (during election campaigns for example). In these instances the primary objective of budgetary negotiations is to determine how to achieve and stay within these pre-stated targets, rather than establishing the expenditure targets that should be achieved.

Delivering the expenditure targets stated in these documents requires changes in both budget organization and procedure. Budget timetables are redesigned to ensure decisions on annual expenditure aggregates and priorities are set *before* decisions on allocation commence. In some countries these specific portfolio targets and limits are decided by a very small number of guardian ministers and officials, and deliberately exclude any participation by spenders. Often these reforms are accompanied by limitations (or indeed the abolition) of the annual bidding process over expenditure on continuing programs (Australia's rolling forward estimates and the British PESC). 'Baseline' expenditures are determined automatically and responsibility for allocating any additional expenditure is devolved to senior representatives of the spending departments (ministers, departmental heads, and senior finance officers). These reforms seek to exclude spenders' from the debates over budget aggregates and thereby increase the authority of guardians.

The establishment of aggregate expenditure controls provides guardian(s) with an external reference point to restrict the expansionary endeavours of spending agencies, and to guide work within the budget agency. A former head of the Australian Department of Finance once stated 'there is nothing that Finance or Treasury loves more than publicly stated expenditure limits, it provides a stick with which they can thrash the spending departments in budget negotiations' (interview Keating, 1998). The promotion of a corporate budget ethos across the public service reduces the efficacy of spenders' arguments based on their position as advocates of particular interest groups. Such arguments are likely to result in an accusation of 'rent-seeking' rather than enhance the validity of spending claims. In addition, clear statements of when and why expenditures have risen or targets not been met, enable an interested public to allocate blame to 'spoilers'. These processes are more likely to locate the political costs of expenditure increases with spenders rather than guardians.

In sum, articulating and developing centralised aggregate expenditure controls typically requires the introduction of hierarchical or top-down budgetary processes that change the position and functions of both guardians and spenders. Many of these reforms deliberately reduce the access of spenders to decision-making on expenditure aggregates and budget formulation. In terms of the more detailed expenditure decisions, spenders are required to perform a rationing function over the expenditures for which they are responsible. At the same time, these reforms increase the strategies and tools available to guardians in controlling claims on the public purse, but require them to engage in quite different budgetary activities. Guardians focus on ensuring bottom-line targets are delivered, rather than on engaging in bidding negotiations with spenders over detailed expenditure levels and policy decisions.

BUDGETARY POLITICS UNDER A FLEXIBLE RESOURCE MANAGEMENT REGIME

NPM reforms designed to increase managerial flexibility focus on two primary themes: devolving financial management, and introducing new modes of service delivery. The first increases flexibility to manage a given resource base even within traditional departmental structures. It aims to make public sector service delivery more efficient by reducing 'inefficient' rules and regulations that limit managerial capacity to improve resource management. The second set of reforms extend the notion of 'managerial flexibility' by challenging traditional notions of governance in which departments are exclusive providers of public services. This new mode of governance is based on the implementation of a purchaser-provider split and market-based price-costing methods (Ewart & Boston, 1993). Rather than rely on the advice of internal service providers, governments seek to determine the lowest 'purchase price' of service delivery through competitive tendering, market-testing, and full cost accounting systems. The government then enters into a formal contractual relationship with either private or public sector providers to deliver the desired provision at a given price. In theory, this enables government to achieve lower prices, avoid client capture and reduce transaction costs. Whilst public sector providers may 'win' government contracts they should operate as commercial units reconstituted on a profit motive (see work on agencification by Pollitt, 1999) and 'hived-off' from the parent department. Under this model, a government 'department' consists of a core group of policy and contract managers. The adoption of either model of 'flexible' management significantly changes the role of and relationship between spenders and guardians.

Devolution of financial management removes some traditional tools of guardianship, while at the same time demanding that spenders assume responsibility for 'rationing' public resources – a function traditionally associated with guardianship. The capacity of central budget agencies to impose detailed financial controls over departmental expenditures stood as the primary tool of traditional guardianship. Claims that these controls were illusionary are probably justifiable, especially as they did not assist resource management (Wilenski, 1986: 231). Nonetheless, traditional central controls allowed guardians to limit the uses and directions of public money and guide the flow of public spending in the economy. Under devolved systems of financial management guardians are not devoid of strategies of budgetary control (and could always reclaim some detailed controls should they wish). Rather, their preferred tools are directed toward questions of aggregate expenditure control, and therefore constitute a shift in the focus of guardian-spender budgetary politics away from controls over how agencies spend money.

Further, the devolution of financial management imposes a responsibility on spenders themselves to perform rationing functions. Wildavsky showed that under the traditional budgetary system spenders and guardians performed specialised functions, and that one set of actors could 'push' because the other would 'push back'. In contrast, the financial management system envisaged by NPM reduces the degree of specialization in budgetary functions *and* the countervailing forces in budget negotiations. Program managers, departmental heads and line ministers – those budget actors traditionally classified as spenders – are required to perform the guardianship function within their own areas of financial responsibility (whether classified as envelopes, portfolios, programs, or product-centres for example). Under the traditional model, spenders made demands to guardians or sought to protect their programs from imminent cuts. In a devolved budgetary system, spending agencies must assume responsibility for allocating available funding to new and on-going policies, identifying areas of expenditure restraint and reallocating existing funds. Under this system, budgetary conflict is localised in specific expenditure areas, and played out between a group of actors that would traditionally be classified as spenders.

The introduction of new modes of service delivery has the potential to undermine the institutional basis upon which spenders are defined. The logic defining their behavior in Wildavsky's model (and their value and legitimacy in budgetary negotiations), rests largely on their role as advocates and experts in particular policy areas. Information exchanged between policy and operational sectors in the spending departments produced detailed policy expertise that was unavailable to the budget agencies at the centre of government. In addition, service deliverers operated at the nexus between government and the public, and as such acted as a conduit providing vital feedback into the policy debates. By removing the service delivery functions from spending departments, NPM reforms devalue 'arguments from expertise' by the remaining department. The delivery of public services by non-government organizations means policy expertise derived from service delivery will be outside the government and therefore excluded from higher-level budgetary considerations.

Moreover, to the extent that budgetary reforms under NPM have formalised procedures for financial control, they reduce the scope for actor behavior to construct ways of routinizing bargaining relations between themselves. Increased formalization and transparency does not entirely do away with relational politics but restricts opportunities for bargaining. Accrual schedules, for instance, will project consistent depreciation costs up to ten years out and indicate long-term liabilities for which agencies are required to make provision. Spending agencies will often now know years ahead of time their firm allocative estimates of expenses and have little opportunity to augment these amounts – and be expected to incorporate new policy initiatives within their existing allocations. They enjoy flexibility to move resources to areas of highest priority or need, and do not need to gain central budgetary approval to redeploy their resources. Of course, spenders could decide or allow themselves to become maverick and not comply with these formal requirements. In such circumstances authorization to operate with devolved discretion is likely to be removed or severely curtailed (losing the agency many internal benefits), or additional other penalties may be imposed on recalcitrant agencies (eg, additional levies if running in 'debt' or any 'over-spending' may be deducted from their next year's estimates – as a 'borrowing'). One indication of the changed logic of rationing is that spending agencies that manage to declare a 'dividend' back to the government (a departmental surplus over their costs) are often most likely to be rewarded with carriage of new policy initiatives being considered by government. Paradoxically, the best rationers may be the agencies that have most growth potential.

Reforms directed toward establishing a split between the policy and operational functions of government complicate budgetary politics even further by introducing the potential for a three-way budgetary relationship. Central agencies act as *principal*; line departments become *policy agents*, and the organization contracted to provide government services becomes the *delivery agent*. Moreover, on some programs multiple policy agents may be involved with hundreds of delivery agents. This clearly does not accord with the simple dichotomy suggested in the guardian-spender model. Increasing the number of service providers fragments the budget process: it is likely to result in more bi-lateral negotiations and temporary relationships. This is especially problematic if service providers are included in budgetary processes. One of the conveniences of the previous system was that one or two guardians dealt with a constant, and relatively small group of spenders. This environment fostered the enduring relationships and 'decisional heuristics' referred to by Wildavsky. In the more complex and fragmented environment of NPM, these tools of budget decision making will become more difficult to develop and less reliable.

Decisions about who will bear responsibility for renegotiating service delivery contracts have a direct bearing on budgetary politics. Will the central or policy agencies renegotiate contracts? Will the funding levels for these contracts be renegotiated between central and policy agencies, or between the policy agent and the service deliver? How will prices be set and what benchmarks be used? If central agencies assume the role of 'strategic investor' then they bear responsibility for both generating claims on the public purse (as investor/purchaser) and rationing the available resources between those claims (as guardian) – in other words, they perform both the rationing and claiming functions. While these two functions are not *necessarily* contradictory, they do fall outside the simple classification system offered in the guardian-spender model. If the policy agents remaining in the spending departments assume responsibility for renegotiating contracts, will they behave as guardians of the public purse or advocates for their policy and program recipients? While we can venture answers to these questions on the basis of theory, much more research and is needed to learn the lessons of practical experience.

ASSESSING THE IMPACT OF NPM ON BUDGETARY POLITICS

The overall thrust of NPM reforms strengthens the position of guardians in budgetary politics. Some reforms remove the traditional tools of guardianship – tight controls over detailed inputs, for example, in general, they are replaced by a broader set of strategies that expand the tool-kit of guardians, especially in terms of aggregate expenditure control. At the same time, NPM reduces the capacity and legitimacy of many strategies adopted by the spenders, and has the potential to undermine their institutional base. Many budget actors who would be classified as spenders under an institutional analysis of their budgetary role, are being encouraged to behave as budget guardians. Consequently, an extensive NPM reform program is likely to change the balance of power within the budget system in favour of guardians and should, therefore, facilitate increased capacity to impose budget discipline.

Therefore, the simple dichotomy between guardians and spenders is difficult to sustain. More complex relationships are emerging (e.g. three way principal, policy agency, and service agent under purchaser provider split) in which it is unclear who is playing which role in the budgetary process. In addition, many of the NPM reforms deliberately blur the line between institutional *role* and *budgetary function*. Increasingly, guardians will be called on to perform both rationing and claiming functions; with spenders required to ration as well as claim. In other words, new budgetary functions do not necessarily align with traditional institutional roles.

Moreover, NPM reforms have the potential to redefine the areas of budgetary conflict, as well as the areas of agreement. Guardians are able to do more unilaterally (eg. negotiating contracts and establishing aggregate expenditure targets), but they must deal with a more fragmented (and perhaps less stable) community of spenders (especially if service deliverers are including in the budget process). Conflict is likely to be decentralised away from central budget agencies – with former spenders acting as guardians over detailed expenditure allocations. Multi-year budgets are likely to result in more intense budgetary conflict despite negotiations occurring less often. The longer-term impact of NPM reforms on budgetary politics will not become evident until regularised patterns can be identified and the more complex relationships become clearer.

The impact on budgetary politics in specific jurisdictions will vary according to numerous factors, not the least of which are the specific NPM reforms that are implemented and the detailed design of those reforms. As mentioned in the previous sections, individual nations have pursued the NPM reform agenda with different degrees of vigour, against different institutional and historical backgrounds, and with a considerable level of national variation. Determining whether our initial findings hold in any one country or the extent to which they can be generalised will require considerably more research.

ARE WILDAVSKY'S GUARDIANS AND SPENDERS STILL RELEVANT?

So, what does our research suggest for the continued relevance of Wildavsky's guardians and spenders? Firstly, it demonstrates the continued relevance of this framework. It provides a useful analytical framework for studying budgetary reforms almost 40 years after its development. Its shows that the guardian-spender framework provides a diagnostic methodology for evaluating the impact of NPM on relations between budget actors; and a means of identifying potential imbalances in a country's budgetary system.

However, the above suggests that the definitional basis of Wildavsky's model of budgetary politics is under challenge from the NPM reforms. Wildavsky's definition of budgetary roles was always inexact: but we know that it accorded with both the institutional position of budgetary actors and could vary according to budgetary systems.[2] The breadth of these classifications allowed analyses of budgetary politics to remain grounded, and placed *functional* rather than *institutional* equivalence at the heart of any comparative analysis.

We suggest an expanded classification that differentiates between the individual budget actors *institutional role* (Wildavsky), and the *function*(s) they perform in budgetary negotiations (Schick, 1990; 1994). Distinguishing between *role* and *function* should facilitate analysis of budgetary politics at a number of levels. It provides more flexibility in classifying the position of budget actors in the budget process. It suggests some actors may perform multiple functions in a single stage of the budgetary process (eg, a central budget agency may simultaneously claim and ration during budget formulation); or perform different functions at various stages in budget decision making (claim during budget formulation but ration during implementation of the budgetary year). It also allows for the possibility that while an actor's institutional role may remain constant, its budgetary functions may change over time.[3] Finally, the distinction enables identification of asymmetry between the institutional role of budget actors, and the functions they are required to perform in the budget process. While such asymmetry may be the deliberate consequence of reform (as in NPM), we believe it is valuable to be able to identify any likely disjuncture between the function a public servant is asked to perform and the incentive or culture associated with their institutional position.

CONCLUDING COMMENTS: NPM AND THE PROBLEMS OF SURPLUS. BUDGETING

NPM reforms gained ascendancy during a particular historical context in which governments were wrestling with problems of restraining growth in government spending, reducing budget deficits and cutting debt (Hood, 1991; Wright, 1979; Hood & Wright, 1981). This drive for fiscal discipline created an environment that required new budgetary methods that strengthened guardians, imposed fiscal limits, and amended the incentive structures shaping bureaucratic behavior. This context clearly dovetailed with the NPM paradigm's emphasis on 'economy and parsimony' (Hood, 1991). NPM reforms contributed to the search for fiscal discipline and budgetary restraint by empowering guardians of the public purse and seeking to ingrain values of the 'bottom-line'. In other words, by shifting the balance of power in the *budgetary* system, NPM reforms contributed to the capacity of governments to budget in an era of restraint.

More recently, however, governments around the world are recording budget surpluses year-on-year, and significantly lower levels of debt (some of which may be directly related to NPM reforms). This development raises questions about whether the mechanisms that helped restrict spending are appropriate or efficacious in an era of surplus. The focus of budget debates has begun to shift from how to cut government debt and deficits, to how to manage and what to do with the budget surpluses (Posner & Gordon, 1999; OECD, 1999). Any relaxation in the impetus for immediate expenditure restraint is likely to shift the relationship between budget actors by:

- challenging or eroding the strategic position gained by guardians *via* aggregate expenditure controls;
- requiring more priority-setting (allocative or rationing) decisions to be undertaken on a policy basis; and
- legitimizing spender arguments for broader inclusion in the budget process.

Paradoxically, having now delivered surpluses the dominant position enjoyed by guardians will come under challenge and their ability to control aggregate expenditure is likely to be eroded. New priorities can ostensibly be afforded

JOANNE KELLY AND JOHN WANNA

and governments may be forced by political pressure to relax their previous
patterns of stringent rationing. Even relatively small policy-driven increases in
spending will soon wipe out the relatively small budget surpluses recorded to
date.

Table 30.2 suggests some of the budget policy options available to
governments in this new budgeting environment, and their implications for
budgetary politics.[4] While spending is the clear alternative to saving annual
budget surpluses, expenditure can be targeted toward different strategies, each
of which has implications for the government's future fiscal capacity and
budgetary politics. No one option is mutually exclusive and some countries are
adopting more than one alternative. Yet, the survey in our table suggests that
each option produces quite different political dynamics and imposes different
requirements on budget actors. Delivering the desired options of a particular
government is likely to require further changes in the budgetary system and
may shift the balance of power in budgetary politics.

Given the findings of our research it is likely that the new budgetary
environment will reveal diminished capacity in those budgetary actors
operating as spenders-claimants. Following the logic of both Schick and
Wildavsky, we expect the difficulties of budgeting in this new 'surplus
environment' will result in either improvizational or *ad hoc* budgeting, or
produce renewed impetus for budgetary reforms that redress the any imbalance
between budget spenders and guardians.

Many OECD nations have shown remarkable capacities to impose fiscal
restraint and create budget surpluses. Success has been achieved by a
combination of political will, a disciplined bureaucracy and electoral
acceptance. Arguably, some governments have managed this process while
addressing issues of equality of sacrifice and providing partial forms of
compensation for austerity measures. This discipline, however, has in turn
produced an emerging orthodoxy that views budget surpluses as the prime
objective of government policy, as opposed to one of its outcomes. Such
surpluses are delivered to enhance the confidence of the financial markets in
government performance. How governments manage and dispense their
surpluses will not only impact on the winners and losers in society, but often
will determine the survival of the government itself. To remain in office
governments have shown they are increasingly prepared to lock themselves into
restrictive fiscal strategies that will further constrain their policy discretion.
'Continuing to manage less' may soon become the new motto of governance.

Table 30.2. Strategies and Options for Continuing Budget Surpluses

Strategy	Options	Potential Implications
1. Aim to Accumulate the surplus; institutional primacy of guardians in setting tight aggregate limits	1.1. Maintain as liquid reserve	A conservative and inactive option in which surpluses are retained as an accumulated financial asset base of the government, but not otherwise utilized. Assets in the liquid reserve are credited against gross debt for calculating lower net debt. There are implicit costs of interest foregone if not utilized and potential erosion of the value of the reserve by inflation. This option is usually not considered preferable in modern economies.
	1.2. Invest or lend	Surpluses can be accumulated for lending to the public or private sector. Government acts as a banker, potentially utilising the government's ability to borrow at lower rates than commercial borrowers. This option can impact on private capital markets and can be exploitative of tax payers. The financial asset base is also counted against gross debt for lower net debt. However, the asset base size and its easy liquidity can produce pressure for one-off grants to spending departments. The option is unlikely to work indefinitely. The purpose of accumulating surpluses will not necessarily be apparent. Perhaps the option is only suitable for simple economies or where governments can extract rents from a resource.
2. Aim to retire public debt: spenders constrained by the long-term strategy of the guardians	2.1. Reduce principal debt levels	Debt principal is progressively retired by governments paying down from each surplus. This is a conservative, financially risk-free option. Most appropriate when debt levels and interest rates are high. Can be used to reduce conflict between guardians and spenders if additional funds are released as lower interest payments are required. Surpluses can be disguised or technically avoided by calculating an

Table 30.2. (Continued)

Strategy	Options	Potential Implications
		amount for debt retirement within the annual budget as an expenditure item. Alternatively the surplus can be declared and debt paid down after the budget year.
		Available to complex economies but probably only over the medium-term and subject to the economic cycle.
3. Aim to reallocate surplus for other strategic purposes; may require increased input from spenders	3.1. Tax reductions	Tax reductions can be used as an electoral incentive or to reduce the size of government. Political/economic decisions can be made on the intended purpose, nature, extent and life-span of tax reductions. However, changes to taxation will have uncertain expansionary or contractionary macro-economic impacts depending upon reaction of corporate and consumer sectors (i.e. balance between private savings and private expenditure). There will also be greater pressure on budgets as the available surpluses decrease.
		Consequently not risk-free in either electoral or economic terms. Note that tax reductions can be illusory given the mix of taxes or the incidence of tax creep under conditions of inflation.
	3.2. Increase expenditure on recurrent items including transfers	Increased expenditures can be presented as a dividend for past parsimony. Governments can re-prioritize their outlays and the promise of future expenditures may be electorally appealing (and constitute an incentive for governments deciding on current expenditure cuts).
		There will be immediate pressure on the size of the surplus and perhaps pressure on maintaining new recurrent allocations. Additional spending will increase the size of government. Will also have uncertain

Table 30.2.   (Continued)

Strategy	Options	Potential Implications
		expansionary or contractionary macro-economic impacts depending upon the use of funds and market reactions.
		Although appearing benevolent, the option poses some electoral and economic risks. Requires a capacity to ration requests for new expenditures on policy benefits vs. loss of surplus criteria, otherwise previous pattern is re-established.
	3.3. Increase expenditure as strategic investment	Guardian agencies provide incentives to enable spending and delivery agencies to 'pay their way' and reduce their dependence on general revenue (i.e. increase their future ability to make income-generating investment expenditure and/or reducing labor and other cost-cutting efficiencies). In Australia 'resource agreements' provided additional resources to reduce the long-term dependence on the budget for resources. But, spending agencies have the incentive and ability to disguise recurrent costs as investment expenditure if resource agreement monitoring is not effective.

NOTES

1. The simple two-player game depicted in Wildavsky's spender-guardian dichotomy has enabled collective choice theorists to analyze budgetary politics using a two-player prisoner's dilemma that broadly accords with Niskanen's bureau-sponsor model of the budgetary process. The main difference between these two models results from the respective models of human behavior that underpin each (see Wildavsky (1974: 189–94) for Wildavsky's comments on 'political rationality').

2. Wildavsky used the terms 'spender' and 'guardian' quite loosely in his writings. Participants are variously classified as 'guardians'. 'reviewers', 'cutters' or 'savers'; and as either 'advocates' and 'spenders'. In his collaborative work with Davis et. al. (1966), Wildavsky dismissed the differentiation between these categories completely.

3. We hypothesise that the *institutional roles* are likely to remain relatively constant over time, while the *function(s)* performed by budget actors can and will change. Validating this hypothesis requires further research.

4. Extracted from Wanna, Kelly and Forster (2001) *Managing Public Expenditure in Australia*, Allen & Unwin, Sydney, forthcoming.

REFERENCES

Aitken, J. (1995). Resource Accounting – Much More Than Just A Technical Change. Chief Secretary to HM Treasury, Speaking to the Social March Foundation, London, 22 February.

Aucoin, P. (1990). Administrative Reform in Public Management: Paradigms, Principles, Paradoxes And Pendulums. *Governance*, *3*, 115–137.

Australian Public Service Board and Department of Finance (1984). Financial Management Improvement Program. Canberra: AGPS.

Blair, T. (1999). Modernising Government. Presentation to Parliament by the Prime Minister and the Minister for the Cabinet Office. Cm 4310, March, London: HMSO.

Boston, J., Martin, J., Pallot, J.,& Walsh, P. (Eds) (1991). *Reshaping the State: New Zealand's Bureaucratic Revolution*. Auckland: Oxford University Press.

Boston, J., Martin, J., Pallot, J., & Walsh, P. (Eds) (1996). *Public Management: The New Zealand Model*. Auckland: Oxford University Press.

Caiden, N. (1998). A New Generation of Budget Reform. In: B. G. Peters & D. J. Savoie (Eds), *Taking Stock: Assessing Public Sector Reforms* (pp. 252–284). Montreal: McGill-Queens University Press.

Caiden, N., & Wildavsky, A. (1974). *Planning and Budgeting in Poor Countries*. New York: Wiley and Sons.

Campos, J. E., & Pradhan, S. (1997). Evaluating Public Expenditure Management Systems: An Experimental Methodology with an Application to the Australia and New Zealand Reforms. *Journal of Policy Analysis and Management*, *16*(3), 423–225.

Dawkins, J. S. (1984). Budget Reform: A Statement of the Government's Achievements and Intentions in Reforming Australian Governmental Financial Administration, Canberra: AGPS.

Dunleavy, P., & Hood, C. (1994). From Old Public Administration to New Public Management. *Public Money and Management*, *1*(3), 9–16.

Ewart, B., & Boston, J. (1993). The Separation of Policy Advice from Operations: the Case of Defence Restructuring in New Zealand. *Australian Journal of Public Administration*, *52*(2), 122–137.

Forster, J., & Wanna, J. (Eds) (1990). *Budgetary Management And Contol: The Public Sector In Australasia*. South Melbourne: MacMillan.

Frederickson, H. G. (1996). Comparing the Reinventing Government Movement with the New Public Administration. *Public Administration Review*, *56*(3), 263–270.

Gore, A. (1993). *Creating a Government That Works Better and Costs Less: The Report of the National Performance Review*. Washington D.C.: National Performance Review.

Gray, A., & Jenkins, B. (1995). From Public Administration To Public Management: Reassessing A Revolution? *Public Administration*, *73*(1), 75–100.

Green, M., & Thompson, F. (1999). Organizational Process Models of Budgeting, unpublished manuscript. Salem, Oregon: Atkinson Graduate School of Management, Willamette University.

Heclo, H., & Wildavsky, A. (1975). *The Private Government of Public Money*. London: Macmillan.

Hood, C. (1987). British Administrative Trends And The Public Choice Revolution. In: J. E. Lane (Ed.), *Bureaucracy and Public Choice* (pp. 146–170). London: Sage.

Hood, C. (1991). A Public Management for All Seasons? *Public Administration, 69*(1), 3–19.

Hood, C. (1995). The New Public Management. In: EDITOR(S)? *The 1990s: Variations on a Theme, Accounting Organizations and Society, 20,* 2/3, 93–109.

Hood, C. (1997). Which Contract State? Four Perspectives on Over-Outsourcing Public Services. *Australian Journal of Public Administration, 56*(3).

Hughes, O. E. (1994). *Public Management and Administration: An Introduction.* New York: St. Martin's Press.

Joint Committee on Public Administration (1989). Submission by the Department of the Prime Minister and Cabinet, Inquiry into the Department of Finance. Parliament of Australia: S10–64.

Jones, L. R., & McCaffery, J. L. (1994). Budgeting According to Aaron Wildavsky: A Bibliographic Essay. *Public Budgeting and Finance, 14*(1), 16–43.

Keating, M. (1989). Quo Vadis: Challenges of Public Administration. Address to Royal Australian Institute of Public Administration. Perth, 12 April.

Keating, M. (1998). Personal Interview. Brisbane, Australia.

Keating M., & Holmes, M. (1990). Australia's Budgetary and Financial Management Reforms. *Governance, 3*(2), 168–185.

Kemp, P. (1990). Next Steps for the British Civil Service. *Governance, 3*(2), 168–196.

Kettl, D. F. (1997). The Global Revolution in Public Management: Driving Themes, Missing Links. *Journal of Policy Analysis and Management, 16*(3), 446–462.

Keraudren, P., & van Mierlo, H. (1998). Theories of Public Management Reform and their Practical Application. In: T. Verheijen, D. Coombes & E. Elgar (Eds), *Innovations in Public Management: Perspectives from East and West Europe* (pp. 39–56). Cheltenham.

Management Advisory Board (1997). *Beyond Bean Counting: Effective Financial Management in the APS – 1998 and Beyond.* Canberra, Australian Government Printing Office.

Milburn, A. (1998). Public Services for the Future: Modernisation, Reform Accountability, Comprehensive Spending Review: Public Service Agreements 1999–2002. Presentation to Parliament by the Chief Secretary to the Treasury, Cm 4181, December.

Moon, J. (1999). The Australian Public Sector and New Governance. *Australian Journal of Public Administration, 58*(2), 112–120.

New Zealand Treasury (1987). Government Management, Brief to the Incoming Government, Volume One. Wellington: Government Printing Office.

OECD (1999). *Budgeting in a Surplus Environment.* Paris: OECD.

OECD (1997). *Modern Budgeting.* Paris: OECD.

OECD (1995). *Governance in Transition: Public Management Reforms in OECD Countries.* Paris: OECD.

Osborne, D., & Gaebler, T. (1992). *Reinventing Government: How the Entrepreneurial Spirit is Transforming the Public Sector.* Reading MA: Addison Wesley.

Pallot, J. (1998). 'Newer than New' Public Management: Financial Management and Collective Strategizing in New Zealand. *International Public Management Journal, 1*(1).

Peters, B. G., & Savoie, D. J. (Eds) (1998). *Taking Stock: Assessing Public Sector Reforms.* Montreal: McGill-Queens University Press.

Pollitt, C. (1998). Managerialism Revisited. In: B. G. Peters & D. J. Savoie (Eds), *Taking Stock: Assessing Public Sector Reforms* (pp. 45–77). Montreal: McGill-Queens University Press.

Pollitt, C. (1993). *Managerialism and the Public Services: Cuts or Cultural Change in the 1990s?* (2nd ed.). Oxford: Blackwell.

Portillo, M. (1994). Transforming the Public Sector. Chief Secretary to HM Treasury Speaking to the Oxford Deregulation Seminar, 7 January.

Prime Minister and Minister for the Cabinet Office (1999). *Modernising Government*. London: HMPO.

Premchand, A. (1998). Umbrella Themes Obscure Real Problems: An Appraisal of Recent Efforts to Improve Financial Management. *Public Budgeting and Finance, 18*(2), 72–87.

Rubin, I. (1990). *The Politics of Public Budgeting: Getting and Spending, Borrowing and Balancing*. New Jersey: Chatham House.

Savoie, D. J. (1990). *The Politics of Budgeting in Canada*. Toronto: University of Toronto Press.

Schick, A. (1990). *The Capacity to Budget*. Washington D.C.: The Urban Institute Press.

Schick, A. (1994). From the Old Politics of Budgeting to the New. *Public Budgeting and Finance, 14*(1), 135–144.

Schick, A. (1997). *The Changing Role of the Central Budget Office*. Paris: OECD.

Schwartz, H. M. (1997). Reinvention and Retrenchment: Lessons from the Application of the New Zealand Model to Alberta, Canada. *Journal of Policy Analysis and Management, 16*(3), 405–422.

Thompson, F. (1998). Public Economics and Public Administration. In: J. Rabin, B. Hildreth & J. Miller (Eds), *Handbook of Public Administration*, 2nd edition (pp. 995–1063). New York: Marcel Dekker.

Verheijen, T., & Coombes, D. (Eds) (1998). *Innovations in Public Management: Perspectives from East and West Europe*. Cheltenham: Edward Elgar.

Von Hagen, J. (1992). Budgeting Procedures and Fiscal Performance in the European Communities, unpublished manuscript. Bloomington, Indiana: University of Mannheim and Indiana University School of Business.

Wildavsky, A. (1961). Political Implications of Budgetary Reform. *Public Administration Review, 21*(3), 183–190.

Wildavsky, A. (1974). *The Politics of the Budgetary Process*, 2nd edition. Boston: Little, Brown & Co.

Wildavsky, A. (1978). A Budget for All Seasons? Why the Traditional Budget Lasts. *Public Administration Review, 6*(2), 501–509.

Wildavsky, A. (1979). *How to Limit Government Spending*. Berkeley: University of California Press.

Wildavsky, A. (1986). *Budgeting: A Comparative Theory of Budgetary Processes*, 2nd edition. New Brunswick: Transaction Books.

Wildavsky, A. (1988). *The New Politics of the Budgetary Process*, fourth edition. Illinois: Scott, Foresman and Co.

Wilenski, P. (1986). *Public Power and Public Administration*. Sydney: Hale and Iremonger.

31. CORRUPTION AND THE NEW PUBLIC MANAGEMENT

Peter DeLeon and Mark T. Green

INTRODUCTION

Part of the appeal of the New Public Management (NPM) is its explicit license permitting government officials to operate relatively independently of direct supervision, or to operate as free-lance agents, that is, as "cowboys" on the periphery of the Weberian control bureaucracy. In so doing, NPM theory generates greater governmental efficiencies in those areas in which they command a comparative advantage. Under a "business as usual" scenario, this condition would provide an opportunity for exemplary public service, assuming the official acts in a publicly responsible and accountable manner. However, in somewhat more anomalous conditions that can prevail in either developed or less developed polities, it is fair to ask what safeguards the NPM has that offer to guard against the errant administrator, i.e. the "cowboy" who goes astray. More specifically, how would NPM address or manage situations of political corruption, not so much to eliminate corruption (few administrative scholars have held out a realistic chance for that particular managerial utopia) as to minimize its causes and effects? The explicit question posed is: given that NPM promotes the entrepreneurial edge and independence of public managers, how does NPM strike a balance between that independence and accountability, in other words, the much less welcomed maladministration?

This chapter examines this relationship by first posing the question: is political corruption an anomalous and maligned managerial or administrative condition? This is succeeded by a brief discussion of the New Public Management paradigm and how it conceptually and practically is constructed

Learning from International Public Management Reform, Volume 11B, pages 615–642.
2001 by Elsevier Science Ltd.
ISBN: 0-7623-0760-9

to minimize corrupt activities. The two sections are juxtaposed in the third part of this chapter, with special focus on corruption in modern administrative societies. Lastly, conclusions and outstanding questions are examined.

CORRUPTION AS AN ADMINISTRATIVE PHENOMENON

Unquestionably, political corruption is not a condition conveniently restricted to less developed polities or an abandoned artifact of ancient history. Rather, it remains an on-going, continuing phenomenon with few regions immune to its effects. Recently, the principal architectural party of post-war German democracy, the Christian Democratic Party, and its long-time leader, Helmut Kohl, were indicted for accepting illegal contributions from parties they do not choose to disclose (Anonymous, 2000b). The International Olympics Committee has admitted that some of its officials took illegal gifts from Salt Lake City officials to sway their IOC vote in favor of the host city and the tremendously lucrative contracts that go with that designation. President Jiang Zemin of the People's Republic of China has railed against what is reported to be "modern China's biggest corruption scandal, creating concern in the communist leadership . . .". (Hutzler, 19A). Even in the United States, corruption has hardly been a rare event; DeLeon (1993) documents how corrupt actions plagued the Reagan and Bush presidencies, and the Clinton administration has had more than its share of corruption exposed. These episodes included such embarrassments as the Savings & Loan scandals, procurement misrepresentations within the Department of Defense, and the Iran-*contra* affair. The succeeding Clinton administration has been racked by numerous scandals and special prosecutors of its own, especially over campaign financing. Steven Greenhouse (2000) recently reported in the *New York Times* how "extensive corruption in the nation's largest union of government workers, the American Federation of State, County, and Municipal Employees" has been uncovered, with losses in one local estimated to be approximately $2.2 million. Even the Inspectors-General office – nominally the bureaucratic watchdogs guarding against malfeasance – has come under corruption charges. In Illinois, former Inspector General Dean Bauer was accused of covering up bribery activities in Illinois' Secretary of State Office as a way to "avoid personal and political embarrassment to the secretary of state [Daniel Ryan, who is now the Governor of Illinois]". (Anonymous, 2000b)

The question, then, is not one of whether corruption exists. There is ample evidence to support this proposition. Nor will we address the possibility of the elimination of corruption; after generations of decrying corruption in almost every governmental venue, one still can identify various hints of corrupt activities around the world, from gentle waifs to outright repugnance. NPM can hardly be expected to succeed where generations of corruption remedies have fallen short. However, we do need to consider what NPM can do to reduce the incidence of political and administrative corruption, or at the very least, to make it more manageable.

Knowing that it exists does not necessarily condone the condition. However, before addressing the NPM to corruption issues, let us briefly review how other cognizant academic disciplines have addressed the corruption phenomena. This provides a beginning set of assumptions and actions from which the NPM can build.

STUDIES OF CORRUPTION

Traditionally, public administration has viewed corruption as a rare occurrence, one that, when it appears, is typically an isolated question in public accountability, one in which ethical behavior and education are inevitably portrayed as the ready remedy. (Caiden & Caiden, 1977) Alternatively, a few (e.g. Quah, 1999) have argued for a stronger central political authority, with his principal example being his native Singapore. Political science – perhaps because it is relatively more removed from the operational implications of its research than public administration – has been much more forthcoming in its recognition of political corruption (e.g. Johnston, 1982; Benson et al., 1978) but even here, the empirical literature has been characterized as "not extensive" (Meier & Holbrook, 1992: 135). Economists have generally paid relatively scant attention to the problem of "side payments" as economists refer to corrupt activities. The most important exception is Susan Rose-Ackerman (1978), who makes two salient observations: first, that corruption is most likely to occur at the intersection between the public and private sectors; and second, that corruption can best be described as a *systemic* activity, as opposed to the relatively anecdotal perspective of public administration scholars. In this latter observation, Rose-Ackerman is in close agreement with sociologist Robert K Merton (1968), who argues persuasively that corruption often serves a manifest, desired social and political function; if the government is unable to provide a good or service, there will be occasion for people to engage in "side payments" to obtain the desired articles or services. In Merton's words:

> Since moral evaluations in a society tend to be largely in terms of the manifest consequences of a practice or code, we should be prepared to find that analysis in terms of latent functions at times runs counter to prevailing moral evaluations. . . . Proceeding from the functional view, therefore, that we should *ordinarily* (not invariably) expect persistent

social patterns and social structures [involving political corruption] to perform positive functions *which are at the time not adequately fulfilled by other existing patterns and structures*, the thought *occurs* that this publicly maligned organization is, *under present conditions*, satisfying basic latent functions. [That is to say,] *the functional deficiencies of the official structure generate an alternative (unofficial) structure to fulfill existing needs somewhat more efficiently* (Merton, 1968: 125–27; Merton's emphases).

Public policy, and, by extension, public management scholars are not afforded the luxury of distance; by any measure, public management is intimately involved in the quotidian operations of governing. As such, if it can be demonstrated that political corruption is "inefficient", that it somehow distracts from the cost-efficient operations of government, then public management must be directly concerned with countering corruption and the costs it entails.

The question then poses itself: granted that corruption exists, is it a problem? In other words, should public management be concerned with it? Some have gone so far as to suggest that corruption might even serve as a *benevolent* management tool in terms of political recruitment (Nye, 1967), that is, to attract new people (often who have been schooled in Europe or the United States to return home) to serve in a governmental bureaucracy. But this recognition extends beyond recruitment activities. For the owner of a diner to give a free lunch to the cop on the beat could easily be construed as a low-level form of bribery, but it might just as justifiably be viewed as a form of direct taxation as pay for a police retainer, services rendered, or maybe as little more than a tip for overtime; similarly, a bribe might be considered a user's fee for overcoming bureaucratic bottleneck, just another (albeit illegal) business expense. Robert Klitgaard, in his thoughtful study of corrupt regimes in Asia (1988: 33; Klitgaard's emphases), summarizes:

> The putative benefits depends upon the assumption that the corruption transgresses a wrong or inefficient economic policy, overcomes limitations in an imperfect political system, or gets around imperfections in organizational rules. In short, *if the prevailing system is bad, then corruption may be good.*

He is saying, in effect, "no harm, no foul". But is this a complete, let alone accurate depiction? We would claim that it is fundamentally mistaken on at least two counts.

The first has to do with economic or opportunity costs. Unquestionably corruption (especially if we include illegal drug activities) diverts large amounts of money from the public sector, money that could easily be spent better (that is to say, less selfishly) elsewhere. In the U.S. in the 1990s, DeLeon (1993: 33) estimated the "costs" of corruption (particularly if one includes the so-called "victimless crimes" such as prostitution) in the tens of billions of dollars; worldwide, that could easily run into the low hundreds of billions of dollars. But in a world economy of tens of trillions of dollars, this is hardly a fatal fiscal hemorrhage. However, a straightforward cost-benefit analysis of the mischief caused by corruption would need to be more than a simple dollar accounting. It would be made much more complex by time frames (what are and will be the present discounted costs of corruption?), the state of specific economies, and, most centrally, the expectations of a nation's people as they see corruption inequitably sapping their economy, and their resulting disillusionment. As Frank Fukuyama (1994) reminds us, "trust" is a precious national resource or commodity – one that is easy to tarnish and arduous to rebuild – but surely necessary in any nation building (or maintaining) exercise.

The second concern counters the "fatalism" argument: if corruption is all-but inevitable, why fight it? Imagine the royal peace of mind if King Knute had not ordered the ocean's waves to cease their crashing on the shoreline. Similarly, if corruption is little more than a "user's" tax and going to happen anyway, why break one's policy lances to ameliorate corruption, that is, why expend valuable resources on something that will happen in any case? The answer is that there are times when one must, like Sysyphus, push against the rock. There are too many examples where people have recognized the functional nature of corruption and still found the means to end its baneful influences. Corruption, at its base, is simply inequitable in terms of governing, its processes, and its people, if not in the immediate term, then surely in the long run (see D. Kaufman, 1997). Governments, by their very nature, represent long-term investments, and therefore must reason and rule as such. Corruption, of course, if left unchecked, could easily become a "growth industry", compiling greater stocks of desired goods and services, and thereby weakening the recognized fabric of law and governance. Again, then, we find the inequitable and debilitating effects of corruption to undermine the utilitarian ends of government. As Klitgaard (1988: 42) cautions, "Whereas an occasional act of corruption may be efficient, corruption once systematized and deeply ingrained never is".

In short, we need to recognize a few benchmarks in the study of corruption. First, most public affairs scholars have recognized the debilitating nature of corruption. However, particularly among public administration scholars, their "remedies" of greater education, higher ethical standards (Frederickson, 1999), or higher wages for administrators or greater centralized authority (Quah, 1999) have not proven effective; the "cowboys" may not be rampant but they are still out there, free-wheeling as ever on the range. Second, corruption is an important area for continued study, both for its specific activities as well as for the more generic question of how the NPM attempts to control administrators who it accords a fair amount of entrepreneurial authority and managerial leeway. Let us now, then, review just how NPM scholars have addressed this problem from a theoretic basis, and particular how NPM articulates the issue of accountability in public sector arena that it characteristically and increasingly recommends intersecting with the private sector.

TENETS OF THE NEW PUBLIC MANAGEMENT

Over the last decade, a popular pastime for academics has been is to criticize both the theory and practice of NPM movement, with particular emphasis on the latter (Lynn, 1998). Of particular interest to critics is the issue of entrepreneurial government – or what we have called "cowboys" – and the incessant charge that this will lead to an unaccountable bureaucracy that will abuse power, disavow democratic responsibility, and eventually lead to widespread self-aggrandizement, or, is this case, political corruption (Frederickson, 1999). In spite of the seriousness of these charges, NPM supporters have not actively engaged their critics in this dialogue for one simple reason: the NPM logic is much more than simple-mindedly letting the public sector be entrepreneurial to the neglect of all other managerial considerations. In fact, from a review of the literature from the often-cited explanations of what typifies NPM (Barzelay, 1992; Osborne & Gaebler, 1993; Holmes & Shand, 1995; Stokes, 1996; OECD, 1996), we find that NPM is never simply nor solely about entrepreneurial government. Depending on whose list of characteristics one goes by, we find anywhere from five to ten key features of NPM.

It is true that all characterizations of NPM do include a common set of managerial values that emphasize entrepreneurial spirit, urge flexibility, and downplay excessive rules. However, after these general principles are a number of subsequent interlocking assumptions that emphasize such managerial components as accountability, transparency, efficiency, and performance. For the most part, NPM critics overlook the complementary nature of these management components and fail to incorporate them into their criticisms.

Arguably, the perceived neglect of NPM proponent to answer their critics' concerns regarding entrepreneurial management on the administrative peripheries and potential abuse of power is because they might feel like they already have. By their tally, NPM advocates have spent a great deal of time, effort, and detail examining how functional NPM reforms work in improving accountability, transparency, efficiency, and, ultimately, management. Certainly, in the minds of NPM scholars, such improvements can only enhance the safeguards surrounding public sector corruption. However, this theme has seemingly been lost in the details of NPM philosophy and the more mundane elements of management. Perhaps NPM scholars simply (and erroneously) assumed that their critics understand the benefits of a cost-based accounting system or how performance budgeting works, or comprehend how the marked improvements in information technology might heighten the chance that any corruption will be detected. and hence, deterred. If so, the corresponding shortcoming lies in the court of the NPM proponents, who have overlooked the possibility that NPM critics have alternative administrative priorities on their minds, and, as such, are not the close students of the NPM, i.e. functional, areas of management.

Thus, the critics who might have overlooked the presumed NPM virtues justifiably approach NPM armed with a differing set of the ideas and values of public administration scholars and practitioners. From the perspectives of the traditional public administrators and their fears of entrepreneurial (read: unbridled) government, the lessening of rules, and increased flexibility can and will only lead to disastrous results when cast in terms of democracy and administrative corruption. Instead of focusing on the critics of NPM and their charges, let us briefly explore how NPM proponents have not made the case sufficiently clear. While we will focus on preventing corrupt activities, the argument should be seen as extending beyond the particular and have a more generic applicability.

Most centrally, NPM proponents have obscured the idea that NPM principles are not simply a buffet table where one picks one item to the neglect of other – possibly less attractive – items (OECD, 1996; PUMA, 1995, 1996a, b, c, 1997; Uhr, 1999). To implement NPM reforms in earnest, one must have a well-balanced selection and the appropriate portion of *both* the values preferred by NPM and its functional approaches (see Table 31.1). Adopting the values of entrepreneurial government, rule flexibility, and privatization also requires the accompanying functional reforms, such as improved management information systems, better reporting procedures, performance based monitoring, and improved incentive structures. Conceptually, NPM does not offer a "pick and choose" system, rather, an integrated, cohesive body of reforms and procedures. If one fails to assemble an appropriate *and* complete package of the values *and* functions, then, logically, NPM reforms are doomed to fail by any and all measures. Perhaps the best examples of the selection of NPM values without the functional safeguards are the 1994 Orange County (California) financial crisis (Cohen & Eimicke, 1999) and the Canadian Human Resources Scandal (The National Post, 2000).

NPM advocates have failed to explain how the functional improvements they advocate can improve accountability, transparency, democratic responsibility, and also prevent corruption (Ferris & Graddy, 1997; Frant, 1998; Jones &

PETER DELEON AND MARK T. GREEN

Table 31.1. NPM Characteristics

Barzelay (1992)	Osborne & Gaebler (1993)	OECD (1996)	Holmes and Shand (1995)
Shift from the public interest to a focus on results and citizen's value	Catalytic government	Closer focus on results in terms of efficiency, effectiveness and quality service	More strategic or results oriented (efficiency, effectiveness, and service quality) approach to decision making
Shift from efficiency to a focus on quality and value	Community owned government	Replacement of highly centralized hierarchical structures by decentralized management environments where decisions on resource allocation are made closer to the point of delivery	The replacement of highly centralized hierarchical organizational structures with decentralized management environments where decisions on resource allocation and service delivery are take closer the point of delivery, where greater relevant information is available and which provide scope for feedback from clients and other interest groups
Shift from administration to a focus on production	Competitive government	The flexibility to explore alternatives to direct public provision and regulation that might yield more cost-effective policy outcomes	Flexibility to explore alternatives to direct public provision which might provide more cost effective policy outcomes
Shift from control to a focus on winning adherence to norms	Mission driven government	A greater focus on efficiency in the services provided directly by the public sector, involving the establishment of productivity target and the creation of competitive environments within and among the public sector organizations	Focus attention on the matching of authority and responsibility as a key to improving performance, including through such mechanisms as explicit performance contracting

Table 31.1. Continued

Shift from specifying functions, authority and structures to focus on identifying missions, services, customers and outcomes	Results oriented government	The creation of competitive environments within and between public sector organizations
Shift form justifying costs to a focus on delivering value	Customer driven	The strengthening of strategic capacities at the center to "steer" government to respond to external changes and diverse interest quickly, flexibly and at least cost
Shift from enforcing responsibility to a focus on building accountability	Enterprising government	Greater accountability and transparency through requirements to report results and their full cost
Shift from simply following rules and procedures to a focus on understanding and applying norms, identifying and solving problems, and continuously improving processes	Anticipatory government	Service-wide budgeting and management systems to support and encourage the changes.
Shift from simply operating administrative systems to a focus on separate service from control, expanding customer choice, encouraging collective action, providing incentives, measuring and analyzing results and enriching feedback	Decentralized government	
	Market-oriented government	

Thompson, 1999). NPM proponents need to articulate more carefully how each measure works and compare it to the extant systems, thus describing their comparative logic, motivation, and research that plays a part in the ontogeny of the NPM approach. Only more integrated analyses can provide a persuasive body of evidence that NPM can make things less corrupt in addition to reducing rules and providing more autonomy for bureaucrats.

We may legitimately ask how NPM proponents can be confident that their prescription of functional measures will help prevent public sector corruption? The answer to this question reflects that the basic NPM functional reforms (such as accrual based accounting, performance budgeting) and improved management information systems were developed on the combination of theoretic (albeit applied) economics coupled with demonstrated (albeit largely private sector) management practice. This combination of theoretic insight and demonstrated practice underpins the NPM argument. Although practice preceded theory, we begin with a brief explanation of the theory underlying NPM's functional reforms.

One fundamental precept of NPM organizational and applied economics is the concept of "transaction cost" (see Williamson & Masten, 1995 and Menard, 1997). Ferris and Graddy (1997: 91) have defined transaction cost as, ". . . the costs (other than price) associated with carrying out two-sided transactions – that is, the exchange of goods or services from one individual to another with agreed-upon payment for performance. These costs vary with the nature of the transaction and the way it is organized". Transaction cost analysis thus allows for detailed analysis of the contractual relationship between parties. Nobel Laureate Ronald Coase (1937) demonstrated that organizations were simply a series of both formal and informal contracts determined by the characteristics of transaction costs. Since it would be prohibitively expensive in the modern industrial organization to negotiate, monitor and coordinate a contract for each transaction, the employer would substitute all of these contracts for one contract, which specifies that the employee would follow the directions of the employer within certain limits (Coase, 1937; Miller, 1992). Coase explained that this relationship between employer and employee resembled a hierarchical "master-servant" relationship that later became known as the "principal-agent" theory. The principal-agent relationship is inherently troubled since, to quote Jones and Thompson, ". . . (a) the efforts of the agent cannot be perfectly observed; (b) the interests of agent and principal diverge; and (c) agents pursue their own interests, i.e. behave opportunistically". (Jones & Thompson, 1999, 1; from a policy perspective, see Friedman, 1984). Furthermore, agents have been hired specifically for their talents, expertise and skills, which often means that the agent has greater information about the workings of the specific parts of the organization than their respective principals, and should be accorded the authority to act upon this "expertise".

Traditional bureaucratic hierarchical organizations have struggled with the principal-agent problem by developing specialized rules that outline clearly which activities are allowed and those that are prohibited, as well as specifying the sanctions for violating the rules (Jones & Thompson, 1999). This, of course, would be a central feature in a typical Weberian hierarchy, which suggests accountability as a function of rule adherence. The problem with the rule-based mode of control, however, is that scarce resources are often wasted on monitoring the rules instead of allocated toward performance. Moreover, at least in theory, there are clear information asymmetries: the principal has an overview of the firm's objective while the agent has a better view of the day-to-day operation in the immediate sector. And neither actor's wishes to reveal his/her information completely, for fear of surrendering her/his comparative (bureaucratic) advantage. Therefore the practical task of the principal-agent relationship is to justify the two.

To overcome the principal-agent problem, NPM logic would suggest that solutions or results – *not* process – provide clearer, more discerning information to principals and thereby lead one to design better incentive systems in line with the organization, that is, the principal's and agent's (respective) preferences. NPM posits two reasons underpinning this rationale. First, by providing sharper information flows to the principal, the agent's activities can be more easily monitored; in the language of organizational economists and managerial accountants, this is referred to as "transparency" (Jones & Thompson, 1999), and is the basis for improved process design. Second, if the respective incentives are made more transparent, organizations can counteract the tendency by agents to serve their self-interest and, in the language of the economist, the tendency to "shirk". Modern information systems and processes promise to provide the vehicles to these realizations.

While this is the theoretic basis behind NPM's functional approach to improving the transparency, accountability, and performance of the public sector, the evidence is these reforms have a long history of application in the private sector. The development of better information systems and improved incentive structures to address the principal-agent relationship was a direct result of the rise of industrialization in the early part of the 20th century. Moving from a craftsman production mode – where formal and informal contracts were easily monitored – to a production system of mass-production assembly line mode – where literally hundreds (or even thousands) of contracts existed – required a more accurate system of monitoring, coordinating, and (in many cases) bargaining. To combat the overwhelming threat of self-serving employees (i.e. principal-agent problem), new approaches were created; in particular, the evolution of modern cost accounting systems and accrual based accounting (Garner, 1999) and the transformation of specialist from book-keepers to professional accountants became a primary source for monitoring the activities of employees ("agents"). At this point, the employer ("principal") could more easily monitor the activities and performance of agents from the perspective of the firm.

These conditions would typify the modern private organization throughout the rest of the 20th century. In addition, however, entrepreneurs such as Henry Ford realized that an important way to overcome the principal-agent problem was to construct an incentive system that counteracted much of the agent's incentive to shirk or move freely to other competitors found in the market. His solution was to offer a wage of $5 (a good wage in that day), which gave both management control and enforced long-term commitment from the employee to align his goals with his employer (Miller, 1992). At the same time, modern accounting procedures were developed that help the principal monitor the agents' commitments. All of these developments in improved management information and accounting greatly and inherently increased the chances that either principals' or agents' opportunities for fraud, theft, or corruption would be caught through the flow of enhanced information surrounding organizational contracts.

There are, of course, noted shortcomings to principal-agents theory when its monitoring activities are applied to the public sector. While Henry Ford might have been a paragon of "enlightened" management at the time, one also needs to recognize that he was diametrically opposed to the unionization of Ford Motor Company and determinedly opposed to collective bargaining. There is a growing awareness that principal-agents are a unidirectionable management procedure, in which the principal somehow manages to ride "herd" on the agents. Alternative managerial protocols would stress such ideas as a participatory managerial concept, in which agents and principals come to open agreements as to goals and missions, a more democratic regimen if you will (see DeLeon & DeLeon, 1997). Furthermore, Moe (1984) has suggested that the public sector is directed by a multitude (or confusion) of principals such as elected representatives, elected executives, and a variety of superior-sub-ordinate relationships (e.g. civil service) within the organization itself. Finally, the ultimate "principals" in the public organization are citizens themselves and depending on their own policy and program preferences, associated principals, and agents can be sent a variety of conflicting signals (Ferris & Graddy, 1998).

In spite of the developments in the private sector to improve and disseminate the principal-agent relationship, the public sector has less likely to adopt the NPM philosophy. The private organization is, of course, largely motivated by the external pressures of competitive markets and thus internal systems are structured by the market demands and mitigating transaction costs. In contrast, the modern public organization is confronted by external political forces that also influence the internal systems and can often override the concern for mitigating transaction costs. Moreover, the public and private sectors are often perceived as driven by differing sets of normative concerns; this distinction can most readily be viewed as their respective emphases of "efficiency" vs. "equity" tenets (Okun, 1975). This apparent disjunction between the external and internal systems and the multitude of pressures facing the public organization result in often obscured systems of managerial transparency and accountability. These lead, naturally, to different managerial concepts and approaches.

This concern is especially true with regard to financial matters such as budgeting, accounting, and performance measurement given that the political process has the greatest influence on the management systems (Jones, 1992). Fund accounting is a poor substitute for accrual and cost based accounting systems because the details of the transaction are not tracked accurately. Traditionally, public sector budgeting, with its emphasis on inputs (not outputs) or even better outcomes does not provide a clear picture of the effectiveness of programs. Without more discriminating tools of information, it is increasingly difficult for both managers and citizens to get a real sense of an agency's activities as well as hindering future decision making. Furthermore, budgeting (Wildavsky, 1964) and even audits (Power, 1993) are primarily driven by politics; likewise any sense of accountability is geared toward politics rather than management. In both sectors, then, accurate evaluations are necessary for a variety of reasons. As the record of GPRA points out (Radin, 1998), however, public sector evaluation is much less than a precise tool, as opposed to one beset by a series of political and methodological compromises that render its precise managerial application problematic.

POLITICAL CORRUPTION AND NPM

Having proposed that political and administrative corruption can generate both normative as well as efficiency problems in a generalized world of government decision making and processes, let us turn to a closer examination of a few specific cases. The purpose is to explain these instances of corruption using the framework advanced by the NPM, in order to understand how it might enlighten our analysis, where it might prove deficient, and, lastly, what remedies it might suggest. The cases have largely been derived from earlier work (e.g. DeLeon, 1993), with no intention of being complete or encyclo- pedic; they are meant to serve more as examples of corruption than definitive arguments. Moreover, they are largely from the United States, that is, an industrialized nation; thus, we make no claim for the universality of these arguments, for they will surely be less applicable in terms of the bureau- cratically underdeveloped nations (see Bardham, 1997). Finally, in keeping with Rose-Ackerman (1978) and the recognition that public and private sectors are increasing being conjoined, the examples will deal with the necessary nexus between the two sectors.

The Savings & Loan Crises

Viewed through the NPM prism, and especially that of principal-agents theory, there is evidence that the primary source of corruption would rest more with the "principal" than with the "agent". In terms of political corruption, this suggests that the primary culpability lies less with the administrative staff and more with the (often politically) appointed head of the agency or department and, in some crucial examples, with political actors who choose to become involved. The clearest example of this proposition had to do with the U.S. Savings & Loan (S&L) crises of the 1980s, whose cumulative "bailout" costs to the American taxpayers were estimated to be over $500 *billion* dollars, or over $2,000 for every man, woman, and child in the nation, that is, a magnitude of corruption that was significant by almost anybody's standards, without even wondering as to the "opportunity costs" incurred. It represented, in the worlds of L. J. Davis, "not simply a debacle but a series of debacles that made a few people preposterously rich and will leave most of us significantly poorer" (Davis, 1980: 51).

The origins of the S&L crisis were embedded in the economy: by the early 1980s, high American inflation rates, coupled with a loan portfolio laced with old (read: low interest) loan, had threatened the survival of the home loan industry, which was central to the American dream of personal home ownership (see DeLeon, 1983, chap. 6 for details; also Kane, 1989, and Mayer, 1990). As its liquidity crisis became acute, the "agent" with the primary responsibilities for federal S&L behavior, the newly appointed head of the Federal Home Loan Bank Board, Edwin Gray (himself a former S&L executive), was effectively hamstrung in his investigatory responsibilities towards federally chartered S&Ls by President Reagan's Chief of Staff (Donald Regan) and the Director of the Office of Management and Budget (David Stockman), who refused his request for the additional staff who were necessary to track down the rampant reports of insolvent S&Ls. To complicate his difficulties, U.S. Representative James Wright (D-TX) repeatedly intervened on behalf of Texas S&L executives, including many who were primary targets of the Bank Board's investigation. Since Wright, as the House Majority Leader, had a sizeable voice in Bank Board's vitally necessary $15 billion S&L recapitalization bill (which was necessary to make sure that the federal loan insurance fund could cover banks' depositors should the S&L become insolvent), his protestations could hardly be ignored by Gray. Similar interventions, although somewhat less egregious, were seen in the U.S. Senate.

In this case, the principals (the Reagan Administration as well as pivotal members of the Congress) resolved the problem with their "agent" when Gray's position was not renewed and a new Back Board chair, the much more compliant M. Danny Wall, was appointed. In the meantime, of course, the principals – largely responding to *their* principals, the S&L banditos – had effectively gutted the S&L system, despite the repeated efforts of the various federal and state S&L staffs ("agents") to carry out their responsibilities; these delays were ultimately to double the costs of the federal payback, since they permitted even more S&Ls to become insolvent.

There were, of course, multiple partners for any failure and the S&L crises were no exception. Representative Wright, for one, was responding to what he claimed was a legitimate responsibility of a congressman, that is, representing his constituents against what they described as undue government pressure. Similarly, Donald Regan was reflecting the distress of major campaign contributors and, just as important, manifesting the ideological movement of the Reagan Administration away from government regulation. Still, in this case, the then-chair of the Federal Deposit Insurance Corporation, William Seidman, commented that the S&L debacle "was a failure of government" (quoted in DeLeon, 1973: 155), in which "government" was effectively reflected by the leadership ("principals") perspectives, not the administrative staff ("agents").

The HUD Scandals

A second example of political corruption seen through the principal-agents "viewfinder" would be the corrupt activities of the U.S. Department of Housing and Urban Development (HUD) during the Reagan Administration (for details, see DeLeon, 1993, chap. 3; and Welfeld, 1992). Under the stewardship of HUD Secretary Samuel Pierce, the Department was later described as "the most complete bureaucratic standard-bearer for political corruption during the eight-year Reagan administration", with multiple convictions among the HUD's Secretariat. Senator George Mitchell (D-ME) put the price tag somewhere between $6–8 billion dollars; putting this in perspective, he noted that "It is astonishing that losses to the agency of the last several years could amount to more than Congress actually appropriated [to HUD] in a single year . . .". (both quotations from DeLeon, 1993: 51–52).

As with the Federal Bank Board, Pierce's HUD was also viewed as a prime candidate for deregulation; a 1982 HUD report suggested that "State and local governments have amply demonstrated that, properly unfettered, they will make better decisions than the federal government acting for them" (quoted in DeLeon, 1993: 53). In particular, the Moderate [Cost Housing] Rehabilitation Program (MRP) was singled out by Secretary Pierce for decimation, even though its funds supported large numbers of low-income tenants: "I . . . considered the MRP to be an economically inefficient program, and during my last six years as Secretary . . . we tried to terminate it. However, each year that MRP was left out of the HUD's budget request, Congress appropriated funds for it anyway" (quoted in DeLeon, 1993: 53).

The genesis of HUD's corruption laid in Pierce's plan to dismantle the MRP program, reducing it from a $1.8 billion program to a bit under $500 million. To confound matters further, Secretary Pierce eliminated the long-standing practice (actually, a legally mandated criterion) of geography-based allocations or equity; Pierce argued that with such limited amounts of money, better to fund one area well than to under-fund numerous regions, and Congress assented. As a result, ten states increased their allocation of MRP funds to 51.6%, whereas under the previous formula, they had received approximately 16%; six states, including California and New York, went from 39% to about 11%. This set the stage for the Secretary and his appointed staff to apply another selection criterion, that of partisan politics, which it fully did, according to several statements to the congressional investigation committees. This led to a series of problematic – well, why not call them "corrupt" since convictions were obtained against Pierce and his staff? – MRP allocations that were almost always approved by the HUD administrative staff after the specific interventions of Secretary Pierce or his staff, often overriding specific administrative objections.

Yet part of the blame must surely fall as well upon HUD's burdensome MRP process; many of the public housing construction firms' executives complained bitterly about the wearisome time and excessive energy (and, of course, money) that it took to get a MRP funded. Housing developer Judith Siegel testimony before an investigating committee is representative:

Mr. Chairman, I am sure you recognize that HUD is not an easy agency to work with. It is an agency in disarray, with confused and conflicting policies, and we need someone who could get it to respond. . . . In do I think this [MRP] selection process was good public policy? No. In summary, do I think a more competitive process would have made better public policy? Of course, but the system was there. . . . Developers must not be blamed for the system they neither created nor administered (Congressional testimony, quoted in DeLeon, 1993: 215).

To review the HUD corruption scandals from a NPM perspective, it is clear that both the principals and the agents were at fault, although the primary "fault" of the administrative staff was adhering to the published regulations. Still, as these were seen by the larger MRP community to be onus (in Merton's terms, they were latently dysfunctional), it is hardly surprising that housing contractors did everything they could to circumvent them, even if it meant acting in a manifestly illegal manner. This *apologia* on behalf of the agents in no way alleviates the culpability of the "principals". The agents were basically doing what the law and regulations required them to do; the principals were going well beyond the letter (and almost surely the spirit) of the law in order to accommodate their particular (and often political) constituencies, even if it meant ignoring well-intended alternative bidders. HUD represented a case in which the hide-bound regulations and administrative staff visibly "created" an opportunity for corruption. But this does not excuse the principals, for they were aware that what they were doing was legally "wrong" although (arguably) functionally appropriate.

This episode should not be viewed as a brief against political criteria. In a political system – which the American federal system surely represents – one naturally expects politics to raise its head in multiple instances, even to the point of intervening in what are supposed to be "objective" regulatory disputes or funding allocations. Still, as Herbert Kaufman (1977) made clear years ago, public representatives instituted regulations (or what is derisively called "red tape") to ensure that equity was the necessary password, that bidders would compete under the assumption that the bidder than best met the initial proposal would receive the contract. To subvert this item of faith would, in fact, undercut the competitive component of the system.

Operation Ill Wind

Around the world, the development and acquisition of weapons systems by national militaries has often been suspected of corrupt activities, if for no other reason than the immense amounts of money involved and the scope of the operations; keeping one's accountability ruler on the entire budget of a defense ministry would be all-but-unmanageable. In the summer of 1986, the U.S.

Department of Justice announced its "Operation Ill Wind", an investigation of
the U.S. Department of Defense (DoD) procurement program that ultimately
led to the convictions or guilty pleas of fifty defense officials, executives, and
consultants; seven major defense contractors were also implicated (for details,
see DeLeon, 1993, chap. 5; or Spector, 1995). From a history of alleged and
genuine weapons' procurement scandals, in which $1800 toilet seats covers
were only one incident, Ill Wind opened the Defense Department's procurement activities to heightened criticism.

It is especially important that we understand the background that led to these
disclosures of illegal activities. By the 1980s, the weapons development
process in the United States was becoming truly desperate to weapons
contractors; as R&D costs soared and procurement budgets grew strained (even
under the Reagan defense budget), it became clear than not all defense
contractors could receive defense contracts; since they basically had no
alternative buyer except the U.S. military services, the necessity for contracts
became paramount. Moreover, the military services and DoD were increasingly
demanding that firms vying for defense needed to spend large amount of their
own money to demonstrate the viability of their proposals. In short, defense
contractors realized that government contracts were becoming increasingly
difficult and expensive to obtain, and, more important, that they desperately
needed government contracts in order to survive financially.

President Reagan appointed John Lehman as his Secretary of the Navy, with
the explicit charge to create a 600-ship Navy to combat the then-perceived
"deep water" capability ascribed to the navy of the Soviet Union. Lehman then
hired a former top associate at the Boeing Corporation, Melvin Paisley, as his
Assistant Secretary for Research, Engineering, and System, that is, to be in
charge of the Navy's procurement system. Secretary Lehman soon admitted
that his 600-ship growth mandate was thoroughly frustrated by the Navy's
procurement requirements, which he called an "incredible and unwieldy
monster". In 1985, Lehman abolished the Navy's Materiel Command, which
had been coordinating the purchase of everything from torpedoes to aircraft
carriers since 1960. For a time, this consolidated Lehman's hold on the Navy's
multi-billion dollar acquisition process by removing a layer of analysts and
others who had stood between him and the Navy's purchasing commands. In
passing it may be noted that this change in organization was only temporary as
under the Defense Management Report initiatives of the Bush administration,
directed by Deputy Comptroller Donald Shycoff in particular, the material
commands in the Navy and other military services all were abolished and
reorganized into a single entity under the Office of the Secretary of Defense,

which perplexed the Navy and other service secretaries to a considerable extent.

In his testimony before Congress, Paisley proclaimed somewhat arrogantly, "We have brought the entire range of R&D functions within the direct management of the Navy Secretary. . . . My immediate staff and I will continue to develop appropriate policy and oversee its implementation (DeLeon, 1993: 118–119). They were abetted in this policy by the "hands-off" management style favored by the Reagan Administration and Secretary of Defense Caspar Weinberger, which was conspicuously permissive from a managerial perspective; the President's logic was dedicated to "defeating" the Soviet Union and was much less concerned as to how that was accomplished.

In June 1986, a former Navy employee indicated to the Naval Investigative Service (NIS) that he had been approached by a military consultant, offering to sell some classified procurement information. Using this as a lead, the NIS was able to expand its investigation to uncover a corrupt ring of consultants, who would obtain confidential, even classified information on vital procurement criteria (i.e. what would be necessary for a company to "win" a bidding competition); this information even included proprietary information on data from competing firms. This information was of invaluable use to the bidding firms, because they would give contractors extraordinary access to closely held information involving competitors' bids on multibillion-dollar military contracts. . . . The information, if disclosed at a critical moment in contract bargaining, could allow a company to reshape its offer or otherwise influence the outcome of the competition (DeLeon, 1993: 120)

In some cases, Pentagon officials, and perhaps even key staff in Congress, were thought to have tacitly agreed to rigging the bidding process to favor certain companies, in exchange for a position after they left government service or even personal favors; indeed, Assistant Secretary Paisley, who left the Department of the Navy in March 1987, later plead guilty to providing classified and proprietary data to free-lance military consultants, many of whom were later convicted or plead guilty. (Among the "personal favors": a major defense contractor bought Paisley's vacation condominium in Sun Valley at an above-market price, reselling it in a year for a loss.)

Secretary of Defense Frank Carlucci (who followed Weinberger) was unambiguous in his actions when the charges were announced. On July 1, 1986 he suspended all payments to the contractors identified with Operation Ill Wind. But ten days later, the Pentagon restored all the contact payments that Carlucci had blocked, out of fear that the suspensions would affect the companies' production lines and their promised delivery of weapons to the armed forces. Members of Congress later chimed in to the effect that to continue the suspensions would hurt completely innocent defense subcontractors (suppliers). Still in all, some of the fines paid by defense contractors – in the case of Unisys Corporation, $190 million – were among the largest fines ever levied. But the point had been made: The Ill Wind corruptions were not viewed by the Reagan Administration as a patently illegal activity, an unvarnished wrong, but rather as a tawdry but perhaps justifiable compromise to the possibility of a Soviet threat.

The principle that underpins the Defense Department's weapons development system is consciously designed with both competition and equity in mind, so that in theory, all qualified bidders have an equal opportunity to win a contract (or, from the perspective of the contractors, to survive institutionally). The voluminous procurement requirements reflect the mandate that the procedures should not be circumvented or compromised or favor accorded to a (covertly) chosen few. Unfortunately, equity loses its normative appeal when viewed from the vantage point of a harried military contractor. When his organizational purposes are joined with a "principals" whose main concern is for efficiency (that is, to ignore the admittedly tedious procurement regulations and administration as well as the lengthy time frame to develop and deliver a new weapons system), it is not hard to understand why one would replace the equity criterion for one of efficiency.

Lehman made no bones about how he saw the procurement situation: He reportedly "scoffed" when asked if his management strategies might have lead to the Ill Wind corruption and convictions, declaring that he, ". . . did not see any possibility of any correlation between good, strong management and wrongdoing". To emphasize his point, he admitted that in many respects, the military's acquisition system "doesn't work efficiently" but the blame should be ascribed to a "bloated" bureaucracy (quoted in Cushman, 1988: 5). Lehman's argument was not contested by Secretary Carlucci's disinterest in the investigations, as fears of the Soviet "evil empire" plus concerns over other threats to U.S. interests world-wide apparently outweighed concern over the legal disposition of this regrettable case. Finally, it is clear where the private defense community stood on this issue of corruption: in a dangerously competitive world, the military procurement complex was acting like perceptive business people would: they were out there purchasing pivotal information from military consultants, even if they were doing it illegally. In the words of Suzanne Garment, "Under these circumstances, middlemen will emerge to fill the gap and profit from it as inexorably as sidewalk vendors appear on the streets of New York". (Garment, 1991: 138)

ADDITIONAL PERSPECTIVES ON CORRUPTION

There are certainly more case of political corruption than these three that occurred in the United States in the 1980s. As mentioned, the distress visited upon the German Christian Democratic Party is just as pervasive as the "clean hands" scandals that generations of Italian Christian Democrats endured in their post-war political dominance. Likewise, France has regularly been plagued by corruption at the national level although, to be fair, generally they are much less publicized and less the occasion for national introspection for reasons probably rooted in the French political culture. As noted, however, the cases above were not meant to be definitive or exhaustive; as was pointed out, each of these cases had its apologists and defenders, who contrived to explain just why these cases did not represent political corruption and, even if they did, the corrupt activities were nothing more or less than the sorry concatenation of unfortunate circumstances, usually a reaction against perceived bureaucratic ineptitude.

Typically, the balkiness of the extant bureaucracy (HUD or the Bank Board, so on ad infinitum) was seen to have somehow and repeatedly managed to thwart managerial initiatives. Likewise, others (e.g. Garment, 1991) have suggested that congressmen and special counsels have held extensive (and expensive) hearings at least partially to gain personal visibility, even when the costs of such hearings far exceeded the costs resulting from the alleged corruptions. The most commonly observed example is Kenneth Starr's Office of the Special Prosecutor, which, in conducting its investigation of the Clinton Administration's various allegations, spent in excess of $40 millions. Given these costs, perhaps it just may be "functional" or at least cost-effective to allow the occasion corrupt activities, a return to the earlier suggestion that corruption be treated as little more than a "cost of doing business". We will directly address this functional statement in our conclusion.

Until then, we need to stress that in the cases reviewed (and we submit they are representative of a larger population of political corrupt activities), the onus seems more on the political leadership or appointed administrations (which we have characterized "principals" in the NPM orientation of the "principal-agents" theory), and less on the actions of the "agents". This is not meant to suggest, of course, that "agents" are always pristine; there are too many examples of (say) police or zoning corruptions for that position to stand on its own merits. Again, we will return to this argument and its implications in the Conclusion.

CONCLUSIONS

We propose two related investigations in this section. The first is an analysis of the New Public Management (NPM) and its ability to monitor or hold accountable actor on the periphery of its control (we called them "cowboys"); to do this, we have used examples of political corruption, for surely such activities are carried out by actors well beyond any legitimate administrative or managerial or entrepreneurial pale. In doing so, we will emphasize some insights NPM might offer, as well as pointing out some possible shortcomings in the NPM framework. The second section, drawing upon the first, reflects what we posed in our Introduction (with such varied corruption scholars as Klitgaard [1988] and Quah [1999]) that the complete elimination of corruption is virtually impossible. If so, then we should at least pose a series of "big questions" (akin to Behn, 1995; and Kirlin, 1996) whose focus might bring us somewhat closer to the reduction of corruption.

One of the more revealing findings of an NPM examination of political corruption is that the principals seen to be more likely to succumb to the opportunities or fruits of corruption than the agents. While this generalization is clearly open to more rigorous examination, it does raise the notion of ameliorative measures. Many (e.g. Garafolo et. al., 1999) have argued for a renewed emphasis on ethical behavior and, hence, accountability, as a way to counter corruption. In Frederickson's (1999: 21) words, "This issue here will be of accountability. Who will be accountable when contractors fail to perform or when they steal or cheat?" To cast an ethics net over both principals and agents would seem to be overkill. Agents, who would seem to be the most accessible for an "ethical education", have already been thoroughly schooled (some would say "socialized") against corruption; Herbert Kaufman's (1960) forest ranger would be a classic example of an agency that had a history of well-removed and insulated agents. On the other hand, principals, who often and legitimately are recruited from outside the civil service, are less likely to bring the necessary ethical training and standards to the administrative table. The corruption question, then, raises itself more distinctly: if the principals are primarily (*not* exclusively) at fault, what can the government do to assure its citizens that they indeed have the moral compass necessary to circumnavigate the shoals of corruption? There is, we submit, not a straightforward answer: the main culprits in the Reagan Administration's Iran-*contra* affair were naval officers sworn to uphold the very Constitution they consciously worked to subvert; nor does the eight-year track record of the Clinton much-investigated Administration's Cabinet offer much confidence.

The NPM philosophy and practice certainly accords well with a reduction in corrupt actions. More thorough accounting and budget ("transparency") procedures would have uncovered the transgressions perpetrated by the S&L executives, possibly early enough to have headed off the worst of their excesses; likewise for the HUD scandals. But information alone does not solve the ethical dilemmas of the controlling authorities. In the HUD scandals, critical Inspector General reports chronicled the managerial wrongdoings of HUD's Secretary and his immediate staff, but – and this is important – they were largely ignored. Former Senator William Proxmire (who chaired the HUD's Senate oversight committee) was asked why he did not ". . . act to prevent this waste and fraud". His answer is revealing and disturbing: "The answer is simple. We had no idea it was going on" (cited in DeLeon,1993: 78). What good, then, is the enhanced information propounded by NPM advocates when the crush of everyday activities precludes it from being monitored or even used? As far back as Roberta Wohlstetter (1962), information theorists have cautioned that information received is not necessarily information acted upon, a condition made even more apparent as administrators today face a growing inundation of data.

New Zealand wags, from the nation that is thought to have the most wide-scale adoption of NPM program (and one of the most corruption-free political environments according to Transparency International), have proposed an NMP aphorism, "If you can't measure it, you can't manage it" (Gregory, 1999: 66). While this might be an arguable proposition, what is less arguable is that NPM has yet to propose an information management system such that the administrators (in this chapter's metaphor, "cowboys") can not only be observed (i.e. held accountable) but the information underlying their accountability can be intelligently processed and acted upon. In addition, one can ask that even if the NPM insistence in precise specification and measurement – the better to enhance financial and managerial accountability – would not degenerate into nothing more than a "numbers" game, not unlike the administrative trajectory of PPBS from a management tool manipulated by the Comptroller in the Office of the Secretary of Defense (OSD) in the early 1960s to the 1970, in which the military services controlled OSD using the self-same PPBS. Gregory comments on this phenomenon of exactitude in New Zealand: "Such an overweening desire for specificity can result in management becoming a numbers game in which what is measured is what can most readily be measured, and in which the judgment necessary for comprehending and assessing the importance of the nonmeasurable becomes undervalued" (Gregory, 1999: 66). Again, NPM must develop a system for handling the increased data it produces.

PETER DELEON AND MARK T. GREEN

A third point might be made, one concerning "greed" or personal aggrandizement, a concept that underlies most analysts' views of corruption. Ivan Boesky, an American financier (and felon who was later fined $100 million) was quoted as telling a University of California (Berkeley) MBA seminar that, "Greed is healthy. You can be greedy and feel good about yourself" (quoted in DeLeon, 1993, p. 41; see Steward, 1991, for further details of Boesky and other Wall Street corruptions). *If* greed and personal financial gain were the only "currency" that motivated personal and political corruption, then NPM measures might indeed be particularly effective. However, as DeLeon (1993) points out, there are many cases in which monetary accumulations were not the case, that corruption in these (and other) cases was motivated by dedication to the President and his programs (Iran-*contra*), political affinities (HUD), and desire to defeat the enemy (Ill Wind), or to prevent friends from being embarrassed. And this says nothing about the "functional" view of corruption (see Merton, 1968), which treats corruption as an alternative mechanism to provide goods and services that the government is thought to be unable to provide on a timely basis. However cognizant NMP might be regarding economic incentives, it would have to be (impossibly) omniscient to ward off these alternative causes of corruption.

A final observation can be made. NPM and its emphasis on transaction costs brings a new perspective to the study of corruption, perhaps replacing, certainly supplementing others. Still, at base, people view the study of corruption as an exercise in norms. The NPM is largely a celebration of an efficiency norm. But governing (read: politics) is not always and exclusively about efficiency. Others (see Frederickson, 1999, and Gregory, 1999) argue that equity is the predominate criterion of governing. Lynn (1999: 120; italics added) has written that, "To the extent that the problems of modern public administration is democratic accountability . . ., then we must once again focus attention *on politics and the role of public law*". Law, of course, suggests equity and the idea of public interests. Which surfaces another important normative question for NPM proponents to address: "Economistic [*sic*] approaches tend to deny the validity of public interest, but if administrative reforms jeopardize the maintenance of high ethical standards, then it is up to the [NPM] reformers to explain why any such decline ought to be a matter of public indifference". (Gregory, 1999: 67) Or, put another way, if NPM takes stock in the ends (results), what does it have to say about the means adopted to reach those ends?

Let us return to the theme of this chapter: what measures does NPM have in its entrepreneurial toolkit that would counter (or, to be fair, support) the proverbial "cowboy" out there on the bureaucratic range? The emphasis on results (preferably contracted) is surely bona fide, and the stress upon accurate measurements is similarly well placed. But this chapter has raised a number of questions that NPM might wish to address. Specifically, how does NPM address the "big" questions revolving around the (admittedly overlapping) issues of:

- *Accountability*: to whom are the principals accountable? To their contracts? To their superiors? To the amorphous public at large? How is accountability demonstrated? And, most centrally, does accountability matter?
- *Ends vs. Means*: If we accept that NPM is results (ends) oriented, does one concern him/herself with the question of "means" to the agreed upon ends? And, accordingly, to the norms ascribed to those means. Simple analogy: If a sheriff is contracted and has the entrepreneurial authority to "clean up Dodge", does it make any difference how the "cleaning" is accomplished?
- *Principal-Agents Theory:* We have some preliminary indications that in matters of political corruption, "principals" seem to bear a larger proportion of the blame. However, we need to go past this observation and inquire if a principal-agents theory *should* be the foundation upon which an office or agency is best managed. Some (including DeLeon and Ewen [1997] and DeLeon and DeLeon [1997]) have argued for a more democratic, participatory managerial style than the "master-servant" relationship posited by Coase (1937). More constructively, are there any harbingers that suggest which agencies might be more (or less) amenable to NPM (or, alternatively, other models)?
- *Normative underpinnings:* What are the underlying norms that support NPM and other administrative philosophies or practices? How does this accord with concepts of the public interest? Gregory (1999: 67) asks how they accord to criteria embedded in a civic culture (or social capital). The distinction broached above between "efficiency" and "equity" is only a starting place for this discussion.
- *Non-pecuniary concerns:* Many aspects of governing are predicated on values that are non-economic in nature. NPM is often defined as drawn from theories of institutional and transaction cost economics. If these two assumptions are true, then one needs to understand how NPM encompasses phenomena outside its intended purview.

None of these questions are meant to undercut the normative or practical standing of the New Public Management. We do, however, suggest that this chapter has pointed out both the present strengths and shortcomings of the NPM paradigm as it is currently posed and exercised. We view NPM, then, as an evolving process, one whose theory and practice is open for amendment and improvement. We hope this exercise in "cowboys on their range" is one step in that process.

REFERENCES

Anonymous. (2000a). Germany's Desperate Right. *The Economist, 3541(8154)*, January 22–28, 49–50.
Anonymous. (2000b). Ex-Ill Inspector General Indicted. *New York Times*. web www.nytimes.com January 12.
Bardham, P. (1997). Corruption and Development: A Review of Issues. *Journal of Economic Literature, 35*, 1320–1346.
Barzelay, M., & Armajani, B. J. (1992). *Breaking Through Bureaucracy: A New Vision For Managing In Government*. Berkeley: University of California Press.
Begley, S. (1999). Lessons from the Frontier. *Newsweek, 134*(24), December 13, 80.
Behn, R. D. (1995). The Big Questions of Public Management. *Public Administration Review, 55*(4), 313–324.
Benson, G. C. S. (1978). *Political Corruption in America*. Lexington, MA: DC Heath.
Benson, G. C. S. et al. (1978). *Polittcal Corruption in America*. Lexington, MA: DC Heath.
Caiden, G. E., & Caiden, N. J. (1977). Administrative Corruption. *Public Administration Review, 37*(3), 295–306.
Coase, R. (1937). The Nature of the Firm. *Economica, 4*, 386–405.
Cohen, S., & Eimicke, W. (1999). Is Public Entrepreneurship Ethical? A Second Look At Theory And Practice. *Public Integrity, 1*(1), 54–74.
Cushman, J. H., Jr. (1988). Former Navy Chief Defends Policies. *The New York Times*, September 17, 5.
Davis, L. J. (1981). Chronicle of a Debacle Foretold: How Deregulation Begat the S&L Scandal. *Harper's Magazine, 281*(1684), September: 45–52.
DeLeon, L., & Ewen, A. J. (1997). Multi-Source Performance Appraisal: Employee Perceptions of Fairness. *Review of Public Personnel Administration, 17*(1), 22–36.
DeLeon, L., & DeLeon, P. (1997). The Democratic Ethos and Public Management. Paper presented at the 4th National Public Management Conference. Athens, GA.
DeLeon, P. (1993). *Thinking About Political Corruption*. Armonk, NY: M. E. Sharpe.
Ferris, J. M., & Graddy, E. A. (1997). New Public Management Theory: Lessons From The Institutional Economics. In: L. R. Jones & K. Schedler (Eds), *International Perspectives On The New Public Management* (pp. 89–104). Greenwich, CT: JAI Press.
Frant, H. (1997). The New Public Management and The New Political Economy: Missing Pieces in Each Other's Puzzles. In: L. R. Jones & K. Schedler (Eds), *International Perspectives On The New Public Management*. (pp. 71–88). Greenwich, CT: JAI Press.
Frederickson, H. G. (1999). Public Ethics and the New Manageralism. Paper presented to the International Institute for Public Ethics, Chateau delaBretesche, Missilac, FR, August.
Friedman, L. S. (1984). *Microeconomic Policy Analysis*. New York: McGraw-Hill.
Fukuyama, F. (1995). *Trust*. New York: The Free Press.
Garafolo, C., Geuras, D., Lynch, T., & Lynch, C. (1999). Applying Virtue Ethics to the Challenge of Corruption. Paper presented to the 5th National Public Management Research Conference, Texas A&M University, College Station TX, December.
Gargan, E. A. (1988). As China's Economy Grows, So Grows Official Corruption. *New York Times*, July 10: A1, A10.
Garment, S. (1991). *Scandal*. New York: Random House.

Greenhouse, S. (2000). Report Details Corruption Within Government Unions. *New York Times*, web: http:www.nytimes.com/yr/mo/day/news/national/unions-corrupt.html, January 21.

Gregory, R. J. (1999). Social Capital Theory and Administrative Reform. *Public Administration Review, 59*(1), 63–75.

Hutschler, C. (2000). China's President Targets Widespread Corruption. Denver *Post*, 21 January: A19.

Johnston, M. (1982). *Political Corruption and Public Policy in America*. Monterey, CA: Cole.

Jones, L. R. (1992). Public Budget Execution and Management Control. In: J. Rabin et al. (Eds), *Handbook of Public Budgeting*. (pp. 147–164). New York: Marcel Dekker.

Jones, L. R., & Thompson, F. (1999). *Public Management: Institutional Renewal for the 21st Century*. Stamford, CT: JAI-Elsevier Press.

Jones, L. R., & Schedler, K. (Eds). (1997). *International Perspectives on The New Public Management*, Greenwich, CT: JAI Press.

Kane, E. J. (1989). *The S&L Insurance Mess: How Did It Happen?* Washington DC: The Urban Institute.

Kaufman, D. (1997). Corruption: The Facts. *Foreign Policy*, No. 107, 114–131.

Kaufman, H. (1960). *The Forest Ranger*. Baltimore, MD: Johns Hopkins Press.

Kaufman, H. (1977). *Red Tape: Its Origins, Uses, and Abuses*. Washington DC: The Brookings Institution.

Kirlin, J. J. (1996). The Big Questions of Public Administration. *Public Administration Review, 56*(5), 416–424.

Klitgaard, R. (1988). *Controlling Corruption*. Berkeley, CA: University of California Press.

Liu, A. P. L. (1982). The Politics of Corruption in China. *American Political Science Review, 77*(2), 602–627.

Lynn Jr., L. (1998). A Critical Analysis of the New Public Management. *International Public Management Journal, 1*(1), 107–123.

Mathiasen, D. G. (1999). The New Public Management And Its Critics. *International Public Management Journal, 2*(1), 90–111.

Mayer, M. (1990). *The Greatest-Ever Little Bank Robber*, New York: Charles Scribner's Sons.

Meier, K. J., & Holbrook, T. M. (1992). I Seen My Opportunities And I Took 'Em: Political Corruption in the American States. *Journal of Politics, 54*(1), 133–155.

Ménard, C. (1997). *Transaction cost economics: Recent Developments*. Cheltenham, U.K.; Brookfield, Vt.: Edward Elgar.

Merton, R. K. (1968). *Social Theory and Social Structure*. New York: The Free Press.

Miller, G. J. (1992). *Managerial Dilemmas: The Political Economy Of Hierarchy*. Cambridge, New York: Cambridge University Press.

Moe, T. M. (1984). The New Economics of Organization. *American Journal of Political Science, 28*(4), 739–777.

North, D. C. (1990). *Institutions, Institutional Change, and Economic Performance*. Cambridge; New York: Cambridge University Press.

Nye, J. S. Jr. (1967). Corruption and Political Development: A Cost-Benefit Analysis. *American Political Science Review, 61*(2), 417–427.

Okun, A. M. (1975). *Equality And Efficiency, The Big Tradeoff*. Washington: The Brookings Institution.

Organisation for Economic Co-operation and Development, Public Management Committee (1996). *Integrating People Management Into Public Service Reform*. Paris and Washington, D.C.: Organisation for Economic Co-operation and Development; OECD Washington Publications and Information Center.

Organisation for Economic Co-operation and Development. Public Management Service (1995). *Governance In Transition : Public Management Reforms In OECD Countries.* Paris, France, Washington, D.C.: Organisation for Economic Co-operation and Development ; OECD Publications and Information Center.

Osborne, D., & Gaebler, T. (1992). *Reinventing Government: How The Entrepreneurial Spirit Is Transforming The Public Sector.* Reading, Mass.: Addison-Wesley Pub. Co.

Pastor, A. (1995). *When the Pentagon Was for Sale: Inside America's Biggest Defense Scandal.* New York: Charles Scribner.

Peters, J. G., & Welch, S. (1978). Political Corruption: A Search for Definition and a Theory. *American Political Science Review, 72*(3), 974–984.

Pilegge, J. (1992). Budget Reforms. In: J. Rabin et al. (Eds), *Handbook of Public Budgeting.* (pp. 67–94). New York: Marcel Dekker.

Power, M. (1993). The Politics of Financial Auditing. *Political Quarterly, 64*(3), 272–285.

PUMA. (1997). Public Management Committee. *Managing Government Ethics.* Paris: OECD/ PUMA.

Quah, J. S. (1999). Corruption in Asian Countries. *Public Administration Review, 59*(6), 483–494.

Radin, B. A. (1998). The Governmental Performance and Results Act: Hyra-Headed Monster or Flexible Management Tool? *Public Administration Review, 58*(4), 307–316.

Rose-Ackerman, S. (1978). *Corruption: A Study in Political Economy.* New York: Academic Press.

Shand, D. A. and Organisation for Economic Co-operation and Development. (1996). *Performance Auditing And The Modernisation Of Government.* Paris: Organisation for Economic Co-operation and Development.

Steward, J. B. (1991). *Den of Thieves.* New York: Simon & Schuster.

Uhr, J. Institutions of Integrity: Balancing Values And Verification In Democratic Governance. *Public Integrity, 1*(1), 94–106.

Washington, S., & Armstrong, E. (1996). *Ethics In The Public Service: Current Issues And Practice,* Public, Management Occasional Papers, No. 14. Paris: Organisation for Economic Co-operation and Development.

Welfed, I. (1992). *HUD Scandals: Howling Headlines and Silent Fiascoes.* New Brunswick, NJ: Transaction Publishers.

Wildavsky, A. B. (1964). *The Politics of The Budgetary Process.* Boston: Little Brown.

Williamson, O. E. (1997). *Transaction Cost Economics: How It Works, Where It Is Headed.* Berkeley: Institute of Management Innovation and Organization, University of Califronia Berkeley.

Williamson, O. E., & Masten, S. E. (1995). *Transaction Cost Economics.* Aldershot, Hants, England, Brookfield, Vt.: Edward Elgar.

Williamson, O. E., Winter, S. G., & Coase, R. H. (1991). *The Nature of the Firm: Origins, Evolution, And Development.* New York: Oxford University Press.

Wohlstetter, R. (1962). *Pearl Harbon: Warning and Decision.* Palo Alto, CA: Stanford University Press.